VALERY BRYUSOV AND THE RIDDLE OF RUSSIAN DECADENCE

Unfinished charcoal, chalk, and crayon portrait of Valery Bryusov, 1906, the last work of the Russian painter Mikhail Vrubel. [Now in the Tretyakov Gallery, Moscow.]

Valery Bryusov and the Riddle of Russian Decadence

JOAN DELANEY GROSSMAN

University of California Press

BERKELEY · LOS ANGELES · LONDON

336455

Chapters 4 and 9 appeared in shorter form in, respectively, *The Russian Review* 39 (1980): 285–300, and
The Slavonic and East European Review 61 (1983):
344–62. They are reproduced with the publishers'
permission.

University of California Press
Berkeley and Los Angeles, California

University of California Press, Ltd.
London, England

Library of Congress Cataloging in Publication Data

Grossman, Joan Delaney.
 Valery Bryusov and the riddle of Russian decadence.

 Bibliography: p.
 Includes index.
 1. Bryusov, Valery Yakovlevich, 1873–1924—
Criticism and interpretation. 2. Decadence (Literary
movement)—Soviet Union. I. Title.
PG3453.B7Z648 1985   891.71'3   83-14470
ISBN 0-520-05141-6

Printed in the United States of America

1 2 3 4 5 6 7 8 9

Contents

Acknowledgments

THE LARGEST PART of the research for this book was accomplished under a fellowship from the John Simon Guggenheim Memorial Foundation and a grant from the International Research and Exchanges Board; the latter afforded me the opportunity of working in Moscow and Leningrad under the sponsorship of the Academy of Sciences of the USSR. I am grateful to these, as well as to the Committee on Research of the University of California, Berkeley, and the Center for Slavic and East European Studies at Berkeley, for generous research support.

Assistance, advice, and encouragement in the work came to me at various crucial times from Vsevolod Setchkarev, Vladimir Markov, Victor Erlich, Robert Belknap, Edward J. Brown, Lazar Fleishman, Robert P. Hughes, Olga R. Hughes, Edward Kasinec, John Malmstad, and Irene Masing-Delic. I wish also to thank friends and colleagues who read the manuscript and offered constructive suggestions: in addition to some of the above, Francis J. Whitfield, Simon Karlinsky, Hugh McLean, Robert Maguire, and Avril Pyman. In Moscow and Leningrad various scholars aided me in important ways. Among these I may mention the senior Soviet specialist on Bryusov, D. E. Maksimov, and the late Academician M. P. Alekseev. I am also indebted to the research staffs of the Institute of World Literature (IMLI) and the Central State Archive of Literature and Art (CGALI) in Moscow and the Institute of Russian Literature (IRLI [Puškinskij Dom]) in Leningrad.

Over the past several years I have been blessed with splendid assistance from Berkeley graduate students, first of all Peter and Susan Scotto, who included in their research duties a photographic tour of the *"Brjusovskie mesta"* in Moscow; John Weeks, whose superb editorial skills helped smooth the text; and Jerry Heil, David Mayberry, Richard Miller, Molly Molloy, Ruth Rischin, and Kate Scanlan. I am extremely grateful also for their kind efficiency to University of California Press editors Marilyn Schwartz and Jane-Ellen Long.

Finally, this book is an all-inclusive thank-you to my husband, Gregory Grossman.

Note on Editions and Transliteration

APPENDIX B GIVES the first-edition tables of contents for the six volumes of Bryusov's poetry treated in the text, keying them to the seven-volume *Sobranie sočinenij* (Moscow, 1973–1975), the only easily accessible edition of his works. Poems referred to in the text may in most cases be found there, though sometimes with revisions. Since Bryusov gave immense importance to the total form of his books, the ordering of poems in the first editions is crucial to an understanding both of his initial inspiration and of the impression created on his early readers. The seven-volume Soviet edition follows, with some omissions, the order Bryusov adopted in the uncompleted *Polnoe sobranie sočinenij i perevodov* (St. Petersburg, 1913–1914), which represents a later rethinking of his early books and lies outside the time scope of this work.

Russian names and words familiar to English readers appear in their accustomed anglicized spelling in the text. Other Russian words and sentences cited in the text and all Russian words and names in the notes and bibliography are spelled according to the international scholarly system of transliteration of Cyrillic.

Abbreviations Used in the Notes

Vol. no., page no. [e.g., I, 35]	Brjusov, Valerij, *Sobranie sočinenij v semi tomax*. Moscow, 1973–1975.
Ašukin	Ašukin, N., ed., *Valerij Brjusov v avtobiografičeskix zapiskax, pis'max, vospominanijax sovremennikov i otzyvax kritiki*. Moscow, 1929.
"Avtobiografija"	Brjusov, Valerij, "Avtobiografija," in *Russkaja literatura XX veka*, ed. S. A. Vengerov, 3 vols., vol. I, pp. 101–119. Moscow, 1914.
Bibliografija	È. S. Danieljan, *Bibliografija Valerija Jakovleviča Brjusova 1884–1973*, ed. K. D. Muratova. Erevan, 1976.
CGALI	Central'nyj gosudarstvennyj arxiv literatury i iskusstva, Academy of Sciences, USSR, Moscow.
Dnevniki	Brjusov, Valerij, *Dnevniki 1891–1910*, ed. I. M. Brjusova, N. S. Ašukin. Moscow, 1927.
IMLI	Institut mirovoj literatury, archival division, Academy of Sciences, USSR, Moscow.
IRLI	Institut russkoj literatury (Puškinskij Dom), archival division, Academy of Sciences, USSR, Leningrad.

LN 27–28   *Literaturnoe nasledstvo.* Vol. 27–28, ed. P. I.
Lebedev-Poljanskij et al. Moscow, 1937.

LN 85   *Literaturnoe nasledstvo. Valerij Brjusov.*
Vol. 85, ed. A. N. Dubovikov and N. A.
Trifonov. Moscow, 1976.

Percovu   Brjusov, Valerij, *Pis'ma V. Ja. Brjusova k
P. P. Percovu*, ed. P. Percov. Moscow,
1927.

Stixotvorenija   Brjusov, Valerij, *Stixotvorenija i poèmy*,
second ed., comp. D. E. Maksimov, ed.
M. I. Dikman. Leningrad, 1961.

Introduction

"IT IS OF GREAT IMPORTANCE what mask we were wearing the first time we appeared before the public. We lie a great deal, not because we want to deceive, but simply because we have to preserve the mask we once assumed."[1] Valery Bryusov wrote this to Ivan Bunin in the summer of 1899, a year before the appearance of his third book of poetry, *Tertia Vigilia*. The mask he had chosen was that of the Decadent poet, and it was to define his activity for many years to come.

Decadence as an esthetic or social category has never admitted of easy definition.[2] Prominent in much of Europe in the last two

---

1.   Ivan Bunin, "Letter to Bunin, August 1899," I, 446. All translations are mine unless otherwise noted.

2.   A recent study of Decadence in French literature is based on the premise that Decadence is a more central, less limited phenomenon in French art and letters than had hitherto been thought (Jean Pierrot, *The Decadent Imagination, 1880–1900*, tr. Derek Coltman [Chicago: University of Chicago Press, 1981]). The author opposes the generally held view that "the emergence of symbolism proper some time in 1885 or 1886 . . . was preceded and prepared by a seven- or eight-year transitional decadent period, the distinguishing features of which faded away once the symbolist doctrine had been definitely formulated" (p. 5). He argues that Decadence, even in poetry, was "much less transitory and much less negative than such a hypothesis might suggest." He proposes instead that "decadence constitutes the common denominator of all the literary trends that emerged during the last two decades of the nineteenth century" (p. 7). A hypothesis touching Russian literature, similar to Pierrot's but less elaborated, has been proposed by Vladimir Markov ("K voprosu o granicax dekadansa v russkoj poèzii [i o liričeskoj poème]," 2: 485–98). It is a subject that invites further investigation, in which the works of Valerij Briusov are certain to play a major role.

1

decades of the nineteenth century, Decadence—like most such movements—had varied sources. The pessimism and disgust with life expressed in various forms, notably in art, were an outgrowth of philosophical and social thought as well as a reaction to recent political events such as the Franco-Prussian War. The writings of Schopenhauer and Darwin combined with studies of heredity, criminality, and neurosis to suggest an irreversible decline in the vitality of the race, or at least of its European part. Art, with its own history and its own responses to man's outer and inner worlds, gave these strains voices and images: in short, an esthetic. Claiming writers such as Flaubert, Poe, and Baudelaire as predecessors, the generation that applauded Verlaine, D'Annunzio, Ibsen, Strindberg, Przybyszewski, Nietzsche, and Oscar Wilde rebelled against the empirical world about them and withdrew into worlds of their own construction. The forms this withdrawal took and their manifestations in art came to be called *Decadence*.

The movement that took shape in France in the mid-1880s found echoes in the literatures of many other countries. Russia's position in all this was, however, anomalous. Inclined during most of two centuries to take its cultural cues from the West, especially from France, Russia nonetheless was conscious of a history into which Western trends were imperfectly assimilated. Although reasons for pessimism and disgust were plentiful in Russian life during the latter part of the nineteenth century, the weariness of the French Decadent spirit did not evoke immediate sympathy, even in Russian poetry, which was emerging with uncertain steps from a period of near-oblivion. The poets of the 1880s were on the whole unimposing heirs to the Pushkin tradition. Their verses were largely elegiac and personal or mildly social in content; their craft was feeble. The early 1890s brought little improvement. Yet few, if any, poets looked for inspiration outside their cultural boundaries. That stagnant and politically reactionary period seemed to drain artists of the energy to look beyond Russia's borders for succor. Critics bemoaned the situation, but the official view, of necessity reflected in the press, was determinedly optimistic and chauvinistic. Decadence was therefore roundly denounced as a foreign phenomenon that might conceivably have some raison d'être in countries such as France but could hardly take root in Russia's fertile soil. The critic of *Messenger of Europe* wrote in 1887:

> Our poetry is still too young to be in need of artificial means of freshening and renewing—artificial means consisting of extraordinary subjects or unheard-of devices of creation. Even in France the future of course belongs not to the so-called *décadents*, boasting monstrosity of inspiration and form; still less is there room for such phenomena on our soil, offering so much untilled virgin land.[3]

Nonetheless, such protestations, more frequent near the turn of the century, themselves bore a nervous character. Some commentators took up the alarm sounded by Max Nordau's sensational tract *Entartung*, translated into Russian in 1894. Nordau undertook to show that most modern art derived from its creators' moral and mental degeneration and, unchecked, could lead to a general Völkerdämmerung. Others, such as the venerable Populist N. K. Mikhailovsky, wrote off Russian manifestations of Decadence as a blend of stupidity, lack of talent, and poor taste. Yet something was surely changing, and a fair part of the public felt some changes to be desirable. But Decadence, or Symbolism, in art—for the terms were then used interchangeably—was not the sort of change they had in mind. Accustomed for half a century to expect inspiration or moral indignation from literature, the public through its literary critics gave voice to sentiments ranging

3. K. K. Arsen'ev, "Soderžanie i forma v novejšej russkoj poèzii," *Vestnik Evropy* (January 1887): 246–47. For a discussion of the reception of Decadence in the Russian press in these years see Joan Delaney Grossman, "Genius and Madness: The Return of the Romantic Concept of the Poet in Russia at the End of the Nineteenth Century," *American Contributions to the Seventh International Congress of Slavists*, ed. Victor Terras, 3 vols. (The Hague: Mouton, 1973), 2, pp. 247–60.

from outrage to ridicule when a thin brochure called *Russian Symbolists* appeared, at its contributors' expense, in 1894. It was published anonymously, but Valery Bryusov was quickly labelled as the brochure's chief perpetrator, and the mask was firmly in place.

A twenty-year-old Moscow University student with ambitions that far outreached his experience or apparent powers, Bryusov was understandably elated at any attention whatsoever. He rejoiced when the newspapers referred to him by his surname alone, even in terms of abuse, and he played the role expected of him with zest. "I was shown off like a trained animal," he wrote of a visit to acquaintances in 1894. "I indulged in all the tricks of a trained beast—talked about Symbolism, recited poetry, waved my arms (a sign of originality)."[4] (His gift for self-irony developed early.) A critic later wrote: "Bryusov began his path as poet in a harlequin costume wearing a jester's cap, grimacing and mincing. . . . No one then guessed that under the thick layer of white and red clown's paint there was immense poetic force."[5] Bryusov would have welcomed a more dignified entry into the arena of art, but his instinct for the new directed him to seize the clues to recent developments in poetry that found their way to Russia and to use them in any way he could. Although his understanding of these developments was not yet deep, he was convinced that Russian poetry needed an infusion of new blood. If the result of his first experiments was a modest *succès de scandale*, at least it was in some small way a success.

The jester's cap was not his standard garb for long; even the dramatic mask of the Decadent poet sometimes cramped his features. Whereas some aspects of the Decadent spirit were alien to Bryusov and to Russian poetry generally, however, others suited

4. *Dnevniki*, p. 19.
5. N. Pojarkov, quoted in Ašukin, p. 68.

his temperament and shaped his conception of the role of the poet—a conception that had an important influence on his followers. At twenty, Bryusov dreamed of renewing and changing the course of Russian poetry; by thirty-five, he could take major credit for the literary transformation that had occurred. In 1923, the year before he died, the plaudits at a jubilee in his honor may have rung hollow to his ear, as his words to Vladimir Mayakovsky on that occasion suggest;[6] for at age fifty he was seeing the future that throughout his life had exercised an almost hypnotic hold on him and it did not meet his expectations. Whatever is to be said of his later years, however, cannot invalidate the contribution to Russian poetry he made in his prime. His old ally and fellow poet Fyodor Sologub interpreted the central goal and meaning of Bryusov's life at a memorial meeting in Leningrad nine days after his death: "The task with which Valery Bryusov charged himself consisted in freeing the art of the word from alien promptings, in returning to art its autonomous freedom, turning it from a mirror of life into a form-creating principle, a free creative action, freely striving for its own goals."[7] Most listeners no doubt understood that Sologub was eulogizing an earlier Bryusov, the leader of the movement to return Russian poetry to the high freedom of its Golden Age as well as the defender of modern poetry from the demands of the younger Symbolists that it be more than poetry. Whether from magnanimity or from personal knowledge, Sologub chose to interpret as submission to historical necessity Bryusov's apparently willing cooperation with the cultural designs of a government that gave freedom low priority. Sologub also saw a consistency in Bryusov that later observers disputed: "Under

6. To Majakovskij's congratulations he reportedly replied, "Thank you, but I wouldn't wish you such a jubilee" (L. Ju. Brik, "Čužie stixi. Glava iz vospominanij," *V. Majakovskij v vospominanijax sovremennikov* [Moscow, 1963], p. 353).

7. Fedor Sologub, "Speech in Memory of V. Ja. Brjusov," pp. 422–23.

all masks he always remained himself, always the same Valery Bryusov."[8]

Bryusov's vision of poet as herald of the future was born of a union between the nineteenth-century idea of progress and the Romantic concept of poet-prophet. The notion found itself in Decadence, where rejection of the present could include flight into the future as well as into the exotic. The close link between Bryusov's particular understanding of Decadence and his identity as a poet is treated in some detail in the following chapters. To him, at least in the 1890s and early 1900s, Decadence was the direction of the future, and the most truly contemporary spirits were those faced in that direction. Far from a mere slogan or device, the notion of poet as not only seer but also mover was fundamental to his self-concept. A man of Bryusov's temperament required satisfactions beyond the making of verses. It has been common enough to categorize Bryusov as a supremely able literary entrepreneur (as indeed he was) and to conclude that performing this role was the real driving force of his existence. Without denying its importance to him, we must see beyond it if we are to understand Bryusov. Whatever the sources of his ideas on poetry and the poet—and they apparently were most various—they combined under the pressures of his personality and circumstances into a coherent belief that dominated his life. To the nineteenth-century idea that poetry is the product of moments of heightened insight into the artist's soul and through it into the universe (Baudelaire provides striking formulations) Bryusov joined a cosmic evolutionism and an extreme individualism, along with theories about the unconscious that were then fermenting in Europe. Giving shape to it all was the vigorous excitement before frontiers to be pushed back that we associate with adventurers from Balboa to those heroes of science whose lives Bryusov read avidly as a boy. The frontiers most promising for Bryusov were those of human

8.   Ibid., p. 423.

consciousness, and the human activity most suited to explore them was poetry. Whatever its other associations, fin-de-siècle meant for artists such as he a mood of urgency in anticipation of a new age. If the zest and ambition with which he began his course eventually turned into less attractive qualities, this transformation is one of the dangers of a commitment that becomes a vested interest or of a prophet who becomes a mere dogmatist.

Poet, novelist, critic, literary activist, and man of letters par excellence, Valery Bryusov has long been a sign of contradiction for many students of Russian literature. Since about 1903 no one has questioned his importance in the history of Russian Symbolism, but few have been willing to grant him, once the excitement of that movement died away, the accolade he most desired: "poet of the Russian land." The purpose of this study is not to provoke a reevaluation of Russian Symbolism that would promote Bryusov to its first rank of poets. Although his poetry may gain in the process of review, whatever reassessment occurs is chiefly in the direction of a better understanding of Bryusov—his aims, his achievements, the man himself—than has hitherto been common, along with a better understanding of the transformations in Russian poetry at the beginning of this century.

In one important sense the time is right for such a reassessment. The revival of Bryusov studies both in the Soviet Union and in the West began in the mid-1950s.[9] In fact, this revival might almost be called a beginning. The earliest posthumous studies, the Formalist critics' writings summing up Bryusov's career, are still of considerable value but bear the mark of both their doctrine and their proximity to his own time. The émigré memoirs of the 1920s and early 1930s that deal with him have almost become period pieces in their own right. Some important

9. A bibliography of Russian and Soviet critical works concerning Brjusov, extending through 1973, with additions, forms the second part of *Bibliografija*.

documentary material was published in the Soviet Union in those years, but, for a variety of reasons, the time before the 1950s produced little substantial scholarship on Bryusov. Bryusov studies, unlike other beginnings of the 1950s, have continued to thrive in a modest way, with the help of official sponsorship and genuine interest by scholars in a period that was earlier largely out of bounds. A two-volume edition of selected works appeared in 1955. In 1969 D. E. Maksimov published a short but important work that significantly updated and corrected his 1940 book on Bryusov's poetry, a lone effort in its time. The centenary of Bryusov's birth in 1973 produced a seven-volume edition including most, though not all, of his poems; his novel *The Fiery Angel;* two other fictional works; and a good selection of his critical writing. In 1975 a volume of the prestigious Soviet documentary series *Literary Heritage* was devoted to Bryusov. Another volume in that series, devoted to his correspondence, is in progress. A good deal of archival material and commentary has found its way into print in other formats, though the larger part of his archive is as yet unpublished. Uneven though the quality of scholarship is, the Western scholar, whose access to Soviet archives is limited, can be grateful for this abundance. Moreover, some first-rate Soviet scholars have taken a hand in the enterprise.

On the other hand, Western scholars who over the years have paid serious attention to Bryusov form a very small cohort.[10] In

10.   The works referred to here are the following: Konstantin Močul'skij, *Valerij Brjusov*; Johannes Holthusen, *Studien zur Ästhetik und Poetik des russischen Symbolismus*; Alexander Schmidt, *Valerij Brjusovs Beitrag zur Literaturtheorie*; T. J. Binyon, "Valery Bryusov and the Nature of Art"; V. Setschkareff, "The Narrative Prose of Brjusov"; Victor Erlich, "The Maker and the Seer: Two Russian Symbolists"; and Martin P. Rice, *Valery Briusov and the Rise of Russian Symbolism*. Among interesting thematic studies are Danylo Struk, "The Great Escape: Principal Themes in Valerij Brjusov's Poetry"; and Irene Masing-Delič, "Limitation and Pain in Bryusov's and Blok's Poetry." An extremely informative and judicious study is the dissertation of T. J. Binyon, "Valery Yakovlevich Bryusov: Life, Literary Theory, Poetry."

1962 Konstantin Mochulsky's *Valery Bryusov* appeared posthumously in Paris. A synthesis of already published materials, it offered little new information. Wladimir Weidlé's introductory essay sought to correct what he took to be an overly favorable view. Both scholars' work manifested the viewpoint of the generation who knew Bryusov in his later years and for whom he had become a literary phenomenon rather than a living figure. Johannes Holthusen, Alexander Schmidt, and T. J. Binyon have studied Bryusov's esthetics; V. M. Setchkarev has dealt authoritatively with his narrative fiction. In a vivid and articulate essay, Victor Erlich expressed a view prominent in discussions of Symbolist poetry for many years, contrasting Bryusov and Alexander Blok as "The Maker and the Seer." Martin P. Rice's brief study, heretofore the only book on Bryusov in English, chronicled Bryusov's career with emphasis on its earlier phases. His most significant contribution may lie in the attempt to undermine the romantically inspired condemnation of Bryusov's esthetic stance expressed in Erlich's essay. Rice invokes the examples of Eliot and Pound to show that another tradition may look on these matters differently.

Several factors have combined to prevent Western scholars from paying Bryusov the attention his importance in the development of Russian poetry would seem to warrant. One obvious factor is the relative inaccessibility of primary materials. Countless documents of importance, including drafts and uncompleted works, remain unpublished. Moreover, some of his poetry and fiction and many critical pieces are found only in the earliest editions. A Decadent who became a Communist of course continues to present official problems: scholarly access to archives touching certain aspects of Bryusov's career is made extremely difficult. Formidable obstacles, then, stand in the way of study of a fascinating topic: a major literary figure who lived through the turmoil in Russia during the first quarter of this century and who reflected aspects of that experience in his career, an innovator to whom can be traced some basic features of modern Russian poetry. When these

obstacles are combined with the difficulty of achieving a balanced
view of the man himself, there emerges a kind of "Bryusov problem" within the larger area of Russian Symbolism (itself a far
from exhausted topic for study).

The problem of Bryusov is not a simple one. It lies both with
the poetry and with the man, along with the tendency to con-
fuse the two. Many people still alive remember Bryusov in his
later years. On balance, this has been a disadvantage for objective
study. Despite official acceptance, Bryusov in his last years (he
died in 1924 at the age of fifty) was not popular with the new
Bolshevik establishment in Russia nor, of course, with the many
outside this group. Some former associates who emigrated took
with them recent unpleasant memories of Bryusov's zeal in the
service of the new Soviet bureaucracy of culture: "poseur, mediocre poet, opportunist, petty dictator" are among the kinder epi-
thets used by several highly gifted memoirists. Zinaida Gippius,
writing before his death, in an essay called "One Possessed" described her former colleague as the slave of overweening ambition.[11] Vladislav Khodasevich, a young follower at the peak of
Bryusov's popularity, later cut his former hero down to life-size
(or perhaps smaller) in two brilliant but unreliable essays.[12] These
essays revealed a good deal about Bryusov but also about the
adulation he had once enjoyed and its consequences. Marina Tsvetaeva's famous "Hero of Labor" is even more clearly the work of a
disappointed hero-worshipper, full of fascinating but highly personal reminiscences.[13] Andrei Bely's memoirs give pictures of
Bryusov generally more favorable than those of Khodasevich and
Tsvetaeva, but heavily colored by Bely's blatant subjectivism.[14]
In recent years, recollections of the mature Bryusov as a kind and
skillful teacher have appeared in Soviet publications. More im-

11.   Gippius, "Oderžimyj (O Brjusove)."
12.   Xodasevič, "Konec Renaty," "Brjusov."
13.   Cvetaeva, "Geroj truda (zapisi o Valerii Brjusove)."
14.   Belyj, *Načalo veka*.

portant, recently published correspondence between Bryusov and such major figures as Bely and Vyacheslav Ivanov has opened new perspectives.[15] Yet, for Western readers at least, an unappealing image of Bryusov has by and large been fixed by earlier impressions.

The question one may ask is: does it matter? Should this inherited image of Bryusov the man affect our study of his poetry? Even if the picture is accurate—and there has always been ample reason to suspect the picture before us to be less than complete—this seems an inappropriate way to judge poetry. Of course, this is not to say that the image of the poet—especially a Symbolist poet who insisted that the essence of poetry was the poet's personality—should not be taken into account. The main problem here is the usual one of stereotypes: they discourage further investigation. The result is that our knowledge of a crucial period in modern Russian literature is significantly poorer than it might be. Bryusov was a shaper of modern Russian poetry in its initial stages—this much is acknowledged. It seems strange, then, that scholarly curiosity has not overcome the psychological barrier to a thorough study of this poet.

Another barrier exists, however: Bryusov's poetry itself. At the peak of his fame, around 1905, Bryusov was acclaimed as Russia's leading poet by, among others, Bely and Alexander Blok, both soon to rival him in the poetic firmament. This enthusiasm faded within a few years. Shortly after 1910, the Symbolist enterprise was pushed aside by a new generation of poets. While they anxiously watched the pages of *Russian Thought* for Bryusov's judgments of their new books, in their bumptious manifestoes they rejected him along with the rest of the Symbolist movement. Of course, this in itself is not enough to explain why Bryusov's poems have failed to achieve even a modest perennial popularity. Literary history is full of such abrupt shifts in taste. The question

15.   These and other selected letters appear in *LN* 85.

is why others rebounded and Bryusov, despite the reputation he once enjoyed, has not.

One obvious answer is that the hieratic language and exotic imagery used by the Symbolists rapidly became outdated. Perhaps Bryusov used more of these locutions, or perhaps the poems especially so marked are the ones that made him most popular. However, there are many poems in his *œuvre* that, to a reader coming on them freshly, sound anything but dated, and even the poems steeped in Symbolist imagery are sometimes reminiscent of the gracefully distorting forms of Art Nouveau. It thus seems unfair and inaccurate to dismiss him as "primarily a purveyor of well-wrought period pieces."[16] The problem is not so easily resolved. By almost any standards Bryusov wrote some splendid poetry. Without magnifying his talent beyond measure, other considerations may put the picture in fairer perspective.

The Formalist critic Yuri Tynyanov, in an essay written just after Bryusov's death, stated that the distinctive and valuable feature in Bryusov's work was its "tendency," not its poetic results.[17] Perceptive and judicious though the essay generally is, Tynyanov was writing at the ebb of Bryusov's poetic fortunes and, considering his own theories of literary development, could have been expected to reach just such a conclusion. He also offered a comment that speaks to the present problem: "If we pause on the question of what is new, what original in Bryusov as a literary phenomenon, we simply do not recall any one thing, any feature which absolutely marks him, any turn of verse which belongs to him alone, any intonation inseparably linked with him."[18] Bryusov seemingly developed no truly distinctive voice to ring in the ears of generations of readers.

Underlying this complaint is a comparison that has somehow

16.   Erlich, p. 97.

17.   "Valerij Brjusov," *Arxaisty i novatory* (Leningrad, 1929; reprinted, Wilhelm Fink Verlag, 1967), pp. 521–40.

18.   Ibid., p. 522.

become obligatory with Russian critics and readers: that of Bryusov with the younger poet Alexander Blok. In these terms Bryusov is regarded as emotionally shallow, a versifier of skill, a groundbreaker of some merit, but lacking the soul to produce genuine poetry. At the time the obvious comparison was with Konstantin Balmont, his fellow–pioneer Symbolist and Decadent. But for the later Russian reader turning to modern poetry, the lyrical magic of Blok, supported by the personal myth of the dreamer-seeker broken by his fate, has an almost hypnotic power, and Bryusov has often come to mind as a natural antithesis. This is not the place to consider in detail reasons for Blok's being regarded as a profoundly Russian poet. Yet one inviting field of exploration is that which Maksimov has called the "myth of the poet's path—*put'*," the poet's sense of passing through stages of artistic development that manifest the stages of his inner growth.[19] Blok and Bryusov were both strongly directed by this sense, but Blok, a few years younger, felt his "path" to be identified with his country's spiritual movement. Bryusov had a narrower preoccupation—his profound concern with poetry.

The non-Russian observer of Russian literary history may be struck by a "great man" theory of literature that does not seem to exist, at least to such a degree, in France or England. The names of Pushkin, Gogol, Tolstoy, Dostoevsky, and Blok seem to blot out those around them. The explanation may lie in the fact that the modern period of Russian literature dates from Pushkin, that is, from the early nineteenth century, and perhaps as a result is still permeated to a striking degree by certain Romantic conceptions of greatness. (Bryusov himself shared many of these conceptions, as will shortly be seen.) Moreover, the peculiar "Russian-

19.   Maksimov developed this notion in "Ideja puti v poetičeskom soznanii Al. Bloka," *Blokovskij sbornik II* (Tartu, 1972), pp. 25–121. See also Z. G. Minc and N. Pustygina, "'Mif o puti' i evoljucija pisatelej-simvolistov," in *Tezisy I vsesojuznoj (III) konferencii Tvorčestvo A. A. Bloka i russkaja kul'tura XX veka* (Tartu, 1975), pp. 147–52.

ness" of these authors has become an article of faith. Certainly, Bryusov thought of himself as a truly Russian poet, yet his poetic bias inevitably set him outside the mainstream. Much of Bryusov's poetry, whatever its ostensible topic, is metapoetry. The emotion may well be genuine, yet the poetry informed by it may seem less full-blooded than poetry whose primary inspiration is felt to be personal experience. T. S. Eliot has remarked that "there are many people who appreciate the expression of sincere emotion in verse, and there is a smaller number of people who can appreciate technical excellence. But very few know when there is an expression of *significant* emotion, emotion which has its life in the poem and not in the history of the poet." [20] All Symbolist poets, including Bryusov, believed that the poet's life and his poetry were inseparable, a view of which Eliot would hardly have approved. Nonetheless, even Symbolist poems may be judged by Eliot's criterion, that is, on their own merits and divorced from the personalities of the poets.

Bryusov's voice, then, to the ears of the generation that followed him contained no melody to be remembered. He dazzled and he moved on, leaving only traces of his past creation for the guidance of others. What Tynyanov does not consider is that this was the result of a deliberate artistic decision required by Bryusov's concept of the role of the poet. Examination of these matters forms an important theme of this book. Let it be recalled, however, that Bryusov was indeed, as Zinaida Gippius has said, obsessed by ambition, if not in just the sense she meant. For him to be a poet was to have the ambition to explore and enlarge the known universe by means of poetic language and images. Words, sounds, in all their variety and in continually new concatenations, were both the means and the object of investigation. Moreover, Bryusov's code put much stress on the act of exploration

20. "Tradition and the Individual Talent," *Selected Essays* (new edition, New York: Harcourt, Brace & World, 1960), p. 11.

itself. The poet had no right to stand in one place, however advantageous the viewpoint, and to paint essentially the same landscape over and over again. He must ever be off and over the next range of mountains, for his eye may see differently, his voice sound different in different surroundings.

The image of the adventurer-poet whose poetry was essentially the record of his spiritual travels was recognized and prized in Bryusov's own time. The origins of such a notion go back at least to Dante, but Bryusov's conception of his poetry as the sustained history of a contemporary soul struck his readers as new and important. Russian poets at the start of the twentieth century were aware that the Russian poetic tradition had subsided almost to quiescence during the third quarter of the last century, and its slow revival in the 1880s was generally only a pallid and less technically skilled reflection of the poetry of the first half of the century. Even those who, like Dmitri Merezhkovsky,[21] announced the coming change were relatively timid in their first steps in a new direction. Indeed, the image Merezhkovsky presented in his poems of that time was that of a pilgrim caught between night and daybreak, trapped in the cold predawn hours of whatever new day was ahead. This was not an image likely to energize and unite. Young Valery Bryusov was not by temperament the person to wait for a leader to emerge; he decided to be that figure himself. Finding little support in the work of recent Russian poets, he turned to the available models in France and Belgium. There was a good deal of the accidental in the first clues he seized upon, but of one thing he quickly became convinced: Symbolism, or Decadence, offered poetry a future. In Russia a leader was needed,

21.   Dmitrij Merežkovskij's essay "O pričinax upadka i o novyx tečenijax sovremennoj russkoj literatury [On the Reasons for the Decline and on New Currents in Contemporary Russian Literature]" (St. Petersburg, 1893) is generally regarded as a landmark. His collection *Simvoly* (St. Petersburg, 1892), poems which could hardly be called Symbolist, also raised hopes among those who looked for literary change.

a prophet in contemporary garb. For that role he volunteered, and because of the force of his personality and conviction, his contemporaries by and large accepted him. The peculiar sense of themselves as a new breed of men experiencing emotions and sensations unknown to their predecessors, which marked some of his generation in Russia and elsewhere, was only partially derived from Nietzsche. As has been seen, it was in the air. From the first Bryusov believed firmly that his was an eminently contemporary soul. The new word he had to say was simply the record of that soul—its moods, its experiences, its perceptions—in his poetry. The result might appear to be totally solipsistic: the image of a man who regards everything and everyone only in relation to himself. Bryusov's public image eventually came close to that. But some of his contemporaries, especially younger poets, were undeterred and even fascinated by such confidence in one's own vision. It was the Romantic concept of the poet reinstated, but with so strong an infusion of the fin-de-siècle spirit as to present a face that for a time seemed totally new.

Many readers recognize Bryusov easily as the author of such lines as "worship art, / Only art, unfalteringly, without reckoning," or "Love only yourself without limit" (both are from his "To a Young Poet"). In Bryusov's philosophy of poetry, these two counsels amounted to the same thing. Bryusov saw poetry as made up of insights into the universe caught through the window of the poet's soul at moments when the soul's nonrational powers were at their peak. Both the insights and the process interested him mightily. Some poems, such as the one cited above, deal overtly with this subject, and these are often anthologized. However, he also wrote of love, war, the city, civic turmoil, history, personal desires, frustration, loss. Many readers are dissatisfied, as has been remarked, because they fail to find in some of these poems the ring of authentic, appropriate human emotion. It may not remove their dissatisfaction or exculpate Bryusov entirely to recognize that love, war, and frustration are often not the primary subject, that these poems are often in fact about poetry.

An additional problem of interpretation arises here: to yield their full meaning, most of his poems need the context of other poems. While this problem is of Bryusov's own making, it is also connected with one of his more interesting artistic achievements. Bryusov's well-formulated conception of a book of poems as an integrated text rather than a mere collection of poems was an early and important contribution to modern Russian poetry. This means that his books, when read in their entirety, whatever their overt content, form a running narrative of the poet's exploration and expansion of his poetic universe. While some poems are explicit on this subject and some allegorical, many are neither. Yet the total corpus of each of his books bears this central theme. The advantage to such a system lies in the possibility of new layers of meaning and beauty emerging in individual poems from the more complex design of the whole. Its chief disadvantage lies in the difficulty of endowing both the whole and the individual parts with significance. The temptation to include, for the sake of the larger meaning, poems weak in themselves is not always resistible. The problem is compounded if the poet, especially over time, is known chiefly through selected works, as has been the case with Bryusov.

Bryusov's obsession with poetry and the poet narrowed the appeal of his work. That which was a reason for his powerful attraction for contemporaries who took courage and inspiration from his example and his words turned against him in a relatively short time. His concept of the poet as standing on the forward edge of the evolutionary movement of art held a danger he had not foreseen. Inevitably, he entered the generation of the "fathers," while the "sons" proclaimed with some justice that they were now the monitors of contemporaneity. After 1909 or 1910, Bryusov's position underwent an irreversible change. Yuri Tynyanov described the fate of Bryusov's poetic principle: in the first half of his career its drive coincided with the line of literary evolution and history, therefore having a complex development, but in the second half it moved by inertia, forsaking that line, and was consequently impoverished.[22] Formalist principles so applied may well oversimplify the phenomenon; nonetheless, it is undeniable that the Symbolist movement, which Bryusov fostered and for a time almost personified, grew, flowered, and withered in the first decade of this century. Both Bryusov's popularity and the direct influence of his poetry rose and fell with it.

There is excellent reason, then, to look at this phase of Bryusov's life as in some degree self-contained. It may be argued convincingly that the poetic features that defined his work in this period continued and even achieved their highest perfection in poetry written after 1910, and that his influence on the development of Russian poetry did not terminate with the decade. It may also be pointed out that Bryusov's career embraced more than poetry, and that some of his important critical work appeared in the later years. It is true that most of his prose fiction, including his novel *The Fiery Angel*, was written before 1910, and that his publicistic and organizational activity directed to securing the new art's position belonged to that time. But Bryusov always defined himself as a poet, and the impulse to be a poet, to live and write as one and to be so valued by the world at large, sustained, propelled, and provided an inner form to his activity. The image of poet-explorer which gave direction and excitement to the young Moscow Decadent and which he used to dazzle his early followers had long since ceased to be a mere mask; it had become the inner form of the man. When this self-image came into serious and prolonged question after the appearance of *Stephanos* in 1906, the effect on Bryusov can hardly be exaggerated. No matter if poetic techniques and some themes remained the same, the poet who

22. Tynjanov, p. 523.

employed them had entered another and quite distinct period of his career. This study attempts to trace the development of Bryusov's poetry in terms of his developing self-concept as poet. When this development reached its term, Bryusov's path necessarily took another direction, and a phase in many ways the most creative of his life was over.

The treatment of the subject is chronological, beginning with his discovery of Symbolism and his earliest published poetry in the three miscellanies of 1894 and 1895 called *Russian Symbolists*. The two editions of his first book *Chefs d'œuvre* (1895, 1896), with their clues to his poetic origins, set lines that reappeared in his mature poetry, while *Me eum esse* (1897) recorded his first spiritual pilgrimage and its results. Drafts and fragments of early critical pieces, largely unpublished, show him defining his understanding of the poetic tradition and his relation to it. Three volumes mark his rise to the summit of his career: they are *Tertia Vigilia* (1900), *Urbi et Orbi* (1903), and *Stephanos* (1906).[23] His 1909 volume, *All Melodies* [*Vse napevy*], was in his own view a kind of summation. Throughout, events of his personal life and career are discussed where relevant.

The present work does not pretend to be a full literary biography of Bryusov, even for the part of his life which is covered. This seems unfeasible at the present time for several reasons. Too much archival material remains unpublished and inaccessible. Too few preliminary studies of real critical substance on Bryusov have been published. Full assessment of a thirty-year career that included the most varied literary activity and crossed several literary epochs should probably await the filling in of many lacunae.

23. *Tertia Vigilia* referred to the third watch of the Roman sentry's night duty, i.e., on the brink of morning. *Urbi et Orbi* is the formula by which the Roman pontiff speaks as bishop of Rome and head of the universal church. He addresses himself "to the city and the world." *Stephanos*, which Brjusov translated into Russian as *venok*, referred to the laurel crown awarded the victor, a picture of which appeared on the cover of the book.

However, something is to be said for venturing now on a more limited enterprise, subject to later correction, with the hope of forwarding some well-equipped scholar in the task of a genuine history of Russian Symbolism.

A word should be said about the approaches employed here. First of all, chronology has been emphasized with special intent. The Bryusov of 1895 was not the Bryusov of 1910 or 1920, but too often critical, especially thematic, appraisals have made it seem as if he were. The tag "poet of marble," meant to describe the sculpted finish of his best poems, has been extended to his personality, and from there to the corpus of his works, treating them as monolithic. Bryusov himself was perhaps *overly* concerned with tracing his own development, but development there was, and struggle, victory, and defeat. He begged friends to read his books from start to finish, as the history of his soul. (In those days it went without saying that that was what readers wanted to know.) He kept diaries and wrote quantities of autobiographical sketches, all meant as commentary on his poetry and, of course, all arranged chronologically. Material newly available makes investigation along this line, and particularly of his earliest, formative period, particularly rewarding.

The desire to stay within decent limits of length precludes certain other attractive approaches. Analysis of the poems per se has been kept to a minimum; it is employed chiefly in support of other points in the discussion. Moreover, as has been noted, aspects of biography loom large in the assessment of a Symbolist poet. Bryusov's love affairs, particularly those with Nina Petrovskaya and Nadezhda Lvova, are generally seen as supporting the image of a callous exploiter, draining personal relations for the sake of art. Khodasevich, especially, recorded this image. Bryusov's letters to Nina and her memoir of him, which have been published in part in the *Literary Heritage* volume, put the case in a somewhat different light, and additional letters known to this writer substantially change the picture. Another revealing aspect of Bryusov is his interest in spiritualism, which needs interpretation in the light of his general world-view. Both these subjects are being dealt with in other work in preparation. More can certainly be said about Bryusov's relations with other poets, and his work in genres such as theater needs consideration. Finally, the termination of this study with the end of the first decade after 1900 is not meant to deny the substantial interest of his poetry and other activities thereafter. All these restrictions were dictated simply by the wish to give the fullest attention possible to that period of Bryusov's life unified by his poetic production and by its impact on the development of modern Russian poetry.

Photographs of Bryusov taken between 1900 and 1914 usually show a serious young man neatly dressed in a dark suit, with an appropriately thoughtful look in his dark eyes. Even the famous Vrubel portrait painted in 1906 conformed to this image. At no time, even during his earliest years as a Decadent, did Bryusov try to draw attention by extravagant dress or demeanor, by yellow vests or elaborate boutonnieres. In fact, the severity of his dress and visage became part of his personal legend. The first Moscow Symbolists, or Decadents, were relatively mild people who emulated their heroes, Edgar Allan Poe and Huysmans' Des Esseintes, chiefly in spirit. There were exceptions, and some Petersburg cousins such as the notorious Alexander Dobrolyubov were of a different cut. But Valery Bryusov was a young man bent not so much on overthrowing the establishment as on taking it over and transforming it. This he ultimately succeeded in doing to a large degree. The kind of notoriety early awarded him was only an incidental and transitory prize. From the very first he wanted something bigger, and he was remarkably single-minded in pursuing his goal.

His very efficiency told against him in some quarters. Khodasevich and Zinaida Gippius both spoke of his ordinariness, especially in his youth. After describing the pleasantly slim, modest-mannered youth in a tightly buttoned black jacket, Gippius offhandedly compared him to a chimpanzee.[24] His light tenor voice reminded her of that of a young salesclerk or the son of a merchant family—as, in fact, he was. Khodasevich added that such young men sold haberdashery in Moscow.[25] As Victor Erlich has written, "the Symbolist movement was the swan song of that part of the Russian intelligentsia which was drawn from the gentry or upper middle class. It was the product of a culture which achieved a high degree of intellectual and esthetic sophistication only to find itself faced with the prospect of inevitable extinction."[26]

The fact that Bryusov was not by inheritance a part of that world most likely affected his approach. Certainly he never found it necessary to reject his origins. In fact, long before it became politically advantageous, he publicized them. An autobiographical tale begun in the summer of 1900 opened with the words: "By descent I am a Kostroma peasant."[27] His paternal grandfather, an enterprising serf who bought his freedom, became a wealthy Moscow cork merchant. His maternal grandfather was a small farmer with literary pretensions, who published a book of original fables and looked for the day when posterity would place his name alongside those of Derzhavin, Krylov, and Pushkin. Mother and father were people of the sixties who read Darwin and Marx and Buckle, and they brought up their eldest son in this spirit. "I heard about the ideas of Darwin and the principles of materialism before I learned the multiplication tables," he wrote.[28] Not surprisingly, then, his brand of youthful revolt consisted in part of reading modern poetry and attending spiritualist seances.

24.   Gippius, p. 78.
25.   Xodasevič, p. 26.
26.   *Russian Formalism: History—Doctrine* (third ed. New Haven: Yale University Press, 1981), p. 34.
27.   "Moja junost'," *Iz moej žizni* (Moscow, 1927), p. 9.
28.   "Avtobiografija," p. 102.

Before reaching this stage, however, he developed a strong interest in natural history and, by extension, in the biographies of great men of science. From this it was only a step, as he said, to the novels of Jules Verne, Fenimore Cooper, and Mayne Reed. Entering Kreiman Gymnasium at eleven, he was far ahead of his schoolmates in scientific information and far behind in other respects. Some of his schoolmates were already "poets" and well read for their years in Russian literature. He rushed to catch up. However, apparently he learned less edifying things also from his schoolmates, and taking advantage of a distracted home situation (his brother was ill, his father was losing money on horses), early made the acquaintance of brothels, with which his neighborhood was well supplied. Dismissed from Kreiman's for insubordination, he was fortunate enough to be accepted after a lapse of time at a much better school, the Polivanov Gymnasium, headed by the noted educator and Pushkin scholar Lev Polivanov. Polivanov both appreciated and disciplined the active mind of his new pupil. Bryusov's great interests were now mathematics and philosophy, which he paraded before classmates and teachers. His published diary begins with spirited epigrams by classmates on "Valery Bryusov-genius." They translate badly, but one of them is worth rendering for the sense: "Mathematician and poet, / And passionate philosopher. / 'What, is he a phenomenon, then? Oh, no! / Just a terrible braggart.'"[29] One day Polivanov entered the game by walking into a classroom and handing Bryusov "Confessions of a Pseudo-Poet-Frenchman," a parody on a poem that Bryusov had proudly recited before his French teacher.[30] Bryusov enjoyed the joke enough to preserve it.

At this stage Bryusov began the attempt to define his vocation as a poet, though without solid ground beneath his feet. In 1892 he encountered Symbolism and began to assimilate it. In 1894,

29. *Dnevniki*, p. 3.
30. Ibid., p. 11.

the year after he entered Moscow University, he met Konstantin Balmont. Together the two wrote and recited poetry. Bryusov soon produced his first independent book. After his second book, he retired to take stock and equip himself seriously for the task of reviving Russian poetry and becoming a real poet. His passage through Moscow University took six years instead of four, in part because he was pursuing both philosophy and history and in part because his literary concerns occupied much of his time. He published little poetry between 1897 and 1899; instead, he plunged into the Russian poetic tradition, thinking and writing steadily about poetry itself and about the poets. Some of his writings of that time, largely unpublished, help to provide the outline of Bryusov's intellectual and artistic formation presented in this book. In 1899 he published an essay *About Art*, conceived as a response to Leo Tolstoy's *What Is Art?* Tolstoy ignored it, but others did not, and Bryusov was launched in a modest way in his career as literary theorist. In 1900, with the publication of *Tertia Vigilia*, he felt he had attained not only a high level of technical excellence but a clear conception of where he was going, what poetry was, and what it meant to be a poet. This book exhibits some of his poetry's most striking features. His next two books, *Urbi et Orbi* and *Stephanos*, established him in the view of many as Russia's foremost poet.

Meanwhile, literary undertakings seemed to spring up around Bryusov. The new movement was taking shape, largely through his efforts. He was cofounder and a moving force of the publishing house Scorpio, devoted to propagating the new art, both Russian and Western. Other literary enterprises increasingly sought his cooperation. In modern terms we would say he infiltrated the artistic establishment, represented by the Moscow Literary-Artistic Circle, in 1902, and from 1908 till after the 1917 Revolution he was its director. As de facto editor of the elegant Symbolist monthly *The Balance* through most of its six-year existence, he held a guiding position in the movement. When *The Balance* ceased publication at the end of 1909, its directors claimed with considerable justification that its purposes of propagating the new art and the ideas behind it had largely been accomplished. But Symbolism was then rent by inward tensions. The Petersburg journal *Apollo*, whose first issue almost coincided with the last of *The Balance*, seemed initially the logical place for one who, like Bryusov, had regarded Symbolism as an esthetic mode and rejected its extension to matters of religion and philosophy. Perhaps the last important Symbolist debate appeared on its pages in 1910, when Vyacheslav Ivanov and Alexander Blok stated the case for a theurgic poetry and Bryusov strongly restated his position in favor of a free poetry subservient to no external goals. Andrei Bely's response charged Bryusov with betrayal. With that the Symbolist consensus, which had existed only minimally for some years, came openly to an end.

For some time Bryusov had been looking about for other fields of endeavor, and in 1910 he took over the literary section of the solid monthly *Russian Thought*, edited and published by Peter Struve, leader of the Constitutional Democrats. Bryusov and other Symbolists had already been publishing in this journal, and Merezhkovsky was for a time its literary editor. Bryusov now hoped to steer it more firmly in the Symbolist direction, but his success was limited. Over the next two or three years, moreover, the center of interest and controversy in literature shifted to new movements, proclaimed as Futurism and Acmeism. Bryusov judged their productions astutely from his seat on *Russian Thought*.

In 1912, leaving his post as the literary editor of *Russian Thought*, Bryusov turned to other activities. Volumes of poetry appeared at quite regular intervals for the rest of his life: *Mirror of Shadows* [*Zerkalo tenej*] in 1912, *Seven Colors of the Rainbow* [*Sem' cvetov radugi*] in 1916, *Experiments* [*Opyty*] in 1918, *Last Dreams* [*Poslednie mečty*] in 1920, *In Such Days* [*V takie dni*] in 1921, *Instant* [*Mig*] and *Distances* [*Dali*] in 1922, and *Mea* in 1924. In 1913 a small volume appeared called *Verses by/to Nellie* (the Russian *Stixi*

Nelli is ambiguous). It purported to be the work of a woman, presumably Nadezhda Lvova, but Bryusov's authorship or major collaboration has long been inferred. Various volumes of translations appeared also during these years: of Verlaine, Verhaeren, Ausonius, and Poe, as well as a selection of French nineteenth-century poetry.

In 1908 Bryusov began a project which suggests the conscious termination of a phase of his career. This was a collected edition in three volumes of all his poetry thus far. *Roads and Crossroads* [*Puti i pereput'ja*] preserved the shape of each previous collection, though the two editions of *Chefs d'œuvre* were collapsed into one and augmented by other poems to form a section called "Youthful Poems: 1892–1896." The other books were revised and their titles translated into Russian. The third volume was his new *All Melodies* (1909). (What this project meant to him in terms of ends and beginnings is taken up in Chapter Ten, below.) In 1913 a yet larger summary project got underway. This was to be a complete scholarly edition of his original works and translations, in twenty-five volumes. Volumes I–IV, XII, XIII, XV, and XXI appeared in 1913 and 1914. With that the series was terminated, for the publisher encountered difficulties, and Bryusov was unable to find another publisher willing to take it on at that time. Thus he suffered a severe blow both financially and personally.

When war broke out in August 1914, Bryusov went to the front as a war correspondent. At first he was filled with patriotic exaltation. Difficult access to the front (he was confined for much of the time in Warsaw) and problems getting his dispatches published supported other reasons for dissatisfaction and disillusion. He returned home in mid-1915. Immediately thereafter he undertook, at Gorky's recommendation, the editing of an anthology of Armenian verse in Russian translation, a project in support of the Armenian people then under persecution in Turkey. Bryusov threw himself into the task, studying the language as well as Armenian history and culture, making translations himself and re-

cruiting his fellow Symbolists to make others. Eventually he travelled to Transcaucasia to give a series of benefit lectures. This
project absorbed much of his time and energy until the beginning
of 1917.

The February 1917 Revolution found Bryusov in weak health.
Despite the impression of robustness he gave in his earlier years,
he had suffered intermittent bouts of illness. More serious than
these was his addiction to morphine, which began during his prolonged affair with Nina Petrovskaya. Efforts at a cure were unsuccessful, and photos of Bryusov in his later forties show a prematurely aged man. Nonetheless, he greeted February 1917 with
an enthusiasm that was consistent with his attitudes for years past
and with those of most of his fellow poets. Basically apolitical,
Bryusov shared the general ecstatic hope that a new Russian day
was dawning. The ineffectual conduct of the war by the Tsar
could only have intensified his disgust with the old regime. As
his brief flurry of excitement over the 1905 Revolution demonstrated, Bryusov was a strong nationalist, detested vacillation in
government, and admired shows of strength.

When the October Revolution came, Bryusov was ill and de-
spondent. It is noteworthy that over a decade earlier he had expressed distrust of Lenin's party for its intolerance of opposing
views and had opined that the situation of art would be no better
under them than before. Whatever his motives in 1917—and
they were probably mixed—Bryusov, like many other literary
figures, went to work for the Bolshevik regime. A position in its
cultural apparatus, including censorship, no doubt provided him
with the sense and to a degree the actuality of at last being able to
influence the shape of art in days to come. In his new situation he
made new enemies, and old ones took satisfaction in pointing out
the correctness of their assessments of his character, to say nothing
of his art. He edited, he censored, he administered, he sat on endless committees. For Bryusov, the most satisfying of his multi-
tudinous activities in those years was his teaching. He held vari-

ous posts in rapid succession and sometimes simultaneously. He taught Greek and Latin literature, the history of Russian literature, the techniques of poetry. The institute which he headed from the summer of 1921, the Higher Institute of Literature and Art, gave him an audience of would-be poets as large as any that had ever listened to him in the heady days of Moscow Symbolism. The students before him were largely proletarians, and no important writers emerged from among them, but at least he was engaged in raising the cultural level of the masses, which presumably gave him some satisfaction.

This orgy of activity may have been a narcotic of another kind to numb Bryusov's increasing sense of isolation. As Elena Pasternak wrote in an important article on the relations of Bryusov and Boris Pasternak, by that time Bryusov had fallen from the status of a public idol to "the ambiguous position of an official personage and at the same time the target for attacks by the artistic youth and the educated class. His recognition by the government was taken as a statement of the death of creative power and the end of any real biography, which Bryusov was forced, with bitterness and pain, to acknowledge and accept."[31]

One bright aspect of Bryusov's life in those last years was his relationship with Boris Pasternak. Nearly twenty years younger than Bryusov, Pasternak belonged to the generation of "sons" who displaced and largely disowned their Symbolist "fathers." Pasternak occupied an independent position among the Futurists, shown not least in his ability to value the historical contribution and even the poetry of the generation before him, while taking a very different path. Quite early in his career he rejected what he called the Romantic manner, the conception of life as show, which contemporaries (among whom Mayakovsky was foremost)

31. Elena Pasternak, "Pasternak i Brjusov. K istorii otnošenij," *Rossija. Russia* 3 (1977): 243.

had taken over from the Symbolists.[32] This and other features apparently separated him from Bryusov. However, two letters written to Bryusov in 1922 reveal a remarkable sympathy between the two and do much to illuminate the poem that Pasternak presented at the ill-fated 1923 jubilee.[33] Elena Pasternak notes that the warmth of attention which Boris Pasternak showed Bryusov in 1922 and 1923 was prompted in part by his sensitive awareness of Bryusov's painful position. Beyond this, Pasternak valued Bryusov's professional devotion to literature. While separating himself from Khodasevich and others whose beginnings were directly influenced by Bryusov, Pasternak acknowledged yet another connection. More than any external model, Bryusov had provided a kind of inwardly held image difficult for Pasternak to describe, but strongly felt: "Most of all I am grateful to you for this, that while, it seems, not imitating you, sometimes I feel Bryusov in me—that is when I feel over me, behind me, and in me—the poet."[34]

In the jubilee poem "To Bryusov," Pasternak expresses sympathy as well as congratulations to a master who was also in some sense a father, with whom he talks as Hamlet with his father's ghost. In none of this was there much indication of Pasternak's attitude toward Bryusov's poetry as such. Over twenty years later Pasternak's annotated copy of a 1945 edition of selected poems by Bryusov revealed his judgments, as Elena Pasternak says, "from new positions in his [Pasternak's] biography, of the creative line he had chosen, and the mastery and maturity he had achieved."[35]

32. Boris Pasternak, "Oxrannaja gramota," *Sočinenija: Proza 1915–1958* (Ann Arbor: University of Michigan Press, 1961), pp. 281–82.

33. "Brjusovu," *Sočinenija: Stixi i poèmy 1912–1932*, pp. 236–37. This relationship is discussed in Lazar Fleishman, *Boris Pasternak v dvadcatye gody* (Munich: Wilhelm Fink Verlag, [1981]), pp. 34–39. See also K. A. Paxanjanc, "V. Brjusov i B. Pasternak," *Brjusovskie čtenija 1973* (Erevan, 1976), pp. 278–94.

34. Quoted by Elena Pasternak, p. 246.

35. Ibid., p. 252.

30   INTRODUCTION

There is no guarantee that these judgments, made at a later stage
in his artistic development, mixed as they were, were identical
with Pasternak's earlier ones. He underlined sentiments of Bryusov's with which he could have agreed, for example: "The essence
of works of art is the personality of the artist."[36]

Yet much about Pasternak's attitude toward Bryusov, both early
and late, points to the watershed that separated Symbolism from
all that came after it. The Futurist and Acmeist movements and
the Formalist school of criticism that grew up in their immediate
wake marked a shift of sensibility so acute that, allowing for vari-
ations, especially in the case of Blok, the kind of sympathy that
makes an audience receptive to an artist no longer existed for the
Symbolists. A clear early example of this can be seen in the review
of the third and fourth volumes of Bryusov's collected works,
published in 1915, by the young soon-to-be-Formalist critic
Boris Eikhenbaum.[37] These volumes contained the three books
that represent Bryusov at the peak of his powers and popularity:
Urbi et Orbi, *Stephanos*, and *All Melodies*, published originally in
1903, 1906, and 1909. Only a few years later, to a critic speaking
from a new esthetic position, they seemed lifeless things: "We
have somehow become accustomed to think that the poet is dif-
ferentiated from other people, non-poets, by one mysterious gift
almost inspiring terror, the gift of direct knowledge of the nou-
menal world," wrote Eikhenbaum. ". . . We saw in the poet not
only a singer but a prophet. Such was our tradition, coming from
Pushkin, from Venevitinov. . . . In every poet we have loved to
feel that he *knows* something. But here—that tradition has been
broken. Bryusov is a poet, but he is not a prophet."[38] The history
of a poet's soul turns out, from the viewpoint of another era, to
have led nowhere, but in fact that other era was impatient with
the whole search. Bryusov, like Balmont, is "alien to the earth,"

36. Ibid., p. 253.
37. *Severnye zapiski* (April 1915): 223–25.
38. Ibid., pp. 223–24.

while what that earth wants, as this new generation sees it, is to be loved for itself. There seems to be a contradiction in Eikhenbaum's position: not even a successful prophet could expect a hearing where prophecy had gone out of fashion.

The temper of a new era thus colors critical judgment, and the very strength of the Symbolist movement in its own time is shown in the reaction against it. What we might have liked to hear from so able a critic as Eikenbaum is not merely what Bryusov lacked as a prophet but what kind of poet he was deemed to be. As Tynyanov and others have demonstrated, the Formalists viewed literature through a lens that effectually filtered out those elements that gave Symbolist poetry its particular character, and some other important ones as well. Yet their judgments, along with a few other influential ones, have been allowed to stand. We thus have again the reasons for reviewing the case of Valery Bryusov to understand better his achievement and his rightful place in the history of Russian poetry. The chapters that follow, it is hoped, will contribute to that process.

ONE

Russian Symbolists

A SURVEY of the Russian literature of 1891 in
Russian Thought anxiously posed the questions: "How does the
past year in fact stand out in regard to literature? Was it distinguished in any way from any year of the past decade, did it have
its own physiognomy, did it leave us any worthwhile bequest?"
And the answers came: "No, it was not distinguished, it had
none, it left nothing!"[1] Most critics writing in the major journals
at that time looked for the kinds of literature that offered social
and moral uplift. They were not ready to applaud new writing
that did not fit this category. Others were also discontented with
the present state of Russian letters, though for different reasons.
In the fall of 1892 Valery Bryusov was nearly nineteen and beginning his final year in Polivanov's Gymnasium in Moscow. Earlier
that year he had come upon the diary of the young artist Marie
Bashkirtseff, who, dying in Paris in 1884, left a compelling record of her ambitions, talents, and unfulfilled hopes.[2] In this document Bryusov recognized his own immense uncertainties, fears,
and frustrations, along with a kindred conviction of talent and
mission. In August he had written in his diary, perhaps to convince himself: "I was born a poet. Yes! Yes! Yes!"[3] But the prob-

1.   M. A. Protopopov, "Pis'ma o literature," *Russkaja mysl'* no. 1 (January
1892): sec. 2, p. 41.
2.   *Dnevniki*, pp. 5–6, 146–47. A Russian translation appeared in *Severnyj vestnik* during 1892.
3.   ·Ibid., p. 8.

lem was to find a direction: Russian literature seemed at that point to have nothing inspiring to offer.

Bryusov came to Russian poetry relatively late. In his childhood he had pored óver biographies of great inventors and men of science. From those he moved on to the novels of Jules Verne, James Fenimore Cooper, and others. However, by the time he reached Polivanov's he already considered himself a poet, writing variously in the styles of Lermontov, Nekrasov, and Nadson. At Polivanov's he turned enthusiastically to Pushkin and discovered Tyutchev and Fet. His notebooks now were full of clippings and copies of Fofanov, Lokhvitskaya, and other poets of the eighties. His newest discovery in the fall of 1892 was Merezhkovsky's *Symbols.* Yet nowhere did he find the guidance he wanted. Then the September 1892 issue of *Messenger of Europe* carried Zinaida Vengerova's article "Symbolist Poets in France."[4] Bryusov read it and was enthralled. His new departure was at hand.

Vengerova's article was a reasonably comprehensive summary of recent events in French poetry, directed to a readership that knew next to nothing about the subject. Many of the points she elaborated must have seemed to Bryusov like answers to questions that he had not known how to formulate. He absorbed her information hungrily and doubtless rushed out to the bookstore on Kuznetsky Most owned by the father of his friend Alexander Lang to find books by Mallarmé, Verlaine, and other poets whose names he had read for the first time. The effect of the Symbolist revelation on Bryusov's literary activity was immediate. His first

---

4. Zinaida Vengerova, "Poèty simvolisty vo Francii," *Vestnik Evropy* no. 9 (1892): 115–43. Zinaida Vengerova, sister of the noted literary historian and Pushkin scholar S. A. Vengerov, specialized through her critical writing and translation in bringing Western writers, especially English ones, to Russian attention. She also wrote on Russian literature for foreign journals and was an early translator of Tolstoj into English. Not much older than Brjusov (she was born in 1867), she had established a reputation as a journalist well before 1900.

venture was into translation. By December he was translating Verlaine, whom he still found necessary to label in his diary as "(Symbolist Poet)." On 2 January he dispatched these translations to *News of Foreign Literature*, in the first of several unsuccessful efforts to ride to fame on the coattails of the new French poets introduced to Russian readers by the respectable *Messenger of Europe*. In March he was working at translations from Mallarmé, but here too his efforts at publication failed. However, the significance of the experience is shown by two portentous diary entries of this period. On 4 March he wrote in words reminiscent of Marie Bashkirtseff: "Talent, even genius, by honest means earns only gradual success, if that. That's not enough! For me it's not enough. I must choose another way. . . . Find a lodestar in the mist." Then comes the well-known moment of illumination: "And I see it: Decadence. Yes! Whatever one may say, whether it is false, or ridiculous, it is moving ahead, developing, and the future belongs to it, especially when it finds a worthy leader. And that leader will be *I!* Yes, *I!*"[5]

The nineteen-year-old who hoped to set Russian poetry moving again now believed he had found his direction. The attitude which became so characteristic of him, that of listening for the future, was here formulated possibly for the first time. A short time later he returned to the point: "What if I tried to write a treatise on spectral analysis couched in the language of Homer? I wouldn't have the words or the expressions. The same thing if I try to express fin-de-siècle sensations in Pushkin's language. Yes, Symbolism is necessary!"[6] Art must be with the times or ahead of them, for art is the expression of the poet's soul, and the artist, almost by definition, is the most contemporary of men. More sensitive than his peers to the winds of the future, he is destined at times to prophesy to them. These were the convictions already

5. *Dnevniki*, p. 12.   6. Ibid., p. 13.

forming in Bryusov. They served as a powerful stimulus for a
young man possessed of extraordinary ambition and talent.

Ever practical, Bryusov promptly saw the necessity of creating
a Russian Symbolist movement or at least the illusion of one. If
Russian poetry was to be transformed, it was imperative to draw
public attention and eventually, he hoped, support. He tested his
powers of leadership in a small way among his schoolmates,
whipping up enthusiasm first for Merezhkovsky's *Symbols* and
then for Decadence.[7] But beyond this, it was absolutely required
that he, the future chief, publish and be noticed. Efforts at placing translations had so far failed. Now during the summer of
1893, with his friend Alexander Lang, Bryusov devised another
means of breaking into print. His inspiration probably came from
Verlaine's *Poètes maudits*, which he discovered that spring. When,
in 1883, these sketches began to appear, they reportedly transformed literary fashion in Paris overnight. Verlaine's series combined critical and biographical introductions with poems. However, he dealt with poets of some repute and stature (his first series
included Tristan Corbière, Rimbaud, and Mallarmé). Bryusov
was forced to take another tack. By fall he and Lang had ready for
the censor a small volume entitled *Russian Symbolists*, hopefully
designated "No. 1." Only these two, Bryusov and Miropolsky
(Lang) appeared, along with the fictional publisher V. A. Maslov,
who was Bryusov himself.[8] The censor's permission was granted
on 30 December, and the book was out by the end of February
1894. This was Bryusov's poetic debut.

Bryusov later maintained that the purpose of these volumes
was to provide models of various poetic forms.[9] Moreover, by as-

7.   Ibid.
8.   The name *Maslov* was a tribute, one of many, to Elena Maslova, his
first "Decadent" love, who died of smallpox in May 1893. His diary, in both
published and unpublished sections, contains extreme expressions of grief at her
death (*Dnevniki*, pp. 13ff.; Ašukin, pp. 52–53; I, 566).
9.   K. Loks, "Brjusov—teoretik simvolizma," *LN* 27–28, p. 266.

serting that there *was* a Russian Symbolist school, he hoped to create one and ultimately to win acceptance for the new poetry. The reception given the first issue made clear, however, that neither result would soon be forthcoming. The first volume contained two sections. Eighteen lyrics over Bryusov's name occupied twenty-five pages. The contribution of Miropolsky (Lang) included two selections in poetic prose and two lyrics, taking up in all ten pages. Bryusov's section used an epigraph from Mallarmé: "Une dentelle s'abolit / Dans le doute du jeu suprême." The first poem in the section bore in manuscript the notation "From M.(?) Mallarmé (sonnet)." [10] However, the resemblance to a sonnet by Mallarmé was limited to the attempt at approximating Mallarmé's mood and technique through unlikely images and word combinations. Nonetheless, the form, a trochaic tetrameter sonnet, was novel in Russian. [11] Bryusov's first section was completed by a translation of Verlaine's "Il pleure dans mon cœur" and a poem "From Maeterlinck." [12]

Having established the Symbolist tone of his contribution, Bryusov changed key in a section entitled "First Happiness" that was dedicated to the memory of "E." [13] Here translations from Verlaine ("Cythère" and "Voeu" from *Fêtes galantes* and *Poèmes saturniens*) mingled with poems showing the influences of Fet and Heine, and in the midst an echo of Pushkin. "From the Portuguese" is an interesting example of Bryusov's use of allusion, echo, quotation, and adaptation. In manuscript he used an epi-

10. I, 33–34, 567.
11. N. Gudzij, "Iz istorii rannego russkogo simvolizma," p. 202.
12. I, 567.
13. "E." was of course Elena Maslova. Brjusov also dedicated poems of this period to "Talja," (Natal'ja Daruzes), "Manja" (Marija Širjaeva), and others, but the Elena Maslova ("Lëlja") poems are usually those associated with lost love and death [III, 592]. The manuscript of "S portugal'skogo" (later "Polutëmnoe okoško") bears, along with the epigraph from Pushkin, the notation: "To Lëlja. 4 May. After the rendezvous (posle svidanija)" [I, 569]. This is of course a vivid early illustration of how Brjusov converted life experience to literary use.

graph from Pushkin's free translation under the same title of a
love song by the Brazilian poet T. A. Gonzaga. The use he made
of Pushkin's piece accords well with the method of free adaptation
Bryusov had used for Mallarmé. His meter here is that of Pushkin—trochaic tetrameter with strong second and fourth stresses.
The rhyme scheme, however, is different: Bryusov's alternating
rhymes replacing Pushkin's rhymed couplets change the intonation, and indeed the whole emotional tone of Bryusov's poem differs from Pushkin's. Pushkin's—or Gonzaga's—hero is a simple
shepherd who watches his beloved from a distance as he tends her
favorite lamb with special care. When she approaches, he cheers
her heart with his love song, but the bliss passes, and his song is
replaced by hopeless tears. Pushkin's poem has eleven quatrains,
chiefly devoted to narrative frame for the brief song, with moments of intimacy only implied. Bryusov's focus is on that intimacy. Of its four quatrains, one exhorts the beloved to prepare for
his coming and two look ahead to the actual moments of love. In
the concluding stanza there is a sudden Symbolist elevation of
"dream" (*mečta*) at the end, where the dream becomes the most
important and lasting part of the experience: "Under cover of
darkness everything will drown for us in enchanting languor, except the intoxicating dream." Pushkin's poem is evoked to under-
line Bryusov's method: perennial motifs are updated in a way
which he conceived to be peculiarly modern.

Despite the mixture of ingredients in this second section,
Bryusov achieved in these seven poems something of that inner
logic that would mark the cycles and sections in his later collections. From the first meeting to the closing sonnet from Verlaine,
the episode of first love is traced through its development to its
sad conclusion, culminating with recognition of man's dependence on woman. The third section, also containing seven poems,
was entitled "New Fancies" (*Novye grezy*). These brief love poems
sketch a second love with a "sadder-but-wiser" motif. While they
owe something to French Symbolist inspiration, they also show

mingled Russian influences: Fet, Tyutchev, Fofanov, and others.[14] However, Bryusov closed his part of the volume with a rousing reassertion of Symbolist pretensions (in the poem that so appealed to Vladimir Solovyov's sense of humor, as will be seen below): "Golden-hued fairies / In a satin garden."

Russian Symbolists, No. 1, was barely out when the second volume was being planned by the two collaborators. Despite reviews almost exclusively bad, other budding Symbolists began to communicate with Bryusov. Two or possibly three new contributors were admitted to the circle.[15] For a brief moment in June 1894, Bryusov thought he had secured two allies of superior talent: Alexander Dobrolyubov and Vladimir Gippius, young poets from Petersburg, came to visit him. Bryusov's diary tells how Dobrolyubov especially impressed him with his poems, his views on literature, and in part his "arch-Symbolist" behavior, including the taking of opium. The alliance fell apart when the visitors tried to throw out half the contributions and drastically rewrite the rest (though Bryusov subsequently decided their criticisms were right).[16] Nonetheless, they did not lose touch, and their visit left its mark on Bryusov's thinking, as will be seen later. Of the eight

---

14. Gudzij, pp. 207–8.

15. The new contributors in *Russkie simvolisty*, No. 2, were Erl. Martov (pseudonym of Bugon); N. Novič (pseudonym of N. Baxtin); Z. Fuks, Sozontov, Darov, M., and *** (all pseudonyms of Brjusov); and A. Bronin (Gudzij, 183ff.). Writing to his literary Petersburg friend Petr Percov, Brjusov confessed to several of his pseudonyms but not to "Darov" or "Fuks" (*Percovu*, p. 34). He maintained the fiction further by remarking somewhat later to Percov, "How many Zinaidas we have!—Gippius, Vengerova, Fuks!—and they are all sympathetic to Symbolism!" (*Percovu*, p. 52). Gudzij reported that manuscripts of the poem signed "Z. Fuks" were written by Brjusov (Gudzij, p. 184). The case of "Darov" is more complicated and will be treated in Chapter Three. Of the genuine contributors, only one made any subsequent contribution to literature. He was a minor translator and also a bibliographer of some note, compiler of the "Kartoteka Baxtina," a catalogue of translations from foreign literatures into Russian which is kept in IRLI.

16. *Dnevniki*, pp. 17–18.

new signatures in the second issue, five belonged to Bryusov. While four poems were actually signed with his name, in fact six more, plus a prose translation from Mallarmé, were from his pen.

The new volume advanced the theme of music in vaguely Symbolist fashion.[17] The four sections were called "Notes," "Scales," "Chords," and "Suites," though no obvious reason for these titles is suggested by the poems themselves. Each section had from five to seven items, and Bryusov assigned one poem in his own name to each. This of course enabled him to place his own contributions advantageously. This strategy was already guessed by Vladimir Gippius at the time of the June visit. Going over the materials planned for inclusion, Gippius noticed what he considered skulduggery on the part of Bryusov and Miropolsky: "'You're purposely printing your . . . un-Decadent poems and other people's Decadent ones. That way the critics, who are generally hostile to Decadents, will start praising you. But it's terrible and dishonorable to act from such motives in a serious matter.' The wretch was right," Bryusov continued his report to Lang, "though of course I defended us to the last degree."[18]

Bryusov apparently chose to play down his position as contributor to this volume, perhaps to give weight to his signed introduction, which endeavored to present a serious explanation of Symbolism (see Chapter Three). His acknowledged contributions were conservative as well as few. Two were translations: one of Verlaine's "La lune blanche," the other "From a Letter" by Marceline Desbordes-Valmore, who, though she died in 1859, was

---

17.   Aleksandr Dobroljubov's volume *Natura Naturans: Natura Naturata* used musical designations equally idiosyncratically ([St. Petersburg, 1895]; reprinted in *Sočinenija*, ed. Joan Delaney Grossman [Berkeley: Berkeley Slavic Specialties, 1981]). Dobroljubov was much enamored of the notion that poetry at its highest level merged with music (Vengerov, *Russkaja literatura XX veka*, I, 276).

18.   Gudzij, p. 192.

included in Verlaine's *Poètes maudits*. Both pieces are simple and musical.[19]

Bryusov's pseudonymous offerings, on the other hand, were designed to shock. They are gathered chiefly in the third section, "Suites" (numbered IV). Two are by "Darov," one by "Sozontov," and one is signed "***." Sozontov's "Saga," with its determined use of synaesthesia, reads like a parody. Darov's "The black waves advanced, they gushed" ends with a line Vladimir Solovyov might well have singled out for mockery: "They rise, they go . . . , but where? To an exploit / Or to shame?" The second Darov poem, which closes the section, is a tour de force of Russian hushing sounds, anticipating some of the more extreme performances of Balmont and later experimenters. But Bryusov saved the greatest shock till last: a Baudelairean vision of "A woman's corpse, rotting and stinking," signed "Z. Fuks." Solovyov devoutly hoped that "Z." was "Zakhar," not "Zinaida," but "Zinaida" it was.[20]

Several months after the appearance of *Russian Symbolists*, No. 2, Vladimir Solovyov decided to direct his considerable powers of ridicule to the new phenomenon. His review of the first issue appeared in the August 1894 issue of *Messenger of Europe*, his review of the second in the January 1895 number. Like many critics, Solovyov refused to take seriously the "Russian Symbolists'" effort to identify themselves with their French models. Instead, he concentrated on unmasking their supposed "Symbolism" as homegrown frippery. The chief target was Bryusov: Solovyov dismissed his translations and mercilessly ridiculed his two attempts

19.   One original poem, "Ne dremljut teni," later named "V sadu," used the meter of the Verlaine poem [I, 47]. The other original piece was "V serebrjanoj pyli," later "Otveržennyj geroj" [I, 36].

20.   Solov'ev's first two reviews appeared over the signature "Vl. S." in the section "Xronika.—Literaturnoe obozrenie," *Vestnik Evropy* no. 8 (1894): 890–92, and no. 1 (1895): 421–24. These two reviews, with a third, are also to be found in V. S. Solov'ev, *Sobranie sočinenij*, vol. 7, pp. 159–70.

at Mallarmean obscurity. The "golden-hued fairies in a satin garden" and the "silvery splashing of naiads in love," guarded from
sight by "jealous boards," were gleefully revealed as "female persons" bathing behind a board fence, and the poet as a young voyeur, for whom there was still hope as a poet if he was no more
than fourteen years old. In the second volume, Solovyov found his
target in the Bryusov poem that eventually received the title "The
Rejected Hero" and was dedicated to Denis Panin, one of the inventors of the steam engine, to whom adhered a legend that his
steamboat had been destroyed by rival boatmen.[21] With little
foundation, Solovyov took this poem to be a description of Bryusov taking a bath. Having shrewdly guessed that the increase
from two to ten contributors in the second volume had no basis in
fact, he fixed on Bryusov as the ringleader.

When the third volume of *Russian Symbolists* came out, it bore
only the designation "Summer 1895," the censor possibly having
decided that this lessened the implication that succeeding volumes would appear. The series had not managed to gather a talented group of poets (one new contributor appeared with two
poems and two more with one poem each). But the appearance of
a third issue served in itself to reinforce the illusion of the existence of a school.[22] Two-thirds of the volume consisted of translations, including an entire section of poems by Prisca de Landelle
translated by Bryusov.

The most memorable items in the third *Russian Symbolists*
were the original poems by Bryusov. Three poems over his signature led off the book; of these, two became famous immediately

21.   I, 36, 569.
22.   Though Miropol'skij did not appear, Brjusov kept his synthetic coterie
of Darov, Fuks, and ***, along with collaborators, Martov, Bronin, and Novič.
These were joined by Zaronin, Xrisonopulo, and F. K., names which quickly
disappeared from literature. Zaronin (whose name was signed to two poems in
the volume) was the pseudonym of Aleksandr Gippius, brother of Vladimir and
Vasilij (Gudzij, p. 189).

through a *succès de scandale*. The poem later entitled "Creation
[Tvorčestvo]" was ridiculed by Solovyov for its unlikely figures
and paradoxical images.[23]

Tén' nesózdannyx sozdánij
Kolyxáetsja vo sné,
Slovno lópasti latánij
Na èmálevoj stené.

Fiolétovye rúki
Na èmálevoj stené
Polusónno čértjat zvúki
V zvonko-zvúčnoj tišiné.

I prozráčnye kióski
V zvonko-zvúčnoj glubiné
Vyrastájut točno blёstki
Pri lazórevoj luné.

Vsxódit mésjac obnažёnnyj
Pri lazorevoj luné;
Zvúki réjut polusónno,
Zvúki lástjatsja ko mné.

Tájny sózdannyx sozdánij
S láskoj lástjatsja ko mné,
I trepéščet tén' latánij
Na èmálevoj stené.

[The shadow of uncreated creations
Sways in a dream,
Like the laminae of palm fronds
On a wall of enamel.

Violet hands
On a wall of enamel
Half-drowsily sketch sounds
In a ringing-sonorous stillness.

23. "Ešče o simvolistax," *Vestnik Evropy* 10 (1895): 847–51. Solov'ev
pointed with mock seriousness to the indecency of having the crescent moon—
mesjac, masculine in Russian—rise naked before the feminine *luna*, full moon.

And translucent kiosks
In a ringing-sonorous depth
Swell like spangles
In the presence of the azure full moon.

A nude crescent moon rises
In the presence of the azure full moon;
Sounds hover drowsily,
Sounds fawn on me.

Secrets of created creations
With fondness fawn on me,
And the shadow of palm laminae quivers
On a wall of enamel.]

A decade later, Khodasevich cited this poem as a prime example of creation of a fantasy-world from the everyday environment.[24] In this combination of fantasy with daily life, he claimed, lay the special charm of Bryusov's early poetry. Many years later, Alexander Bryusov recalled his older brother composing this poem at twilight in a sitting room with potted palms and an enameled stove.[25] It was a room Khodasevich no doubt knew, but this confirmation is unnecessary, for the subject of description is the poet in the act of creating a "real world" of fantasy into which he retreats in order to create further dreams.

The first stanza of "Creation" describes the poet's condition of readiness, with the shadows of the palms suggesting "uncreated creations" waiting to be evoked. In the second stanza, the imagination becomes more active: violet shadows, now "violet hands," sketch sounds. This is an indication of how the poem begins in the poet's consciousness: with sounds that fill the silence around him. Next, images arise, to "swell like spangles," and another

24.   V. Xodasevič, "'Juvenilia' Brjusova," *Sofia* no. 2 (1914): 64–67.
25.   A. Brjusov, "Vospominanija o brate," *Brjusovskie čtenija 1962 goda* (Erevan, 1963), pp. 296–97. Brjusov's wife identified the "moon" in question as a large lamp outside the circus, which was opposite Brjusov's house [I, 568].

moon appears—the reflection on the enameled stove, to be sure, but also a poetic creation which is, according to Bryusov's then determinedly Decadent credo, superior to material reality. As the poem grows, the poet is surrounded by its sounds. In the final stanza, he and his creations stand in a world apart, as the shadows of palm fronds continue to quiver on the enameled stove wall.

Sounds and images blend ingeniously in this poem. A glance at the transliterated Russian text above will show how one sound, the sonorant *n*, serves as a motif accompanying the description of the creative process. A second motif, carried by the liquid *l* supported by *r*, enters almost immediately. The *l* is attached to the two most suggestive features of the "real" world, the palm fronds ("lopasti latanij") and the azure moon ("lazorevoj lune"), but crosses over to the world of creative fantasy as the poet finds himself "fawned on" ("lastjatsja") by the sounds his imagination evokes. Sounds in their own right play a prominent part in the poem's central section. The nearly onomatopoetic phrase "V *zv*onko-*zv*učnoj tišine" introduces the *zv* combination (*zvuk* = sound) that rings through stanzas 2–4, then partly merges into the *zd* of the "created creations" ("sozdannyx sozdanij") in the last stanza. Assonance is also used effectively: the stressed *e–o–a* of the first stanza swell to the insistent *u* in the "sound" stanzas.

Images in the poem tend to fall into two groups, those associated with the material world and those belonging to the creative state, though the line between them is deliberately faint. The palms, the enamel wall, and the full moon of course belong to the former, their transformations to the latter. The three principal dream images—"violet hands," "translucent kiosks," and "nude crescent moon"—are placed in the first lines of successive stanzas. They are only secondarily tied into the above-described sound pattern, allowing full attention to their visual aspect. In the final stanza, individually distinct sounds and images have disappeared into the "secrets" of the poet's created world, leaving behind the mere shadows and reflections of the material one.

"Creation" is the best example of the poetry of suggestion in Bryusov's early work. It shows the poet in the process of distancing himself from the empirical world by creating, in the best Decadent manner, a synthetic world, employing images and methods associated with the new poetry. However, the chances of such a poem being widely appreciated were slim. Perhaps for this reason he did not scruple to follow it with the one-liner that became surely the most notorious "poem" in Russian at the end of the nineteenth century:

> Oh, cover your pale legs.

> [O zakroj svoi blednye nogi.]

Solovyov's irony did not fail: according to him, the second line obviously had been omitted: "Or you will catch cold."[26] In fact, though he must have anticipated the uproar, Bryusov's intent was at least partly serious. He wrote to Peter Pertsov, who had not yet

26.   The "pale legs" became a tag for Decadent poets. I am indebted to my colleague Simon Karlinsky for calling to my attention several such uses, including two by Anton Čexov. (See *Anton Chekhov's Life and Thought: Selected Letters and Commentary*, tr. Michael Henry Heim with Simon Karlinsky, commentary by Simon Karlinsky [Berkeley and Los Angeles: University of California Press, 1975], pp. 431–32.) In October 1902, Čexov sent Ivan Bunin a postcard: "Milyj Žan! Ukroj svoi blednye nogi! (Dear Jean, Put something over your pale legs!)" The joke related to the photo on the reverse, supposedly of A. N. Emel'janov-Koxanskij (A. P. Čexov, *Polnoe sobranie sočinenij i pisem*, 30 vols. [Moscow, 1982], 11, p. 383). Emel'janov-Koxanskij's collection of very weak Decadent verse entitled *Obnažennye nervy* appeared in 1895 with a frontispiece showing the author, actually the singer A. P. Xoxlov in the role of "Demon." This prank did not exhaust Čexov's use of the phrase to express his mixed scorn and amusement at the Decadents, whom he accused of being not Decadents at all but swindlers. He was reported to have said, "And their legs are not pale at all, but hairy like everyone else's" (Karlinsky, p. 432). Finally, evidence of the tag's viability may be seen in its use in Alla Ktorova's novel: two modern adolescent girls wander restlessly about Moscow, deciding how to amaze their family and friends: "Buy a shanty and raise pumpkins? Or cover our pale legs?" (*Lico Žar-Pticy* [Washington, D.C.: Victor Kamkin, 1969], p. 132).

seen it, "My third poem in the third volume [of *Russian Symbolists*] is neither more nor less than a bold foray ahead."[27] He strongly defended the concept of the single-line poem (which, he later claimed, had been known in Roman poetry).[28] How often, he reminded Pertsov, does one know by heart only a single line from a poem! Quoting a line from Konstantin Balmont, Bryusov claimed, "For that line the other fifteen were written." The conclusion followed: why not stop with the single exquisite line? The notion was one that he had discussed with Balmont, with whom he had been friendly since the fall of 1894.[29] It also may have grown out of discussions with Alexander Dobrolyubov, who, he later said, had taught him to value the poetic line *as line*.[30] At any rate, the experiment was regarded by most readers as a failure, and Bryusov abandoned it.

Bryusov's translations in the third volume of *Russian Symbolists* included poems by Rimbaud, Mallarmé, Maeterlinck, and Tailhade. Earlier, as has been seen, he interested himself especially in

27. *Percovu*, p. 35.
28. A. Izmajlov, *Literaturnyj Olimp* (Moscow, 1911), p. 395.
29. I, 568. Brjusov's relationship with Konstantin Bal'mont was one of the most important and enduring of his life. (It will be treated in detail in succeeding chapters.) Not surprisingly, much of their discourse concerned poetry. Vladimir Markov put this present matter finally into perspective in an informative article accompanied by a sampling of one-line poems from Greek and Roman as well as modern European literatures, including Russian, and accompanied by thirty "odnostroki" of his own composition. He also provided seven one-line poems by Brjusov in addition to "pale legs" (Vladimir Markov, "Odnostroki," *Vozdušnye puti. Al'manax III* [New York: R. N. Grynberg, 1963], pp. 242–58.
30. "Avtobiografija," p. 112. Twice in his first collection Dobroljubov used the image "white feet" (Sočinenija, pp. 27, 77). This source, which contains other religious motifs, makes somewhat more likely than at first seems the suggestion that Brjusov's poem referred to the Crucifixion, though Brjusov rejected this interpretation when it was put to him by the critic A. Izmajlov (*Birževye vedomosti*, morning ed., 25 March 1910, cited by L. K. Dolgopolov, *Poèmy Bloka i russkaja poèma konca XIX-načala XX vekov* [Moscow and Leningrad, 1964], p. 37).

Mallarmé and Verlaine. Translation for these young would-be Russian innovators was a labor dictated not only by the wish to introduce these poets to Russian readers and thereby form a new taste, it was also a method of forming their own poetic style. In 1911, Bryusov described how he and Balmont had to teach fellow poets such devices as internal rhyme and alliteration as if Pushkin, Tyutchev, and Baratynsky had never written.[31] To learn these things themselves, their French models were important: "The influence of Pushkin and that of the 'elder' Symbolists blended strangely in me. I now sought the classic severity of Pushkin's verse, now dreamed of the new freedoms for poetry discovered by the French poets."[32] Bryusov's ties with French Symbolism and its forerunners have always been taken for granted, though he later admitted that in the summer of 1894 he knew French poetry only in fragments.[33] He had much to learn, and translation was an excellent school.

The French poet who meant most to Bryusov at that time was almost certainly Verlaine. While this link has long been recognized, there has been little useful effort to establish the answer to a key question: during this formative stage, what elements in Verlaine's teaching and in his poetic craft made the greatest appeal to Bryusov? From his study of *Poètes maudits*, which he acquired in March 1893, Bryusov probably derived several valuable counsels. Attacking Parnassian perfection, Verlaine praised poetry that was far from impeccable but was indubitably interest-

31.   VI, 293.
32.   "Avtobiografija," p. 107.
33.   Ibid. Cf. also M. L. Mirza-Avakjan, "O rabote Brjusova nad perevodom 'Romances sans paroles' Verlena," *Brjusovskie čtenija 1966 goda* (Erevan, 1968), pp. 489–510. Mirza-Avakjan points out that, despite Brjusov's enthusiasm for Verlaine and other French poets whose poetry he had recently encountered, he drew freely on Russian poets of the 1880s and 1890s for lexicon and other features. (It must be said that the many French passages cited in this article are rendered almost unrecognizable by printing errors. These and other mistakes detract greatly from this article's usefulness.)

ing. Of Tristan Corbière he wrote: "Son vers vit, rit, pleure très peu, se moque bien, et blague encore mieux."[34] Rimbaud's poetry was commended for many features, including the variety of his short forms. Moreover, "le choix des mots est toujours exquis, quelquefois pédant à dessein." His language always remains clear.[35] Though contemporary Russian poetry offered Bryusov no Parnassian perfection of form to combat—indeed, he sought this very quality—Verlaine's arguments must have fortified his viewpoint in many ways and helped formulate his goals. Variety of form, clarity of language (if not of sense), and, above all, novelty of theme characterized Bryusov's earliest poetry, especially that collected in his first book, *Chefs d'œuvre*.

The nature of Bryusov's attraction to Verlaine, as well as certain strategies regarding Symbolism, was illuminated in an unpublished essay he wrote during the first months of 1894. Entitled "Paul Verlaine and His Poetry," it seems to have been designed for publication in one of the serious journals.[36] Though Zinaida Vengerova's precedent no doubt encouraged him, he had no reputation as a critic. Therefore, he assumed a posture more conservative than Vengerova's, one of basic solidarity with a readership that wished to be abreast of the latest developments in art but was not prepared to embrace them immediately. Bryusov presented Verlaine as a Decadent, yet a genuine and interesting exception among all these "Mallarmés, Ghils, Péladans" who are mere curiosities. He referred to Verlaine's lack of moral principle as shown in some poems, which, he said, he preferred not to describe. In view of the poems Bryusov was to publish within the year in *Chefs d'œuvre*, these remarks were patently a strategy. However, one or two notes possibly ring true—for example, his

34. Paul Verlaine, *Œuvres complètes*, ed. Yves-Gérard le Dantec, 5 vols. (Paris: Editions Messein, 1948–1953), 4, p. 12.
35. Ibid., p. 21.
36. Prepared for publication by S. I. Gindin. See also Mirza-Avakjan, pp. 491–92.

distaste for and distrust of Verlaine's repentance and conversion to Catholicism. When he spoke of Verlaine as a product of the West's decaying civilization, Bryusov was echoing popular conceptions recently reinforced by the Russian translation of Max Nordau's *Entartung*.[37] By addressing his readers' prejudices he clearly was hoping to disarm them, for he had made his choice: "Whether it is false, or ridiculous . . . the future belongs to [Decadence]."[38] And, resolving to be the leader of Russian Decadence, he had chosen Verlaine as his guide.

Bryusov's article gave special praise to *Romances sans paroles*. In this volume in which, he felt, Verlaine found his poetic voice, Bryusov saw special values for Decadents and Symbolists. Yet he gave little direct attention to the artistic qualities of *Romances*, except to note the kinship of "Il pleure dans mon cœur" with poems by Fet. The elegance of technique and innovative subject-matter of the earlier *Poèmes saturniens* and *Fêtes galantes* drew his attention. And he focused on "Art poétique," from the later volume *Jadis et naguère*, which opens with the famous line "De la musique avant toute chose."[39] This poem stated the two principles which Verlaine called essential to poetry and which Bryusov took to be basic to the new style: there must be musicality, and there must be nuance. Musicality in poetry of course did not mean the same thing to all: for Mallarmé it meant giving a poem the structure of a musical composition, while for Baudelaire individual words had the value of musical notes.[40] For Verlaine it meant combining words so that their recurrent sounds create an effect on

37.   Max Nordau, *Entartung* (Berlin: C. Duncker, 1892–1893), and *Vyrož-denie* (St. Petersburg, 1894). See also Joan Grossman, "Genius and Madness: The Return of the Romantic Concept of the Poet in Russia at the End of the Nineteenth Century," *American Contributions to the Seventh International Congress of Slavists*, ed. Victor Terras, 3 vols. (The Hague: Mouton, 1973), 2, pp. 247–60.

38.   *Dnevniki*, p. 12.

39.   Verlaine, 1, pp. 295–96.

40.   Anna Balakian, *The Symbolist Movement: A Critical Appraisal* (New York: New York University Press, 1977), p. 64.

the hearer like that of music. Sometimes, then, the sound becomes more important than the word and its meaning in achieving the desired end of poetry. Deliberate irregularity, avoidance of
strong chords and resolutions, were to help create the lightness
and fluidity Verlaine sought:

> De la musique avant toute chose,
> Et pour cela préfère l'Impair,
> Plus vague et plus soluble dans l'air,
> Sans rien en lui qui pèse ou qui pose.
>
> Il faut aussi que tu n'ailles point
> Choisir tes mots sans quelque méprise:
> Rien de plus cher que la chanson grise
> Où l'Indécis au Précis se joint.

The poetry of suggestion is evoked in the further lines:

> Car nous voulons la Nuance encor,
> Pas la Couleur, rien que la nuance!
> Oh! la nuance seule fiance
> Le rêve au rêve et la flûte au cor!

When Verlaine wrote these lines in 1874, he had recently completed *Romances sans paroles*. It was the period when he was especially close to Impressionism. The young French poets of the
eighties perhaps saw in the poem more of a manifesto than Verlaine had intended, and it was received in the same way by Valery
Bryusov. Verlaine's preference for irregular lines and for shadow
rather than color, and his warnings against the tyranny of exact
rhyme, were directed against the Parnassians, but they gave Bryusov a warrant to replace the tired conventions which were almost
all that remained by 1890 of Russia's poetic tradition. At the
same time, Verlaine's "elegance of form" supported the standard
which Bryusov wanted to reinstate in Russian poetry.

In August 1894, Bryusov completed his translation of *Romances
sans paroles* and published it in a printing of one thousand copies.

The lengthy essay just described was perhaps intended to appear at the same time. No doubt with considerable pride, Bryusov sent a copy to Verlaine—or at least he planned to do so, for a notebook entry for 23 November 1894 contains the following:

"ON SENDING TO P. VERLAINE THE
TRANSLATION OF 'ROMANCES SANS PAROLES'"

Still your humble vassal,
I send a gift to my suzerain,
Proud and happy to have bound
The Seine in Russian granite.

III, 214

Later he was more modest. In the foreword to his 1911 translation of Verlaine's poems Bryusov wrote: "I was almost the first who began to translate Verlaine into Russian. . . . In these attempts there was much more zeal and enthusiasm over Verlaine's poetry than real rendition of his lines into Russian" [III, 592]. In fact, at least some of Bryusov's early Verlaine translations show not only ingenuity but occasional inspiration. More significantly for the study of a beginning poet's craft, they indicate certain aspects of his original's method which had a particular appeal for him, and they show how he went about applying these lessons in Russian. A useful example is his translation of Verlaine's "Il pleure dans mon cœur."[41]

Il pleure dans mon cœur
Comme il pleut sur la ville.
Quelle est cette langueur
Qui pénètre mon cœur?

O bruit doux de la pluie
Par terre et sur les toits!

41.   Verlaine, 1, p. 143. Brjusov's translation is here given as it appeared in *Russkie simvolisty*. It was later revised; see *Stixotvorenija i poèmy*, p. 598.

Pour un cœur qui s'ennuie,
O le chant de la pluie!

Il pleure sans raison
Dans ce cœur qui s'écœure.
Quoi! nulle trahison?
Ce deuil est sans raison.

C'est bien la pire peine
De ne savoir pourquoi,
Sans amour et sans haine,
Mon cœur a tant de peine.

Nébo nad górodom pláčet,
Pláčet i sérdce moë;
Čtó ono, čtó ono znáčit
Èto unýn'e moë?

I po zemlé i po krýše
Šúm neumólčnyj doždjá;
Sérdcu pečál'nomu slýšen
Šúm neumólčnyj doždjá.

Pláčet nevnjátno nenást'e;
Sérdca pečál' bez pričín';
Dá, ni izmény, ni sčást'ja —
Pláčet ono bez pričín.

Kák-to osóbenno ból'no
Tak gorevát' ni o čëm;
Pláču, no pláču nevól'no
Pláču, ne znája o čëm.

Bryusov's first problem concerned meter. His substitution of dactylic trimeter, without dactylic endings, for Verlaine's syllabic verse made the Russian line slightly longer. The falling dactylic intonation with its regular beat was substituted for the more flowing subtle monotony of Verlaine's line. For rhyme scheme he chose the common *AbAb*, instead of Verlaine's more marked *abaa*.

Lexically the translation strives to be reasonably faithful, with one major exception. "Rain" is the basic term of the comparison on which Verlaine's poem was built: "It weeps, (*pleure*) in my heart / as it rains (*pleut*) on the town."[42] This suggestive feature returns in the second stanza, where the external description is developed: "Oh sweet sound of rain (*pluie*)." By the third stanza the comparison is no longer needed, for the external world has been internalized: "It weeps without reason / In my disheartened heart." The final stanza abandons the figure entirely for the analytical "It's far the worst pain / Not to know why. . . ." "Weeping" becomes simply "pain."

Russian did not provide Bryusov with any terms for "weep" and "rain" that were closely allied in sound. He was thus deprived of the "*pleure–pleut–pluie*" series so essential to Verlaine's poem. His decision to use *plačet*, "weeps," in both terms of the comparison introduces into the first stanza a metaphor instead of the simile in the original. Bryusov's version reads: "The sky weeps on the town, / And my heart weeps also." In the second stanza, forced at last to use the Russian *dožd'*, "rain," Bryusov temporarily lost his advantage. In the third stanza he regained *plačet* but was forced to sacrifice precision: "The gloomy weather weeps faintly; / The heart's sadness is without reason." And while the first half of the fourth stanza is translated quite literally, the closing departs importantly from Verlaine: "Without love or disdain, / My heart has such pain" becomes "I weep, but I weep involuntarily / I weep, not knowing why."

Clearly shades of meaning are lost in the translation. Equally clearly, the reason for most departures from the literal meaning of the original is the desire to approximate Verlaine's pattern of sound. Bryusov was fortunate in that Russian provided him with *plačet* (or *plaču*) to match at least the initial sounds of *pleure–pleut–pluie*. Moreover, while reduced to repeating *plačet–plaču* perhaps excessively he made good use of *pečal'* and *pečal'nyi* (sadness, sad)—nearly the same sounds in different combination—to

42. Translation of C. F. MacIntyre, *Paul Verlaine: Selected Poems* (Berkeley and Los Angeles: University of California Press, 1948), p. 103.

suggest Verlaine's intricate effect. Beyond this, he undertook to match insofar as possible the original's delicate arrangements of liquids and sonorants, *r*, *l*, *m*, and *n*. He also attempted to approximate other patterns of instrumentation, taking advantage of the sound qualities of Russian. And in the matter of phrasing he attentively sought to create equivalents, if not absolute parallels. It can be said, then, that Bryusov grasped Verlaine's musical intention and showed some sensitivity in his efforts to duplicate that effect. The sound here is decidedly more important than the sense, or, rather, it *is* the sense—the mood is conveyed by the music of the words. When in 1911 Bryusov revised his translation, the alterations were all in the direction of more liquid sound, none for a more literal translation. While deploring, as did Verlaine himself, some of the extremes to which the suggestions of "Art poétique" were carried (it was, after all, a lyric, not a dogmatic statement), Bryusov applauded the principles and, especially for the next several years, concentrated on applying them in his own poetry.

Bryusov's hope two years earlier, for at least a modicum of favorable attention for *Russian Symbolists* and for his translation of *Romances sans paroles* was demolished by the reviewers. The translation was treated as harshly as the original work. However, at least one end was attained: Verlaine was frequently exalted by those who excoriated his translator. One reviewer, after contrasting the two, concluded: "To call oneself a Symbolist does not yet mean to become a talented poet and translator; anyone reading the verses of Bryusov will easily be convinced of this."[43]

The press did give an extraordinary amount of attention to these meager beginnings. This fact suggests the vacuum which then existed in the realm of new writing. *Russian Thought*'s reviewer of 1891 might have repeated his complaints—as others indeed did—in the years immediately following. It was this vacuum that initially encouraged Bryusov. In hopes of receiving a

43.   Ašukin, p. 71, quoting from a review in *Novosti*, 6 January 1895.

hearing, he had written the foreword to the first issue of *Russian Symbolists* in a judicious tone, and in the second he set forth the principles of Symbolism as he then understood them. The third foreword found him wholeheartedly adopting the polemical stance thrust upon him. To the Zoiluses and Aristarchuses of the press he wrote that they were obviously totally unprepared to evaluate a new phenomenon in art. He then dissected reviewers' comments with some of the keenness and wit that were to stand him in good stead in many future clashes.[44] Citing a round dozen reviews dealing with the previous two issues of *Russian Symbolists*, Bryusov marshalled most of them into three categories, which he then proceeded to demolish. He showed his opponents to be uninformed, illogical, unsophisticated, and in some cases not even to have read the books. Only Vladimir Solovyov was spared: instead Bryusov suggested somewhat disingenuously that Solovyov had merely wished to amuse the public. Solovyov could not seriously have disapproved, since he himself had recently published at least one genuinely Symbolist poem.[45]

From *Russian Symbolists* and from the translation of *Romances sans paroles* Bryusov had learned something of value both for his craft and for his role as leader of the Decadents. But he had a good deal more to do before he could consider himself a fully formed poet. He had yet to produce an entire book of his own poems, and he had yet to answer satisfactorily—even for himself—essential questions about the nature of poetry and the role of the poet. He was hard at work in both areas during 1895.

44.   VI, 32–34.
45.   Brjusov referred to Solov'ev's poem "Začem slova?" which appeared in *Vestnik Evropy* 10 (1892): 811. See also Vladimir Solov'ev, *Stixotvorenija i šutočnye p'esy* (2nd ed. Leningrad, 1974), pp. 91–92. It would be hard to prove Brjusov wrong on this point. However, Solov'ev responded in the review of the third issue of *Russkie simvolisty* with several parodies, which, as he noted, gave Brjusov the right to say that he, "Vlasij Semenov" (his pseudonym), had published some Symbolist poems.

TWO

Chefs d'œuvre:
The Start of a Career

"THE THIRD VOLUME of *Russian Symbolists* will be sent to the censor in a few days; I'm not bothering much about it, however, since I have become as disillusioned with Russian Symbolist poets as with non-Symbolists. I am more interested in my new book *Chefs d'œuvre*, which will come out in the fall. These will be masterpieces, not of my own poetry (in the future I will doubtless write even more significant things), but masterpieces of contemporary poetry, which . . . is certainly not hard." [1] Bryusov thus announced his new project to his Petersburg friend Peter Pertsov on 12 March 1895. The title of the new book was frankly provocative, but *épater le bourgeois* came easily after his recent experiences. The foreword repeated the above statement in almost so many words, softening it only with the parenthetical remark "(At twenty-one it is permissible to make promises!)" [I, 572]. However, stung by reactions to his previous efforts, Bryusov made it clear that his satisfaction did not depend on critical response: he bequeathed this book "to eternity and to art" [I, 572].

The author was actually considerably less confident than these statements suggest; his hopes fluctuated wildly. In June, with the proofs before him, he wrote to Pertsov: "I repeat, poetry is perish-

---

1. *Percovu*, p. 11. Plans were made for a fourth volume of *Russkie simvolisty*, but it did not materialize.

ing. It needs a revolution—and alas! my *Chefs d'œuvre* is inca-
pable of effecting it. When I think of them again, I blush."[2] The
position between extremes was expressed, also in June, to another
correspondent, his boyhood friend and schoolmate Vladimir Stanyukovich, to whom he usually spoke without affectation: "You'll
find no masterpieces there, but you will find several quite original
(in all senses of the word) pieces; they have one undoubted virtue:
there is nothing run-of-the-mill either in idea or in form."[3]

"The last book of my youth," Bryusov called *Chefs d'œuvre*
{I, 572}. In retrospect, *Me eum esse* (1897) better qualifies for this
title, but the sense of his own rapid growth, his developing art
and the vision of its possibilities was at times intoxicating, and it
no doubt seemed to him that full stature as a poet could hardly be
far off. Just now, though, he was still very much in the throes of
dealing with some crucial questions about poetry, about Symbolism and Decadence, and about himself as a poet. His exploration of these matters will be discussed in the next chapter, but
some of their practical reflections can be seen in *Chefs d'œuvre*.

In August 1895, shortly before the book's publication, Bryusov
wrote to Pertsov: "I—the Symbolist, and I—the author of *Chefs
d'œuvre*—are two extreme opposites. But I openly acknowledge
both one and the other as mine."[4] Indeed, most of the poems in
this, his first independent book, suggest other models than the
"poetry of hints." In *Chefs d'œuvre* Bryusov set himself a series of
artistic problems. The choice of extremely varied subject-matter,
theme, and tone involved rejection of hackneyed materials and
their conventional links to certain poetic forms. He had earlier
written of the impossibility of expressing fin-de-siècle sensations

2.   Ibid., p. 28.
3.   V. K. Stanjukovič, "Vospominanija o V. Ja. Brjusove," *LN* 85, p. 736.
In fact Brjusov was wounded by Stanjukovič's blunt criticism of a number of
these poems (*LN* 85, p. 738).
4.   *Percovu*, p. 35. To Stanjukovič he also insisted that there was no Symbolism in his most recent book (*LN*, 85, p. 738).

in Pushkin's language. He was now groping for both the new sensations and a new language of expression. To this end he drew on French Parnassian poetry and on the most innovative Russian sources, as well as on Western Symbolism's predecessors: Poe, Baudelaire, and Verlaine. The thematic core of the book was love, but not the conventional, often elegiac emotion of generations of Russian writers. The experience of love had to be seen and felt anew, and to some extent new poetic forms could aid in this renovation.

Perhaps Bryusov's greatest concern was to give a coherent structure to the book. To Pertsov he insisted: *"Chefs d'œuvre* is not at any rate a cento, it is a complete book, with a head, a trunk, and a tail. This is the way you have to look at it."* He begged Pertsov to read straight through without a break, "from the foreword to the table of contents inclusive, for everything has a fixed purpose."[5] At first inspection it is not obvious that the book's five sections make up an organic whole; however, the notebooks for 1894–1895 show that a great deal of thought went into the plan. Several variants exhibit different organizing principles.[6] The first plan was primarily thematic: "Love," "Death," *"Poèmy,"* "Ideas," "Nature." The use of a genre designation, *poèma,* here is less exceptional than it might seem—in Russian literary terminology the *poèma* is defined broadly as a poem of some length containing narrative elements and often used for lofty subject-matter; hence it carried some thematic weight. The second plan was divided into four sections without headings, but "Small *poèmy"* and "Exotic *poèmy"* were set apart. In the third, genre asserted itself more defi-

5. Ibid., p. 37.
6. M. L. Mirza-Avakjan, "Rabota Brjusova nad sbornikom 'Šedevry,'" in *Brjusovskie čtenija 1973 goda* (Erevan, 1976), p. 49. Aside from this presumably accurate information, this article is highly misleading, since the author is unaware that there were two editions of *Chefs d'œuvre* and regards the second, 1896 edition as the only one: see p. 50, where she cautions the researcher against using the Sirin edition of 1913 as if it were the primary one.

nitely. There were five headings: *"Poèmy,"* "Small *poèmy,"* "Sonnets," "Sounds," and "Ideas." The final version returned to titles that were thematic, though less categorical than those originally proposed. The first two are simply titles of *poèmy*: "Autumn Day" and "Snows." The remaining section-headings are "Cryptomeria," "Last Kisses," and "Meditations."

Behind the concern with coherent form and preoccupation with the *poèma* surely lie the literary discussions and exchanges about poetry with Konstantin Balmont which were so important a part of Bryusov's life in the fall of 1894 and the early months of 1895, that is, exactly the period when he was devising the form and writing the poems for *Chefs d'œuvre*. Bryusov later remembered: "The evenings and nights which Balmont and I spent together, when we endlessly recited to one another our own poems and those of our favorite poets—he to me, Shelley and Edgar Poe, I to him, Verlaine, Tyutchev (whom he did not yet know), Karolina Pavlova—, these evenings and nights when we talked *de omni re scibili* will ever remain among the most significant happenings of my life."[7] These poetic evenings presumably affected Balmont as well. Having just published *Under Northern Skies*, his first venture into modernist poetry, he was now writing the poems that would appear as *In Boundlessness* at the end of 1895, just a few months after the first edition of *Chefs d'œuvre*. A pattern that might almost be called antiphonal developed between Bryusov's books and Balmont's in the next few years which surely reflects their close association and intense interest in each other's work and ideas.

At the time of their first meeting, Balmont was translating Shelley and preparing his first translated volume of Poe's poetry, and Bryusov became the beneficiary of his enthusiasms. Immediate echoes of either in Bryusov's poetry are slight, though over the next several years Poe's influence on Bryusov took interesting

7.   "Avtobiografija," p. 111.

forms. Nonetheless, one feature of "Ulalume," "Annabel Lee," and other favorites which presumably was discussed by the two was, rather surprisingly, their genre. Bryusov and Balmont were apparently fascinated by what they regarded as promising mutations of the Romantic *poèma*. For the Romantics, Western and Russian, the narrative line of the form tended to be weakened as it became a vehicle for personal meditation on external events and interior states. Moreover, its psychological and philosophical content often called for heightened lyricism.[8] Successors to the Romantics—in Russia, Nekrasov and A. K. Tolstoy—turned the form to other uses, including the expression of historical and folkloric themes. In the 1880s the subjective aspect of the genre was further strengthened in the work of writers such as Golenishchev-Kutuzov. Yet Bryusov and Balmont might not have found the form so intensely interesting had they not encountered Shelley and Poe. Though he belonged to the Romantic period, Poe in particular seemed in this as in other features a truly modern figure, a Decadent before his time.[9] They saw in his longer poems a traditional genre transformed so that it could express "fin-de-siècle sensations" and moods in appropriate form. That Bryusov linked their experiments with the *poèma* to Poe is indicated in his letter of 29 June 1896 to Alexander Kursinsky, a young poet whom Bryusov regarded as unoriginal. After discouraging him from trying to write a novel, Bryusov added, "And you've written a *poèma*. That I understand even less. Even more hopelessly cliché, unless in the style of Edgar Poe or [Balmont's]

8.   The topic is discussed by L. K. Dolgopolov in "Osnovnye tipy poèmy v 80-90-e gody. Liričeskaja poèma," Chapter I in his *Poèmy Bloka i russkaja poèma konca XIX-načala XX vekov* (Moscow and Leningrad, 1964), pp. 8–35. The "*liričeskaja poèma*" in relation to Decadence is treated by Vladimir Markov, "K voprosu o granicax dekadansa v russkoj poèzii (i o liričeskoj poème)," pp. 487–90.

9.   See Joan Delaney Grossman, *Edgar Allan Poe in Russia: A Study in Legend and Literary Influence* (Wurzburg: JAL Verlag, 1973), especially ch. 4.

'Dead Ships.' But then it is something new."[10] (That Bryusov's own efforts in the *poèma* were closely linked to Poe will be evident in the discussion of "Snows" below.)

In Bryusov's and Balmont's interpretation of the *poèma*, the narrative element tends to be decidedly weak. In 1897, when Balmont published *Stillness: Lyrical poèmy*, some of the "*poèmy*" seemed to be no more than a series of lyrics under a single thematic title. Vladimir Markov in his seminal discussion of the "lyrical *poèma*" distinguished the modern *poèma* from the Romantic variant by its outstanding flexibility. He noted in the blurring of genre lines of Balmont's *Stillness* a deliberate feature that set the new *poèma* apart from its predecessors.

The blurring of genre boundaries linked with other characteristics to make the lyrical *poèma* a form particularly suited to the Decadents' inspiration. Obviously closely related was another formal development in the work of both poets, but especially in Bryusov's, at about this time: the phenomenon that later came to be called cyclization. Thematic unity in grouping poems had already occasionally been employed in Russian poetry. The chief innovator in this direction was Fet, whose collections of 1850, 1856, and 1863 showed the same division into sections and the mixture of thematic and generic designations used in *Chefs d'œuvre*. L. K. Dolgopolov noted in his book on Blok and the *poèma* that this tendency toward larger lyrical foci developed into cyclization in the Symbolist period when organization on thematic-generic lines was enriched by a broad unity of poetic mood, a psychological unity.[11] Bryusov and Balmont were at the forefront of a development which was to be found in the work of nearly all the major poets within a few years after 1895. It was Bryusov who taught other poets how to extend this feature to include the entire book

10.   CGALI, fond 1223, op. 1, ed. xr. 3. Bal'mont's "Mertvye korabli" appeared in his *Tišina*.
11.   Dolgopolov, pp. 13–14. There is no mention here of Poe's possible role, however.

of poetry and ultimately to make the poetic corpus a chronicle of the poet's spiritual path. *Chefs d'œuvre*, his first effort in this direction, was not so closely organized as his next book, *Me eum esse*, nor had he yet developed an autobiographical "lyrical hero" to act as the focus of the book. For the time being he used instead a central theme, love treated in various keys and varied poetic forms, as the organizing core of his work.

Given the importance of this unified poetic structure in the subsequent course of Russian poetry, the question is bound to arise: what gave Bryusov the impetus in this direction? What prompted the move from thematic groupings to the notion of a book of poems as a unified whole "with a head, a trunk, and a tail"? (Of this neither Poe nor Shelley offered a model.) Was there a work which suggested that a more complex kind of unity might serve the complex modern demands upon poetry envisioned by Bryusov? The enjoyment of art, he wrote in the foreword to *Chefs d'œuvre*, lies in communion with the artist's soul,[12] that essentially contemporary spirit, which required new language and new forms for its expression. One source suggests itself: *Les Fleurs du mal*. And the circumstances bear out the conjecture.

In 1892 Balmont became acquainted with the wealthy Moscow lawyer and art patron Prince Andrei Urusov, whose knowledge of and taste in poetry, especially French poetry, played an important role in Balmont's artistic education. Urusov's knowledge of Baudelaire could hardly be bettered in Russia. In 1896 a volume called *Le Tombeau de Charles Baudelaire* came out in Paris with the participation of some three dozen French luminaries headed by Stéphane Mallarmé. The centerpiece of the volume was "une étude sur les textes de *Les Fleurs du mal*. Commentaire et variantes, par le prince Alexandre Ourousof." The study was a milestone. As Martin Turnell wrote: "It was not until the appearance in 1896 of Prince Ourousof's essay that writers on Baudelaire began to pay

12. I, 572.

proper attention to the architecture of the *Fleurs du mal*." [13] If, as seems likely, it was Urusov who brought this highly important feature of Baudelaire's masterpiece to Balmont's attention and, through him, to Bryusov's, a significant side effect of Urusov's study of *Les Fleurs du mal*—its impact on Russian poetry—has gone unnoticed.

Urusov took as his point of departure Barbey d'Aurevilly's 1857 review of the first edition, which pointed out that, beyond its individual merit, each poem in Baudelaire's book had "*une valeur très importante d'ensemble et de situation* qu'il ne faut pas lui faire perdre en la détachant," and referred to "*une architecture secrète*, un plan calculé par le poëte." [14] D'Aurevilly's insight was lost to subsequent Baudelaire criticism because of the editorial errors and addition of poems in the third, posthumous edition. To reestablish and verify D'Aurevilly's assertion, Urusov reproduced detailed tables of contents of the first three editions, the first two planned by Baudelaire himself. Urusov laid special stress on the relation of the author's arrangement of the poems (not identical with chronological order of composition) and the inner contours of the poet's spirit: "Toutes les parties de son œuvre correspondent à des particularités de son tempérament et de son génie qui, unies entre elles par des liens mystérieux, concourent à former un individu sans précédents, d'une originalité sans exemple. Ce livre est bien l'âme et la vie du poëte *tout entière*." [15] It was a concept which, newly articulated and applied to a poet of prime importance to the Symbolists, must have singularly excited Bryusov. One can only speculate on the connection between Urusov's insights into the relation between poet and poetry in Baudelaire,

13.   Martin Turnell, *Baudelaire: A Study of His Poetry* (New York: New Directions, 1972), p. 92.

14.   Quoted in A. Ourousof [Urusov], "L'Architecture secrète des 'Fleurs du Mal,'" in *Le Tombeau de Charles Baudelaire* (Paris: Bibliothèque Artistique et Littéraire, 1896), p. 9. Emphasis in original.

15.   Urusov, p. 9.

and Bryusov's rapidly evolving ideas on the same subject. It is of some interest, though perhaps coincidental, that a letter of Baudelaire to Alfred de Vigny, which accompanied a presentation copy of the second edition of *Les Fleurs du mal*, expressed the same sentiment in words very similar to those Bryusov used to Pertsov (cited above). Baudelaire wrote:

> Le seul éloge que je sollicite pour ce livre est qu'on reconnaisse qu'il n'est pas un pur album et qu'il a un commencement et une fin. Tous les poëmes nouveaux ont été faits pour être adaptés à un cadre singulier que j'avais choisi.[16]

That Bryusov's first attempt at creating a similar *cadre singulier* for his poems fell short of his model hardly needs saying. But it seems significant of his intentions that he sent a copy of the second, 1896 edition of *Chefs d'œuvre* to the man who he hoped would understand its design, the man who had earlier made him a gift of *Les Fleurs du mal*—Andrei Urusov.[17]

The first edition of *Chefs d'œuvre* opened with two *poèmy* which seem to represent the "before and after" of the influence of Poe on Bryusov's conception of that form. "Autumn Day" was dated in manuscript 25 September 1894, just three days before his first meeting with Balmont. Bryusov later spoke of it in the most deprecating terms, as nothing more than a link to his previous poetry.[18] The *poèma* consists of a series of nine short lyrics narrating

16. Letter of December 1861 to Alfred de Vigny, *Œuvres complètes de Charles Baudelaire*, ed. F.-F. Gautier and Y.-G. le Dantec, *Correspondance*. I: *1841–1863* (Paris: Editions de la Nouvelle Revue Française, 1933), pp. 395–96.

17. A brief account of Brjusov's relations with Urusov is given in Valerij Brjusov, "Iz pis'ma k izdateljam," *Knjaz' Aleksandr Ivanovič Urusov. Stat'i ego. Pis'ma ego. Vospominanija o nem*, ed. A. Andreeva, O. Gol'dovskij, 3 vols. (Moscow, 1907), 3, p. 288. According to his report, Brjusov read his Baudelaire translations to Urusov. The presentation copy of *Chefs d'œuvres* is now in Puškinskij Dom in Leningrad. It is inscribed: "kn. Aleksandru Ivanoviču Urusovu. V znak neizmennogo uvaženija, ot avtora. 4 apr. 96."

18. *Percovu*, p. 38.

an autumn visit with the new beloved to the first love's grave.[19] It is reminiscent of Verlaine's sonnet sequence "Melancholia" from *Poèmes saturniens*, where the poems "Nevermore" and "Après trois ans" play on shared memory in an autumn wood.[20]

The second *poèma*, "Snows," held a higher place in its author's evaluation of his work. To Pertsov, who ranked it much lower than did Bryusov, the author declared, "I consider this the best work in the whole collection. The hero of these tercets (by the way, ringing and true) after an orgy finds himself by chance outside the city, and he converses with an imagined companion, his forgotten beloved. In the first address to her is the divine line— 'Speak, are we phantoms, Maria?'"[21] Divine or not, Bryusov rightly valued the graceful stanza form. He could boast as well of the artful development of theme from section to section to the final stanza, where the hero realizes that he stands alone on the snowy field under the cold moonlight and the distant gleam of Vega. Here, through a shift of perspective, he becomes a figure in a landscape, and the landscape a picture distanced by the final word: "Vega." Interestingly, when Bryusov found himself defending "Snows" to Stanyukovich, he maintained that its only fault was a possibly excessive dependence on motifs from Poe.[22] Without analyzing the use of these motifs in detail, we may note the echoes of Poe's "To Helen," where the hero meets with memory as does Bryusov's and like him is left "in the sad, silent watches of my night," kneeling to the stars.[23] This poem is dated 27–29 November 1894, only two months after the other, but in Bryu-

---

19.   The poem was dedicated in manuscript to Maria Pavlovna Širjaeva, sister-in-law of Aleksandr Lang [I, 571].

20.   Paul Verlaine, *Œuvres complètes*, ed. Yves-Gérard le Dantec, 5 vols. (Paris: Editions Messeins, 1953), 1, pp. 8–9.

21.   *Percovu*, p. 41. "Snega" was written in *terza rima*.

22.   *LN* 85, p. 738.

23.   Edgar Allan Poe, *Works*, ed. Edmund Clarence Stedman and George Edward Woodberry, 10 vols. (Chicago: Stone and Kimball, 1894–1895), 10, p. 84.

sov's estimation is separated from it by light years of artistic experience. After all, for a full two months he and Balmont had been meeting to recite and discourse on poetry.

The theme of love, which in "Autumn Day" and "Snows" was given a distinctly contemporary setting and tone, moves into a different key entirely in the book's third section, "Cryptomeria." *Cryptomeria*, a genus of evergreen belonging to the pine family, is native only to eastern Asia. Thus the poems in this section may be regarded as exotic plants. (One thinks of Huysmans' Des Esseintes ordering a selection of the most hideously *unnatural* plants for contemplation in his exotic retreat.) In the eight poems of "Cryptomeria," erotic motifs range from the delicate hints of "On the Murmuring Godaveri" to the strongly sadomasochistic tones of "Long Ago." However, the exoticism of setting and sometimes of speaker or speaker's psychological experience places both events and emotions in a curiously wrought frame. Six of the eight poems are distanced in space or time or both: passion in a tropical garden ending in death; an Indian temple dancer supplicating her goddess by the Godaveri; two lovers on a comet speculating on the emotions felt on earth; a young girl at some distant time shamed publicly and put to death for love, earthly or divine; a wizard on Easter Island pondering the origin of monumental prehistoric statues; a medieval Venetian nun meditating on her lover and her hopeless fate. Two poems are specifically related to visual art forms. "The Leper" is subtitled "drawing in charcoal"; "The Priest" bears the subtitle "bronze statuette." To Stanyukovich's indignation at the eroticism of these poems Bryusov responded somewhat disingenuously: "Take almost all of 'Cryptomeria'—it is made up of motifs from Leconte de Lisle and Hérédia, whom no one calls erotic poets."[24] Leconte de Lisle's "Les Eléphants" and other poems may have contributed the boa, the lianas, and the glimpse of tropical jungle seen in "Premonition," but its serene

24.   *LN* 85, p. 738.

scene-painting is far from the mood of Bryusov's poem. On the other hand, "On the Easter Islands [*sic*]" and even more "The Priest" do recall Leconte de Lisle's "Sûryâ (Hymne védique)." [25] However, elements of theme and style suggest also the inspiration of Gautier and Baudelaire.

That summer of 1895, awaiting the publication of *Chefs d'œuvre*, Bryusov wrote to Pertsov on a subject much on his mind: "And they exist, these new, unknown forms! I foretold them in the foreword of *Chefs d'œuvre*, I feel them, but I don't know them. It's the same sensation as groping for a word which hovers just beyond your memory but won't be caught." [26] A week later to Pertsov he warmly supported Balmont's use of exotic subjects because of the lexical opportunities these gave:

> And do you count for nothing the fact that his avoidance of reality gives Balmont the chance to introduce words as yet unheard in poetry, to revel in exotic names? How strange and wonderful alien words sound, especially in rhyme! Is it possible you don't know the enjoyment of poetry per se—outside its content, only sounds, only images, only rhymes. . . . I'm not saying that there is nothing else in poetry. There is, there is another kind of poetry altogether. But both kinds are splendid. [27]

Bryusov's enthusiasm for this kind is especially apparent in "Cryptomeria," where unusual settings permit the use of rhymes like *Yavy—udavy* (Java—boas); *allei—orkhidei* (garden paths—orchids); *lian—stan* (lianas—human form), all from "Premonition"; *banana—rano—tumana* (banana—early—fog), *Godaveri—vere—bayadere* (Godaveri—faith—temple dancer) from "On the Murmuring Godaveri"; *gondole—zheltofioli—Anatoly—voli* (gondola—wallflower—Anatolio—

---

25.   Leconte De Lisle, *Œuvres*, 4 vols. (Paris: Société D'Edition "Les Belles Lettres"): "Sûryâ," vol. 1, *Poèmes antiques* (1977), pp. 3–5; "Les Eléphants," vol. 2, *Poèmes barbares* (1976), pp. 159–60.

26.   *Percovu*, p. 32.

27.   Ibid., p. 36.

open space) from "Anatolio." There are also rhymes based on the names of pagan deities, sometimes synthetic, as Èatuya and Atomi, the divinities of Easter Island.

New forms were of course not confined to exotic rhymes and sounds. Nor in his quest for the new did Bryusov scorn forms that had already reached high perfection in other hands. Besides themes, the Parnassian cult of form offered him models to explore. Several pieces in *Chefs d'œuvre* are sonnets, a form for which he might have found models in Russian poetry, but which was brought to a particularly high level by the French Parnassian Hérédia. A more striking debt to Hérédia may be surmised in a form first used by Bryusov in "Cryptomeria" and later employed in some of his most successful and characteristic poems. This is the lyric monologue, placed in the mouth of a mythical or historical personage or an historical type, such as Hérédia's "L'Esclave."[28] The wizard of Easter Island addresses the silent figures that loom over the sea, their frowns concealing lost legends. The simple people now inhabiting the island know nothing of the statues' origin. Only the wise man, as he roams solitary among them, dimly surmises the past bloodshed and wrath. Closer to the dramatic monologue form is the sonnet "Anatolio," where the hapless nun sees from her window her lover's gondola gliding away from the monastery walls, then turns to slip from her cell into the procession of her sisters descending to the chapel. In the final three lines of the sestet the words of the common prayer mingle with her private sorrow.

The fourth section, "Last Kisses," is in several ways a continuation of "Cryptomeria," extending the exotic themes and further exploring aspects of form, especially meter. The first poem, "In Night Shadows," is a playful erotic/exotic poem that reaches back to "Premonition" and forward to "Pro domo sua," the con-

28.   José-Maria de Hérédia, *Les Trophées* (Paris: Alphonse Lemerre, n.d.), p. 47.

cluding poem of this section. "Premonition" consists of an extended metaphor: "My love is the torrid noon of Java." All the
events, down to the lethal embrace, are on the metaphorical
plane. "In Night Shadows," on the other hand, is a playful vision. The lover lying in a "blue alcove" imagines a "forest of
cryptomeria." In the first edition his companion is turned into a
young native girl. Suddenly he hears a rustle in the imaginary
forest—is it the mischievous monkey "vauvau"? No, it is something more dangerous, with gleaming eyes. "Valery, you're dream-
ing, what's the matter?" Bryusov categorized this poem as a joke,
and he probably should be believed.[29] But it is a joke with a function. The playful vision has a horrible variant in "Pro domo sua,"
where the dream leaves the protagonist telling his beloved of the
terrible vision that has driven songs of love from his mind: prosti-
tutes waiting for a convoy are left bleeding and broken on the
road amid the neighing of horses and chatter of children. "And
you, my darling, in vain / Cling to me with a smile—do not call
me back, / I no longer know songs of love."

So far none of the poems in this section qualifies as a song of
love, and in that respect they are linked to the three preceding
sections. Yet several of them are about love's negation. The speaker
in "A Dream" wishes for a return to innocence, as does the prostitute in "Stanzas." In "Phantom" the protagonist flees a brothel,
pursued by a frightful vision, and the love affair chronicled in
"Three Trysts" ends in separation. Only two poems seem oddly
placed thematically. "At the Window" is a sparkling evocation of
a winter scene, playing with the transformation of reality by
dream, while "Madman" takes place in the recesses of a twisted
mind. In fact their placement among poems of love brings into
clear relief another theme which is equally important in the book:
the transformation of experience by dream, subjective vision,
memory. Experience, especially that of love, is passed through

29. *Percovu*, p. 47.

the prism of the poet's personality in its many states, under many influences, and itself assuming various characters.

In this section Bryusov applies with a vengeance the lessons about variety of form that he had learned through Verlaine. Each of the eight poems uses a different meter. Amphibrachic trimeter, trochaic tetrameter, anapestic trimeter, iambic tetrameter, and amphibrachic tetrameter are interspersed with poems of variable lines. The strong tendency toward ternary meters was evident also in the work of some of Bryusov's Russian contemporaries. In Bryusov it is marked by lively efforts to coordinate meter with other elements of the poem. "Three Trysts" is especially interesting in this regard. The three sections sketch the beginning, middle, and end of an affair. The setting is naturalistic. The love is neither exalted nor mysteriously depraved, but merely casual. A tone of conversational intimacy is achieved by diction and by somewhat elastic ternary meter.

"There is another kind of poetry altogether," Bryusov had assured Pertsov, when speaking of the poetry of images and sound-play, and in the final section of *Chefs d'œuvre* he turned his attention to this "other kind" of poetry. To Stanyukovich he wrote, "You are looking for connections—these very 'Méditations' constitute a connected narrative of the life of my soul." [30] To Pertsov, a more literary and less intimate friend, he explained, "In 'Méditations' there is a good deal of prose, but this is after all poetry of 'ideas,' a small *poèma* of the soul, which is revealed in the consecutiveness of the poems." [31] The seven poems trace by means of various images the young poet's embarkation on the life of mind and imagination through stages of suffering and discovery, thirst and despair, to a point that is indeed the beginning of another trek. In "It is fine here alone by the window," love is dismissed,

30. *LN* 85, p. 738.
31. *Percov*, p. 43. Again note the near-equivalence of cycle and *poèma* in Brjusov's thinking at that time.

the will and the mind are free: "I can grasp all, understand all, / And I need not kiss you, / O my sweet, here by the window at night." But the second poem shows the poet already experiencing a brief dark night of the soul. All about is rot and slime, and death's forgetfulness is the only answer. The third shows his soul hemmed in by the world's smallness, deprived of a sweeping view of the horizon; when he looks to heaven in reproach, the answer is a falling meteor. In the fourth the hero lounges on a divan in a luxurious house of pleasure; he is overcome by a dream in which he is wounded and imprisoned in a crypt, and when he awakes, he is weeping for someone, he knows not whom. The fifth describes a barren shrine in a desert, where, on a bare wall, are depicted two demons in embrace: "Good and evil; two brothers and friends. / Their way is one, their lots the same," says the windworn inscription. The final line is unexpected: "The cliff is silent. To the answers there is no question." The sixth poem tells of a thirsty man's vision of a beautiful garden where there is no water for him. Finally comes a programmatic summons from above to the poet and his fellows to proceed in the perilous climb higher.

For the poems of his final section Bryusov apparently found models not among the French Symbolists but closer to home, in Fet, Tyutchev, and Merezhkovsky. Fet and especially Tyutchev at that time stood outside the canon of Russian poetry. Afanasy Fet published several collections in the 1850s and early 1860s but was hounded out of literature in the later sixties by the utilitarian critics, whose activity effectively stifled poetry in Russia for several decades. While Fet continued to write, he did not publish again until 1883 and was truly revived only in the Symbolist period, through the attention of Bryusov and Solovyov. Fyodor Tyutchev's work underwent the same eclipse and revival. Both these poets played significant roles in Bryusov's development in the next few years, and Bryusov's scholarship later was important in reestablishing the reputations of both. All the Symbolists came to value the two as links with the Pushkin epoch, the culture of which they looked upon nostalgically. Dmitri Merezhkovsky, a poet senior to Bryusov by about a decade, was himself strongly drawn to Tyutchev. Merezhkovsky's approach to Symbolism was gradual and uneven, but as one of the first to begin looking for a new direction he was for Bryusov a figure of importance.

On the whole Bryusov's "Méditations" represented a rather feeble attempt at philosophical poetry. The section is mildly interesting as the "narrative of the life of my soul" which Bryusov assured Stanyukovich it was, but it is more interesting in another way to the student of Bryusov or to anyone curious about the migration of images and themes in poetry. Some of the influences felt by Bryusov in these early days ultimately had deep and significant effects. Here, however, especially in the case of Fet, Bryusov's appreciation of the poetry shows up superficially in easily identifiable—and sometimes amusing—borrowings. For example, Fet's poem "At the Window" and Bryusov's of the same name have little in common besides the winter landscape.[32] Curiously, the mood and imagery of Bryusov's poem seem the more typically "Fet-like," temporarily imposing the sparkling impression of "a whole world of silver" on a more humdrum landscape. On the other hand, Fet's poem used the kind of imagery favored by Bryusov in his more exotic poems: palm trees, pearly fountains, crystal grottoes. In fact one of Fet's lines tempted Bryusov to appropriate it for quite another context: "Beneath the vivid leaves of the banana tree [Pod list'ja jarkie banana]" Bryusov transferred to its native habitat, the banks of the Godaveri, as "Leaf of the tall banana tree [list vysokogo banana]."

Of Tyutchev, Bryusov wrote to Pertsov in July 1895: "Tyutchev has for a long time been my most treasured poet."[33] Yet in a careful study of Tyutchev's relation to the Russian Symbolists,

32. A. A. Fet, *Večernye ogni* (Moscow, 1971), p. 33. In the article cited above, footnote 6, Mirza-Avakian calls Brjusov's poem "U okna" "programmatic" for its treatment of the building of a poetic world (p. 51).

33. *Percovu*, p. 33.

N. K. Gudzy questioned the depth of his influence, either poetic or philosophical, on Bryusov.[34] Epigraphs from Tyutchev often appeared with Bryusov's poems, and Gudzy suggests that Bryusov's debt to Tyutchev consisted chiefly in the impulse toward certain themes and, occasionally, certain images. Certainly none of Tyutchev's mystical pantheism can be found. (Other links of Bryusov with Tyutchev will be discussed in connection with later stages of his career.)

One poem in "Méditations," while it may bear out Gudzy's comment concerning Tyutchev, also demonstrates interestingly the kind of variation on a theme already seen in "From the Portuguese," with its allusion to Pushkin. "Toward a bench by a marble cistern" has its referent in Tyutchev, as indicated in later editions by the epigraph: "Send, Lord, your joy."[35] Tyutchev's poem prays for relief for all poor plodders along life's burning pavement, to whom the greenery and cool fountains of a secluded garden are inaccessible. Bryusov narrates the thirsty wanderer's situation in the first person, thereby intensifying the experience and narrowing the focus. (The prayer for poor sufferers is relegated to another poem in the same section.) An important new feature introduced by Bryusov is the picture within a picture, or the second level of consciousness. The narrator collapses on the moss before he can reach the cistern, and the "graceful Grecian girls" at play do not hear his parched cries. In the hallucination that follows, he enters a magical garden full of many charming features but without water. Again he collapses on the moss, and again his cries go unheard. The perspective is potentially endless.

Bryusov's connection with Merezhkovsky is still a different matter. Generally the two had little in common on any level, ar-

34.   N. K. Gudzij, "Tjutčev v poètičeskoj kul'ture russkogo simvolizma," pp. 490–91.

35.   "Pošli, gospod', svoju otradu": F. I. Tjutčev, *Stixotvorenija. Pis'ma* (Moscow, 1957), p. 166.

tistic or personal, aside from Merezhkovsky's position as an early
proponent of the new poetry. Yet their work occasionally touched.
The link between the closing poem of Bryusov's book, "Pale
shadows entwine," and Merezhkovsky's "Children of Night" is
worth exploring. "Children of Night" appeared first in *Russian
Thought* in September 1894 and was regarded as programmatic. It
rendered in poetic form views expressed the year before in his
much-talked-of essay *On the Reasons for the Decline and on New Currents in Contemporary Russian Literature.*[36] Merezhkovsky saw the
task of his generation of poets as that of leaping the gap between
the old period and the new, between which lay a fearful abyss (to
use the favored image). Born between two historical and cultural
eras, they were afflicted with inherited feebleness of spirit, along
with insatiable hunger for the new. "Children of Night" employed no striking new features; its first lines expressed the preva-
lent mood—the hour before the dawn. Bryusov, while using the
same diction, took issue with Merezhkovsky's defeatism. He acknowledged the perils: "And mutely above the eternal abyss / Our
pathway sways." And he addresses his comrades as "Wayfarers of a
starless night, / Searchers for an uncertain paradise." However,
the final stanza brings encouragement. In the cycle as a whole
Bryusov seems to call for a new mood of exploration, even of the
abyss, if so indicated.

In his more optimistic moods, Bryusov hoped that *Chefs
d'œuvre* would be perceived as a new programmatic statement replacing Merezhkovsky's comparatively fainthearted one. However, the book's immediate reception justified his worst fears. In
his diary for 30 August 1895, a few days after *Chefs d'œuvre* appeared, he noted that it had produced the worst possible impres-

36.   Dmitrij Merežkovskij, "Deti noči," *Polnoe sobranie sočinenij*, 24 vols.
(Moscow, 1914; reprinted Hildesheim and New York: Georg Olms Verlag,
1973), 22, p. 171; "O pričinax upadka i o novyx tečenijax sovremennoj literatury" (St. Petersburg, 1893), *Polnoe sobranie sočinenij*, 18, pp. 175–275.

sion on his friends: "They don't condemn it outright, but they keep silent, which is worse." [37] His natural resilience assisted his recovery, and by late September he could report to Pertsov that *Chefs d'œuvre* had begun to receive a few bouquets: "One young lady unknown to me even sent her photograph!" [38] Nonetheless, he felt deeply the desertion of some friends from whom he had expected support, if not total understanding. And he scorned the praise of those, such as Balmont, who gave their approval belatedly.

Bryusov's revenge took an unusual but characteristic form: he rushed into print with a second, enlarged and revised edition, containing a foreword that said in effect that he was completely indifferent to his audience. Actually, the foreword was full of defiance and smacked considerably of hurt ego. He wrote in part:

> Not all the newly added poems were written *after* the first edition of *Chefs d'œuvre*. Some belong to those rejected earlier, because there was a time when I did not want to publish poems in which I myself saw faults; at that time I still dimly hoped that my poems would find genuine readers. Now I am deprived entirely of such a hope. The critics and the public, as well as those persons whose opinion I especially prized and those whom I had a right to consider admirers of my poetry, have shown such crude lack of understanding of it that I now only laugh at their judgments. I no longer consider it necessary because of secondary flaws to conceal works in which there are remarkable features, all the more in that they belong fully to *Chefs d'œuvre* in both spirit and style.
>
> [I, 573]

With hauteur he reiterated his dedication of the book to eternity and art, closing with the lofty reminder: "All on earth is transitory except works of art."

37. *Dnevniki*, p. 22.
38. *Percovu*, p. 40. Nor was the press unanimous in its condemnation: *Dnevniki*, pp. 22–23.

Bryusov aimed his slap much more at the faces of his erstwhile comrades than at the press or public. The pain of the first reaction had not faded. Indeed, a real sense of betrayal lay behind his outburst to Pertsov in August: "Damn it! My friends have caused me a lot of harm; Balmont doted on ["Autumn Day"] and made me recite it to him at least five times." "Premonition" was praised by Lyalechkin, a young poet whom he admired, and even by Urusov. "What could I say? It went so far that their praise made me include 'Stanzas'—the most banal of banalities."[39] Since the printing expenses came from the author's pocket—printing the first edition had involved the attempt to pawn a gold watch—his revenge was costly.[40] But presumably it was worth it to him.

The second edition came out in the spring of 1896, when Bryusov had already embarked on his next project. It was largely ignored, except that he received a fair number of unpleasant anonymous letters. Equally unpleasant, but predictable, were letters from those to whom he had sent copies with inscriptions like "To one of those whose opinion I once valued" and "To the author of 'Half-Shadows' [Kursinsky], half-poet and half-friend."[41]

It is rare, however, that two editions of a poet's book appear within a year, and if the poet, as in Bryusov's case, is actively developing both his art and his ideas of what a book of poems should be, the second book merits some attention. In the second edition of *Chefs d'œuvre* the alterations were considerable. Poems were added, some were moved, and a few were revised or retitled. The most obvious and significant changes were in the order and number of sections. "Cryptomeria" and "Last Kisses" now headed the book. Then came a new section, "The Everyday," followed by "Méditations," with title now in Russian as well as French. Next came another new section, "Poems about Love," and finally *Poèmy.* A one-page commentary explained certain terms in the

39. Ibid., p. 38.   40. *Dnevniki*, p. 21.
41. *Percovu*, pp. 72–73.

text. The book had grown from twenty-three short lyrics and two *poèmy* to thirty-five lyrics and four *poèmy*. To the extent that Bryusov had assimilated Baudelaire's method in constructing his *cadre singulier*, these changes might both change and strengthen the meaning of the book as a total work. Presumably his careful attention to the matter indicated the value he placed on it.

A shift in emphasis is signaled by the placement of "Cryptomeria" in opening position. Moreover, the new, programmatic poem that opens the section makes an even greater change. In "My Dream" the poet's imagination, or dream, scorns the role of well-nurtured, sheltered slave-girl; instead, she inhabits the solitary desert, roams the mountains like a chamois. But when she reaches the Hill of Abandoned Shrines, she trembles in alarm, gazes, then leaves with bowed head. The poet's free imagination, then, has been to the holy mountain and has seen more than is given to those who remain in peopled places. The section and the book that follow are to be regarded as issuing in some fashion from this superior vision. In the first edition, as has been seen, in "Cryptomeria" the poems were set in a distant and exotic time or place. In the second edition, three poems are added, one removed, and the sequence altered, without changing this thematic format. However, the section seems to have gained a new meaning. "Premonition," with its lush eroticism and necrophilic theme, has been transferred, and the new arrangement plays down the erotic motif. Love continues to be a central theme, but inclusion of "My Dream" changes the tonality. Exotic sensuality is now subordinated to forays into the realm of mystery. The other two new poems in the section enhance this impression. "In Old Paris" has the quality of an etching. Cold moonlight on the Seine reveals shadows of duels and intrigues on its banks, but the lighting is from far above, and the delicate *terza rima* creates an impersonal distance. "In the Future" portrays a brief wave of love and sympathy reaching the poet from a being on another planet. Three poems in the section now refer to a heavenly body, and three speak of mysterious gods and goddesses. A sense of otherness pervades the section, coloring its themes of love and death.

The eroticism thus muted in "Cryptomeria" reappears emphatically, though in various keys, in all the subsequent sections except "Méditations." Four of the earlier poems remain in "Last Kisses," and the two added are heavily erotic. "Vestalis Virgo" is also fiercely sadistic. The second additional poem, "The Bat," is a more elusive piece easily classed as Symbolist.[42] Like the "laminae of palm fronds" in "Creation," the bat and windowsill are transformed by the mood infusing the poem. The amphibrachic rhythm dictated by *letučaja myš'* ("bat") is hypnotic. The protagonist is held captive by his own passion, which comes to be embodied in the brooding emblematic bat clinging to the windowshade.

After these pungent "Last Kisses," the reader may turn with some expectation to "The Everyday." Startlingly, the first poem is "Premonition." We are back in the tropical garden where the play of passion leads to death, much as in "Vestalis Virgo." A change from first to third person is not particularly successful (Bryusov later changed it back), but it does serve to shift attention to a female protagonist. Five of the seven poems in this section focus on the love experiences of a young woman. Russian coloration replaces, in several of them, the exoticism of the previous section. The section closes with a new poem, "A Village," showing a pensive figure in a skiff (*čelnok*) among the reeds.[43] With light and

42.   In a letter of 13 December 1895 Brjusov amusingly recounted to Percov the imaginative discussion among several friends, including Bal'mont, over the "gray window ledge" in the poem. They invested it with mystical meanings until Brjusov pointed to a windowsill in his own room (ibid., pp. 55–56).

43.   The image of a *čeln* on dark waters easily evokes Tjutčev ("Son na more"). However, Brjusov's *čelnok* had a more immediate purpose. His poem calls up a landscape similar to that in Bal'mont's "Kamyši" (*V bezbrežnosti* [Moscow, 1895], p. 9). Brjusov wrote to Percov that Bal'mont expressed a peculiarly Decadent terror of death in such poems as "Kamyši," where nature's indifference to man is shown either by the absence of human beings or by their deaths. Brjusov put a human figure in his sketch (*Percovu*, pp. 59–60).

dark, moonlight and river depths, mysteriously illuminated distance and dark human habitation, "A Village" creates a meditative mood leading easily into "Méditations."

No longer the keystone of the book, "Méditations" is reproduced almost intact. The move to fourth position, with two sections following, undeniably reduces its importance and also suggests the shift in focus of the book. It is also possible that Bryusov wanted to play down the message of the final poem of this section, the invitation to fellow poets to climb higher. At the end of 1895, Bryusov was deeply disillusioned with his fellow poets and their sympathizers. He had decided for the time being to pursue an independent—and higher—path. This is indicated by the choice of "My Dream" as the poem to introduce the book, and it is abundantly clear in the light of *Me eum esse*, the book he was now planning.

"Méditations" is followed by a brief new section, "Poems about Love." Like "Last Kisses," where passion dissolves into madness, this section is ironic. The four poems all celebrate or ironically lament the absence of love. The first has a charm derived in part from the formal delicacy of touch at which Bryusov had become skilled. Two five-line stanzas in dactylic tetrameter are followed by a single line repeating the first and last lines of the first stanza: "Stupid heart, what is there to grieve you!" The *ABABA* rhyme-scheme minimizes the contrast offered by alternating masculine-feminine rhymes, but achieves a more subtle one through use of inexactly rhyming words: *pečálit'sja / celoválisja* in the first stanza, *snéžnoe / ínee* in the second. In the first stanza the poet reasons with his heart, explaining that nothing has been lost, while memories of happy moments remain. The second suggests the heart's reply: with no transition, it describes a cheerless winter landscape with a particularly gloomy sky. The heart knows better than the mind; the reprise in the eleventh line, now ironic, makes this clear. A diary notation from just the time when the poem was written puts the experience in personal terms: "Elena Vladimirovna

[Burova] was a shadow that stirred the stagnant water of my life. There was no love, but without her I am twice as solitary" [I, 574]. As often happens with poets, the poem probably meant more than the relationship. Its dactylic rhythm and endings, the slightly off-center caesura, the sound-play and play on roots all support the mood of playful sadness, a mood well within the poet's reach at that time, neither pretentious nor overambitious.

In the second edition the section "*Poèmy*" took on a new importance, not only by its placement but by a clearer conception of what the form was to be, and consequently a surer use of its possibilities. The "lyrical *epos*," as Bryusov once called it, required a narrative thread, but much could be left unsaid.[44] The section is introduced by a short poem designated "Motto"; its title, "Il Bacio," alludes to Verlaine's poem by the same name. Indeed, it seems to be a polemic. Verlaine's lyric glorifies the kiss, "rose trémière au jardin des caresses!"[45] Moreover, he invokes a long literary tradition in so doing: "Will" and Goethe. But Bryusov, in the name of modernity, takes issue with this. Beyond the kiss—and the joys of love—lies another satisfaction; beyond the limits of desire are other mysteries accessible only to art. At least, this seems to be implied in the *poèmy* that follow. "Ideal" is in fact an etherealized version of the discarded "Autumn Day," with something of Poe's "Annabel Lee," where the angels guard the purity of the young lovers. Bryusov's poem contains one striking image, of a meteor suddenly frozen in the heavens, shedding its light henceforward and forever—the experience of love made permanent in art.

The second *poèma* seems at first a very different matter, yet it also shows the poet encountering his Muse. Here she is a nighttime creature, a vampire who herself succumbs to the embrace. She represents a force whose periodic summons draws the poet to

44.   "Profession de foi," unpublished essay written probably in June 1894. Prepared for publication by S. I. Gindin.
45.   Paul Verlaine, "Il Bacio," *Œuvres complètes*, 1, p. 45.

the dark side of human experience. That a poet's Muse knows no limitation in this or any other regard was a cardinal principle for Bryusov. The vampire of "And Once Again" reappears many times in his work, both poetry and prose, in various guises. The figure embodying passion is the recurrent reminder of something lying beyond the rational in human nature, while at the same time it offers the key to the mystery.

The poet in "Snows" has lost his Maria—his ideal love, his Muse—through careless debauchery. The debauchery is in fact to be interpreted as infidelity to his Muse, however. He perhaps has not answered the call which came "and once again," in the time of the new moon. In "Snows" he stands ultimately solitary under the cold light of that same heavenly body, and from an even greater, colder height shines the passionless distant Vega.

The final *poèma* is the sequence "Three Trysts," earlier found in "Last Kisses." Its new placement greatly enhances its meaning. In case the love motif has been taken too seriously in the preceding pieces, it is here definitively subordinated to art. In each of the three sections the intimate scene is distanced by the poet's perception of it within some sort of frame. The first rendezvous finds the lovers looking down from "somewhere"—a window?—on a crowd metonymized into scarfs, caps, and epaulettes: "What a wonderful frame for trysts!" This consciousness of setting throws some doubt on his closing words, "Darling, no, I'm not lying when I say I love you." The second vignette finds the lovers vaguely reflected in a mirror, "like sweetly imperfect rhymes." The poet-protagonist is acutely aware of the clichés that apply to such meetings. There it is, he says, that "quiver of love, which / I have so often repeated in triolets, / There it is—'the sweet tears of nights.'" Finally, on a railroad platform the protagonist bids farewell to a companion who "weeps and weeps, / Like the final scene of a novel."

A single protagonist, the poet, is present in all four of the *poèmy*. However, Bryusov had not yet created a lyrical hero in the usual sense. The poet-figure in the *poèmy* was only the beginning of a consistent lyrical persona that would be developed in later books. The relationship of poet and muse became central to *Me eum esse*, but in much of *Chefs d'œuvre* this is only suggested. In many cases, the autobiographical element was very apparent—at least to his friends—and was meant to be so; on the other hand, many of the erotic scenes were used as figures with further meaning. Speaking of the first edition, Bryusov's literal-minded friend Stanyukovich complained that the book consisted of "some fragmentary thoughts linked only by erotic escapades." To this Bryusov replied: "The first two *poèmy* ["Autumn Day" and "Snows"] and 'Three Trysts'—these are all the places where I speak of my own love." [46] By the time of the second edition he had taken steps to give "Snows" and "Three Trysts" a meaning that overshadowed the autobiographical. Mistaken identity or attribution was of course a constant danger. He wrote to Pertsov in August 1895 that up to now all critics have made the mistake of assuming that a lyric poet expressed only his own thoughts in poetry. "Why so? Can I not embody in a lyric poem moods completely alien to me and, even more, thoughts that are not mine!" [47] He was beginning to work his way out of his own confusion, but the problem of the naive reader would continue to dog a poet whose subject matter often ranged beyond the bounds of conventional morality and sensibility.

The second edition of *Chefs d'œuvre* sacrificed none of the first edition's exuberant play on exotic rhyme and other sound patterns—assonance, alliteration, internal rhyme and its variants. The slight textual alterations and additions were all in the direction of greater exploitation of sound features in support of meaning or mood. His preference for ternary meters has already been noted. He also employed mixed rhythms in several poems, and

46. *LN* 85, p. 738.   47. *Percovu*, p. 36.

the first signs of the *dol'nik* are to be found, where a variable number of syllables occur between stresses.[48] In addition to sonnet, *ottava rima*, and *terza rima*, Bryusov used a wide range of stanza forms, including those of irregular length or with irregular line length, though the quatrain continued to be his favorite. He employed approximate rhymes with considerable frequency.[49] Some of the poems added in the second edition showed particular virtuosity in these matters. Intricate and effective sound structure is a feature of "Vestalis Virgo," both poems entitled "Alone," "Foggy Nights," and "In the Future." Others, especially in "Poems about Love," show a clever interplay of stanzaic structure and meaning.

In December 1895, while preparing the second edition for the censor, Bryusov wrote in his diary: "Perhaps it's a good thing that I am 'not acknowledged.' If I were in favor with the public, I might fall to the level of such as Korinfsky and dance to someone else's pipe."[50] Since general approbation was out of the question—at least for the time being—he felt free to experiment, to test the limits of his powers. The crashing failure of the first edition badly damaged his self-confidence. However, soon he was able to survey his work with a measure of detachment. Acknowledging that the book contained some bad along with the good, he told Pertsov that, if he had the choice of publishing the book again as it was and not publishing it at all, he would choose the former.[51] As has been seen, he did better—he printed a second, enlarged edition: in the book that appeared early in 1896 Bryusov displayed both his poetic powers and his artistic values as they were, without much heed for immediate critical reaction, indeed,

48.   See Chapter Six, footnote 17.
49.   Mirza-Avakjan (see above, footnote 6) includes a table of approximate rhymes found in the second edition of *Chefs d'œuvre* (pp. 60–61).
50.   *Dnevniki*, p. 23. Apollon Korinfskij was a second-rate poet and devotee of "pure art," who began publishing at the end of the 1880s.
51.   *Percovu*, p. 40.

with demonstrative disregard. After all, the poet whose Muse wandered on the Hill of Abandoned Shrines presumably had access to sources beyond the common reach. This was not to claim too much, as he said: it was not hard to exceed the standard of most of the poetry being published at the time. Bryusov's response to criticism was already contained in the foreword to the first edition: "In the future I shall write far more significant things (at twenty-one it is permissible to make promises!)"

THREE

Symbolism or Decadence?

FROM CONCEPTION OF THE FIRST *Russian Symbolists* to completion of the second *Chefs d'œuvre*—that is, from 1893 to early 1896—Bryusov was much occupied with working out a rationale and a direction for the revolution he planned for Russian poetry. A bewildering variety of new ideas, as well as poetic styles, had recently come from France. Chief among these new ideas were the notions of Symbolism and Decadence. Not yet fully understood in Russia, they were nonetheless perceived to be laden with significance. To Bryusov the first task seemed to be one of definition. What exactly was Symbolism and what was Decadence, and what was the relation between them? Beyond these questions, the dimensions of the problem grew to include an effort at defining poetry itself in the light of its latest development. Finally Bryusov's deliberations issued in a plan to write a history of the Russian lyric and thus to trace the development of Russian poetry up to the advent of Symbolism. These were long-range plans; the problems of the new theorist of Russian Symbolism had not been solved by the beginning of 1896. However, the period 1893–1896 formed an epoch both in Bryusov's poetic practice and in his thinking about poetry. His second volume of poetry, *Me eum esse*, completed in the fall of 1896, marked a temporary departure from the line of thought begun earlier. After it he returned to pursue further many of the ideas that had been started in this first period.

The names *Symbolism* and *Decadence* can be traced back into the melee of manifestos, slogans, and small journals that emerged in France in the 1880s. In Russia they were generally used interchangeably, and largely as terms of opprobrium. The terms received almost their only honorable use from Akim Volynsky, the leading force in the late eighties and early nineties of the journal *Northern Messenger*, the only journal then publishing poems and even novels by Merezhkovsky, Nikolai Minsky, Zinaida Gippius, Fyodor Sologub, and Konstantin Balmont.[1] These works mingled with Realist writings, and translations of Maeterlinck were flanked by articles on popular education and international law. As director of the literary section, Volynsky propagated his own ideas on the new art. He apparently visualized himself as mentor of a new literary movement which in rejecting Realism and Naturalism would accord with his own philosophical idealism. The notion of poetry in the service of spiritual values which came to characterize the second generation of Symbolists had an early propagandist here. Volynsky's conception of Symbolism in art required that symbols be employed "with one stroke to awaken in man his whole inner being—with all his poetic contemplativeness, with all his moral ideals."[2] Though willing to tolerate Decadence temporarily insofar as it protested against positivist, materialist culture, Volynsky saw it as essentially a negative phenomenon, soon to be replaced by his brand of Symbolism. His

---

1.   In *Severnyj vestnik* for 1895, along with shorter works by these writers, two novels appeared: Merežkovskij's *Otveržennyj [Julian Otstupnik]* (nos. 1–6) and Sologub's *Tjažëlye sny* (nos. 7–12). The role of Akim Volynskij (Flekser) and *Severnyj vestnik* in the discussions of this period is discussed by D. E. Maksimov in "'Severnyj vestnik' i simvolisty," in V. Evgen'ev-Maksimov and D. E. Maksimov, *Iz prošlogo russkoj žurnalistiki* (Leningrad, 1930), pp. 85–128. See also E. V. Ivanova, "Severnyj vestnik," in *Literaturnyj process i russkaja žurnalistika konca XIX-načala XX veka 1890–1904. Buržuazno-liberal'nye i modernistskie izdanija*, ed. B. A. Bjalik et al. (Moscow, 1982), pp. 91–128.

2.   "Literaturnye zametki," *Severnyj vestnik* no. 7 (1892): 148.

alliance with the authors mentioned above was not lasting, and Bryusov was never published in *Northern Messenger*.

As a reader of *Northern Messenger* Bryusov could not have over-looked Volynsky's views, but he would have found them unacceptable. He was taking another route. His diary entries of March 1893 show him using *Symbolism* and *Decadence* almost interchangeably, but with a slight distinction which suggested that he took his cues from Zinaida Vengerova's "Symbolist Poets in France."[3] Vengerova had explained to the Russian public that "the name 'Decadents' was given to the new poets as a joke . . . but they accepted the challenge and began to declare themselves the representatives of the Latin *décadence* [*sic*], with its morbid thirst for unknown sensations and desire to create a new language, a new music of sounds capable of embodying their dream of the unattainable ideal."[4] The name *Symbolism*, she continued, had been adopted to indicate the most essential feature of their poetic devices. This was to become for Bryusov an important distinction. Decadence for him was the larger phenomenon relating to world outlook and lifestyle, while Symbolism was specifically the artistic method developed to express the perceptions, intuitions, and feelings of Decadence. However, the process of definition was not simple: it came to involve Bryusov's entire conception of poetry and of the nature and role of the poet. His intellectual struggles may be traced in part in writings dating from that time.

Some of the relevant critical pieces that Bryusov wrote between 1893 and 1896 were published, others were not. The latter were sometimes incomplete or were designed as forewords to works that never saw the light of day. The published texts include the forewords to the three issues of *Russian Symbolists* and the two editions of *Chefs d'œuvre*, the introduction to his translation of *Romances sans paroles*, and an interview (in fact an article written by

3.   *Dnevniki*, pp. 12–13.
4.   Zinaida Vengerova, "Poèty simvolisty vo Francii," *Vestnik Evropy* no. 9 (1892): 117.

Bryusov) in *News of the Day* for 29 August 1894.[5] His thoughts
on poetry also appear in letters of that time—notably, to Peter
Pertsov—and in his diary.[6] Taken together, these show a young
poet strenuously trying to understand and formulate the meaning
of the role he had assumed. His position developed, shifted, sometimes contradicted itself, and generally showed the characteristics
of growth. Those writing about Bryusov have not always treated
these texts with the requisite caution, and they have often ne-
glected the chronology.[7] While Bryusov arrived at some of his
ideas on poetry early and retained them throughout his career,
many he later replaced by other insights, drawn from the most
varied sources. Bryusov held firm convictions about art, which he
passionately defended in debates over three decades, but for him
adherence to a notion for the sake of consistency had no value,
while the capacity for absorbing new ideas had a very great one.

"What if I tried to write a treatise on spectral analysis couched
in the language of Homer? I wouldn't have the words or expressions. The same thing if I try to express fin-de-siècle sensations in
Pushkin's language. Yes, Symbolism is necessary!"[8] Bryusov was
profoundly convinced of the need for new forms of literary expression for contemporary spiritual experience. Following his intro-

---

5.   The forewords to the three *Russkie simvolisty* are to be found in VI, 27,
28–31, 32–34. The forewords to the two *Chefs d'œuvre* appear in I, 572, 573.
The *Novosti dnja* interview is reprinted in *LN* 27–28, p. 268. The foreword to
Romances sans paroles is excerpted in Ašukin, p. 69.

6.   Brjusov's correspondence with Percov between 1894 and 1896 is the
richest available source (*Percovu*). Another correspondence that dealt in part with
literary matters was that with Stanjukovič, printed with his memoir of Brjusov
(*LN* 85, pp. 713–58).

7.   For example, M. L. Mirza-Avakjan, "Rabota Brjusova nad sbornikom'
Šedevry'," *Brjusovskie čtenija 1973* (Erevan, 1976), pp. 44–61. Besides her un-
awareness that the 1896 *Chefs d'œuvre* was the second, not the first, edition, she
considered it suitable to group together critical statements of Brjusov's from
1895 and 1905 on the subject of literary schools—a risky procedure, as these
pages hope to show.

8.   *Dnevniki*, p. 13.

duction to French Symbolism in Vengerova's article, he turned quickly to obtaining and translating the works of French Symbolist poets, trying to deduce from these samples the essence of Symbolism as a literary method. This was in a sense a thankless task, since Bryusov could obtain at best only fragmentary glimpses of the kaleidoscopic literary scene in France. Nonetheless, his own habits of mind as well as his immediate purpose of organizing and publicizing the new art in Russia required clear formulations. One completed but never published project, antedating *Russian Symbolists*, was a collection he intended to call *Symbolism. (Imitations and Translations)*. His earlier submissions to journals having been rejected, he apparently decided to provide his own vehicle. The foreword he wrote for this book is valuable as his first available statement on Symbolism.[9]

Like Bryusov's unpublished study of Verlaine, this brief introduction took a measured tone toward the new trend. Acknowledging the excesses which were drawing so much attention, the author stressed that, by avoiding precise descriptions of objects, Symbolism aimed to force the reader to use his imagination. This was the only essential feature. All other alleged aspects of Symbolism were accidental. He explained how some of these features came about. Symbolists tried to portray the world as it is reflected in the soul of contemporary man, and, in their view, these new, refined sensations required new metaphors and similes. Striving for beauty of form, they paid great attention to the sounds of words, desiring to bring poetry close to music. The results sometimes struck readers as extreme. Moreover, the attempt to align poetry with contemporary moods sometimes led to use of images in questionable taste. Finally, in an effort to avoid banality, the new poets often deliberately made their work incomprehensible

9.   "[Vstupitel'naja stat'ja k sborniku 'Simvolizm. (Podražanija i perevody)'], " text prepared by S. I. Gindin, in press (U.S.S.R.). A comprehensive description of the development of Symbolist approaches to art in the period here concerned is A. G. Lehmann, *The Symbolist Aesthetic in France, 1885–1895* (Oxford: Basil Blackwell, 1950).

to all but a small coterie. But Bryusov concluded reassuringly that true Symbolist writings are more simple and understandable than they may at first seem to the unaccustomed reader. With these soothing and moderate words Bryusov apparently hoped to smooth the way for the new Russian poetry.

At the end of 1893, Bryusov composed a foreword for the first volume of *Russian Symbolists*. Signing the name of the fictitious publisher, V. A. Maslov, he again took a detached tone toward the new movement. Now he clearly distinguished between Symbolism and Decadence. The language of the Decadents, "strange, unusual tropes and figures," was not an essential element of Symbolism. The aim of Symbolism was "by a series of juxtaposed images to, as it were, hypnotize the reader, to evoke in him a certain mood" [VI, 27]. His disclaimers regarding Decadence were disingenuous, considering his private remarks and intentions at this time. However, they may have been prompted at least in part by his genuine interest in isolating the essence of Symbolism.

Half a year later in his diary, Bryusov wrote that he was "painfully hatching an article *'Profession de foi'* for the second issue of *Russian Symbolists*." [10] The article, never completed, contains a greatly clarified theory of Symbolism. By this time his ideas had been fortified by further acquaintance with French writers. As he now saw it, French Symbolism was accompanied by three trends not truly related to it: (1) Romanticism with medieval coloration, founded by Jean Moréas, which used medieval language and imitated the songs of that period; (2) mysticism, which followed Verlaine's religious poetry; and (3) the semi-spiritualist theories propagated in the novels of Saâr Péladan. [11] In Symbolism itself he distinguished four trends, any one of which could make a work

10. *Dnevniki*, p. 17. *"Profession de foi."* Text prepared for publication by S. I. Gindin.

11. It is interesting that Brjusov himself was soon involved in the first and third of these currents. He was already becoming adept in spiritualism, though this did not appear in his poetry (Stanjukovič, *LN* 85, p. 727). And a few years later, as will be seen below, he became intrigued by Russian folksongs.

Symbolist, but which in fact seldom occurred singly. These were: (1) the tendency to bring poetry close to music; (2) the trend that followed Gautier and Baudelaire in affecting strange turns of speech and bold metaphors and similes, and in general strove to renew language; (3) Symbolism proper, which provided a series of symbols or, better, images that were seemingly unconnected but actually designed to produce a certain mood; and (4) the trend represented by Maeterlinck's dramas, where external content hides a second meaning, bringing the work close to allegory. It has been observed that Bryusov's insistence on seeing Symbolism as essentially a poetry of suggestion was at first dictated as much by his own artistic experience, especially in translating Verlaine, as by theoretical considerations.[12] This may be the case; certainly, his second category looks toward the poems which he was soon to publish as *Chefs d'œuvre*.

At about this time a rich new source of ideas and information on the French Symbolists presented itself to him in the person of Alexander Dobrolyubov, whose visit to Bryusov in June 1894 has already been described. Bryusov wrote later that Dobrolyubov was "in the highest degree knowledgeable about the 'new poetry' (French), of which I actually knew only fragments. Mallarmé, Rimbaud, Laforgue, Vielé-Griffin, not to speak of Verlaine and of the forerunners of the 'new art' such as Baudelaire, Théophile Gautier, and other 'Parnassians,' were known to him cover to cover."[13] Dobrolyubov's revelations were probably the single most important influence on Bryusov's ideas at this time. It is not clear whether *"Profession de foi"* was written just before or after Dobrolyubov's visit, but if before, it must surely have undergone revision afterward. Heretofore Bryusov had excluded the first trend mentioned in the article—the rapprochement of poetry to music—from the list of Symbolism's central features. However,

12.   K. Loks, "Brjusov—teoretik simvolizma," *LN* 27–28, p. 266.
13.   "Avtobiografija," pp. 112–13.

it was one of Dobrolyubov's cardinal principles, which he tried to exemplify in his 1895 book *Natura naturans. Natura naturata.*[14] It may have been he who temporarily persuaded Bryusov of the importance of this trend for Symbolism.

For whatever reasons, Bryusov decided against using *"Profession de foi"* in the second *Russian Symbolists*. The new foreword must have been completed before 23 August 1894, the date of the censor's approval.[15] Addressed to "a charming stranger" and signed by Bryusov, it is his fullest and most serious attempt up to this point to deal with the question of Symbolism. While in many ways a reworking of *"Profession de foi,"* it represents a new step in Bryusov's development. Having perhaps shaken off the immediate hypnotic effect of Dobrolyubov's visit, he was now confident enough to distinguish his Symbolism from other varieties. While recognizing that Symbolism perhaps could not be reduced to a single form, he could assert positively what it was for him. His list of secondary elements remained the same, but several core elements—innovation in language and imagery, alignment of poetry with music, and approximation of poetry to allegory—were demoted from ends to means. Thus he returned to the position of his first, unpublished statement, written before his encounter with Dobrolyubov. Symbolism continued in his vision as supremely the poetry of suggestion.

Bryusov's ideas on Symbolism and on poetry in general were still relatively limited in that summer of 1894. However, the foreword to the second *Russian Symbolists* exhibits key features of Bryusov's position which were to figure in debates for years to come. Mysticism in poetry or the use of poetry to attain mystical experience, advocated by some later Russian Symbolists, was permanently excluded from Bryusov's canon of esthetics. He held,

14.   Vladimir Gippius, "Aleksandr Dobroljubov," in Vengerov, *Russkaja literatura XX veka 1890–1910*, 1, p. 276.
15.   VI, 28–31.

then and always, that poetry must never be subordinated to any end outside itself. Subject matter as such was not to be a determining feature in deciding what was Symbolist poetry: fin-de-siècle moods and feelings were not enough to qualify a poem as Symbolist. Moreover, the poetry of suggestion permitted a wide range of forms, from a picture left intentionally incomplete, to a narrative with scenes included chiefly to create an impression, to a series of seemingly unlinked images. Bryusov justified this kind of poetry in the following way. Literary schools vary in the stage of development at which poets embody their thought; Symbolism seizes the first glimmer of thought or emotion—the dream (*mečta*). Hence both the Symbolist poet and his reader need sensitive souls; thus, the circle of qualified readers may be very small. Apparently this explanation owes much to Dobrolyubov.[16] At any rate the notion of exclusiveness on the basis of special sensitivities was to be a cardinal point in Bryusov's credo for at least the next quarter of a century.

Another statement of Bryusov's appeared in print even before the *Russian Symbolists* foreword. On 30 August the Moscow daily *News of the Day* printed a supposed interview with Bryusov that had actually been written by him. The newspaper had published the previous day an interview with Lang and E. Martov, a new collaborator, mistakenly treating them as leaders of the Symbolist movement in Moscow who expressed views with which Bryusov disagreed. He hastened to put matters right by claiming that the offending views in fact belonged to Petersburg Symbolists and specifically to Dobrolyubov.[17] While diversity of approach was to

16.   *Dnevniki*, p. 17. Considerable evidence of Dobroljubov's influence on Brjusov in this and other matters at this time is adduced by E. V. Ivanova, "Valerij Brjusov i Aleksandr Dobroljubov," pp. 255–65, esp. p. 257.

17.   *LN* 27–28, p. 269. Ivanova (p. 257). The editors of *Bibliografija* (p. 237) attribute both interviews to Brjusov. However, in his diary entry for 29 August Brjusov identifies Martov and Miropol'skij as the interviewees and mentions going to the newspaper office that day and the day before to straighten

be expected among members of a new school, Bryusov stressed that the majority viewed Symbolism as the poetry of suggestion and nuance, suited to the refined sensibilities of contemporary man. Some, he acknowledged, did see Symbolism as a search for new means of expressiveness because modern man's sensibilities required strong stimulants. In addition Bryusov tested a new idea, attributing it to his pseudonymous creation "Darov," "one of the most passionate followers of Symbolism,"[18] namely, that Symbolism alone constituted true poetry and that all preceding it was only prelude.

Meanwhile, Bryusov turned his attention from construing

---

out matters. On 30 August he reports the interview with himself. Ivanova quotes, without giving its date, a letter from Vladimir Gippius accusing Brjusov of plagiarizing Dobroljubov's ideas (p. 257). Given the editors' mistaken attribution, Gippius may have accused the wrong person. This would account for Brjusov's eagerness to place his own statement in the newspaper. On the other hand, it is entirely possible that Brjusov was indeed indebted to Dobroljubov for some of the ideas in his statement.

18. "Darov" was useful to Brjusov also as the "author" of some of the more daringly Decadent verses in the two collections in which his name appears. However, "Darov's" appearances in *Russkie simvolisty* formed only the tip of the iceberg: N. K. Gudzij discovered much more about this creation of Brjusov's ("Iz istorii simvolizma," pp. 185–88). "Darov's" first appearance was as the protagonist in Brjusov's one-act play "Proza," which was presented in an amateur performance as a benefit in the German Club in Moscow in November 1893. "Darov," a Decadent poet, was played by Brjusov. (See *LN* 27–28, p. 727. In "Literaturnoe nasledstvo Valerija Brjusova," *LN* 27–28, p. 492, Aleksandr Il'inskij reported "interesnaja xarakteristika poèta Darova" in an early notebook of Brjusov's, but he did not elaborate.) In 1894, Brjusov planned to put his own poems before the public without risk to his reputation. He drafted two forewords to a collection of supposedly original poems and other writings by the prematurely deceased genius "Darov." As late as the writing of his "Avtobiografija" for the 1914 Vengerov *Russkaja literatura XX veka*, Brjusov chose to resurrect Darov. There he wrote that "V. Darov (pseudonym) turned to commerce and at the present time is known in the financial world but continues to write poems" (p. 109n). Mirza-Avakjan wrote that "Darov" was a pseudonym for Dobroljubov (*Brjusovskie čtenija 1963* [Erevan, 1964], p. 88). This is patently incorrect, which is not to deny that "Darov" may have advocated some of Dobroljubov's ideas.

French Symbolism to examining the recent history and present
state of Russian poetry. His aim was twofold: on one level, he
wanted to establish the recent lineage of the new Russian movement; on another, he was intent on clearing the debris and edu-
cating public, or at least critical, taste—insofar as that was possible. At the end of 1894 he drafted what is probably his first
attempt to deal with the subject.[19] This may have been conceived
as the introduction to a book on which he began work a little
later. The variable title shows a certain indecision about its scope:
"The Russian lyric of the last decade," "of the last twenty years,"
and finally, "of the last fifteen years." Briefly describing the persecution of poetry during the 1860s, he noted the fate during that
time of those he considered the period's three real poets, Fet,
Tyutchev, and A. K. Tolstoy. For contemporary poetry he saw
two chief formative influences: Fet, to whose genius, especially in
the realm of love and nature poetry, Bryusov awarded an honorable place in world literature, and Semyon Nadson, who reflected
the barrenness of the most recent era. (Bryusov saw the harmful
effect of Nadson's influence in the banality of his elegiac theme,
which was widely imitated.) Minsky, Merezhkovsky, and Konstantin Fofanov, who appeared during the eighties, were that decade's only lights but even they seldom expressed a new point of
view on any subject. Only very recently, claimed Bryusov, had
Russian poetry begun to abandon such topics as "What is truth?"
and "How she told me 'I love you' on a warm summer night."
The new voices included Konstantin Balmont and the poets publishing in *Russian Symbolists*, along with one other, Ivan Lyalechkin.[20] The essay ends with a quick survey of the scene and general

19.   "Russkaja lirika za poslednie 15 let," prepared by S. I. Gindin, in
press.
20.   Fofanov was a poet of considerable lyrical gifts, valued by Brjusov and
regarded as in some measure a forerunner of the Decadents. Minskij (Vilenkin),
owing to an article published in 1884 in which he set forth the principles of
individualism, is considered the first spokesman for Decadence in Russia. His

condemnation of the poetasters who crowded the literary journals and popular press.

This unpublished draft gives notice of a project that Bryusov described to Pertsov a few months later. Bryusov's acquaintance with Pertsov had begun with the latter's request to reprint one of Bryusov's pseudonymous contributions to *Russian Symbolists*, No. 2, in Pertsov's collection *Young Russian Poetry*. Pleased by the invitation, Bryusov nonetheless was extremely unhappy with the volume for what it revealed of the state of Russian poetry in the mid-nineties. In a letter of 27 July 1895 he told Pertsov that *Young Russian Poetry* provided him with the occasion for a small book of criticism which he was preparing, "a collection of remarks, not so much critical as polemical, rather thoughts *occasioned* by the newest works of our poets than *about* them."[21] This work, to be called *Russian Poetry in {18}95*, also remained unfinished, but considerable material for it was assembled.[22]

That fall Bryusov returned once more, this time in his correspondence with Pertsov, to the definition of Symbolism.[23] The latter apparently supported, on the basis of Maeterlinck's dramas, the notion that a Symbolist work must have both a direct and an oblique meaning. In a letter of 18 November Bryusov dissented sharply from this point of view. Such a definition would exclude

---

earliest poetry reflected a Populist point of view; he then moved on through Decadence to a paradoxical idealist theory that he called "Meonism." By 1905 he was working with Lenin on the newspaper *Novaja žizn'*, where he published a poem with the famous line: *"Proletarii vsex stran, soedinjajtes'!"* ("Workers of the world, unite!"). Minskij died in Paris in 1937. Ivan Ljalečkin was a young poet with whom Brjusov had been in correspondence but whom he had never met. Ljalečkin's death at the age of 25, in 1895, shortly after this was written, shocked Brjusov (*Dnevniki*, p. 20, entry for March 1895).

21.   *Percovu*, p. 32.

22.   Brjusov wrote about this work to friends like Percov (*Percovu*, pp. 32–33) and Stanjukovič (*LN* 85, pp. 737–55). Fragments of work possibly destined for it have been described by Gudzij (pp. 195–96), Ivanova (pp. 180–82), and others.

23.   *Percovu*, pp. 46–47.

many of the newest poets, he pointed out, consigning them to
the category of "classical," while assigning the tag "Symbolist" to
Goethe, Dante, and Milton. This was exactly what some critics
were doing, but, asked Bryusov, "What does the solution of our
problem gain from such a play of names?" Regarding the troublesome problem of definition, he insisted that his view had not
changed "in its general features" since the summer of 1894. But
in the course of the present discussion with Pertsov, he found
himself dealing not with Symbolism but with poetry itself. For
when Pertsov denied that some of the new writing, including
Mallarmé's, deserved to be called poetry, Bryusov was provoked
to the assertion which he had earlier attributed to "Darov": outside of Symbolism there is no poetry. However, anticipating Pertsov's demand for clear definitions, he wrote:

> In what do this essence of poetry and these distinguishing features of
> Symbolism consist? I cannot answer you directly. In any case, not in
> symbols. I seek the solution first of all in form, in the harmony of
> images or, better, in the harmony of those impressions which images
> evoke, in the conciliation of those ideas which become clear under
> their influence. Words lose their usual sense, figures lose their con-
> crete meaning; there remain the means of controlling the elements of
> the soul, of giving them that sensuous-sweet combination that we
> call esthetic pleasure. If one's soul is not sufficiently flexible, it will
> fail to yield to many things. This is why we do not wish to consider
> Mallarmé or Dobrolyubov to be a poet. But poetry is broader than
> we imagine her to be: there are many forms not yet foreseen by us.
> The future is limitless.[24]

This last remark is noteworthy. Throughout his career Bryusov
was drawn ever onward by the exhilarating prospect of a continuing road of discovery. His definition of Decadence involved this
probing of the unknown, as will be seen below. Meanwhile, his

24.   Ibid., p. 48.

optimism about the progress of the new art had some grounds, despite the frigid reception of *Chefs d'œuvre* in the late summer and fall of 1895. First of all, Bryusov received encouragement as well as ridicule. In a diary entry for 21 November he wrote: "After the well-inclined remarks of the *Russian Bulletin*, after the sympathetic interview in the [Petersburg paper] *News*, I see how my fellow students behave toward me. The 'O-o-oh, Decadent' of not so long ago has disappeared without a trace. 'Yes,' said N. N., as Samygin tells it, '*Chefs d'œuvre* is a very remarkable book. There is much in it for the psychologist and for the philosopher and for the pure esthetician.'"[25] More broadly, the year 1895 was marked by a burst of Symbolist publications. In addition to Bryusov's own books and Dobrolyubov's *Natura naturans. Natura naturata*, Balmont's *In Boundlessness* was printed, a second volume of Minsky's poems appeared, and Zinaida Gippius published her first volume of prose and poetry, *New People*. Merezhkovsky's novel *Julian the Apostate* and Fyodor Sologub's novel *Bad Dreams* gave the movement a more solid appearance. Balmont's translations of Poe appeared, along with two others.[26] While Pertsov's *Young Russian Poetry* was not generally Symbolist in content, and some of its contributors were not especially young, it helped sustain the impression of new activity. There were lesser phenom-

25. *Dnevniki*, pp. 22–23. The interview referred to is to be found in Ašukin, pp. 84–86. Samygin, close to Brjusov in the 1890s, published fiction as "Mark Krinickij."

26. K. Bal'mont, *V bezbrežnosti* (Moscow, 1895); Nikolaj Minskij, *Stixotvorenija* (St. Petersburg, 1895); Zinaida Gippius, *Novye ljudi* (St. Petersburg, 1896; appeared December 1895). Merežkovskij's and Sologub's novels appeared in *Severnyj vestnik* (see footnote 1 above). Bal'mont published two volumes of Poe's prose and poetry: *Ballady i fantazii* and *Tainstvennye rasskazy* (Moscow, 1895). The other translations of Poe were: *Polnoe sobranie sočinenij*, tr. G. Klepackij (Kišinev, 1895; no other volumes of the "complete works" appeared) and *Izbrannye sočinenija*, tr. S. Dobrodeev (supplement to *Živopisnoe obozrenie*, July 1895). See Joan Delaney Grossman, *Edgar Allan Poe in Russia: A Study in Legend and Literary Influence* (Wurzburg: JAL Verlag, 1973), p. 196.

ena, such as Alexander Kursinsky's *Half-Shadows*, and negative ones, such as *Bared Nerves* by A. N. Emelyanov-Kokhansky.[27] If not yet crowded, the scene was at least more encouraging than two years earlier for those who put their hope in the new tendencies.

Much that Bryusov included in the 18 November letter to Pertsov showed up in a substantial, though uncompleted, author's foreword, clearly intended for *Russian Poetry in {18}95*.[28] Bryusov probably worked on this foreword in late 1895 and early 1896. The essay opens with an explicit renunciation of Bryusov's earlier, qualified view of Symbolism's position and asserts that Symbolism and poetry are in fact equivalent terms. Bryusov then turned to refuting the notion—supported at that time by Minsky, Balmont, and others—that Symbolist poetry is distinguished by the fact that it has two levels of meaning and thus comes close to allegory. This was the position advanced in *Northern Messenger* by Volynsky. Bryusov remarked that in the foreword to his translations of Poe [*Ballady i fantasii*, 1895] Balmont had defined a Symbolist work as one that has an oblique as well as a direct meaning and had then claimed that the works of Goethe, Dante, and many

27.   Aleksandr Kursinskij, *Poluteni* (Moscow, 1896; appeared in 1895); A. N. Emel'janov-Koxanskij, *Obnažennye nervy* (Moscow, 1895). Aleksandr Kursinskij, one-time tutor of Tolstoj's children, was a university colleague of Brjusov's. A. N. Emel'janov-Koxanskij's lavender-colored booklet, dedicated "To Me and Queen Cleopatra," justified everything the most hostile critics could say about the new poetry. Brjusov wrote to warn Percov about this "Russian *Fleurs du mal*," which he considered much ado (by the author) about nothing. However, he added a footnote: "The most interesting point of all is that these verses, which I anathematize, were half written by me." Emel'janov-Koxanskij, he said, had once begged him for a notebook of verses which Brjusov had written in his early teens, and he had now published them over his own signature (*Percovu*, p. 30. See *Bibliografija*, pp. 11–12). Emel'janov-Koxanskij thus played out the comedy that Brjusov had considered for "Darov."

28.   Prepared by S. I. Gindin; in press.

others could be called Symbolist. Bryusov wondered why in that case Symbolism had become such an object of derision and Symbolists considered harmful innovators. His general refutation followed the lines taken in the letter to Pertsov, but with more detailed argument and example; by this criterion, he noted, Verlaine's *Romances sans paroles* and Maeterlinck's *Serres chaudes* would not qualify as Symbolism. He attacked the derivation of the term *Symbolism* from the word *symbol* in its usual sense. Balmont, Minsky, and others who support this idea will have to admit this error, he said, or disqualify the poems of Verlaine and Tyutchev and Poe's "The Raven" and "Ulalume." Balmont in particular was easy game for a rigorous reasoner like Bryusov. Had this piece reached print, it would have foretold some acerbic disputes of years following.

As in the November letter to Pertsov, Bryusov here avoided any categorical definition of Symbolism. Clearly he had come far since the summer of 1894, when he had spelled out his conception with such precision in *Russian Symbolists*, No. 2. The belief that poetry and Symbolism are one made the situation much more complex. Symbolism was now not merely a school like Romanticism, which had the specific charge of destroying its predecessor, Pseudo-Classicism; Symbolism's task was the total transformation of poetry into its true self. It protested not merely against one school but against views that had lasted thousands of years. Consequently Symbolism might require centuries before an adequate self-concept was formed.

Sobered by the dimensions Symbolism had assumed in his thinking, Bryusov offered now, as in his letter to Pertsov, only to point out some of the characteristic features. Every Symbolist work, he said, consists of a series of images, i.e., symbols, linked for the purpose of producing a certain impression. It matters not at all whether these images form an entire picture or merely a sequence; what is important is that in this process the word loses its function as carrier of ideas.[29] Words, worn out by common usage, are ungrateful material for the artist. This is the reason why Symbolist poets have come to emphasize the musical quality of words; as lexical meanings are forgotten, poetry has been brought close to music. Here Bryusov developed a new idea mentioned only recently to Pertsov. While poetry may produce a mood, this is not its goal—as he had learned from studying the poems of Gautier. Poetry is "first of all the conciliation of ideas, meaning all psychic facts in the life of man and [illeg.] of the universe in general, and this conciliation, this harmonic disposal of them, gives a sensually sweet feeling which is called esthetic enjoyment."[30]

The next step toward the transformation of Russian poetry was, as Bryusov saw it, to attempt a fuller understanding of its past and present, so as to define the problem more clearly. He announced in this foreword an ambitious project, the history of the Russian lyric, which was to occupy him for several years to come. The present project was to be a smaller book dealing primarily with three poets whose collections had appeared that year: Dobrolyubov, Balmont, and Apollon Korinfsky. Bryusov classified them as follows: Dobrolyubov represented the pure Symbolists; Balmont stood with those who, not satisfied with the old forms, were not yet united with the new movement; and Korinfsky represented the worst of contemporary poets. The foreword, which began with the promising discussion outlined above, lost itself in discriminations and exceptions and was never completed. Nor was the book written. Again, seemingly, Bryusov's widening

29.   "Pri ètom rol' slov kak vyrazitelej *ponjatij* soveršenno uničtožaetsja—i èto odno iz važnejsix priobretenij simvolizma."
30.   This notion recurs in later writings, notably in the 1924 essay "Sintetika poèzii" [VI, 557–70]. It is of course a very old notion in poetic theory. Some of its possible sources are briefly discussed by René Wellek, *A History of Modern Criticism 1750–1950*, vol. 1 (New Haven and London: Yale University Press, 1955), pp. 3–4.

horizon and deepening conception of what he was about drew his attention and efforts elsewhere.

Another piece, probably undertaken in February 1896, was entitled "Apologia for Symbolism."[31] It continued the attack on the notion of Symbolism as allegory. The authoritative spokesman for the objectionable theory was named as Brunetière,[32] but the real targets were Minsky, Merezhkovsky, and especially Balmont, whom Bryusov attacked with relish. A narrow polemic probably motivated at least in part by discussions with Balmont, this article contributes little to an understanding of Bryusov's concept of Symbolism.

Of great importance to Bryusov was the project alluded to in the foreword to *Russian Poetry in {18}95*, the history of the Russian lyric. The first indication of this work appeared on the back cover of *Chefs d'œuvre* in the summer of 1895.[33] In December of that year he drew up a brief plan and expressed the optimistic belief that it would take "a year, possibly even two." His diary a year later cited this work as "the most immediate goal of my life," with the still optimistic expectation that it would require three more years, if he had free time, but otherwise five.[34] (Though it was never finished, a great deal of work was done on it between 1897 and 1899.)

During the period between early 1893 and early 1896, then, Bryusov worked strenuously at clarifying and formulating his ideas on Symbolism and on poetry itself. By the end of this period the task had taken on unforeseen dimensions. His essay projects were at first largely publicistic in aim. By mid-1894 he had defined to his (temporary) satisfaction the nature of Symbolism, or

31. "Apologija simvolizma," ed. D. E. Maksimov, *Učenye zapiski*, Fakul'tet jazyka i literatury, Leningradskij Gosudarstvennyj Pedigogičeskij Institut, vol. 4, no. 2 (Leningrad, 1940).
32. F. Brunetière, *Evolution de la poésie lyrique en France* (Paris, 1894).
33. S. I. Gindin, "Neosuščestvlennyj zamysel Brjusova," p. 191.
34. *Dnevniki*, p. 26.

at least the variant of French Symbolism that he hoped to foster in Russia. However, within the year his thinking had changed. What once seemed a fairly straightforward project, that of providing models and translations of French Symbolist poetry and thereby attracting a group of young poets to form a Russian Symbolist school, had become much more complex. Conflicting views among Symbolism's Russian sympathizers brought to light conflicting understandings of art itself. Moreover, the Russian poetic tradition needed to be better understood in order to determine what was viable, onto which branches the new could be grafted. Formulating a set of questions, Bryusov was laying the groundwork for critical, historical, and philosophical projects that would compete with his poetry in the years following the completion of *Me eum esse*—and, indeed, for the rest of his life.

The second major topic to engross Bryusov's attention during the mid-1890s was Decadence. In March 1893 he had seen Decadence as his guiding star: "the future belongs to it." [35] From the start, this aspect of Decadence justified for Bryusov whatever else the notion contained. Through a curious combination of ideas (partly his own, partly acquired), he came to see an orientation toward the future as its leading characteristic, and this in spite of the associations with decline, decay, and death that Decadence had acquired in Western literature. Initially he must have noted Zinaida Vengerova's description of the "morbid thirst for unknown sensations" which generated the "desire to create a new language" to express those sensations. [36] If Symbolism was chiefly

35.   Ibid., p. 12.
36.   Vengerova, p. 117. Though they were barely—and not favorably—mentioned in Vengerova's article, one faction among the new French poets might have drawn Brjusov's attention and even influenced his perception of French Decadence. This group was gathered around the periodical *Le Décadent*. Whether it represented their orientation accurately, an article by Paul Pradet, called "Décadence et Décadence," in the 15 May 1886 issue supports the conception that Brjusov espoused early and continued to hold. Distinguishing between two

concerned with the mode of expression, Decadence defined the content of the modern spirit that expressed itself in Symbolist poetry. Persuaded of its central importance and its irresistibility, Bryusov welcomed Decadence and was at pains to penetrate its meaning. Not so the contemporary critics. They excoriated the new trend in art indiscriminately, attacking with equal force "inadmissible" subjects, bizarre language and imagery, and the lifestyle and psychology of some of the artists. The general disapprobation ranged from distaste to alarm. Translation into Russian in 1892 of Max Nordau's *Entartung* created a sensation, while providing the new movement's Russian critics with all the ammunition they could desire.[37] Young Moscow bourgeois that he was, despite his declared Decadence Bryusov occasionally adopted the typical Russian tone of moral superiority toward a new trend from the decaying West. Yet the restless, forward-thrusting aspect of his nature soon overcame this tendency.

The unpublished *"Profession de foi"* of June 1894 contains what was probably Bryusov's first formal attempt to explore the notion of Decadence. In the ten years since the term had become current, it had taken on a widened meaning, he believed, until now it "designates the attempt to bring poetry close to the contemporary, even more, to the most extreme implications of contemporary civilization."[38] Its opponents, he noted, considered Deca-

---

kinds of Decadence, Pradet wrote that the true Decadence had one goal: "faire exprimer à la langue toutes les idées, toutes les sensations, toutes les nuances si atténuées soient-elles; créer des vocables nouveaux capable de serrer l'idée dans ses reflets les plus fugitifs." It was, like other such labels, he maintained, "un écriteau collé au tournant de la route littéraire, pour indiquer à la nouvelle génération une voie inexplorée." Nothing could have better satisfied Brjusov's sense of what the new poetry was about.

37. See Joan Grossman, "Genius and Madness: The Return of the Romantic Concept of the Poet at the End of the Nineteenth Century," *American Contributions to the Seventh International Congress of Slavists*, ed. Victor Terras, 3 vols. (The Hague: Mouton, 1973), 2, pp. 247–60.

38. Here his ideas seem close to those expressed in *Le Décadent* (see footnote 36, above).

dents to be feeble individuals who, unable to sustain the pace of contemporary development, preferred to distort it, and who embodied the undesirable traits of Western man, such as vacuity, in their most extreme forms. Whether Decadence was the direction of the future, he noted guardedly, only the future could tell. However, the pace of historical development seemed to him to argue in its favor. His argument then turned to a phenomenon that much interested him: the inner development of the range of human emotions that accompanies outward historical change. "What if I tried to express in Pushkin's language fin-de-siècle sensations!" he had written over a year before. Now he observed that feelings were known today which poets from the Greeks to Heine only gradually and distantly approached. In particular he explained that the great attention paid to love in contemporary writing was due to the new forms and feelings of love in modern times.

Despite his obvious attraction to the trend, there is no indication that, as of June 1894, Bryusov had come into close contact with anyone who could conceivably be called a Decadent in the new French meaning of the word. The advanced development of civilization, which had brought the new movement into being, took place after all in the West, not in Russia. Bryusov sensed the new feelings and ideas that were circulating there, but like the new poetic forms of which he wrote to Pertsov, they continued in large part to spin just beyond the reach of his own experience. His understanding of Symbolism developed first from reading French Symbolist poetry and gradually from his own practice in writing and translation, but Decadence was not solely a literary style. While reading could and did play a role in its assimilation, for Bryusov it was of crucial importance that he encounter it in practice. This occurred when he came into close contact with Alexander Dobrolyubov and Konstantin Balmont.

Dobrolyubov, despite his youth, was exceptionally well versed in the new trends. Bryusov later wrote: "[Dobrolyubov] was saturated with the very *spirit* of Decadence and, so to say, revealed to me that world of ideas, tastes, and opinions portrayed by Huysmans in his *A rebours*."[39] In his diary account of Dobrolyubov's June 1894 visit Bryusov remarked rather ironically that Dobrolyubov performed like the perfect arch-Symbolist, that is, Decadent: "He indulged in all kinds of oddities, took opium."[40] However, Bryusov was captivated by the version of Decadence that Dobrolyubov personified: "'I seek new perfumes, larger blossoms, pleasures still untasted.'"[41] Huysmans's protagonist Des Esseintes shuddered when he heard these words of Flaubert's Chimera. Dobrolyubov was involved in the same pursuit. He had very early given himself to the kind of extreme estheticism that was linked with extreme individualism. He preached complete freedom of the personality, and in poetry he rejected any limitations. As his friend and, for a time, fellow Decadent Vladimir Gippius wrote of him, he worshipped art as "the absolutely free manifestation of the unfettered, self-affirming personality, striving toward and beyond the bounds of the knowable, the given. . . . Dobrolyubov went to extremes in everything. . . . Having come into contact with Decadence, he went to its very depths and touched them, because Decadence, as a psychological doctrine, is the idealization of direct personal perception of the world."[42] No doubt Bryusov at first understood little of what Dobrolyubov said (Dobrolyubov's esthetic ideal was "to speak of the incomprehensible incomprehensibly"),[43] but he was tremendously impressed. Bryusov's own strong-willed individualism was partly instinctive, but the example of Dobrolyubov doubtless had a considerable shaping influence. A central feature of Dobrolyubov's Dec-

39. "Avtobiografija," p. 112.
40. *Dnevniki*, pp. 17–18.
41. J.-K. Huysmans, *Against Nature*, tr. Robert Baldick (Baltimore: Penguin, 1959), p. 114.
42. Gippius, "Aleksandr Dobroljubov," pp. 275–76.
43. Ibid.

adence was infatuation with death, the ultimate freedom. *Natura naturans* was full of this theme, though it was not rendered in the usual Decadent imagery. Moreover, Dobrolyubov's life, as well as his writing, was permeated with thoughts of death. Bryusov's attitude to this typical Decadent preoccupation was ambivalent and most of the time merely speculative.[44] He eagerly accepted the Decadent requirement of strenuous exploration of all the possibilities of existence and of stepping beyond the usual bounds of experience, but only in extreme moments did he consider the adventure of "easeful death."

The second important encounter of that year, that with Balmont, took place toward the end of September. They met on 28 September 1894, at the first meeting of a small student group, the Society of Lovers of Western Literature. Both were published authors, though Balmont had the edge and was six years older besides. They were immediately attracted to each other, and after the meeting, by Bryusov's account they "wandered drunk about the streets till eight in the morning and swore eternal love."[45] This performance was repeated after the next meeting, when they roamed all night "in poetical fantasies." The contacts continued, with mutual visits and conversations about poetry that inspired Bryusov at least to furious productivity. Equally important were the attitudes Bryusov was absorbing from Balmont. He considered Balmont a Decadent, the first with whom he was in frequent touch and, moreover, one who seemed to be a natural Russian example of the new type. Balmont was steeped in Baudelaire and Edgar Poe, yet his personality was spontaneous and, most important, full of contemporary moods. Moreover, he was exciting. In

44. In a school notebook for 1890–1891, when he was in the sixth class of Polivanov's gymnasium, Brjusov worked out a table analyzing the causes and probabilities of suicide in the abstract (IRLI, manuscript division, fond 444, no. 87, p. 21). Suicide became a concrete possibility in his life several times, as will be seen in subsequent chapters.

45. *Dnevniki*, p. 19.

his autobiography Bryusov wrote of the Balmont of those days that he was "exuberant and full of the most varied literary projects. His mad love for poetry, his fine sense of the beauty of the poetic line, his whole original personality produced an exceptional impression on me. . . . He uncovered in my soul that which slept in it and which without his influence might have slept for a long time yet."[46] Much that Bryusov learned from Balmont concerned poetry per se, and their discussions and reading together affected the work of both poets.

Throughout their uneven relationship and especially in the next several years, Balmont's image carried a special meaning for Bryusov and his influence was at times strong. Balmont exemplified the free, unfettered personality existing beyond the reach of convention. To follow the untrammeled imagination in pursuit of pure beauty was his only rule. Bryusov tried to live up to Balmont's idea of him, and in turn he resented Balmont when the latter slipped from his ideal. Not surprisingly, Balmont did not always sustain his role. The following February Bryusov wrote: "Have seen Balmont several times. Most of the meetings were half-Decadent, but—alas—they ended in a tavern and a 'dive.' Balmont has appeared before me in a clear light and, again alas! he has lost much of his former attractiveness."[47] Two points should be noted here. First, Decadent behavior to Bryusov had no connection with drinking and debauchery. Second, it was exactly Balmont's Decadence that surrounded him with an aura. He was most attractive when he projected the image of Edgar Allan Poe. Some years later, Bryusov analyzed what it was that made Balmont the epitome of Decadence for him:

> Balmont is first of all a "new man." He did not come to the "new poetry" through conscious choice. He did not reject the "old art" as a result of rational criticism; he did not set himself the task of being the spokesman of a certain esthetic. Balmont forges his poems, car-

46. "Avtobiografija," p. 111.   47. *Dnevniki*, p. 20.

ing only that they be beautiful according to his own taste, interesting in the same way, and if his poetry belongs to the "new art," this has happened without his willing it. He simply tells what is in his soul, but his soul is one of those which has only recently blossomed on this earth. So in his time it was with Verlaine.

[VI, 250]

Bryusov's words show the central place held by contemporaneity in his notion of Decadence. Bryusov, too, felt himself a contemporary spirit, one of those who had only recently appeared on earth. He learned much from Balmont in this regard. The Decadent poet is he who, looking into his own soul, finds the image of the world as it is in this moment and the next. Hence his individualism: no other authority can begin to match that of the spirit finely attuned to the successive instants in the world's changing life. Bryusov did not have to learn from Dobrolyubov and Balmont that he himself was a contemporary spirit. In them, however, he could see the contemporary spirit embodied, and in their society he could best learn and remember who he was.

Was Bryusov, then, both a Symbolist and a Decadent? According to his own definition of these terms he was. The real debates on Symbolism lay well ahead and there is no question that by the measure of the majority of his colleagues at a later date he was not a true Symbolist, but by that time the label was well affixed to him. He had, after all, the rights of early occupancy. As for his Decadence, there is no doubt that he was a Decadent at the time of which we are speaking and that he remained in that camp for at least a decade to come.

FOUR

Me eum esse:
Decadence and the
Caucasus Tradition

ON 9 JUNE 1896, Bryusov left Moscow for an
extended trip to the watering places of the Caucasus.[1] He was absent from Moscow for nearly three months and during that time
produced a book of poetry that marked an entirely new phase of
his work. The months preceding this journey had been difficult
ones with little promise of creative energy. He awaited the second
edition of *Chefs d'œuvre* with no hope at all of encouragement or
approval, and in this his expectations were well founded. Moreover, in December he contracted a rheumatic illness that kept
him more or less bedridden until February. The illness was both
serious and painful, though Bryusov himself suspected a psycho-
somatic origin. He wrote half-jokingly to Pertsov on Christmas
Day: "If I die, do me the final favor of placing in some little newspaper the obituary of a young poet 'having some talent but destroyed by Symbolism.'"[2]

In this dark period of germination there were, however, bright

---

1.   This journey is not mentioned in the originally printed sections of
Brjusov's diary; the major source for information on it is his correspondence. An
informative treatment based on this is V. Dronov, "Pjatigorskoe leto Valerija
Brjusova," pp. 158–77. Relatively little information is added in the material
more recently published by the same scholar: "Iz neopublikovannyx stranic dnev-
nika Brjusova," in *V. Brjusov i literatura konca XIX–XX veka*, pp. 107–124.

2.   *Percovu*, p. 59.

111

moments. In the same Christmas letter to Pertsov, Bryusov wrote enthusiastically of Balmont's volume *In Boundlessness*, which had just appeared, and later described how he had taken this book into the hospital with him to read and reread.[3] Many of these poems were known to him already from the sessions of poetry-reading in which the two had engaged throughout the previous year. Nonetheless, the impact of *In Boundlessness* in its totality and at just this point in his career was greater than the sum of its parts. His admiration for Balmont's poetry was not uncritical, as his running literary commentary to Pertsov in previous months had shown.[4] Nor did he regard him as particularly innovative, but simply as one of the best poets writing in Russia at that time. The poems that he admired shared one quality, marvellous mastery of the poetic line: "Such harmony has not been heard for a long time in Russian poetry."[5] Though a few poems in this volume exhibit that insistent use of alliteration which overrides sense and which later became Balmont's hallmark, Bryusov prized the subtle, melodious interplay of sounds, achieved by alliteration and assonance, by judicious repetition and variation of sound clusters, which was at its best when knit closely to the images to form the texture of the poem. These were qualities he had already admired in Verlaine and which he strove to embody in his own poems.

Another feature of the book also appealed to Bryusov. Balmont had not fully adopted the method of cyclization which Bryusov had already used and was to employ with exceptional effect in *Me eum esse*,[6] but the loose thematic unity of *In Boundlessness* brought

3.   Ibid., p. 61.
4.   See, for example, the letter of 12 March 1895, where he spoke of Bal'mont's talent as "very, very narrow."
5.   *Percovu*, p. 65. At this stage he placed him after Konstantin Fofanov.
6.   Brjusov's penchant for non-Russian titles for his books began with *Chefs d'œuvre* [sic] and ended with his last book, *Mea* (1924). However, most such titles were concentrated in the period covered by *Me eum esse*: one French, three Latin, and one Greek. The choice of French for the first is not surprising,

together in the first of its three sections poems which Bryusov valued highly. As we have seen, Balmont's personality, along with his deliberate imitations of Poe and Baudelaire, taught Bryusov much about the Decadent spirit. A December diary entry reads: "Balmont just dropped in, exultant, mad, Edgar-like. A great deal in his mood is of course artificial, but all the same he cheered me up and distracted me. As if a moonbeam slid through the clouds and scorched the waves with a brief kiss."[7] The reference is to Balmont's "Moonbeam" in this same collection, which expressed the exhilaration that Balmont at his best imparted to Bryusov. But there was more to Balmont's Decadence, and it showed itself to Bryusov in the yearning to step "beyond the limits." "I cannot live by the present," announces Balmont's poem "The Wind." The keynote poem of *In Boundlessness* contains a similar defiance of the constraints of existence. The poet at dusk triumphantly climbs a quivering stair to the point where night is finally below him and the distances appear bathed in the light of a sun visible to him alone.[8] Distance may be said to be the theme of the first section. Many of its poems deal with unpeopled places,

---

given his literary leanings in 1895. The change to Latin is also suggestive. Brjusov was a student of classical philology at Moscow University, but his interest in and admiration for the powerful figures of Roman antiquity went back at least to the gymnasium. In those days he was writing dramas, among them three entitled "Julius Caesar," "Pompey the Great," and "Caracalla" (*Dnevniki*, pp. 6ff.). For Brjusov such images fused with Nietzschean ideas circulating at the time. The grammar of the phrase *me eum esse* is difficult to construe. Since he was a serious Latin student, this was probably not a simple misconstruction. Possibly there was a source, but it may be presumed to be Brjusov's own deliberately idiosyncratic distortion. When he referred to the book in Russian, as he often did, he called it simply *Èto ja* [*It is I*].

7. *Dnevniki*, p. 23.

8. "Ja mečtoju lovil uxodjaščie teni" in K. D. Bal'mont, *Stixotvorenija*, ed. V. Orlov (2nd ed. Leningrad, 1969), p. 93. There seems to be a sequential connection between Merežkovskij's "Deti noči" (Chapter Two, footnote 36), Brjusov's closing poem of *Chefs d'œuvre*, "Svivajutsja blednye teni" [I, 88], and this poem.

unknown to humankind and all but unknowable: the desert, mountain heights, the floor of the sea, the place where the mountain stream is born. Uninhabited nature is everywhere, often personified, and treated now playfully, now with reverence. Traces of both Lermontov and Tyutchev can be found in these poems. Bryusov favored the more original ones, including a sonnet called "Aquatic Plants," which describes wraithlike growths stretching their pale leaves upward toward light and life. But the cold water is silent; only sharks swim by, and fragments of shipwrecks and corpses descend from time to time. Bryusov considered this an almost perfect work.[9] The book's final poem underlines the element of Balmont's thought which probably most appealed to Bryusov at this time: "Beyond the limits of the limited, / To the depths of radiant boundlessness! / . . . / We shall speed to a marvellous world, / to unknown / Beauty!"[10] Abandonment of the world of material reality in order to search by means of poetry for a higher world of beauty became Bryusov's obsession in the months to come.

The influence of Balmont and Poe converged in Bryusov's consciousness with other important influences, among which was the reading of Leibniz, begun the summer before. For Bryusov, Leibniz was the philosopher of individualism.[11] Leibniz's thought, setting forth the total independence of the "I," was in full consonance with the position that Bryusov adopted almost by instinct.

Nietzsche's ideas, too, probably influenced Bryusov at this time. Ten years later, agonizing over his inability to move on to new paths and still seeking new "distances," Bryusov wrote to Nina Petrovskaya, his mistress, "I can no longer live by 'dec-

9. *Percovu*, p. 35.

10. "Za predely predel'nogo," Bal'mont, *Stixotvorenija*, p. 112.

11. R. E. Pomirčij, "Iz idejnyx iskanij V. Ja. Brjusova (Brjusov i Lejbnic)," *Brjusovskie čtenija 1971 goda* (Erevan, 1973), p. 164. Pomirčij quotes from unpublished notebooks of Brjusov of a slightly later date (1897). However, Brjusov's diary records his enthusiasm of the summer of 1895 (*Dnevniki*, p. 21).

adence' and 'Nietzscheanism,' in which I believe, believe." [12] But Bryusov's response to Nietzsche was certainly selective and may have been gradual. The notion of the Superman took root in him very early, probably from a multitude of sources. Heroes, men of might and daring, had from childhood played a large part in his personal ideal. His early poetry exalted such figures as Alexander the Great and Napoleon, and his study of Roman history enlarged this gallery. His growing conception of the artist as an ideally free agent, subject to no demands and no laws in pursuit of his art, grafted easily onto his natural inclinations as well as his formed ideas. At this juncture certain words of Nietzsche's could have provided a critical impetus: "He shall be the greatest who can be the most solitary, the most concealed, the most divergent, the man beyond good and evil, the master of his virtues, superabundant of will; this shall be called greatness: the ability to be as manifold as whole, as vast as full." [13]

The spark between Nietzsche's ideas and Bryusov's spiritual condition may have been provided by an encounter that spring. On 5 March 1895 Bryusov eloquently described in his diary the low state of his morale: "I have been feeling that to live as I now live is impossible. Monotonous sameness, silence, and longing. On Sunday I was in such despair that I couldn't even read Edgar Poe." [14] On this occasion he was rescued by Balmont. However, shortly afterward he left for a three-week trip to Petersburg, Riga, Vilna, and Warsaw, apparently timed to ensure his absence from Moscow when the new *Chefs d'œuvre* appeared. (He later told Pertsov that his flight was in vain, for the packet of anonymous letters increased appreciably during his absence.) [15] During his stay in Petersburg he saw Vladimir Gippius, who now seemed a

12. *LN* 85, p. 791, letter of 13–14 June 1906.
13. Friedrich Nietzsche, *Beyond Good and Evil*, tr. R. J. Hollingdale (Harmondsworth: Penguin, 1973), p. 125.
14. *Dnevniki*, p. 24.
15. *Percovu*, p. 72.

man fated to carry all before him.[16] This meeting coincided with the peak of Gippius's attraction to Nietzsche.[17] Bryusov was by temperament a challenger and an individualist, who had just suffered a sharp check to his artistic ambitions. He was therefore in the most receptive mind possible for whatever lessons Gippius, the "man of victory," might impart.

In a mood of despair mingled with defiance, then, Bryusov approached the Caucasus, throughout the nineteenth century a haven for disgraced and persecuted Russian poets and heroes. Bryusov was acutely conscious of that tradition as he set out for the destination of Lermontov's Pechorin. Bryusov's Pyatigorsk summer cannot be described simply. Besides being a Decadent poet, he was a young Moscow University student enjoying his freedom, climbing mountains in congenial company, engaging in mild flirtations and other diversions, writing lively letters to friends and family and begging for replies. On another level, he had recently recovered from an acute illness that had hospitalized him for several weeks, and he had also recently suffered the severe psychological buffeting resulting from his catastrophic debut as a poet. Like so many, he came to the waters half-seriously seeking a cure but also searching for distraction, which he duly found.

His descriptions of the trip reflect not only the high spirits of the journey, but certain contradictory attitudes.[18] He carried to the South the young Northerner's curiosity and excitement, plus

16. *Dnevniki*, p. 24.

17. Vladimir Gippius, "Aleksandr Dobroljubov," in Vengerov, *Russkaja literatura XX veka 1890–1910*, 1, p. 277. Vladimir Gippius, a distant relative of the poet Zinaida Gippius, came from a literary family; his younger brother Vasilij Gippius was a noted scholar and translator. Vladimir, who also engaged in literary scholarship, later became director of the Tenišev Gymnasium in Petersburg, where he taught literature to, among others, Osip Mandel'štam and Vladimir Nabokov.

18. Letters containing Brjusov's accounts of that summer's adventures are found in the following: V. S. Dronov, "Dva pis'ma Valerija Brjusova Aleksandru Kursinskomu," *Russkaja literatura i Kavkaz* (Stavropol', 1974); V. K. Stanjukovič, "Vospominanija o Brjusove," *LN* 85, pp. 739–44; V. S. Dronov, "Pis'ma

an unwillingness to be easily overwhelmed. And he carried considerable literary baggage. First and foremost was his own Decadence, but pressing upon this was the whole corpus of Russian literature, from Pushkin and Lermontov down to Merezhkovsky's "Vera," a tale in verse. As a Decadent, his flight from society could not be, like that of most Romantics, to the consolations of nature in its primitive grandeur: a cardinal Decadent principle was the inferiority of nature to art. Thus his flight to the Caucasus had to be a journey, not to a refuge or a challenge in nature, but into his own poet's world, constructed from the materials of life but transformed by the all-powerful imagination. In this undertaking nature was both friend and foe.

What did Bryusov the Decadent expect from the Romantic South? Did he come to see the best that nature could offer in order to assert more surely the superiority of art? Clearly this was part of it. His letters written while en route to Pyatigorsk and on first arrival nearly all spoke of his disillusionment with nature. Recounting to two correspondents his first view of the Black Sea and the Crimean coast, he challenged Pushkin's lines, "You are splendid, shores of Taurus, / When you are seen / From a ship." And to one of them he summed up his reaction: "I gazed and in vain sought ecstasy in myself. The most second-rate artist, if he were given real stones, water, and greenery instead of paint and canvas, would create something a thousand times more majestic and splendid. I'm sorry for nature." [19] Much later he confessed, "I did not want to yield to the charm of nature, and I stubbornly forced myself to see imperfections in her." [20] But even then he sometimes confessed to a deeper impression, especially in his di-

---

Valerija Brjusova k Marii Pavlovne Širjaevoj," *Russkaja literatura i Kavkaz*, pp. 93–104; *Percovu*, pp. 77–79. Additional letters to Kursinskij are found in CGALI, fond 1223, op. 1, ed. xr. 3. Letters to Brjusov's family are found in IRLI, fond 444, no. 35.

19. *Percovu*, p. 77.

20. N. Ašukin, "Iz prošlogo: Iz arxiva Valerija Brjusova," *Novyj mir* (December 1926): 118.

ary, where he spoke of distant snowy crests which caused him to "gaze and pray."[21] We have not here a pure dichotomy between the public Decadent Bryusov, scorning nature, and the natural, private Bryusov, admiring it. The emotion aroused in him by the distant crests belonged to the former as well as to the latter. An adjective provides the clue: *netlennyj*, imperishable. For him the lush Crimean shore and the low but still impressive mountains Mashuk and Beshtau all belonged to the category of perishable nature, but the distant, inaccessible heights were different. One recalls the awe of Tolstoy's Olenin before "the mountains, the mountains!" Sometimes visible, sometimes disappearing into the blue of the sky, these snowy peaks were detached from tangible reality. They represented for Bryusov that remote, untouchable, imperishable beauty for which his soul longed, as—to use Poe's words—"the moth for the star."

The imagery of *Me eum esse* reflects this distinction, especially in the first, theme-setting cycle. These are not in any sense descriptive poems. Surrounding scenery is identified, if at all, only to be annihilated in the face of eternal beauty. Alleys and ravines may form labyrinths for the poet's elusive muse, but the waters, steppes, and cliffs are mere dust before the dream. The star, the remote crests, and the distant light of the heavens: these are the elements that alone deserve to be called imperishable, unchanging.

Even the twenty-two-year-old Bryusov's perceptions of women were at least partly literary. Recounting to Kursinsky one of his summer adventures, he wrote, "And as befits a poet in the South— I fell in love!"[22] Like all his amorous exploits on this journey, the first adventure was a mild one. And it resulted in a poem.[23] This was to be a pattern throughout. The women who attracted him

21.   Quoted in Dronov, "Dva pis'ma . . . Kursinskomu," p. 67.
22.   Ibid., p. 72.
23.   "I snova drožat oni" [I, 115] (see footnote 29 below).

that summer were young, elusive, and in some way ethereal. Passion, except the passion for art, was given no quarter.

The problem of the relation of art to reality is never a simple one, and apparently each generation of artists must formulate it anew in its own terms. For the Decadent, reality had first to be transformed by the artistic imagination into something as alien as possible from life before art could yield that esthetic pleasure which poetry alone can give. Lyric poets sing of nature, love, and death. During his Caucasian summer Bryusov sought a new stance toward all three themes. Love was temporarily swept from his horizon—surprisingly, after the erotic poetry of *Chefs d'œuvre*—to become merely a code for the search for true poetry. Nature, in that dramatic setting, seemed to provide the Decadent's great test. The temptation to feel humble before her or to lapse into pantheism was to be resolutely resisted. The poet, conscious of his power to transform and immortalize, must remember that he stood above nature. Bryusov was not always faithful to this doctrine, but his recitation of Lermontov and Pushkin as he climbed some of the higher mountains may have signified more than the impulse to add the beauty of familiar lines to that of the panorama. It may also have been the effort to understand *how* nature is transformed in poetry. Most important for him was the poet's internalization of an experience and transformation of it into art. Thus the mood conveyed, for example, in Pushkin's sequence of Caucasus poems and the method by which that mood was evoked were of primary interest.[24] As Bryusov wrote to a friend that summer, "The goal of poetry is to give 'esthetic pleasure.' . . . Esthetic pleasure consists in an innumerable series of moods which can be evoked only by poetry (not by life)."[25]

Me eum esse, its largest part composed within a few weeks, of-

24.   A. S. Puškin, "Kavkaz," "Obval," "Delibaš," "Monastyr' na Kazbeke," *Polnoe sobranie sočinenij*, 10 vols. (Moscow, 1957), 3, pp. 137–41.

25.   Stanjukovič, p. 740.

fered a capsule history of the poet's soul over the previous year or
more and a statement of his present beliefs and goals in art. Simply described, it is a book about poetry and the poet. It contains a
foreword and thirty-six poems arranged in six cycles: "Counsels,"
"Visions," "Wanderings," "Love," "Intimations of Death," and
"In the Struggle." The last two are subtitled "The Past." As a
whole *Me eum esse* is an extraordinary exemplar, probably the first
in Russian poetry, of the kind of close-fitting organization of
theme and imagery that later became customary among modern
Russian poets.[26] Bryusov's conception of a book of poems as a unified structure eminently fitted it to serve as a vehicle for spiritual
autobiography. Embodying his present lofty vision of the poet,
Me eum esse traced the path followed and the pains undergone in
achieving that eminence. The title "It Is I" is usually, and correctly, taken as a statement of the poet's strongly individualistic
stance at this stage of his development. From the start Bryusov
had insisted that the basic meaning of poetry lay in the poet's
communication of his spiritual discoveries, since the poet, gifted
with superior sensitivity, had a unique vision to impart to his
readers. The cyclization of this book represented Bryusov's consciousness of having completed a cycle of experience which demanded expression in some connected and unified form. The programmatic poems of the first section, "Counsels," represent the
position he had now arrived at in his meditation on the poet and
his art. The following sections, "Visions," "Wanderings," and
"Love," retrace his sometimes painful pursuit of the ideal beauty
he longed to worship, and the fifth and sixth sections portray the
"dark night" through which his soul had passed to reach its present relative certainty and authority. All of this had to be seen as
an ordered whole if the experience was to be conveyed at all.

26.   An interesting study of this method in the work of Boris Pasternak is
that of Katherine Tiernan O'Connor, "Boris Pasternak's 'My Sister—Life': The
Book behind the Verse," *Slavic Review* (July 1980): 398–411.

The section "Counsels" contains some of the poems most often quoted to show Bryusov's cold egoism and devotion to art above all other values. This is exactly the effect he intended, since this was indeed the ideal to which he was now committed. "Counsels" contains eight poems, of which the first four form a special unity by virtue of their strong statements about art. The first, the famous "To a Young Poet," was occasioned by his acquaintance in Pyatigorsk with the thirteen-year-old Alexander Brailovsky.[27] To the "pale youth with burning gaze" he offered three precepts: first, do not live by the present, for the future alone is the realm of the poet; second, do not love, do not sympathize, worship only yourself without limit; third, bow down before art alone, without a backward glance, with no other goals. He assured the youth, "If you accept my three counsels, / I will die proudly, a conquered warrior, / Knowing that in the world I have left a poet." It was Bryusov's passionate orientation toward the future that propelled him initially into Decadence and no doubt determined his understanding of it. The poet is a seer, who ranges over time and space and "beyond the boundaries," but his mission is always to reveal the new. His art constantly develops, he learns from the past, but he must never repeat. Moreover, he must be free of entanglements which would prevent his following his inspiration, wherever it might lead. And he must worship his own soul without distraction, since that is where his inspiration is found. His service is thus totally and solely to art. It is arguable that Bryusov followed these principles to unbelievable extremes. In any event, he now projected them as his course for the future.

The second poem reinforces these precepts. Later entitled "Cold" [I, 581], its initial image is of snow, suggesting an uninhabited land. He may have gotten the image from Balmont's "At the Far Pole," or both Balmont and Bryusov may have taken inspiration from Poe's "The Narrative of A. Gordon Pym." Bryusov

27. *Dnevniki*, pp. 24–25.

goes beyond Balmont to the essence of Decadent withdrawal into
another reality: "As the kingdom of white snow / My soul is
cold." "Cold snow" becomes "cold dream," playing on the Russian forms *snega/sna*, "of snow—of dream." In that remote territory the world's sounds of victory and love, its curses and wails,
pass by as pale shades, "like the spells of a wizard," and the poet,
given over to "cold fantasy," prays unceasingly to "unearthly
beauty." The third poem continues logically, carrying withdrawal
from reality to the extreme: "Our reality I do not see, / I do not
know our age, / I hate my homeland,— / I love the ideal of
man." This complete rejection of everything mundane in favor of
the ideal releases the poet's lonely imagination to range over time
and space, penetrating the secrets of another life. However—and
here he returns to a note sounded in the foreword of the book—
when new beings emerge, his revelations will sound to them like
native songs. The poet's homeland is found where—and when—
he is understood. The fourth and shortest poem pictures the
poet's ideal state: "And abandoning people / I went away into
quietness, / Solitary as a dream, I live by dream." There is great
bliss in hiding one's dreams, in repeating the words of the revelation to oneself alone and watching in the desert the ascent of a
star.

These four poems, which form a unit within a unit, state the
poet's position with great force. In form they are simple, although in the second and third poems meter is treated with some
freedom. In each case the three stresses of the line are separated by
a varying number of syllables, one, two, or three, an early instance of Bryusov's *dol'nik*. In the third poem the irregularity is
much more pronounced. The stretching and displacing of rhythmic elements form a counterpoint to the series of straightforward
"I" statements of the first stanza, and a complex though not ob-
trusive play of sounds enriches the poem. Bryusov's handling of
rhyme is remarkable throughout the four poems chiefly for regularity and even repetition.

Of the remaining four poems of the first cycle, the first three comment on the program outlined in the first quartet. "Branches" seems initially to return to the everyday world, where branches sway at a window and a shade billows on its white ribbon. However, the poet gazes out through this tangible frame to that remote world of stillness and light where "beauty and death are unchangeably one." This line, the cycle's epigraph, articulates the fundamental Decadent belief that true beauty is unattainable on earth. From this belief stem all of the Decadents' efforts to withdraw their poetry from life and to come as close as possible to life's negation. For some, like Sologub, this meant a preoccupation with death and an attraction to it. For others, like Zinaida Gippius, there was both attraction and fear. For still others, like Baudelaire, Maeterlinck, and Balmont—or so thought Bryusov—terror of death was dominant.[28] Bryusov himself belonged to none of these groups. For him at this stage, withdrawal from life had only one purpose: pursuit of beauty into those realms that lie furthest from nature's corrupting power, "there where no movement, no malice are found, / There shines eternally the longed-for light." In a later revision "longed-for light" becomes "imperishable." Nature's great flaw was its impermanence. Poetry was located "in boundlessness" or "beyond the limits"; death was only incidental.

The cycle's sixth poem, "Concerning *Chefs d'œuvre*," fits this history of a Decadent poet's development by explaining his previous book's position: "earthly steps to the unearthly." In "Morning," the penultimate poem, the poet turns again to his successor with counsel on dealing with the world's intrusions. The final poem, "Renunciation," introduces an oracular Voice which confers final authority on his earlier counsels: "Greet only the visions of art, / Seek only eternal love." Renunciation is the path "without end!"

28. *Percovu*, pp. 59–60.

Erotica as a theme seems to have been discarded from Bryusov's poetry for the time being. However, two sections of *Me eum esse* deal in some fashion with love. The book's second cycle, "Visions," is made up of five poems, the first of which, "Spring," suggests the early poetry of Alexander Blok. A girl (surely Pushkin's Tatyana) scratches initials on a frosted window and waits in grief and longing—for whom? Another world of roses exists in a distant spring, but does she know, or only sense, its existence? The delicate parallelism of the poem's couplets is full of suggestion, and its highly melodic quality, created by assonance and use of liquids, reinforces the lyrical mood. The second poem, "With lowered glance," is also built on a "here/there" opposition. However, its central figure is a young prostitute. Like Dostoevsky's Sonya Marmeladova, she passes timidly, in white, with downcast eyes, and the moment is one of intuition for the poet. He and his companion stand abashed on the noisy boulevard; only the remote sky breathes poetry. Is he struck, then, by a vision of beauty about to be smirched by life? Seemingly, only "there" in the realm of art can beauty be preserved. The next poem, "An Instant," is a companion piece. It likewise portrays a momentary apparition, though now in no concrete setting. Both poems are written in tercets, which underlines their relationship. However, the second is a symbolic version of the first. Where the first female figure passes timidly with lowered gaze, "her" glance in the second poem is more dazzling than thousands of stars. Beauty is clad no more in timid white but shines with diamond brilliance. Abashed before his first vision, the poet cries out before the second apparition, "Die, die, words and dreams!"

A similar pairing occurs between the first and the fourth poems, "Spring" and "She was in mourning." Again the stanzaic form is parallel—four couplets—though the meter differs. In the first two couplets of each, the grieving female figure is juxtaposed with a glimpse of another reality which she senses dimly if at all. The problem is left unresolved in the first poem, but the fourth offers the solution we have been led to expect: art is capable of catching and reconciling both the brilliant heaven and the thoughts of sadness; art lives forever. The final lines containing the solution serve as epigraph for the section and no doubt were intended as its climax. The fifth and final poem in a sense stands alone in the cycle, though its heroine is another young prostitute. The "here/there" opposition so prominent elsewhere in these five poems is merely hinted: the young girl seems a captive in her bright red gown and vulgar surroundings. But her dream of blue firmament and green leaves makes her also a figure of trapped innocence and therefore of beauty. More than the other four, this poem shows how Bryusov made meaning dependent on the poem's place in a cycle. Anthologized, this would be merely a somewhat naturalistic lyric with a sentimental slant; capping the cycle "Visions," it brings forward the meaning of these visions collectively. The female figure in all of her guises is seen to embody beauty. She is the poet's Muse—the term was not too old-fashioned for Bryusov—straining to escape the corrupting influence of temporal things and take ultimate refuge in the eternal. The moments of vision in which the poet now and then glimpses her essence are foretastes of that eternal love which the oracle in "Renunciation" commanded the poet to seek.

The third cycle, "Wanderings," continues the poet's quest, developing the contrast of fleeting, crumbling earthly nature with the "unchangeable" sky, moon, and stars symbolizing ideal nature. The final poem makes a striking statement of this position. "There is something shameful in nature's might, / A dumb enmity to beauty's rays." But the years waft over it all, and only the world of dream proves eternal. The second quatrain sounds a note of vindictive triumph. Let the "unchanging ocean" rage— and here "unchanging" is used ironically; let the icy crests sleep proudly. Nature's "shameful" might will come to an end. The world will end, "and only the world of dream is eternal." The eight lines of this poem are given special force by the artful use of rhythm and meter to support the thought. The thought pattern moves from nature's inappropriate assumption of grandeur to its ultimate annihilation, with only the world of dream surviving eternally. This pattern is followed in both stanzas, which conclude with the simple statement of the ultimate fact. Each stanza begins with a strong amphibrachic tetrameter line (see below) and gradually contracts, the stresses moving closer together, to a final line of iambic tetrameter with four realized stresses. This may also be regarded as a *dol'nik*, but the metrical pattern is not to be disregarded. It looks like this:

$$(1) \; \smile \acute{-} \smile \smile \acute{-} \smile \smile \acute{-} \smile \smile \acute{-} \smile \qquad 2) \; \smile \acute{-} \smile \smile \acute{-} \smile \smile \acute{-} \smile \smile \acute{-} \smile$$
$$\smile \acute{-} \smile \smile \acute{-} \smile \acute{-} \smile \smile \acute{-} \qquad \smile \acute{-} \smile \acute{-} \smile \smile \acute{-} \smile \smile \acute{-}$$
$$\smile \acute{-} \smile \acute{-} \smile \acute{-} \smile \smile \acute{-} \smile \qquad \smile \acute{-} \smile \acute{-} \smile \acute{-} \smile \smile \acute{-} \smile$$
$$\smile \acute{-} \smile \acute{-} \smile \acute{-} \smile \acute{-} \qquad \smile \acute{-} \smile \acute{-} \smile \acute{-} \smile \acute{-}$$

This stanzaic stress-pattern underlines the movement from temporal splendor to eternal simplicity. Moreover, throughout this section both meter and sound instrumentation are employed with growing mastery. The ideal nature which Bryusov sought to create through his "dream" expressed itself through the superbly modeled structure of these poems. It was perhaps to direct attention to this achievement that he used as epigraph to this cycle the second stanza of "The mountains' sharp line": "I have created with my dream / A world of ideal nature; / Oh, how paltry before this / Are steppes, and cliffs, and waters!"

The fourth cycle, "Love," returns to the central motif of "Visions," that of the elusive Muse. Again, as with "Visions," the five poems of "Love" receive their meaning from their places in the cycle and the book, a meaning which is hardly perceived if they are read separately. The epigraph is taken from the first lines of the opening poem: "And again they tremble, the impotent dreams, / The impotent dreams of unneeded love." This is the love supposedly left behind with *Chefs d'œuvre.*[29] Bryusov now shows in slow motion, as it were, how flirtation with an earthly girl becomes transformed into the humble pursuit of his Muse in the rarefied regions where he might hope to find her. The second poem, "I remember an evening palely modest," evokes Pushkin's famous "I remember a marvellous instant," where the loved one appears before the poet "Like a fleeting vision, / Like the genius of pure beauty."[30] Bryusov—no doubt intentionally—used Pushkin's characteristic iambic tetrameter, though with fewer unrealized stresses. Pushkin's six-quatrain poem consists of a lyrical narrative connecting two identical apparitions separated by years and suffering. But Bryusov very likely wished to point out that for Pushkin, as for himself, it was neither the woman nor the sufferings of absence, but the *vision*, that was all-important. Hence his condensed, impressionistic narrative: the evening, the somewhat wilted flowers, and the girl's gaze, which reminds him of the eyes of Egyptian goddesses—and the leap is made. Now nothing else exists for him; he is transported in dreams to where she—now "She," transfigured—presides over roaring crowds and burning fires, with her Memphian eyes, *memfisskie glaza*.

The cycle's third poem, "The faded stars trembled," similarly shows the transformation of a real woman—or is she now his Muse?—into poetry. The poem falls into two nearly equal parts. The first quatrain describes her appearance in an alley of poplars,

29.   This poem was the product of a brief infatuation. In the cycle it takes on a very different meaning.

30.   Puškin, 2, p. 267. The opening also evokes Tjutčev's "Ja pomnju vremja zolotoe" (F. I. Tjutčev, *Stixotvorenija: Pis'ma* [Moscow, 1957], p. 99). A synthetic epithet like "bledno-skromnyj" would hardly have been used by either Puškin or Tjutčev. The incident underlying this poem was amusingly recorded in a passage of Brjusov's diary only recently published. Fascinated by Maria's eyes, he determined to attract her attention. Continually frustrated by the presence of other young men, Brjusov ended by breaking the glass of an outdoor light with his cane. "My God! He's gone mad!" shrieked her mother. And Maria finally turned her frightened eyes on him (Dronov, "Iz . . . Brjusova," pp. 121–22).

"like the quiet dream of sadness." The second begins with her quick passage and disappearance. After the vision comes the inspiration: while the poet awaits the desired dawn, his sadness is suddenly illumined by the "silvery rhyme Maria." The real woman has merged with his Muse, the fleeting vision of whom leaves him ready to create his poem.

But the path of the poet and his Muse, like that of true love, does not run smooth. The final poem of the cycle, "The Rendezvous," at the most obvious level of meaning describes a rather unsuccessful meeting between lovers. Hints establish the real meaning of both poem and cycle. When the woman tries to speak her thoughts, the words resound with an "impossible dissonance" that disturbs nature around them. Flower stalks sway in alarm, and the grass whispers and trembles. This shattering sound is of course disproportionate to broken sentences uttered by a hesitant woman. Furthermore, the "impossible / Dissonance" is conveyed by an enjambement, extremely rare in Bryusov, with his regard for the integrity of the line. Thus from the troubled encounter of two lovers beneath a yellow moon, the experience becomes one of much greater artistic moment: the struggle of the poet and his Muse to unite in beautiful utterance.

A feature of "The Rendezvous" that heightens its poetic tension appreciably is the artful use of sound features, including repetition. While Bryusov early reached sophistication in handling the auditory aspect of a poem and showed by his comments on the poetry of others a keen ear for harmony, he did not often indulge himself in the fashion seen here. Both he and Balmont, it will be recalled, were much under the influence of Poe in the years just preceding this, but such striking reminiscences are more commonly found in the latter's work. However, as will be seen further on, Poe had even more influence on *Me eum esse* than Baudelaire and Verlaine had on *Chefs d'œuvre*. The Poe poem evoked by "The Rendezvous" is "Ulalume," and the parallel becomes irresistible when the opening stanzas of the two are compared:

ULALUME

The skies they were ashen and sober;
    The leaves they were crispèd and sere—
    The leaves they were withering and sere;
It was night in the lonesome October
    Of my most immemorial year;
It was hard by the dim lake of Auber,
    In the misty mid region of Weir—
It was down by the dank tarn of Auber,
    In the ghoul-haunted woodland of Weir.

SVIDANIE
(THE RENDEZVOUS)

My brodíli vdvojëm i pečál'ny
Meždu tónkix vysókix stvolóv,
Bespoščádnye, žádnye tájny
Nas tomíli; tomíli bez slóv.
My brodíli vdvojëm i pečál'ny
Meždu tónkix vysókix stvolóv.

[We roamed together and sad
Among slim tall treetrunks,
Merciless, hungry mysteries
Tormented us; tormented without words.
We roamed, etc.]

"The Rendezvous" is written in anapestic trimeter, which is, in combination with amphibrachic lines, the dominant meter in "Ulalume."[31] Though Poe's stanza is more complex, Bryusov's rhythmic and sound composition clearly belong to the same family. Once the connection is registered, other links can be noted. The protagonist in "Ulalume" strolls through an alley of cypresses

31.   Edgar Allan Poe, *Works*, ed. Edmund Clarence Stedman and George Edward Woodberry. Bal'mont's translation, which appears in Bal'mont, *Stixotvorenija*, pp. 509–511, uses Poe's rhythm. It was first printed in 1899. Brjusov may have heard Bal'mont reading his own translation in an early draft, or Bal'mont reading the original aloud.

with Psyche, forgetful of his lost Ulalume until confronted with her tomb. Ulalume provides the image of elusive beauty, ever enticing the poet from beyond the boundaries of human existence. It was from Poe more than from any other source that Bryusov drew the cult of ideal beauty which was the inspiration of *Me eum esse*. His choice of a model was a happy one. "The lost Ulalume" was the perfect avatar of poetry alien from daily reality.

The end of the cycle "Love" left the poet in close contact with his Muse but not in full possession of her. This was only the truth, as far as Bryusov's progress in poetry was concerned. Yet he felt he had come a long way. The fifth and sixth cycles, subtitled "The Past," reviewed the path of the poet to his present stage. The fifth, "Intimations of Death," in its brevity does less than justice to a supposed journey to the far banks of Lethe, which represents part of the process by which the poet is confirmed in his vocation. The final poem, "I returned to the bright earth," announces victory over death. Yet, though he has returned from the other world, the poet hears the voices of this one but dimly, for he cannot forget the "fields of asphodel" on Lethe's mute farther shore. The book's last cycle, "In the Struggle," shows a hard-won and possibly tentative victory. It is the longest cycle, with ten poems, and it makes reference to the mood of *Chefs d'œuvre*. Several poems portray his effort to sustain his new vision against the onslaughts of temptation to return to old ways. He is now without regrets or fears for the future. In "It was a dim evening in May" he longs for one final meeting with his old love, his old Muse: "Before death to fall in a kiss / On the dear fading lips." Both cycle and book close on a note of cautious triumph. His "Last thoughts" find the poet in the position from which he issued the precepts of the first cycle. And though threatened by creeping shadows, "evil lemurs of perished passions," he stands protected within a magic circle as the passionless mage. For the first time Bryusov steps forth in the guise which, some years later as will be seen, Andrei Bely assigned to his person as well as to his character as poet.

Whether the magic circle will hold or not and whether the "magician" can in fact operate in such confined quarters are questions with which Bryusov had to deal later on. But one thing is certain: in *Me eum esse* he demonstrated his ability to, as it were, close a circle. The remarkable unity and coherence of the volume brought something new into Russian poetry. The quality of the poems themselves evinces Bryusov's great and growing artistry with words. Not surprisingly, they are uneven in value. Some of them were probably included for their relevance to a given cycle, or even, as in the case of "Concerning *Chefs d'œuvre*," to refer to an earlier phase of his career. Nonetheless, the modest experiments attempted in *Me eum esse* were fruitful. The sense of rhythm and rhyme and their relation to meaning which was soon a major concern of Bryusov's theoretical work is evident in many of these poems. So is the *vertical* interworking of sense with sound harmony, notable in such poems as "Like the kingdom of white snow," where the play of combinations like *snega/strannaia nega/sna* and *neizmenno/nezemnoi/vselennoi* occurring in different lines of the same stanza bind together the poem's sound and meaning. Bryusov had abandoned the experiment with stanza form that marked *Chefs d'œuvre*. The effect of *Me eum esse* is at once more severe and more polished—which does not prevent some poems and even whole cycles, such as the final one, from being remarkably melodic. This, then, in summary is the book whose foreword acknowledged that it was far from finished and whose author hoped these hints would convey his intention to a "future friend," the symbolic "young poet" to whom the first poem is addressed.

Another significant aspect of Bryusov's Caucasian summer was his strong sense of following in the footsteps of Lermontov. Indeed, Lermontov's presence is almost as pervasive in *Me eum esse* as is Poe's, and it determined much in Bryusov's behavior and his attitudes toward his experiences of that summer. Lermontov's influence on him was not limited to recitation of nature passages from Lermontov's poems. Later he recalled how, admiring from Pyatigorsk the distant panorama of the mountains, greeting the rising sun on Bermamut and exploring the ravines near Kislovodsk, he remembered Lermontov's "Demon" and A Hero of Our Time.[32] At first sight the reminiscences were unremarkable and even frivolous. For example, in letters to Manya Shiryaeva, his most loyal female correspondent of the summer, there occur lighthearted reminders of Lermontov's novel. We find him consciously and with amusement reconstructing there the plot of "Princess Mary" with himself in the role of Pechorin. And since Manya Shiryaeva apparently was not a literary young lady, he had all the fun of knowing that she would not get the point. Further, to both Manya and others, he adopted a truly Pechorinesque irony toward the local scene, the patrons of the spa, and the tourist attractions, which by now included the Lermontov memorial.[33]

However, the remembering went much deeper. At the beginning of the 1890s Bryusov had immersed himself thoroughly in Lermontov's poetry. "My ecstasy before Lermontov knew no measure. I knew him by heart and recited 'Demon' for days on end. I even began writing a large essay on the types of the Demon in literature," he wrote much later.[34] Other enthusiasms caused this one to recede for a time, but Lermontov ultimately ranked high in Bryusov's pantheon of poets. The Caucasian sojourn may have speeded his ascent. At any rate, the Demon and his earthly vari-

32.   Ašukin, "Iz prošlogo," p. 118.
33.   Letter of 1 July to Kursinskij (CGALI; see footnote 18 above) is written on stationery bearing a picture of the Lermontov monument, of which Brjusov makes outrageous fun. He points out that Lermontov is sitting partly on nothing at all, with one foot dangling and his chin resting on a hand whose arm is also resting on nothing.
34.   "Moja junost'," in Iz moej žizni, p. 74.

ant Pechorin were surely for Bryusov the deities of the place. In
the spiritual world of Pechorin he could find support for his disdain of the world he had temporarily left behind, as well as its
extension in the Caucasian watering places. In Pechorin's deliberate isolation he could find a model for the spiritual isolation
which, despite the record of frivolous amusements, he also en-
dured. He relied on this loneliness to strengthen himself as an
artist. And if Pechorin had admired the mountains from his window in Pyatigorsk and from the back of his horse, he took neither
consolation nor refuge in nature. Freedom was Pechorin's prize,
fate his only master, and he sought both in this wild setting. Was
Bryusov perhaps bent on finding in himself a capacity for this
same bitter freedom?

An even more attractive spiritual model for a Decadent was the
Demon himself. "Beyond good and evil" in his cosmic boredom,
the Demon soared above peaks and ravines, contemplating the
grandeur below him with neither hate nor love but with disdain.
Bryusov underlined in his copy of Lermontov's works lines from
an early draft of "Demon": "His gaze filled with scorn / He turned
on the sinful earth."[35] This image, which had attracted Bryusov
from adolescence, blended well with the Nietzschean themes he
had assimilated. Rejection of the terrestrial and of accepted human values could free the spirit who wanted to step beyond the
bounds.

Lermontov's Demon is the type of sated experience. That peculiar blend of conscious pose and genuine desire to experience *all*
may have led to Bryusov's flirtation that summer with the ultimate Decadent act, suicide. Many of the Decadents claimed to
feel death's attraction, and some came closer to it than their poetry required. It would be simple and possibly justified to dismiss
Bryusov's avowedly suicidal episode of those days as a brief Dec-

35.   Dronov, "Pomety Brjusova na poljax sočinenii Lermontova," *Literatura
i Kavkaz* (Stavropol', 1972), p. 100.

adent experiment. Hints to friends in letters before the crisis did
not sound serious, and his account written afterward was laconic
and offhand.[36] However, a letter to his friend and collaborator Alexander Lang, written on 20 July 1896, is unequivocal: "I have
fallen desperately and finally ill. I am in a condition close to death
and to suicide. . . . P.S. The manuscript of *Me eum esse* is completed and *in the event* will be forwarded to you" [I, 586]. Although "the event" did not occur, a manuscript of *Me eum esse* was
sent to Lang.[37] It differs considerably in arrangement (and slightly
in content) from the final version and contains a publisher's foreword which reads:

> *Me eum esse* is the last book of Valery Bryusov, who passed away
> [space indicated for date] 1896 in Pyatigorsk. Shortly before his
> death the author himself prepared the manuscript of this book,
> though he considered it far from finished. The publishers hope in the
> near future to gather in a separate volume as well all the translations
> by Valery Bryusov that have appeared in print.
>
> A. L. Miropolsky [Lang]
> *Moscow, 1896*

A hoax? Perhaps. There are some curious features to this story.
First, the illness supposedly came on Bryusov suddenly, when he
had left Pyatigorsk for Vladikavkaz en route to Samarkand, and it
lasted about a week. A letter written to Pertsov the day before the
letter to Lang makes no mention of illness, and three days after,
on 23 July, he was already able to write to Manya Shiryaeva.[38]

If the thoughts of suicide were induced by the sudden illness,
how could the foreword be written on such short notice by an
author in such physical condition and the entire volume carefully
planned in the guise of a last testament by an expiring poet? Another conclusion strongly suggests itself, one in keeping with the

36.   V. S. Dronov, "Dva pis'ma . . . Kursinskomu," p. 74.
37.   CGALI, fond 56, op. 2, ed. xr. 10.
38.   Dronov, "Pis'ma . . . Širjaevoj," pp. 102–103.

Caucasus setting. It seems probable that the Pyatigorsk manuscript version was the original plan of the book, while the published edition was the result of later revision. Indeed, the setting
and its literary associations may have greatly influenced the shape
of this early version. The number of poems in this, as in the
printed 1897 version, is thirty-six. Substitutions and omissions
occurred in revision, but the most significant difference is in emphasis. By means of the foreword and the same careful arrangement in cycles that characterizes the final edition, the early book
also creates a unified effect—but a different one. Whereas the
final version makes *Me eum esse* a book about poetry and the poet,
the early one focuses on the death of the poet. But it is not a death
brought about merely by defeat and despair. Death, like nature
and love, has undergone the Decadent treatment. The epigraph
to the first section in both versions is: "Beauty and death are unchangeably one." In the Pyatigorsk version this sentiment receives startling emphasis. There the poet's course is traced through
his struggles and trials to their culmination in his death and, presumably, his final union with the Beautiful. The plan here, as in
the later version, is too carefully thought out to be the work of a
hasty, melodramatic decision. It is most likely that all along, until another inspiration prevailed at the end of the summer or in
the early fall, Bryusov intended the book to have this character.
Yet, unless suicide actually figured in his plans throughout this
time, the plan presented certain obvious difficulties. I have been
told of an outline of *Me eum esse* with a plan ascribing the authorship to a suicide, "V. Darov," one of the fictional authors
Bryusov had created for the second and third *Russian Symbolists*.
The existence of such a variant would support the notion that
Bryusov attempted to find a device for publishing *Me eum esse* in
its death-centered form. However, in the end the plan must have
seemed impracticable.

The question of why Bryusov abandoned this plan is less important to the present study than the question of why he devised

it in the first place. There was first of all the sentiment of the epigraph "Beauty and death are unchangeably one," which seems to emanate from Poe and Baudelaire. The Decadent fascination with death and a desire to test this proposition perhaps urged Bryusov to the psychological feat of approaching it in his poetry as closely as a living poet might hope to come. Another aspect of the phenomenon links it to the setting where he composed most of the book. Russian poets since Lermontov have occasionally chosen to foresee their own deaths in their poetry. This is more common in the twentieth century than it was in the nineteenth, and Bryusov may have been one of the first after Lermontov to experiment with this possibility.[39] Pechorin's duel anticipated the circumstances and setting of the duel in which Lermontov himself perished. Possibly even more germane to Bryusov's case is Lermontov's famous lyric "The Dream." There the hero lies wounded "in a vale of Dagestan." The dying hero is enabled to see his death, as it were, in art, framed and shaped by the sympathetic imagination. The cause of death—if death it was—is not clear from the poem. Occurring in the wilds of the Caucasus, it may have resulted from a mountaineer's bullet. Or it may have been a suicide. In any event, the speaker's own death, distanced and made the subject of art, is an object of contemplation, a thing of beauty. The concept is genuinely Decadent. Lermontov made the enshrining of a vision of one's death in art a Caucasian paradigm, and Bryusov could have been tempted to follow it, up to the penultimate point.

During June and July 1896, the months when most of *Me eum esse* was written, Bryusov looked in only one direction: "and abandoning men I went into stillness."[40] If poetry meant alienation

39. This point is discussed in relation to Pasternak and several other poets by Olga Raevsky Hughes in *The Poetic World of Boris Pasternak* (Princeton: Princeton University Press, 1974), p. 163 and n. 93.

40. This is the first line of the fourth poem in *Me eum esse* [I, 100].

from the transitory and earthly and the transfiguration of reality, then his own life, especially its most recent episodes, was also subject to poetic transformation. The final printed version of *Me eum esse* represents that transformation.

Yet with all of this said, there is still something not clearly explained about this book. Bryusov's state of mind in the spring of 1896, the contact with Balmont and with the ideas of Leibniz and Nietzsche, the general mood of Decadence beginning to infiltrate that part of the Russian scene in which Bryusov aspired to play a leading role: all of these together fail to quite explain either the dramatic sharpening of focus that took place in Bryusov's thinking about poetry in the months leading up to *Me eum esse*, or its direction. In the brief span between *Chefs d'œuvre* and *Me eum esse*, a view had been formulated that put downright ascetic demands on the poet. Standing on his snowy mountaintop or crouching in the desert watching the ascent of a star, Bryusov's poet recalls the young neophyte who, in his first fervor, has undertaken feats of renunciation which an older ascetic would attempt only after prayer and fasting. Indeed, perhaps Bryusov regarded his sojourn in the mountains as just that: a time of prayer and abstinence, in preparation for the revelation he hoped would come. His incautious insistence that the old spirit had been vanquished is thrown into some doubt by his account of the struggle, and the poet-magician's confidence in the magic circle which he has drawn about him seems somewhat premature. Specifically, one wonders what possessed him to think of stripping his poetry permanently of the theme of passionate love which, however distasteful to some of his critics and some of his friends, was so central to his earlier book and, in a particular rendition, to his peculiar genius. He speaks like the newly converted, and we naturally ask, what was that powerful message, and who was the preacher?

The probable answer was hinted at by Bryusov in the diary entry of 5 March 1896, when he spoke of being in such despair that "I could not even read Edgar Poe."[41] What he might have read is unfortunately left unstated. However, since Balmont had introduced him to Poe over a year earlier, Bryusov had had ample time to become acquainted with most or all of Poe's slim corpus. And not only time but opportunity, since Baudelaire's French translations could have supplied him with those works that Balmont had not yet rendered into Russian. That Bryusov soon became interested not only in Poe's poems but also in his prose, including his essays, is known from the existence in final but unprinted form of an essay on Poe's *Eureka*, dated 1897, and by the inclusion of Poe in the 1897 plan for a book to be called "Philosophical Studies."[42]

Of Poe's essays on literary questions, one stands out as the most likely source of inspiration for the direction Bryusov's ideas on poetry took early in 1896. "The Poetic Principle" stated in succinct form Poe's theory of poetry, which an early editor called "his most religious belief."[43] Poe's condemnation of the "heresy of the Didactic," by which he insisted that poetry had nothing to do with inculcation of morals, must initially have endeared him to Balmont and Bryusov. Beyond this, his doctrine was full of guidance for them both. The glimpses of their conversations recorded in Bryusov's diary suggest the formation of an ideal of the poet which each tried to embody in his own style, and from which each lapsed at various times, causing bitterness and disillusion on the part of the other.[44] Poe clearly fed this ideal. The Bryusov of *Me eum esse* seems to have been nourished by the pages of "The Poetic Principle." The sense of the beautiful is innate in man, affirmed Poe, but, while he may delight in nature, a mere recitation of its charms is not poetry. There is still "a something in the

41. *Dnevniki*, p. 24.
42. Ibid., p. 29. The unpublished essay is probably the piece referred to.
43. Poe, *Works*, VI, Stedman introduction, p. xxv.
44. For example, *Dnevniki*, pp. 23, 24, 26–27, 29ff.

distance" which the would-be poet has been unable to attain. Poetry addresses itself to this thirst, which is "the desire of the moth for the star. It is no mere appreciation of the Beauty before us, but a wild effort to reach the Beauty above. Inspired by an ecstatic prescience of the glories beyond the grave, we struggle by multiform combinations among the things and thoughts of Time, to attain a portion of that Loveliness whose very elements, perhaps, appertain to eternity alone."[45]

Poe's description of the realm of true poetry held up to the poet an ideal both circumscribed and lofty. "The struggle to apprehend the supernal Loveliness—this struggle, on the part of souls fittingly constituted—has given to the world all that which it (the world) has ever been enabled at once to understand and to feel as poetic."[46] These "souls fittingly constituted" must by implication withdraw from that world, however, in order to strike from their harps "notes which cannot have been unfamiliar to the angels."[47] The unearthly tinge of Poe's language and imagery in this essay is of course even more evident in his poetry. His teaching carried authority: he had been recommended by Baudelaire, he was acknowledged as the first Symbolist. To one like Bryusov, whose lyre had not so long ago given forth notes having little to do with the angels, acceptance of this teaching meant repentance and cleansing. However, what was the alternative? The immediate past offered nothing but recollections of failure and humiliation. *Chefs d'œuvre* had fallen between two stools, trying to appeal both to the reading public and to the Symbolist circle. He had resolved to be much bolder in his next book.[48] But how? Where lay the new direction? Poe's words were like a call, and the poems in "Counsels" were a direct response: "and abandoning men, I went into stillness; / Solitary as a dream, I live by dream. / For-

45. Poe, *Works*, VI, p. 11.   46. Ibid.   47. Ibid., p. 12.
48. *Dnevniki*, p. 23.

getting the charm of aimless hopes, / I gaze at the gleaming of sympathetic stars."[49]

The renunciation required by this calling is amply treated in subsequent sections of *Me eum esse*. In particular, Bryusov found it painful to renounce his eroticism. But he had to do so if he was to follow Poe. As a recent critic put it, "For Poe, such *materia poetica* as physical love, the influence of the natural world upon human sensibility, and human history simply aren't on the page. Not in poetry."[50] In "The Poetic Principle" Poe made it clear that passion must be eliminated: "Alas! its tendency is to degrade rather than elevate the Soul."[51] He went on to make a distinction between the "Uranian" and the "Dionaean Venus," which may have helped Bryusov distinguish his two Muses, she who languished in a window awaiting the onset of night and passion, and she who was glimpsed at the end of shady garden paths, leading him toward the attainment of true poetry, perfect beauty, and eternal love. Poe's was a hard teaching, but for a certain period Bryusov embraced it and preached it.

The confident, didactic tone in which he addressed the "young poet" must have been largely bravado, for Bryusov still had many unanswered questions about poetry. They arose again troublesomely upon his return to Moscow in early September 1896. The next chapter of his life was in many ways a painful one, but it brought him closer to answers with which he could live more comfortably than with the artistic asceticism imposed upon him by Poe's poetic principle.

49.   From "And abandoning men I went into stillness."
50.   Daniel Hoffman, *Poe Poe Poe Poe Poe Poe Poe* (Garden City, N.Y.: Anchor Press, 1973), p. 36.
51.   Poe, *Works*, VI, 28.

FIVE

Art and the Individual Talent

BRYUSOV FOUND REENTRY into ordinary Moscow life difficult after his spiritually eventful Pyatigorsk summer. In September 1896 his friends had scattered. Balmont had married and gone abroad, Kursinsky was in Kiev; Lang, married and thoroughly domesticated, was fast becoming useless as a colleague. Bryusov felt isolated and depressed. Attending classes at the university helped not at all, since the psychological position he had developed over the past months made him aloof and arrogant toward former acquaintances. He managed by November to put *Me eum esse* into final form and see it off to the printer. However, for the present his poetic source had run dry. His return to the "bright earth"—if Moscow in autumn could be called so— had been every bit as traumatic as the poem had prophesied.[1] The memory of "the fields of asphodel" was both tantalizing and elusive. What had happened to the mage's vision? And what was to come next?

Bryusov's diary from November to March records not so much the struggle against external opposition as his effort to renew his spirit and prepare for the gift of poetry when it should come again. His declaration of intent contained light self-mockery, indicated by his use of quotation marks. Yet it was serious:

1. "Ja vernulsja na jarkuju zemlju," the final poem in the section "In the Battle" in *Me eum esse*, represented the poet wandering among people as if befogged and unable to accustom his senses to the sights and sounds of earth.

"Now, several weeks before the publication of my newest book of verses, I solemnly and seriously give my word to abstain from literary activity for two years. I would like to write nothing in that time, and of all books to leave myself only three—the Bible, Homer, and Shakespeare. But even if this is impossible, I'll try to approach this ideal. I will read only what is great and write only in those moments when I have something to say to the whole world. I bid farewell to the noisy life of a journalistic warrior and the loud pretensions of a Symbolist poet. I will withdraw into life, submerge myself in its trifles, and permit my imagination, my pride, my ego to slumber. But this sleep will be only seeming. Thus a tiger closes its eyes, the better to watch its victim. And my quarry is already doomed to be mine. I am on my way. Trumpets, cease!"[2]

By mid-December he felt sufficiently revived to analyze what had happened to him since his return: "The reasons for my 'withdrawal' were many: both internal—exhaustion from the struggle, from reaction after finishing *Me eum esse*, new ideas—and external—scattering of all my friends and suddenly much money."[3] His period of extreme withdrawal was thus very short, but its spirit was prolonged. Moreover, the worry that accompanied it was intense: was he still to be a poet? And if so, what kind? While reading proofs for *Me eum esse*, he felt a yearning to write poetry. But the thirst came without the inspiration. "Muse, where are you!" he exclaimed. "Alas, my former Muse is dead, and the new one, which appeared to me among the cliffs of the Caucasus, has hidden her face and abandoned me, seeing how I offend against her best precepts."[4] The old Muse of *Chefs d'œuvre*, she of questionable virtue, indeed seemed to have left him. The new Muse was the elusive Muse of pure beauty, whom he had learned to love in the months before Pyatigorsk. Severe and unattainable, she demanded of her devotees a renunciation of mundane interests and attachments which Bryusov was in fact beginning to find

2.   *Dnevniki*, p. 26.
3.   Ibid. He is referring to an inheritance.
4.   Ibid.

constraining. The phrase "I am withdrawing into life" signified an attempt to rest a little from these high demands and possibly to harmonize them with other movements of his imagination. Occasionally he experienced moments of rebellion. A lyric dated 17 October 1896, entitled "I looked back in horror," contains the poet's dialogue with a commanding Voice.[5] As we have seen, Bryusov rarely used this device. The last notable instance was "Renunciation," which capped the first cycle of *Me eum esse*. There the Voice summoned the poet to renounce earthly hopes and feelings for the sake of "dreams of art" and the quest for eternal love. Now the poet raises querulous questions: where is truth, where is the road, where is salvation? And when the oracle tells him that salvation is in following its will, he rebels: "I was no slave in life's madness, / Nor will I be for the sake of bliss!" The Voice therefore condemns him to empty seeking, with no hope of ultimate happiness. At the end of *Me eum esse* the poet had hopefully pictured himself standing in a magic circle that would keep the old earthly temptations at bay. He was now beginning to realize that he who stands within a circle is effectively immobilized. He was not quite ready in the fall of 1896 to give up the ideal of pure beauty, but he was having second thoughts.

Sometime in the year following the completion of *Me eum esse*, Bryusov's convictions about art underwent an important change. By the start of 1898, when he began writing *About Art*, he had ceased to believe in beauty as art's object. This essay was first conceived as a response to Tolstoy's *What Is Art?* but its origins lay in Bryusov's own thoughts and experience. The thesis he now rejected had not figured in his writings on art prior to the period of *Me eum esse*. The infatuation with unearthly beauty had its source in the combined influence of Balmont and Poe, and it began to evaporate when Bryusov returned to a Moscow without Balmont. Other ideas were beginning to absorb him. The first copy of *Me*

5.   "I v užase ja ogljanulsja nazad" [I, 131–32].

eum esse brought all the past back in a wave of nostalgia, and he continued periodically to suffer pangs of conscience over his infidelities to the Muse who had inspired it. Nonetheless, his spirit chafed under subjection to the narrow ideal that had enthralled him during spring and summer of 1896.

In January 1897 Bryusov made a short trip to Petersburg to work in the public library, for he had several projects in hand, of which one was a history of the Russian lyric. However, these interests did not distract him from his main concern. He was meant to be a poet, but poetry was a gift which came only to the soul that was ready and worthy. His diary entry for 8 February reflects his inner trials and uncertainties: "My voluntary isolation subjects me to a severe trial. Have I enough spiritual strength to preserve my aspiration amid the petty vulgarity of the life surrounding me? Have I perceived my path clearly enough to follow it firmly amid gossip about money and conversations about women, amidst cards and drinking, alone in the whirlpool? My bright star! Stay pure and blessed. Do not fade."[6] In March he experienced a burst of energy. There were plans for stories, dramas, translations, and a novel. He was at work on the foreword to "History of the Russian Lyric," he was reading the historian Georg Weber, Maeterlinck, the Bible, and Sumarokov. He planned to read Kant, Novalis, and Boileau. Yet immediately after outlining these ambitious plans, he was brought up sharply by the same thought that had prompted his resolve of three months before to abstain from literature for two years: "Writing? Writing isn't hard. I could write many novels and plays in six months. But it is *necessary*, *essential*, to have something to write about."

A poem written a year earlier sums up Bryusov's spiritual state during this difficult winter, giving it the best possible interpretation: "For the chosen there are years of silence. / They come— /

6.   *Dnevniki*, p. 28.

And condemn former desires . . . / O stern judgment!"[7] However, he later wrote to Stanyukovich about this period, "I tried to
console myself with poems about the holiness of solitude, but I
felt awful. And *Me eum esse* was thoroughly ignored. In the whole
world only one man, Fyodor Sologub, was found who sent me a
congratulatory letter. Day after day I fell into a sort of depression,
apathy."[8] A letter from Vladimir Gippius in Petersburg apparently typified the reaction of his friends. To it Bryusov replied:
"In regard to *Me eum*, I will tell you 'why.' I published this book
so that in the eyes of my readers—intelligent or otherwise—I
would not remain the author of *Chefs d'œuvre*. That is all. Now as
a poet I shall be silent, probably for a long time."[9]

In the late spring of 1897, as soon as the university term ended,
Bryusov left for his first trip to Western Europe. This was a flight
as desperate as that to the Caucasus the previous year, but without the same tangible results for his poetry. In a letter to Vladimir
Gippius from Aix-la-Chapelle, dated 17 May, he wrote: "I am
leaving Russia (perhaps for a long time, perhaps not) and more
and more I am losing the hope of returning to poetry."[10] Writing
to Stanyukovich the following Christmas, he described the trip as
a complete loss. "I was in Berlin, in Cologne, travelled along the
Rhine, was in Holland briefly, but saw nothing. For example, I
didn't go as far as Paris, though I was quite close and could easily
have done so. I passed Dresden and hadn't enough curiosity even
to look at the Madonna."[11]

Given this state of mind, it is not surprising that he returned
earlier than planned. But soon a startling change of mood became
evident. By July he was installed in a dacha at Ostankino outside

7.   "Est' dlja izbrannyx gody molčanija" [I, 131].
8.   *LN* 85, p. 745.
9.   IMLI, fond 77, ed. xr. 9.
10. Ibid.
11. *LN* 85, p. 745.

Moscow and was able to write to his friend Samygin: "I am beginning a new life. I swear, it's a resurrection."[12] All thought of *Me
eum esse* and its failure was far from him. He continued: "I now
have so many ideas and images, so much material, that I could
work without stopping for many years. I am working a good deal
on the 'History of the Russian Lyric.' This will be an immense
work, huge. It ought to create the science of the history of literature. . . . It grows with every step; I have years, years ahead of
me." Considering his previous mood and the failure of his European trip, this change would be inexplicable were it not for a factor that had entered his life the previous spring: the arrival in his
family of Joanna Matveevna Runt, the teacher of French who took
up her duties with the younger Bryusovs in February 1897.

Bryusov's way of life did not alter immediately upon Joanna
Matveevna's arrival. She later described his regimen that grim
winter as follows:

> In the family Bryusov lived a separate life "in the other half," as they
> called a separate adjoining apartment. . . . He appeared in our half
> only for dinner. He would come in, silently greet everyone, sit
> down, open a book and stand it before his plate and read, paying no
> attention to anyone and taking no part in any conversation. After
> dinner . . . he would remain in the dining room for half an hour, no
> more, drinking tea, joking with his father and playing cards with
> him, some kind of game that went on day after day. Then he would
> go off, work with his sister (Nadezhda Yakovlevna) on her studies,
> and no one spoke about him until the next day.[13]

That spring his parents went to Paris, and Bryusov began to
spend more time in the family half of the house after dinner, re-
laxing and talking with his sisters and especially with the new
governess. In her recollections Joanna Matveevna pinpointed the

---

12.   "Neizdannyj Brjusov," *Moskovskij komsomolec* 28 December 1973. Letter dated 5 July 1897.
13.   Ašukin, pp. 113–14.

inception of his interest. She had found a paper on which he had copied two of his poems put to the inglorious use of covering a milk jug. In horror she removed and smoothed it. As she stood reading the poems, she was surprised by Bryusov, who thereafter treated her with great respect and attention, sharing French novels and the journal *La Plume* with her.[14]

The printed recollections of Bryusov's future wife are reserved on the subject of their courtship, as indeed on all personal matters. However, it is obvious that his premature return from the West and, possibly, his lack of interest in what he saw there were linked to his new interest at home. Her one remark tells enough: "From [Germany] he sent me a letter, more tender than might have been expected."[15] A poem dated 26 June 1897 was dedicated to "Eda," his name for her after they had read together Baratynsky's poem by that title. His poem "Polycrates" [III, 244] seems to mark the progress of matters between them. Intoxicated with happiness, the poet, like a second Polycrates, thinks of appeasing the gods with a few bad poems, so that they will not destroy his bliss out of envy.

The wedding took place on 28 September with a minimum of pomp. A letter Bryusov wrote to Samygin in the days just before the event is quoted with ironic detachment by Joanna Bryusova in her memoir. It reveals a good deal about both parties, both at the time and in their future relationship:

> My friend, honest and dear to me! I am going to speak to you more frankly than we sometimes speak alone to ourselves. I will try to answer all your questions, both stated and implied. First of all, this is a description of my future wife. She is not one of the number of remarkable women; there are many like her. She does not have that originality, that independent cast of mind which amazed both of us

14. Ibid., p. 114.
15. I. M. Brjusova, "Materialy k biografii Valerija Brjusova," in V. Brjusov, *Izbrannye stixi*, p. 126.

in the letters of Evgenia Ilinychna. She is a character out of a romance. She was brought up as if in a monastery. In poetry she reveres Boileau's "Art poétique," from which she knows long passages. She is dogmatic, naive, but—like all romantic characters—inclined to fleeting though boundless protest. (This does not mean that she is capricious. . . .) I must add that she is far from beautiful and not too young (she is twenty-one). You have met her, in fact.

No, this marriage will not be that ideal union which you preach. A special soul, who would be my equal in talent, in strength of thought, in knowledge—no doubt that would be splendid. But can you assure me that I will meet such a one and that we will fall in love? Perhaps we might hate each other? Yes, remember George Sand and Alfred de Musset. In the past I have had women like that who tower over others. I have spent nights with a woman who rhymed as well as I, and in bed we competed in making up verses for comic poems. Finally, there was that same Evgenia Ilinychna, with her tortuous thoughts about people's happiness, about good, about God. But I wouldn't want any one of these as a constant companion. They are all independent, talented, but nonetheless (believe me!) lower than I, and in the intellectual sphere I have had to condescend to them. And that eternal position as teacher, with whom they quarrel and whom they condemn (because they will never understand me), is unbearable. And she might begin to criticize my poems! I prefer to have with me a child who trusts me. I need peace, a cell for my work, but there I would have everlasting, and for me fruitless, struggle. You see that this marriage is almost one of calculation. But of course these arguments are not the whole story! There is one great argument before which all the others are nothing—this is love, her love. Could I be so stupidly proud as to pass by, saying to myself: "Oh, I can find as much of that as I want."

I treasure your opinion, and it would be very painful if you thought I was behaving unwisely. My God, I am not blinded by passion, that would be comic. For ten years I have been leading the splendid life of a neo-Romantic, an idle poet, taking my satisfaction in stanzas about my mood. Therefore you know I don't need *that*.

So many plans, so many projects before me! To accomplish it *all*, of course, life isn't long enough. And here I am, locking myself in my cell. You'll say that I am talking a lot about myself and haven't given a thought to what *she* needs. Not so. I have thought and am thinking about it. I do not at all want to force her to live only on my joys. I love ordinary, common life, although it's true I love it more as an observer. Oh, I have in me enough youthfulness to fool around and have fun like a schoolboy. You will say further that I must "instruct" her. Yes—up to a point. Now we are reading Shakespeare, sometime we will read—Maeterlinck. But in the last analysis you are right—I am thinking more of myself. My motto in this marriage is: one need not throw away the lamp just because it is not the sun.

With warm regards,
Valery Bryusov.[16]

Bryusov later wrote to Stanyukovich, "My 'rebirth' began with the fall of 1897—exactly from the time of my marriage (you can guess yourself whether this was cause or effect)."[17] Returning from their wedding trip to Petersburg, the young Bryusovs took up residence for a time in furnished rooms away from the family home. In April 1898 they went with other members of the family to spend several weeks in the Crimea. For Bryusov this was a self-conscious return to the South and to memories of his confrontation with nature nearly two years before. He now promised himself to learn to love nature. Indeed, he wrote several lyrics which became the nucleus of a section in his next volume of poems, *Tertia Vigilia*. Nature now conquered him entirely, and he filled his diary with careful and delighted observations. Reflecting on the difference between this and the last journey south he wrote:

I was not young in youth, I experienced all the tortures of a divided soul. From my earliest years, I dared not give in to feelings. I spoke to many about love but for a long time dared not love. Two years ago, travelling in the Crimea, I couldn't make up my mind to enjoy nature without thinking. I was the slave of preconceptions and self-

16. I. M. Brjusova, "Materialy," pp. 126–28. The reference is probably to Evgenija Il'inyčna Pavlovskaja, who was also for a short time a governess in the Brjusov household. Of her Brjusov wrote that she was the best woman he had ever met. In September 1897, just before his marriage, he travelled to visit her in her birthplace, where she was dying of tuberculosis [I, 599].

17. *LN* 85, p. 745.

set goals. . . . Oh, it took a great deal of struggling to understand that highest of all is one's own soul.[18]

The twelve months from June 1897 to June 1898, then, saw the start of a truly new stage in Bryusov's life—intellectual, spiritual, artistic, emotional. His individualism was far from dead, as the final remark in the above-quoted passage shows. However, happiness seemed to free him from the ultimately stifling bonds of his previous personal and artistic creed. Moreover, for the first time in his life, apparently, he experienced real closeness with another person. The diary entry of 2 October 1897, soon after the wedding, serves to counterbalance his laboriously analytical letter to Samygin: "For so long I sought that closeness with another soul, that total merging of two beings. I was born for just such endless love, for endless tenderness. I have come into my native sphere—I was destined to know bliss."[19]

That this was no emotional cocoon excluding all other interests is shown by his plans and activities just before and after the marriage. In the summer of 1897, after the ill-fated trip West, Bryusov was able to crystallize his thoughts about the history of the Russian lyric in a new plan more detailed and comprehensive than any he had drawn up before. Though never completed, this project was important in the development and refinement of his ideas about the goals and nature of poetry and it deepened his understanding of the Russian tradition.

In the fall of 1897 Bryusov returned to his university studies with renewed verve. Another long-standing interest now crowded his project on Russian lyric poetry. This was philosophy. "Perhaps before 'Corona' [provisional name for his next volume of poetry] and before the first volume of the 'History of the Lyric' I will write 'Philosophical Essays.' (Contents: I. Leibniz. II. Edgar Poe. III. Maeterlinck. IV. Idealism. V. The Basis of All Metaphysics.

18.　*Dnevniki*, p. 37.　　19.　Ibid., p. 29.

VI. Love [Two]. VII. Christianity.)"[20] A paper written for Professor Leo Lopatin, one of his favorite instructors, may have stimulated this project. Its title was "The Theory of Knowledge in Leibniz."[21] For Bryusov, as we have seen, Leibniz was the philosopher of individualism. His theory of monads, which stressed the self-containedness of the soul with all its powers drawn from inner resources, supported the viewpoint which emerged so strongly in *Me eum esse*.

Bryusov did not abandon either Leibniz or individualism when his esthetic views underwent a change. Rather, he sought a deeper philosophical grounding for his basic intuition. "The dominance of individuality—this is the nerve of his whole system," he wrote. "Leibniz recognized that force which filled his being, recognized the total independence of his 'I.'"[22] Leibniz taught that the human spirit receives nothing from outside itself; it creates only from its own inner perceptions. But owing to the fact that it is the highest order of monad, it contains in itself the features of all the lower orders. Thus each soul is a microcosm of the universe, and its resources are endlessly rich. Moreover, it refracts the universe in a way uniquely its own but equal to all others. Here Bryusov found the basis for his contention that *every* human insight is worthy of respect and preservation. And on this same foundation he was soon to plant his conviction that truth is multiple and endlessly varied.

Furthermore, Leibniz was among the first philosophers to suspect the presence in man of perception below the conscious level: within the soul are areas of darkness and mystery to be probed. All of this supported Bryusov's ideal of an inner life superior to and largely free of outside influences, a feature evident in his ear-

20.   Ibid.
21.   "Avtobiografija," p. 108.
22.   Quoted in R. E. Pomirčij, "Iz idejnyx iskanij V. Ja. Brjusova (Brjusov i Lejbnic)," *Brjusovskie čtenija 1971 goda*, p. 164.

liest poetry and pronouncements. If this inner-directedness came to a climax of sorts in *Me eum esse*, it did not thereafter ebb away. After his withdrawal from the cult of pure beauty, the task was to find another matrix for his conviction that the further one carried exploration of the soul, the richer might be the discoveries.

Another figure who commanded his personal empathy and respect as a thinker was Poe. Two or three years before, Bryusov and Balmont had regarded Poe as a visionary, a chosen seer, a suffering outcast, and an artist of finest fibre. That Bryusov now prized him as a man of extraordinary intellectual power would have gratified Poe, who had hoped to leave his mark on the history of thought with his cosmological essay *Eureka*. In January 1898 Bryusov lay ill with pleurisy. During his recuperation he made remarkable inroads into his list of "books to read." Among the works read, besides Kant's *Prolegomena*, Taine's *History of English Literature*, *On the Question of the Development of a Monistic View of History* by Beltov (Plekhanov), and two books on spiritualism and mysticism, was Poe's *Eureka*. Bryusov's archive contains drafts and an apparently finished version of an essay on Poe which he called "Eureca." This essay presumably dates from sometime just before or just after January 1898, since the projected literary/philosophical essays soon gave place to other undertakings.

Bryusov's philosophical attractions and spiritual searchings of this time place his study of *Eureka* in an interesting light. In the essay he traced Poe's progress from firm belief in reason, through a period of conviction about man's basic perversity, to a strong belief in intuition as the instrument of growth in human knowledge. Most significant is his interpretation of Poe's cosmogony. Poe conceived of creation as a dispersion of innumerable atoms along radii in a motion that will continue as long as the initial impulse retains its strength. As that impulse weakens, he believed, it is replaced by an urge to unification, but not of return to the center. These two forces, repulsion (initial dispersion) and attraction, explain all phenomena. Bryusov's choice among Poe's ideas of those for special attention is revealing. One of these ideas appeared to overcome the state of incommunicability that Leibniz posited for monads. Poe spoke of the reverberations the smallest physical action made throughout the universe, owing to the mutual dependence through mutual attraction of all atoms. Bryusov seized upon this idea with an enthusiasm betraying his deepest concern: "But if all exists in such a state of interconnection, then there *is* a way to the deepest secrets of the world, and nothing in the whole universe can happen without exerting an influence on me as well. There is truth in the ancient teachings of the wizards, and especially the astrologers: the microcosm of man reflects the life of the macrocosm of the universe, and the fate of the stars is able to foretell my personal fate." [23] This leap of intuition is both characteristic of Bryusov and symptomatic of his intense striving at this time to expand the inner universe of consciousness. He was quick to relate Poe's imaginative projection of the universe to Leibniz's doctrine of preestablished harmony. Poe also opened out possibilities appealing to Bryusov's pluralistic leanings, for Poe's chain of universes was without end, and at the heart of each of them lay its own God. "Here," said Bryusov regretfully, "is the limit of philosophy. There is no further way open even for intuition." [24]

However, Bryusov did not stop at the limits of philosophy in his probing of the range of the human spirit. The works of two other authors perused during that fruitful convalescence show the varied directions of his search. The authors were Baron Carl Du-

23.   In press, prepared by S. I. Gindin.

24.   Ibid. Brjusov may have read Kant's *Universal Natural History and Theory of the Heavens*, where some of the elements of Poe's construct are found, though without their most dynamic features. He may also have been familiar with the source Poe indicated in his dedication—Alexander von Humboldt. Poe called his work "A Prose Poem," a fact that may have touched Brjusov's imagination. It is interesting to note Brjusov's later account of Aleksandr Dobroljubov's theory, dating from his Decadent days, that a time would come when science would constitute "a very detailed song" about the universe (*Dnevniki*, p. 43).

Prel, German philosopher and occultist, and Allan Kardec (Leon H. D. Rivail), founder of the French journal *Revue Spirite*. Du-Prel's major work, *Die Philosophie der Mystik* (1884), was translated into Russian in 1895 and was one of four works listed as references following the article on mysticism by Vladimir Solovyov in a volume of the *Encyclopedic Dictionary* published in St. Petersburg in 1896.[25] DuPrel's book explored what he called "the subjective foundation of all mysticism."[26] One of the students of the unconscious who flourished in Germany in the later nineteenth century, DuPrel based his theories on the belief that the ego is not wholly embraced by self-consciousness, that a part lies beyond the threshold of sensibility and is accessible only in states other than normal wakefulness. Calling upon, in different combinations, Kant, Leibniz, and Schopenhauer, Hartmann and the philosophy of the unconscious, as well as the theory of evolution, DuPrel advanced the possibility of expanding the scope of consciousness, as well as of developing certain rudimentary powers of the soul. These ideas appealed to Bryusov immensely, both for the vistas they opened and for their stress on the individual soul and its potential. For DuPrel explicitly rejected any notion of pantheistic dissolution of the soul into a larger entity, stressing the preservation of individuality.[27] He also rejected a dualistic interpretation of the soul and its powers. Indeed, the last third of his work is called "The Monistic Doctrine of the Soul." Two persons in one subject: this is the phrase he frequently used to describe the separate operations of the soul above and below the threshold of sensibility. Mysticism is possible, then, without the strictly supernatural, since "sense and transcendental functions go on side by side together, that is, we are beings of simultaneous

25.   Vl. S., *Enciklopedičeskij slovar'*, vol. 19 (Bk. 37), ed. K. K. Arsen'ev and F. F. Petruševskij (St. Petersburg, 1896), pp. 454–56 s.v. *Mistika, -cizm*.
26.   Carl DuPrel, *The Philosophy of Mysticism*, tr. C. C. Massey (London: George Redway, 1889), 1, p. xxv.
27.   Ibid., p. xxiii.

membership in the world of sense and in the transcendental world. . . . It is not at death that we are transported for the first time into the supersensuous world; rather, we already live in it, only as earthly persons we know nothing of it."[28]

Though DuPrel offered the kind of natural basis for occultism that Bryusov found congenial, he remained open to other possibilities. For some time he had been interested in spiritualism and mediumistic phenomena.[29] For many years he attended séances and was even considered a talented medium. He may have read both of Kardec's books, *Philosophie spiritualiste: Le livre des esprits* and *Spiritisme expérimental: Le livre des médiums*.[30] Kardec's teaching seemed to contradict DuPrel's but also to complement it. Du-Prel's monistic doctrine of the soul apparently precluded a world of spirits of deceased humans seeking contact with the living. On the other hand, his stress on little-explored or -developed powers in that area of the soul that is unilluminated by self-consciousness accommodated nicely the concept of mediumism. Bryusov would have appreciated Kardec's sober assertion: "Les communications entre le monde spirite et le monde corporel sont dans la nature des choses, et ne constituent aucun fait surnaturel."[31]

Kardec distinguished levels of spirits, dismissing the lower spirits and their vulgar manifestations and affirming the importance of contact with higher ones, who have much to impart.[32] Writing several years later, Bryusov called on his fellow modernist poets to give a hearing to spiritualism. He reminded them

28. Ibid., 2, p. 192. I have altered the translation somewhat.
29. *Dnevniki*, p. 8.
30. Ibid., p. 33. *Le livre des esprits* (6th ed. Paris: Didier, 1862); *Le livre des médiums* (2nd ed. Paris: Didier, 1862). See also Pomirčij, p. 165 n. 2.
31. Kardec, *Le livre des esprits*, p. xli.
32. The distinction between inferior and superior spirits and their manifestations helps explain Brjusov's continued interest in his mature years along with his sometimes mocking attitude toward the séances in which he participated. His seriousness is attested to by the skeptical Stanjukovič in his memoir, *LN* 85, p. 728.

that their favorite writers, Dostoevsky and Poe, Tyutchev and Fet, all pointed to the existence of something beyond the earthly. He wrote: "Seeing that the knowable has its limits, that beyond them is the unknowable, we cannot fail to burn with the desire to see into those inaccessible worlds." [33] Truth was manifold, Bryusov believed, and must be pursued along all paths, in all directions.

The same period of convalescence in January 1898 that allowed Bryusov to fuel his spirit by reading philosophy witnessed a shock to his literary plans and self-esteem which could hardly have helped his recovery. In his diary for 18 January he noted: "The most important event of these days has been the appearance of Count [Leo] Tolstoy's article on art. Tolstoy's ideas so coincide with mine that at first I was in despair and wanted to write 'Letters to the Editor' to protest. Now I've calmed down and contented myself with a letter to Tolstoy himself." [34] The first five chapters of Tolstoy's *What Is Art?* were published in the November–December 1897 issue of *Problems of Philosophy and Psychology.* [35] The journal appeared in December, but Bryusov did not see it until the following month. His letter to Tolstoy, dated 20 January, was courteous and brief, though it betrayed the distraught condition of its writer. "It did not surprise me," he wrote, "that you did not mention my name among your predecessors, since doubtless you did not even know my views on art. However, I should have occupied first place on that list, because my views coincide almost word for word with your own." [36] Enclosing

33.   "Ko vsem, kto iščet," Foreword to A. Miropolskij [Lang], *Lestvica* (Moscow, 1902), p. 12.

34.   *Dnevniki*, p. 32.

35.   "Čto takoe iskusstvo?" *Voprosy filosofii i psixologii* (November–December 1897): 979–1027; (January–February 1898): 1–137. A standard English translation is that of Aylmer Maude, *What Is Art?* (London: Oxford University Press, 1930).

36.   *Dnevniki*, p. 156.

the foreword to the first edition of *Chefs d'œuvre*, where he believed he anticipated Tolstoy, Bryusov asked Tolstoy to make known his oversight "either by a note to the second half of your article, or to its separate edition, or finally by a special letter to the newspapers." A final remark no doubt intended as a graceful plea betrayed Bryusov's panic at being thought an imitator when he would finally bring forth the developed theory he had been nourishing: "You of course would not wish to take from me, like the rich man in the prophet Nathan's parable, my 'only lamb.'" The confrontation was of course ludicrous: Count Leo Tolstoy, world-famous literary figure and moral leader, challenged by a young poet of no reputation. The young poet, claiming to have anticipated the revolutionary views on art contained in Tolstoy's essay and backed by his tremendous prestige, requires that the great man acknowledge this fact publicly. The poet's words are modest, but his deed is not. Nor did Bryusov conceive the indignation that this stern patriarch might feel at the suggestion that any view of his coincided with those of a Decadent, a school of writers he considered at best obscurantists, at worst perhaps scoundrels. No wonder Tolstoy wrote on the envelope of Bryusov's letter: "No answer." [37]

Bryusov's uncharacteristic behavior—in a calmer mood he would hardly have risked humiliation—suggests the strain under which he labored in putting his esthetic house in order. The question of the nature and purpose of art stood in the path of any progress he might make. In December he had written, "I cannot publish 'The History of the Russian Lyric' until I have finally found my views on poetry and criticism." [38] Now Tolstoy forced

---

37. A summary discussion of Brjusov's attitude toward Tolstoj and especially of this incident is found in S. I. Gindin, "Stanovlenie brjusovskogo otnošenija k Tolstomu," *V. Brjusov i literatura konca XIX–XX veka* (Stavropol', 1979), pp. 18–31.

38. Cited in an article prepared for publication by S. I. Gindin: in press.

his hand. Bryusov first conceived an answer to Tolstoy. Reacting initially to the first five of Tolstoy's twenty chapters, Bryusov thought he saw more similarity of views than really existed. In his first five chapters Tolstoy examined previous estheticians' answers to the question "What is art?" and found nearly all of them based on conceptions of beauty; he considered these to be useless as definitions, since all must in the end be subjective. Bryusov, as we have seen, had likewise discarded beauty as a criterion and therefore was much in sympathy with Tolstoy's view in this regard. In his fifth chapter Tolstoy reviewed those few modern definitions of art that rested on some other basis. These he criticized because they were concerned chiefly with the pleasure art can give and not with its function in life. Yet once this is considered, he said, "we cannot fail to observe that art is one of the means of intercourse between man and man." [39] Moreover, Tolstoy asserted, art differs from other means of communication in that it transmits not thoughts but feelings. He summed up his definition in words that surely struck note after familiar note for Bryusov:

> To evoke in oneself a feeling one has once experienced and having evoked it in oneself then by means of movements, lines, colors, sounds, or forms expressed in words, so to transmit that feeling that others experience the same feeling—this is the activity of art. Art is a human activity consisting in this, that one man consciously by means of certain external signs, hands on to others feelings he has lived through, and that others are infected by these feelings and also experience them. [40]

As far back as in the 1893 foreword to the first *Russian Symbolists*, Bryusov had insisted that the goal of Symbolism was to evoke in the reader a certain mood by means of images. He repeated this in the unpublished *"Profession de foi"* (1894). And in the foreword to the first *Chefs d'œuvre* (1895), which he sent to Tolstoy, he had

39.   Tolstoj, Maude tr., p. 120.   40.   Ibid., p. 123.

written: "Enjoyment of a work of art consists in communication with the soul of the artist." Bryusov's claim to originality was not preposterous. Yet to whatever degree he may have anticipated Tolstoy's essay in one or two printed remarks, the fact remained that Tolstoy's 1897 essay was a fully developed statement, while Bryusov was still groping.

The great service to Bryusov of Tolstoy's essay was that it galvanized him into formulating his own position. His first step was to compare his views and Tolstoy's on various points.[41] He deduced that in the second part of the essay Tolstoy would insist on the comprehensibility of art to the receiver, for which he would lay the responsibility on the artist. Bryusov, however, insisted that the potential receiver must share the effort: he must approach the work of art with an open mind, remembering that a new world is opening before him and that he should attempt to enter it. Here was a basic difference between Bryusov and Tolstoy:

> I say: if the goal of art is communication, then that work is truly artistic in which the author opens his soul and makes possible for him who desires it to enter into communication with him, to experience the same feelings. Tolstoy judges otherwise; if art is a means of communication, he says, only that is true art which is understandable to all, which leads all to share the feelings of the artist.[42]

The second and final installment of Tolstoy's essay was printed in the January–February 1898 issue of the journal, but publication was delayed until March by the censors' dissatisfaction with Tolstoy's piece.[43] Circumstances required Bryusov to lay aside for some time the work on his response. The university term ended in late March with a flurry of papers and reports. He suddenly found himself writing poetry again, a welcome change from the aridity that had afflicted him. Domestic activities also inter-

---

41.   Cf. Gindin, "Stanovlenie," pp. 27–29.
42.   From text prepared for publication by S. I. Gindin.
43.   *Dnevniki*, p. 34.

vened. In mid-April, with his family, he left for the Crimean vacation which so refreshed his outlook.

In early June, when he returned, he went to a dacha north of Moscow. There he plunged into his essay, now elevated to the level of a book on art.[44] When he finished it, on 13 August, he experienced a considerable sense of achievement. It appeared at the end of November in a printing of five hundred copies. Two years had now passed since any book of his had appeared in print, and, aside from various forewords, it was his first appearance as a literary theorist. He hoped to be taken seriously. Added to that was the possibility of his essay's riding on the attention—not chiefly favorable, to be sure—given to Tolstoy's work. All these hopes were disappointed. Balmont alone wrote him an ecstatic letter; others were silent. In December, just a week after the book's publication, he went to Petersburg. Certainly he expected at the very least to hear some discussion of his ideas by the Petersburg Symbolists. Merezhkovsky condemned the work for what amounted to banality. "There's not even anything to attack because there's nothing in it. I agree with practically everything in it, but without pleasure. When I read Nietzsche I tremble down to my toes; but this, I hardly know why I'm reading it."[45] Nevertheless, there were approving words in some quarters, and Bryusov counted *About Art* among his achievements when he reckoned up his personal accounts at the end of the year.[46]

Though the immediate response had been disappointing, Bryusov's sense of achievement regarding *About Art* was justified. The essay represented an important step toward his mature stance as an artist. Moreover, it articulated new ideas of profound importance to poets who would follow, although before these ideas

44.   *O iskusstve* (Moscow, 1899); VI, 43–54. (Brjusov insisted on this usage: "*O*," not "*Ob*.")

45.   *Dnevniki*, p. 53.

46.   Ibid., p. 59.

could reach their full effectiveness they had to be diffused through Bryusov's own later critical writing and poetic practice and subsequently through that of others. Meanwhile, only Balmont, whose stock with the public was little higher than Bryusov's, saw anything remarkable in the essay. Its initial character of polemic answer to *What Is Art?* disappeared in revision; only three paragraphs of the introduction referred to Tolstoy. Though the sentence "Both Tolstoy and I consider art a means of communication" drew ridicule, Bryusov's statement of his position was largely cool and measured in tone. "This book is in no way a development of [Tolstoy's] ideas, nor a correction of his teaching," he stated. "We start from a common position but go on to opposing conclusions" [VI, 44]. Their most important difference concerned the ends of art. For Tolstoy art must ultimately serve a moral purpose; for Bryusov art must not be subservient to anything at all. Tolstoy would put limitations on art, while Bryusov concluded strongly, "I seek freedom in art."

Bryusov's newly formulated ideas about art drew strongly on his reading of the past year. The epigraph for the essay is drawn from Leibniz, and it appeals to the reader to consider a position that may at first seem repellent. The essay has four chapters, entitled "Counsels to the Artist," "Counsels to the Reader," "On the New School," and "Hopes." Epigraphs to the first, from Gautier, Fet, and Pozharsky (a little-known Russian poet), stress the immortality of art and its superiority to all perishable things. The chapter defends the artist's total freedom to express whatever is in his soul in terms that owe much to Leibniz and to Poe's *Eureka*. Each soul is individual and each moment of its experience is unrepeatable, and it is art's task to preserve these moments. The artist, therefore, must truly know his soul. To this end he must give himself to solitary meditation, in order to strip off that which is not truly himself. Only after long preparation may he present his received revelation to his hearers. Echoing his recent discoveries, Bryusov declared that everything in the universe is interconnected. Thus a truly great spirit may understand the Creator through one segment of creation, his own soul. Indeed, Bryusov proposed as the artist's goal the re-creation of the entire universe through his own perception of it: "Let the artist illuminate his soul from ever new vantage points" [VI, 46]. Here is the basis of Bryusov's fundamental belief that the artist must develop continually and that his art, when it ceases to change, is dead.

The second chapter is headed by three quotations, all from Baratynsky, the poet who was rapidly becoming one of Bryusov's favorites. "All Muses are equal in beauty, / Their difference is only in their dress," reads one of the epigraphs. All themes are equally worthy in art: this is the message of this section. Rules should not be laid down for the artist, whose primary task is, all unhampered, to reveal his soul. However, here Bryusov obliquely challenged one of Tolstoy's cardinal points, the requirement that true art be accessible to all. Bryusov noted that while all true artists are equally valuable, universal comprehensibility is impossible, because readers differ in their ability to comprehend. When the true artist opens his soul to its depths, he must not be constrained by the demands of critic or reader. "Go by the free road where your free mind leads," was Pushkin's counsel "To the Poet." The reader and critic should follow respectfully.

In the third chapter Bryusov turned to the subject of the new art and its place in the history of poetry. He chose epigraphs from Sluchevsky, Fet, and Baratynsky, marking the essential unity of the elite company of true poets, and then proceeded to a lesson in literary theory and history. Those who have learned to use the materials of art in a certain fashion belong to a single school, he averred, though the content of their art may be very different. Although the content of art changes as mankind discovers new feelings, through all schools runs the common thread of progressive liberation of the personality. Here Bryusov paused to define the new art once more in his own terms, striking a blow at the notion that probing another reality behind the visible universe was the essence of Symbolism. "The struggle against constraints is being continued by the new school (Decadence, Symbolism). It has understood more clearly than others what a school of art is: a teaching about artistic devices and nothing more" [VI, 51]. The new school is distinguished by the value it puts on the word as such rather than on the mere reflection of reality. Moreover, idealism is only one tendency in Symbolism. And once more Bryusov reiterated his belief that the essence of art is the soul of the artist, by whatever means he chooses to reveal it.

Bryusov no doubt thought of the fourth and final chapter, "Hopes," as the pièce de résistance of his essay. The epigraphs come from Tyutchev, Lermontov, Baratynsky, and Fet, the pantheon of the new Russian poetry. Their theme is communication. The text contains many of the ideas that had recently excited him, blended in a whole as harmonious as his present state of thought permitted. Human life, we are told, is governed by two laws, the impulse toward perfection and the thirst for communion. The primordial riches of the spirit are measureless but only partially accessible to us now. Movement toward perfection means the illumination of ever-new reaches of the soul—an endless process. Ideas of Leibniz, Poe, and DuPrel are here blended to provide a theoretical basis for the notion Bryusov had long held almost as a matter of instinct.

Turning to the second law, the impulse toward communion, he drew on Leibniz, Schopenhauer, and additional sources. The self-contained ego, with all its riches, is in a sense trapped. "The world is my representation of it. I am endowed with only my sensations, my desires—nothing more and never more" [VI, 52]. Yet union is the soul's bliss. Sexual love is the sole means available on the lower steps of being. It gives a momentary assurance that we are not alone. Other loves spring from the same source. And

from the desire to communicate sprang the word.[47] Then, following a short disquisition on art, science, and philosophy as means
of satisfying the soul's demands, he packed all his "hopes" into
the closing paragraph:

> In our day there are everywhere precursors and indicators of the new.
> In our own souls we glimpse what we had not noticed before: there
> are the phenomena of the disintegration of the soul, double vision,
> hypnotism; the renewed precious teachings of the Middle Ages
> (magic) and attempts at reaching the unseen (spiritism). Conscious-
> ness apparently is preparing yet one more victory. Then there will
> arise a new art and a new science, more perfectly achieving their
> goals.
>
> [VI, 53–54]

About Art sketched the philosophical basis for Bryusov's intuitions about art and the nature of the artist. The will-o'-the-wisp
of beauty he had pursued in *Me eum esse* was now replaced by a
stronger, clearer version of his original position: that the central
fact of art was the soul of the artist. Over the past two years he
had learned a good deal about the range of action implied. Again
in this essay he affirmed, "The future is open to the new school"
[VI, 51]. It was this belief above all that sealed his allegiance.
Bryusov saw himself as an explorer standing on the rim of undis-
covered continents of the spirit. DuPrel's first chapter, "Science:
Its Capability of Development," inflamed him with the idea that
knowledge must advance at certain points by what we would call
quantum leaps. Why should these not take place in the psychic
sphere? And why, asked Bryusov, should art not participate in
them?

Such thoughts as these intoxicated Bryusov at this time and in

---

47. Brjusov's thinking about language was in its early stages. It is not
clear, for example, when he first encountered the work of Aleksandr Potebnja,
though he was much interested in it at a later date, according to Andrej Belyj's
recollections. It seems possible that he had read Potebnja by this time.

fact deflected him from writing poetry. After his impressive reading list of January 1898 he noted, "Concentration on philosophy somehow kills off poetry."[48] However, he had not yet begun to write his best poetry. Inspiration was to return. Meanwhile, the intellectual occupations of 1897 and 1898 permitted him to base his doctrine of individualism on premises more solid than inclination and pose.

In retrospect certain features of this phase of Bryusov's endeavor are particularly striking. Not only had Bryusov made a tremendous advance in formulating his ideas and giving them a philosophical base, in *About Art* he had strongly challenged the utilitarian critical establishment—Populist, Marxist—who controlled the important journals. Yet this essay packed with original thinking received less notice in the press than had his earliest attack on the literary status quo in *Russian Symbolists*. One contemptuous review appeared in *Russian Wealth*, edited by two stalwarts of the Populist camp, the critic N. K. Mikhailovsky and the writer Vladimir Korolenko. The anonymous reviewer easily supplied an explanation for this difference in response: "Mr. Bryusov's theoretical work compares disadvantageously with his poetry in that it is fully comprehensible; thus it is deprived of the chief interest which the author's poetic works inspired: the interest of oddity."[49] The dismissal of Bryusov's ideas as trivial and banal seems disingenuous in view of the fury (the word is hardly too strong) with which the reviewer focused on the central tenet of *About Art*, the assertion of the supremacy of the artist's soul and its sufficiency as a source for his art. And the excoriation of Bryusov's neglect of the theory of language's popular origin suggests that his ideas were considered too dangerous to go unchallenged. The old trick of destroying one's foe by ridicule was wearing thin in the case of the new art and, within a few years,

48. *Dnevniki*, p. 33.
49. *Russkoe bogatstvo* no. 2 (February 1899): pt. 2, p. 56.

would have to be retired from use until another vulnerable target came along. Meanwhile, Bryusov continued to refine and develop his thinking on art, readying it for unknown debates to come.

Another question finally arises: how relevant is Bryusov's philosophy of art to his poetry? Sometime earlier, Bryusov had chided Peter Pertsov for identifying the ideas about poetry expressed in a poet's prose with his philosophy of poetry. The latter, he insisted, was something different: "a special attitude toward the world, to oneself, to the unattainable; and this is the true philosophy of poetry."[50] He cited the case of Rimbaud, whose general worldview seemed trivial in comparison with the philosophy embodied in his poetry. This discrepancy is hardly obligatory, however, and in the case of Bryusov himself the distinction seems inapplicable. The compression of ideas in *About Art* has something of the intensity of poetry. But beyond that a point of central importance should be observed. In *About Art* Bryusov gave inner shape to the lyrical hero, the persona, who was to dominate the poetry of *Tertia Vigilia* and much beyond. The explorers, the adventurers, the discoverers of hidden secrets who people the poetry are moved by the same force that is revealed in art, or at least in Bryusov's conception of it. They are the poet's masks and participate in his freedom. The rejection of limitation on the matter or manner an artist may employ was implicit in Bryusov's poetry from the beginning. In his next book, as both his poetic craft and his poetic personality approached maturity, a kind of exuberance is felt which reveals the widening poetic horizon that was the reward of Bryusov's long abstinence from poetry. Before attaining this new stage, however, Bryusov had at least one more course to complete: he had to interpret for himself the history of Russian lyric poetry.

50.   *Percovu*, p. 74.

Title page of Bryusov's first book of poems, *Chefs d'œuvre,* published in Moscow in 1895. On the facing page he announced other literary achievements and plans: a play, *Prose,* performed once; his contributions to the first two numbers of *Russian Symbolists;* his translation of Verlaine's *Romances sans paroles;* "The History of the Russian Lyric," here mentioned for the first time as "in preparation."

ТОГО ЖЕ АВТОРА:

ПРОЗА. Драматическій этюдъ. Поставленъ въ 1-й разъ на сценѣ Нѣмецкаго клуба въ Москвѣ 30 ноября 1893 г. (Не напечатанъ).

РУССКІЕ СИМВОЛИСТЫ. Изд. В. А. Маслова:
Въ вып. 1. М. 1894. 18 стихотв. (Распроданъ).
Въ вып. 2. М. 1894. Вступительная замѣтка и 4 стихотворенія. Ц. 50 коп.
Вып. 3. (Печатается).

ПОЛЬ ВЕРЛЕНЪ. Романсы безъ словъ. Переводъ. М. 1894. Ц. 40 коп.

ИСТОРІЯ РУССКОЙ ЛИРИКИ. (Готовится.)

Валерій Брюсовъ.

CHEFS D'OEUVRE.

СБОРНИКЪ СТИХОТВОРЕНІЙ.

(Осень 1894 — весна 1895.)

МОСКВА.
Типографія Э. Лисснера и Ю. Романа,
Воздвиженка, Крестовоздвиженскій пер., д. Лисснеръ.
1895.

Unknown, ridiculed, strange,
I have tasted a boundless bliss:
To enjoy the ineffable dream
And the free rapture of passionlessness.

VALERY BRYUSOV
27 Aug. Kislovodsk

This photo was sent by Bryusov to one of his many correspondents just before he left the Caucasus after the sojourn during which he produced *Me eum esse*. The lines are from his poem "It was the madness of a dream [Èto bylo bezumie grezy]." The poem referred to his brief fascination with a certain "Maria," whose acquaintance he failed to make and whose indifference stimulated the writing of several poems. Though the poem was not included until the 1913 edition of the volume, these lines epitomize the attitude of lofty withdrawal elaborated in *Me eum esse*. [Courtesy of Institute of World Literature, Moscow.]

Me eum esse is the last book of Valery Bryusov, who passed away (. date .) 1896 in Pyatigorsk. Shortly before his death the author himself prepared the manuscript of this book, though he considered it far from finished. The publishers hope in the near future to gather in a separate volume as well all the translations by Valery Bryusov which have appeared in print.

A. L. MIROPOLSKY

Moscow, 1896

"Miropolsky" was the pseudonym of Alexander Lang, Bryusov's friend and collaborator in various literary projects. This foreword, which was written in Bryusov's hand, accompanied the draft version of *Me eum esse* which he sent to Lang from Pyatigorsk in August 1896, to be published in case of his demise. (See Chapter Four.) [Central State Archive of Literature and Art, fond 56, op. 2, ed. xr. 10.]

In September 1897 Bryusov married Joanna Matveevna Runt, who had been his sisters' governess. They lived for many years in the family home, a substantial house in Moscow purchased by Bryusov's grandfather, a former serf who bought his freedom and became a wealthy Moscow cork merchant. Pictured here with Bryusov are his wife and parents. [Courtesy of the Institute of World Literature, Moscow.]

The house on Tsvetnoy Boulevard, where Bryusov lived for many years. [Photograph courtesy of Susan and Peter Scotto.]

"The shadow of uncreated creations. . ."

One of Bryusov's most striking early poems was "Creation [Tvorčestvo]," in which the shadow of palm fronds on a "wall of enamel" initiates the process of transforming reality into art. The mysterious fronds—"lopasti latanij"—decorated the sitting room in the Bryusov house. [Courtesy of the Institute of Russian Literature, Leningrad.]

Valery Bryusov in the late 1890s, at about 25. [Courtesy of Institute of Russian Literature, Leningrad.]

Konstantin Balmont.
[Courtesy of the Institute
of World Literature, Moscow.]

TO VALERY BRYUSOV

Yes, quickly, at once, I wish
To say one thing to you:
To you I am committed as to a ray of light,
As that man is forever committed to the sword
Who is fated to be strong.

I was strong when I loved
You, my best dream.
Having cooled to you, I forgot life,
I slew myself with my own hand,
But again I am in love with the vision.

I forgot that I am a soldier,
I discarded the sharp sword.
But your cold, wrathful gaze
Returned me to myself,
For life together—not for mere encounters.

And I love, and I live,
Forever, once more I am "I."
With you I shall tear off all fetters,
With a laugh I shall look into the lion's jaws—
O light, O happiness of the blade!

K. BALMONT

October. 1903. Night.
(Five minutes after your departure.)

In 1903 Konstantin Balmont and Valery Bryusov were considered the ring-leaders of the new literary revolt, but their underlying philosophies were different, and Balmont tended to go his own eccentric way. This poem in typical Decadent language witnesses a repentant moment under Bryusov's strong influence. [Central State Archive for Literature and Art, fond 56, op. 3, ed. xr. 6.]

Bryusov in 1908, at 35. [Courtesy of the Bakhmeteff Archive, Columbia University.]

The Balance no. 12 (1906). [From a series of sketches "Danses Parnassiennes" by J.-J. Frieslander.]

Изъ серіи рисунковъ «Danses Parnassiennes» Дж.-Дж. Фрисляндера.

"*The Balance* (*Vesy*) Scholarly-Literary and Critical-Bibliographic Monthly First Year of Publication. 1904 No. 12." The journal's astrological sign, Libra, often appeared along with the sign Scorpio, the publisher's emblem. *The Balance* appeared from 1904 to 1909, with Bryusov as its editor during most of that time.

В горахъ.   Рисунокъ Макса Волошина.

"In the Mountains," by the Russian artist and poet Maximilian Voloshin, a younger contemporary of Bryusov's. [From *The Balance* no. 8 (1904).]

Valery Bryusov at 49, taken in 1923, one year before his death. [Courtesy of the Institute of Russian Literature, Leningrad.]

SIX

The Poet's Poets

DURING THE YEARS 1897 to 1899, besides addressing basic questions about art, Bryusov was deepening his understanding of the Russian poetic tradition. At the same time he wrestled with theoretical aspects of poetic technique, occupations that were to continue till the end of his life.[1] The growth of his ideas during these early years appears in his successive attempts to frame the large task he had undertaken, that of writing a history of the Russian lyric. This project occupied a central place among his plans from the summer of 1895 till sometime in 1899, when it faded from his designs. The idea apparently arose out of the plan for "Russian Poetry in 1895," begun in the summer of that year.[2] Bryusov quickly realized that to put contemporary poetry in its proper perspective, a background was needed: "I will begin directly with Kantemir and expect to survey [the Russian lyric] according to the following general plan: I. The lyric until Pushkin. II.1. Pushkin's immediate predecessors. 2. Push-

---

1.   Much of Brjusov's theoretical work is contained in articles and reviews in *Vesy* and other journals. One book published after the Revolution contained lectures for his courses for beginning proletarian poets: *Nauka o stixe* (Moscow, 1919). The second edition appeared in 1924 under the title *Osnovy stixovedenija*. Three theoretical articles written during these years have been reprinted in volume six of the collected works: "Pogonja za obrazami," "O rifme," and "Sintetika poèzii." "Remeslo poèta," the introduction to his 1918 collection *Opyty*, appears in *Izbrannye sočinenija*. Some of his most interesting early work on poetic theory was unpublished in his lifetime. See footnote 6 below.

2.   *Percovu*, p. 32.

kin and Tyutchev. III. The Pushkin school and Fet. IV. The most recent lyric poetry."[3]

An outline from the summer of 1897 reflected Bryusov's new interest in the historical development of Russian versification and the technical side of poetry in general, and a conspectus for the first volume prepared a few months later showed the direction of his thought:

> "Contemporary Russian poetry" did not grow organically, like a tree from a seed, out of folk poetry, as did the contemporary poetry of France, Germany, England, and Italy. . . . Our poetry was not even grafted to the aging but healthy trunk of popular creation. We took over all ready-made poetry's forms and devices and the rules of verse.[4]

When he wrote this Bryusov, like many of his contemporaries, still grounded modern Russian poetry in the eighteenth-century adoption of syllabo-tonic verse and Western verse forms and he viewed the historical debt to Europe and the lack of strong native roots as compelling reasons for Russian poetry to keep in close contact with the European tradition. But by the fall of 1898 a new idea had taken hold of him: perhaps modern Russian poetry actually had roots in pre-Petrine times. He had already recognized Pushkin's effectiveness in synthesizing Western models with native linguistic and poetic stock. Bryusov now decided to open his book with a section on Russian folk poetry, in which he hoped to establish this connection in theoretical terms.[5]

Most of Bryusov's forays into theory at this period centered on the question of what form of versification best answered to the spirit and structure of the Russian language.[6] His interest in

3. S. Gindin, "Neosuščestvlennyj zamysel Brjusova," *Voprosy literatury* no. 9 (1970): 191.

4. Ibid., p. 198. This contrast was probably inspired by Brjusov's reading of French and Belgian poets and his awareness of their interest in their folk tradition.

5. Ibid., p. 201.

6. S. I. Gindin, "Iz istorii stixovedenija. Vzgljady V. Ja. Brjusova na ja-

folk poetry itself went back to his days in the Polivanov Gymnasium. Then in fall 1895 at Moscow University he had studied with F. E. Korsh, whose major work on Russian folk versification began to appear the following year.[7] Though some of Korsh's ideas seemed to Bryusov to be brilliant, he was as yet far from finding in folk poetry patterns applicable to contemporary writing. However, in the summer of 1898 an event occurred that brought his book-knowledge of folk poetry alive and simultaneously suggested its relevance to modern poetry. At the end of July, Alexander Dobrolyubov, completely transformed, returned from the north woods in peasant dress and paid Bryusov another momentous visit. A few months earlier Dobrolyubov had made a complete break with his life as Decadent poet and Petersburg University student. Now (and for years hence) he lived as a pious wanderer. Bryusov was entranced by this apparition from another world. While consorting with peasants and hunting bears in the forest, Dobrolyubov had collected folk songs, tales, charms, and laments. Much of this he recited by heart, though he brought manuscripts as well. His own language had changed and become more purely Russian, and he had composed songs and verses in the new vein, which he recited freely.[8] The guest soon departed, to return briefly a few weeks later. This time he left behind a bundle of papers, presumably including the poems printed under Bryusov's editorship in the 1900 *Collected Works*.[9]

zykovuju priemlemost' stixovyx sistem i sud'by russkoj sillabiki (po rukopisjam 90-x godov)," p. 100.

7. "Avtobiografija," p. 108. An archival notation reads: "I was much assisted in clarifying my ideas on syllabo-tonic versification by the course in metrics that I took from Prof. F. Korš in the fall of 1895" (ibid., p. 102). The work in question is F. E. Korš, *O russkom narodnom stixosloženii* (St. Petersburg, 1896–1897).

8. *Dnevniki*, pp. 41–46.

9. Ibid., p. 49. *Sobranie stixov* is reprinted in Aleksandr Dobroljubov, *Sočinenija*, introduction by Joan Delaney Grossman (Berkeley: Berkeley Slavic Specialties, 1981). Both this and a later book by Dobroljubov, *Iz knigi nevidimoj* (1905), were originally published by Scorpio, where Brjusov played a prominent

Bryusov was profoundly impressed on hearing, possibly for the first time in his life, Russian folk verse with something like its authentic intonations. Added to this was the example of Dobrolyubov's new poetry, strongly influenced by the folk mode. Perusing and, ultimately, editing Dobrolyubov's poems gave Bryusov ample opportunity to absorb their new rhythms and images. Moreover, Dobrolyubov offered a new synthesis, for in the background, unforgotten though ostensibly rejected, was his earlier immersion in the work of the new French poets, including especially some who wrote *vers libre*. Bryusov noted: "He could not entirely overcome the artist in him. The old Dobrolyubov is still alive in the reading of poetry." [10]

This crucial encounter gave Bryusov the impetus to clarify his ideas. His essay "On Russian Versification" was written that fall. [11] Bryusov had been fascinated for several years with the notion of the line (*stix*) as the basic unit of poetry. His earliest effort to define this compositional element appeared in an October 1896 draft chapter for *A History of the Russian Lyric*. [12] Here he approached the matter historically by tracing experiments in versification by Russian poets. Now, stimulated by his recent exposure to folk poetry, he determined that the true structure of the poetic line in Russian is that discovered by the folk. His conclusions about folk verse differed strikingly from those of authorities such as Korsh, who analyzed folk poetry on the basis of metric feet. "Whatever scholars say, it is not [syllabo-]tonic," Bryusov insisted. [13] But neither did he opt for the purely accentual theory

editorial role. The latter has also been reprinted (Berkeley: Berkeley Slavic Specialties, 1983), with my introductory essay describing Dobroljubov's life after his Decadent period: "Aleksandr Dobroljubov and the Invisible Book."

10. *Dnevniki*, p. 45.

11. Gindin, "Iz istorii," p. 100. "O russkom stixosloženii" appeared as the introduction to Dobroljubov's *Sobranie stixov*.

12. Gindin, "Neosuščestvlennyj," p. 194.

13. "O russkom stixosloženii," p. 12 [132]. The term *syllabo-tonic* was adopted after Brjusov's time; *tonic* was then generally used for the standard meters of nineteenth-century poetry.

of the Vostokov school, which viewed word-stress alone as the organizing principle of the line in folk poetry. Instead he formulated a theory that owed something, but not everything, to the ideas of Pavel Golokhvastov, an amateur of folk poetry only part of whose work was published in his lifetime.[14] Golokhvastov also saw stress as the organizing feature of the line, a stress based not on grammar but on sense (*"smyslovoe udarenie"*). The foot, or basic unit, was defined by its embodiment of a single notion. The number of words might then vary, but only one stress was permitted. Like most contemporary students of folk verse, Golokhvastov drew his example from the folk-epic *bylina* form. Bryusov also turned to the *bylina* as the best example of Russian folk poetry, but he adapted Golokhvastov's notion of "sense stress" to his own ideas of what made an effective line of poetry. He declared the unit of measurement for the line to be the "important meaningful expression," for which he unfortunately borrowed the term *image* (*obraz*).[15] These images must stand in important positions in the line so as to distribute the reader's attention and establish his expectations: "The essence of the line is balance of images, and sonority is its coloring."[16] Lines should have equal numbers of images, or at least the number of images in different lines should stand in a definite quantitative relation to each other. All other elements, including rhyme, stress, and sound-pattern, cluster around the images to support and enrich them. This theory results in something close to accentual verse. But Bryusov was interested in more than stress. He was moving toward a theory of the *dol'nik*, the elastic form favored by many twentieth-century Russian poets.[17] The image-principle involved a clustering of all

14. Ibid. In a note to this essay Brjusov referred to P. D. Goloxvastov, "Zakony stixa," *Pamjatnik drevnej pis'mennosti* (St. Petersburg, 1883), and again in a review in *Vesy* no. 10 (1907): 46. Roman Jakobson many years later called Brjusov's theory "a vulgarization (*vul'garizacija*)" of Goloxvastov's ideas: "Brjusovskaja stixologija i nauka o stixe," *Naučnye izvestija* 2 (1922): 236.

15. "O russkom stixosloženii," p. 9 [129].

16. Ibid., p. 11 [131].

17. A. Kvjatkovskij in his *Poetičeskij slovar'* (p. 107) credits Brjusov with

the important elements, including word-stress, at strategic points in the line. Ideally the line was an integrated whole of perfect balance and harmony. Unfortunately, Bryusov provided no specific examples from his own or Dobrolyubov's poems.

While Bryusov chose to derive his theory ostensibly from folk verse, Dobrolyubov's manuscripts and recitations were no doubt simply the catalysts for ideas and intuitions with which he had worked for some time. For example, this theory touched the use of rhyme: if the beginning, middle, and end of the line were the key positions for effective images, then the final position, distinguished by rhyme, had an especially important function. Writing of the verse of Yakov Polonsky, whose approximations of folk songs and Gypsy romances may have influenced the young Blok, Bryusov complained, "The rhyme is not only not an important word, but as if purposely casual. The line is not something whole. It's as if he tried to have the thought pass beyond the rhyme and stop in the middle. . . . Sometimes you may ask yourself why he writes in verse."[18]

The theory that Bryusov worked out in 1898 and published in 1900 reappeared in narrowed and abbreviated form in a note on folk verse in his *The Science of Verse*, published twenty years later. There it was thoroughly ridiculed by the young Formalist Roman

---

introducing the term *dol'nik*, which is generally considered a transitional form between syllabo-tonic and pure tonic or accentual verse. Though exact definitions have differed, the *dol'nik* may be understood as a form with a regular number of stresses per line (or standing in definite relation from line to line) with variable intervals between stresses. Brjusov's definition in *Nauka o stixe* (p. 120) allowed one to three, rarely four, unstressed syllables between. Later theoreticians reduced the permissible range to zero–two. For the more expansive form Kvjatkovskij used the term *taktovik*. M. L. Gasparov calls Brjusov the first of the modernist poets to employ the *dol'nik*: *Sovremennyj russkij stix* (Moscow, 1974), p. 71. He overlooks its earlier use by Zinaida Gippius. In fact, occasional instances can be found even in the work of nineteenth-century poets, most memorably in Tjutčev. Only among the Symbolists, however, was the *dol'nik* developed into an important poetic device.

18.   Gindin, "Neosuščestvlennyj," p. 189. See also p. 195 n. 5.

Jakobson. Bryusov wrote that "many folk songs, among them the most ancient, are founded on a *versification of sense* [*smyslovoe stixosloženie*]. This is based upon the quantity of images, generally significant expressions in the line. Every such expression may be regarded as a foot having one basic stress and an indefinite number of unstressed syllables before and after the stressed one." [19] Jakobson disposed shortly of this theory, as of most of Bryusov's book, as anachronistic. [20] *The Science of Verse* was based on a series of lectures to young proletarians beginning the study of poetry in 1918. No doubt Bryusov did his reputation a disservice by printing these in their original form. The book is a compendium, replete with examples, of poetic terminology, much of it esoteric. As pedagogy it raises grave doubts; as literary theory it was quickly found wanting. And as memorialized by such critics as Jakobson and Boris Tomashevsky, it came to represent the totality of Bryusov's contribution to that field. A reevaluation of that contribution began only decades later, in the work of Victor Erlich, Mikhail Gasparov, and Sergei Gindin. Noting the Formalists' indebtedness to Bryusov, Erlich wrote: "He eschewed the purely acoustic approach to verse and emphasized the close connection between the phonic, semantic and grammatical aspects of poetic language. Brjusov was one of the first Russian students of verse to insist on the importance of 'interverbal pauses' (which the Formalists were to rechristen 'word-boundaries') as a factor in verse rhythm." [21] In retrospect the work of Bryusov appears far from irrelevant to the development of Russian poetic theory, though the Formalists, perhaps reacting against a near predecessor, found it

19.   *Nauka o stixe*, p. 121.
20.   Jakobson, pp. 236–37.
21.   Victor Erlich, *Russian Formalism: History—Doctrine* (third ed. New Haven: Yale University Press, 1981), p. 40. Boris Tomaševskij's review of *Nauka o stixe* appeared in *Kniga i revoljucija* no. 10–11 (1921): 32–34. See later works: M. L. Gasparov, "Brjusov-stixoved i Brjusov-stixotvorec," *Brjusovskie čtenija 1973 goda*, pp. 11–43; S. I. Gindin, "Iz istorii."

unscientific. Furthermore, Bryusov's close attention in his own poetry to the connections among euphonics, stress, and meaning in structuring the line had repercussions other than theoretical. His own practice based on these notions may help account for the electrifying effect his next two books, *Tertia Vigilia* and *Urbi et Orbi*, had on Russia's young poets. Andrei Bely testified to the early importance of Bryusov's lessons in poetic craft for his own work.[22] Thus in the first years of Symbolism Bryusov was a teacher of poets on a less formal basis than he was after 1917, but possibly a more effective one. And his theory of the poetic line, as Erlich has shown, was not without consequence.

Meanwhile, as his ideas expanded, "A History of the Russian Lyric" got badly out of hand. His new views of the roots of Russian versification led Bryusov to an enthusiastic study of the seventeenth century. He studied that period in the spring of 1898, under the historian Klyuchevsky. In October 1899 he drew up what was to be his last plan for the work and wrote a new introduction. In the new literature, he wrote, "there emerge a good many features that can be explained only through similar features in the seventeenth century."[23] But the opening section took on alarming breadth. It began: "I. Moscow in the seventeenth century (1. Streets. 2. Churches. 3. The crowd and street amusements. 4. Court and boyar life. 5. The life of average people). II. Country life. III. Esthetics of the Russian seventeenth century.

22.   Andrej Belyj, *Načalo veka*, pp. 164ff.
23.   Gindin, "Neosuščestvlennyj," p. 201. See also N. S. Ašukin, "Iz kommentariev k stixam Valerija Brjusova (Po neizdannym materialam)," *Brjusovskie čtenie 1963 goda*, pp. 531–37. Ašukin describes Brjusov's fascination with the city of Moscow, past and present, including his plan to draw up a guidebook for the city. The title page was to read, "Moskva v načale XX veka. Ee svjatyni, drevnosti, i sovremennye kartiny. Opisal Valerij Brjusov [Moscow at the beginning of the twentieth century. Her shrines, antiquities, and contemporary pictures. Described by Valerij Brjusov]": (p. 532). See also Brjusov's description of visits to old churches in January 1900 with Konevskoj and the artist Ivan Bilibin: *Dnevniki*, p. 80.

Stimuli to ideas: religion, the schism, art (architecture, painting, music) . . . ." and ran through eleven sections, covering almost every conceivable topic. This lack of focus almost assured the failure of his project. No more is heard of the history of the lyric after 1899. But a considerable amount of material had been prepared for it, and these fragments of the history indeed became the foundation of Bryusov's later literary criticism and research.

The *History of the Russian Lyric* originated in Bryusov's effort to define contemporary Russian poetry and differentiate it from previous stages of the tradition. As early as late 1895 or early 1896, he divided poetry into two types, classical and Symbolist. He later changed the division to "poetry" and "lyric."[24] The first category, "poetry," was meant to embrace all those works for which the writer draws his material from life. Authors whom Bryusov assigned to this category were Turgenev, Lermontov, and, at their head, Pushkin. The other category, "lyric," was considered the domain of writers who draw the content of their works exclusively from their own souls. Here he placed Fet, Dostoevsky, and, chief of them among Russian writers, Tyutchev.[25] Pushkin and Tyutchev were thus the two principals in the unfolding action he was tracing. They, along with Baratynsky and Nekrasov, engaged a large proportion of Bryusov's critical attention in these formative years. The purpose here is not to trace Bryusov's development as a literary critic.[26] It is, rather, to examine his critical perceptions in the crucial years just before 1900 in order to see what they reveal about his poetic values of that time. The esthetic judgments formed then tended to remain fairly constant throughout his career, testifying again to the importance of this period in his esthetic formation.

24. Gindin, "Neosuščestvlennyj," p. 193.
25. Ibid., p. 193 n. 2.
26. This has been done by several authors, including T. J. Binyon, "Valery Bryusov and the Nature of Art," pp. 96–111; D. Maksimov, "Brjusov-kritik," VI, 5–23.

Pushkin—then and always—functioned for Bryusov as a touchstone for every other poet's work. This is less surprising today than it must have seemed in the 1890s. Bryusov's notes and sketches of this period are not particularly informative about which specific features of Pushkin's poems appealed to him. However, the conspectus for the history of the lyric, written in late 1897 or early 1898, not only showed that he allotted to Pushkin the central role in the development of Russian poetry but tried to supply the reasons. One passage is worth quoting at length:

> Almost everything there is in Russian poetry was created or marked out by Pushkin. Possessing a stunning gift of synthesis, he blended all the scattered elements of the new into a single whole, he gave finish to the structure of the Russian language, he created a canon for the Russian poetic line, he pointed out the limits of the far-flung goals of poetry. . . . He had no trouble finding immediately in the Russian language the equivalent of any phenomenon in the Western world. . . . At the same time, immersed more completely than other Russian poets in the world of purely Russian folk art, he showed us the incalculable riches of our native antiquity, gave new life to Russian songs and tales and traditions, and for all of these found as well the appropriate forms which had always suited them. To the Russian poetic line he gave musicality unheard-of before him, and incomparable flexibility, and completely new power. . . . Pushkin proved to us that in the realm of poetry the Russian language is capable of anything; he gave us hundreds of precious models, pointed to thousands of paths into the far distance and bequeathed the command: be bold![27]

In later studies Bryusov's more specific observations bear strikingly on the discoveries he was making in 1898 and 1899. He noted, for example, that after 1830, when Pushkin's genius achieved its greatest scope and freedom, he employed meters drawn from the oral tradition and never before used in formal

27.   Gindin, "Neosuščestvlennyj," p. 200.

Russian poetry. Then he "felt that his rhythmic system was completely liberated from the power of the meter" [VI, 89]. Moreover, Bryusov saw in Pushkin's choice of rhyme words a principle corresponding to that which he set forth in "On Russian Versification." Pushkin, he observed, took special care that the rhyme word was not mere decoration, that it "powerfully supported the general artistic impression, that it moved images to the fore, underlined thoughts, brought out the music in the rhythm" [VI, 92]. He also commented in some detail on Pushkin's effective instrumentation, which not only made for a highly musical line but extended over several lines to give musical texture to the whole poem.[28]

If Pushkin was the overarching ideal, Tyutchev served as exemplar and forerunner of the new poetry, the first Russian Symbolist. (In a later essay Bryusov described Tyutchev's thirst to penetrate the secrets of the universe by nonrational means, which allied him with the Decadents.)[29] In his early, less comprehensive essays on Tyutchev published in *Russian Archive*, his immediate concerns of this period show up vividly. In the 1898 piece he noted Tyutchev's mixing of binary and ternary meters as possibly adopted from the German *Knittelvers*,[30] something which Bryusov had already observed in Lomonosov. In his second, 1900 article, protesting the interpretation of Tyutchev as cut off from things Russian during his long German sojourn, Bryusov underlined his interest in Old Russian literature and folklore.[31]

Another article from 1900 is entitled "Nekrasov and Tyutchev," with emphasis on the former.[32] In Nekrasov, from very early on

28. VI, 95ff., and also the article "Zvukopis' Puškina," [VI, 127–48].

29. "F. I. Tjutčev. Smysl ego tvorčestva," VI, 193–208.

30. "O sobranii sočinenii F. I. Tjutčeva," *Russkij arxiv* no. 10 (1898): 255.

31. "Po povodu novogo izdanija sočinenij F. I. Tjutčeva," *Russkij arxiv* no. 3 (1900): 409.

32. *Russkij arxiv* no. 2, (1900), 312–15. In his diary for 18 December 1899 Brjusov noted a vexing error in *Russkij arxiv*: a poem of Nekrasov's had been attributed to Tjutčev. For this reason he had written a brief article in which

an important poet for Bryusov, he admired the perfect adaptation
of meter to content and the freedom of line recalling folk song.
Among Nekrasov's themes Bryusov singled out his pictures of the
northern city, a point of relevance to the urban themes soon to
appear in Bryusov's *Tertia Vigilia*.[33]

One other nineteenth-century poet, Eugene Baratynsky, assumed prominence in Bryusov's thinking about poetry in these
years. Bryusov deserves major credit for reclaiming Baratynsky's
reputation and placing him in the front ranks of poets for twentieth-century Russian readers. He had performed the same service
for Tyutchev and was soon to do so for the nearly forgotten
Karolina Pavlova. His work on the *History of the Russian Lyric* and
his researches for *Russian Archive* under the tutelage of that living
archive of literature Peter Bartenev, helped greatly in giving his
critical intuitions a firm and independent basis. His publications
in that venerable journal were a first step toward challenging the
views established in mid-century by Vissarion Belinsky and his
followers in the civic school of criticism and still propounded in
the serious journals. In his summer 1897 outline for the history

---

he had insisted "that Nekrasov is much more like Tjutčev than is usually
thought" (*Dnevniki*, p. 78). The fault was Brjusov's own, but it was mitigated,
since the table of contents listed the authorship of "Na pojavlenie anglijskogo
flota pod Peterburgom (1854)" as "Tjutčev(?)." Moreover, the mistake was
understandable, given the similarity of the sentiments in the poem, dated
14 June 1854, to those expressed in a letter from Tjutčev on 19 June 1854.
Russkij arxiv had published a long series of Tjutčev's letters in its 1898 and 1899
numbers, translated by Brjusov from the original French. At the end of that
series Brjusov had published a Tjutčev poem that had been omitted from all the
collected works: "N. F. Ščerbine," *Russkij arxiv* no. 11 (1899): 436. Whatever
his motivation, Brjusov did Nekrasov criticism a service by pointing to aspects
of his poetry that had long been ignored.
33.   Brjusov later devoted an article to this theme: "N. A Nekrasov kak
poèt goroda," *Russkie vedomosti* no. 297 (25 December 1912): 3 (cited from *Bibliografija*). The topic of Brjusov's views on Nekrasov has been thoroughly treated by
S. I. Gindin, "Brjusov o Nekrasove" (Kostroma, 1974), pp. 57–80, and a second article of the same title (Jaroslavl', 1975), pp. 101–128.

Bryusov allotted a section to Baratynsky's book *Twilight*.[34] While crediting Baratynsky with a high mastery of verse technique, Bryusov was drawn primarily to another aspect of his poetry. Significantly, in the 1897 outline he placed the discussion of *Twilight* in the same chapter with the discussion of Tyutchev's poems. In an earlier letter to Pertsov, Bryusov had written: "A poet's world-view appears in his works any time he begins to reason in verse. But this has little to do with the essence of poetry. . . . In poetry there is something else—a special attitude toward the world, to oneself, to the unattainable; and this is the real philosophy of poetry."[35] Among those few poets in which these two elements coincide he put Tyutchev and Baratynsky. In October 1898 Bryusov wrote a piece entitled "Baratynsky's World View" [VI, 35–42] (never published in his lifetime), which showed considerable originality and penetration. The first critic to establish the periods in Baratynsky's development, Bryusov traced his growth from youthful epicureanism and a pose of romantic disillusion, through a long period of real despair, to the beginnings of a new stage in *Twilight*. After long yearning for the time when human nature might be changed and the spirit freed from its trammels, Baratynsky turned toward religion. But the new outlook had no time to flower before his sudden death in 1844. Bryusov enlarged on an idea propounded by another critic: "Baratynsky's development is the story of our society's development, only Baratynsky passed through all stages more speedily."[36] This parallel reflected Bryusov's hope that the new trends in art presaged Russia's imminent emergence from cultural stagnation.

"Baratynsky is original with us because he thinks": Bryusov opened his essay with this remark of Pushkin's. Writing at the height of his own attraction to philosophy, Bryusov felt the poet in him almost stifled by this competing preoccupation. Bara-

34. *Sumerki* (1842); Gindin, "Neosuščestvlennyj," p. 196.
35. *Percovu*, pp. 73–74.
36. VI, 42. For likely sources see VI, 578.

tynsky was a poet who seemed to have combined the two attractions fruitfully. Weighing the poet-thinker against the poet of spontaneous creation, Bryusov wrote: "The poet of direct inspiration of course opens his soul more fully before his readers, but no one more faithfully than the poet-thinker acquaints them with his understanding of the world, with that which he considers his own truth" [VI, 35]. Later, in 1900 and 1901, he engaged in a public polemic over whether Pushkin had used Baratynsky as a model for Salieri in his drama *Mozart and Salieri*.[37] While in print he stoutly denied any similarity, Bryusov was nonetheless intrigued by the contrast between two types of artist. The subject subsequently had implications for himself, notably in his relations with Balmont.

Other aspects of Baratynsky interested Bryusov at that time. Baratynsky's tendency to set his narrative poems not in distant or romantic settings but in society and even on the streets, supported Bryusov's own interest in urban and contemporary themes soon to be manifested in *Tertia Vigilia*. Finally, he found support in Baratynsky for his conviction that all subjects and emotions are equally suitable for poetry. It was a major point on which he had differed with Tolstoy.

Other nineteenth-century poets, notably Lermontov and Fet, at various times played important roles in Bryusov's self-definition as a poet or in the development of his craft. In this formative period, the poets discussed above were his dominant influences. And at least three contemporaries—through personal association as much as through their work—markedly affected his values and notions concerning poetry. One of these, Dobrolyubov, has already been discussed. The two remaining are Konstantin Balmont and Ivan Konevskoy.

37.   "Baratynskij i Sal'eri," *Russkij arxiv* No. 8 (1900), pp. 537–45; "Puškin i Baratynskij," *Russkij arxiv* No. 1 (1901), pp. 158–64, "Staroe o g-ne Ščeglove," *Russkij arxiv* No. 12 (1901), pp. 574–79. His opponent was I. Ščeglov, author of works on Puškin.

"Konevskoy" was a pen name adopted by Ivan Oreus when his father, a retired general, objected to the family name being associated with Decadent poetry.[38] Bryusov met Konevskoy, four years his junior, on his trip to Petersburg in December 1898.[39] After hearing him recite one evening at Sologub's, he sought him out, discussed with him the newest French poets, collected a bundle of Dobrolyubov's papers deposited with him—and confessed afterward that they did not hit it off well. A month later Balmont came to Moscow with three notebooks of Konevskoy's poetry. The two read, reread, copied, and memorized, and Bryusov wrote Konevskoy an ecstatic letter.[40] Out of this new acquaintance, apparently, grew Balmont's idea for a joint book publication. Originally he invited several others to contribute, including Sologub and Zinaida Gippius, but in the end the participants in *A Book of Meditations* were only four: Balmont, Bryusov, Konevskoy, and the artist Modest Durnov.

According to most reports, Konevskoy was not an attractive personality. Yet Bryusov, drawn to him as a poet, made allowances for his arrogance and his dogmatic pronouncements. When he came to Moscow in September 1899 for two weeks, Bryusov went far out of his way to be the perfect host. When Konevskoy's book *Dreams and Thoughts* came out late in 1899, Bryusov pronounced these poems to be among the most remarkable literary phenomena of the time.[41] There were other contacts, in person and by letter. Then in the summer of 1901 Konevskoy accidentally drowned in a river near Riga. This shocking event left

38. The fullest biographical sketch of Konevskoj was contributed by Brjusov to Vengerov, *Russkaja literatura XX veka 1890–1910*, 3, pp. 150–63. His family was of Swedish extraction, and his geographical pseudonym referred to this northern origin.

39. *Dnevniki*, p. 57.

40. Ibid., p. 60. See letter of 26 January 1899, published with four others which throw light on the relationship: Valentin Dmitriev, *V. Brjusov i literatura konca XIX–XX veka* (Stavropol', 1979), pp. 139–42.

41. *Dnevniki*, p. 78.

Bryusov feeling extraordinarily alone as a poet. He felt deeply the loss of Konevskoy's talent. Moreover, now there was no one, he wrote to Anna Shesterkina, from whom he could expect full understanding and valuable criticism.[42] In the next few years he wrote several pieces on Konevskoy that go some way toward explaining what in Konevskoy's approach to poetry so struck him. Konevskoy had little interest in the technical matters that engrossed Bryusov at the time of their meeting. For him Konevskoy was a poet of thought, a living successor to Baratynsky, and his attitude toward literature was more reverent even than Bryusov's. Moreover, he was a Decadent. In the essay "Wise Child" [VI, 242–49], Bryusov wrote that like all adherents of the new art, Konevskoy sought power and freedom, but the boundaries he wanted to overcome were not the usual moral ones or the conventions of poetry. His rebellion was against man's enslavement to the spiritual and physical conditions of life itself—heredity, the spirit's dependence on the body. "He sensed that our life, our being, is only one of many possible varieties, that the basis of our earthly, bodily existence is the spirit" [VI, 246]. While many of Konevskoy's ideas held little interest for Bryusov, they both wanted to escape from what they perceived as the narrowness of man's present horizons. And for both, the mode of escape was intuition, exercised through art and in exploration of the poet's own soul.

Finally, and always, there was Balmont. When Bryusov rejected the ideal of poetry embodied in *Me eum esse*, he was rejecting the ideas that he and Balmont together had developed and cherished. Balmont was absent from Moscow from fall 1896 till nearly the end of 1897. That year, eventful for both, had sent them in new and divergent directions. Yet Bryusov found the pull of old attractions and of Balmont's personal persuasiveness

42. *LN* 85, p. 647.

unsettling when their reunion came. For both it was an occasion for mixed emotions. Balmont had written ecstatically to Bryusov from abroad that in all Russia only Bryusov was necessary to him. "Of course the original is not the same as the dream!" wrote Bryusov in his diary.[43] Moreover, he knew that in Balmont's eyes he was guilty of infidelity. Bryusov had paid his tribute to the muse of pure beauty in *Me eum esse*; Balmont was now preparing his own statement in the collection to be entitled *Stillness*.[44] In *Me eum esse* the poet-persona had exchanged thralldom to passion for ascetic pursuit of unearthly beauty. But he had returned to the earth to face the task of sustaining his artistic vision in mundane surroundings. Subsequently for Bryusov the ideal itself, as we have seen, underwent changes. Meanwhile Balmont continued to preach spiritual withdrawal into regions beyond the reach of human noise and struggle. Recent acquaintance with Mme Blavatsky's *The Voice of the Silence* offered him further support for an already ingrained set of attitudes.[45] Words of true wisdom, he learned, are heard only by the one who unites himself with the "Silent Speaker." Several of the most striking poems in *Stillness* describe a translation of once-living beings into a state presumably superior, where they no longer live or breathe but *are*, in splendid, immobile isolation. The opening poem, called "Rebirth," describes Arizona's petrified forest: "Fragments of ancient things are inflamed with new dreams." The remarkable long poem "Dead Ships," with its reminiscences of Coleridge's Ancient Mariner and Poe's Arthur Gordon Pym, shows proud explorers whose quest for new secrets takes them toward the Pole. There the ships and their masters become skeletons trapped in eternal snow and ice. The book's final poem, "Star of the Desert," pre-

---

43. *Dnevniki*, p. 30.

44. *Tišina* (St. Petersburg, 1898).

45. Vladimir Markov, "Balmont: A Reappraisal," *Slavic Review* 28, 2 (June 1969): 229.

sents the vision a faithful listener and watcher may expect: "Beyond the heavens opened the Heaven of heavens."[46]

For Bryusov this line of thought was fundamentally unsound. After their reunion in late 1897 he wrote that Balmont wanted him "splendidly dead and sad." But, he exclaimed, "I have come alive, I live."[47] Yet *Stillness* exerted its charm on him at first reading, arousing self-doubts and, above all, nostalgia. When Balmont came to Moscow in fall 1898, the two roamed the nighttime streets trying to recapture the spirit of former days. "Strange," Bryusov wrote, "the voice of Balmont more readily than anything else returns the past to me."[48] When Balmont left Moscow again, Bryusov felt the loss to the life of his imagination. He also lamented the loss of his best critic, for he had not yet met Konevskoy.

Warm relations between Bryusov and Balmont continued for some time, even while they recognized their differences. Balmont was one of the few who greeted *About Art* enthusiastically. Immediately after receiving his congratulatory letter in December 1898, Bryusov went to Petersburg. There Balmont introduced him to the established poets of the capital. This acquaintance

46. The poems in question are "Vozroždenie," "Mertvye korabli," and "Zvezda pustyni." Brjusov considered "Mertvye korabli" a model for a new direction for the *poèma*, a form beloved by the Romantics.

47. *Dnevniki*, p. 31. The relations between Brjusov and Bal'mont in these years are described extensively but not especially reliably by A. Ninov, "Tak žili poèty," *Neva* no. 6 (1978): 94–129; no. 7 (1978): 86–134. Ninov's article is not referenced and he makes considerable use of unpublished material, so it is difficult to separate his own surmises from conclusions that have a documentary base. Doubt is cast on the article's reliability by the fact that the author bases a discussion of *Tertia Vigilia* at its first appearance on poems that did not appear in the first edition of that book (no. 6, pp. 121–22). A better-documented recent source is T. Kovaleva, "Valerij Brjusov o Bal'monte (K istorii vzaimootnošenij v 90-e gody)," in *V. Brjusov i literatura konca XIX–XX veka*, pp. 53–61. In the same volume are six letters (ed. Valentin Dmitriev) from Brjusov to Bal'mont from 1897 to 1907, pp. 133–39.

48. *Dnevniki*, p. 31.

with a wider circle had important consequences for Bryusov's later range of activities. The visit also started the train of events leading to publication a few months later of the collective project initiated by Balmont, *A Book of Meditations*, for it was at this time that Bryusov met Konevskoy. Bryusov returned to Petersburg the following March for six days of what must have been intensive work on the project. The book was passed by the St. Petersburg censor on March 26.

A Book of Meditations may be a unique example, at least in Russian, of a dialogue in which two major poets poetically and polemically set forth their opposing views on art and life.[49] The four poets who contributed to the volume were represented unequally. The book opens with two cycles by Balmont, "Lyrics of Thought" and "Symbols of Mood," consisting of ten poems each. Bryusov provided eighteen poems, Konevskoy sixteen, and Modest Durnov five. Balmont's first cycle opens with a statement of the ground he shared with Bryusov: "In souls is found all that exists in heaven and much besides. . . . Only one boundlessness I love, / My soul!" However, the cycle quickly turns to an expression of his recently developed interest in Eastern thought. The key poem is "Maya," which advances the notion that life as it appears to the uninitiated is indeed a dream, conjured up, as it were, by a yogi in his cave.[50] Other images in the cycle convey the contingency of what ordinary mortals call life: "Life is the reflection of the moon's face in the water"; with all its ecstasies and glitter it is "the dream of another dream." Certain poems show him attempting to reconcile extreme individualism with Eastern wisdom:

49. *Kniga razdumij* (St. Petersburg, 1899), K. D. Bal'mont, Valerij Brjusov, Modest Durnov, Iv. Konevskoj (reprinted Letchworth, Herts.: Prideaux Press, 1974). For Brjusov's and Bal'mont's poems included in this volume, see Appendix C.
50. K. D. Bal'mont, *Stixotvorenija*, ed. Vl. Orlov (second ed. Leningrad, 1969), pp. 196–97. Other Bal'mont poems contained in *Kniga razdumij* and listed in the appendix are keyed to this volume.

"The world is one, but in that world eternally are two. He, the Unmoving, He, the Unthirsting—and I." [51]

While the first cycle states Balmont's poetic and philosophical stance generally, his second cycle is explicitly directed toward Bryusov. Indeed, this second cycle turns out on careful reading to combine with the first ten of Bryusov's poems to form a unified whole. Read antiphonally, they unfold the same polemic between the two poets that emerges in fragments in their letters and reminiscences. Here it appears in poetry—its proper form, so to speak. Exact dates are not available for the composition of Balmont's poems, but Bryusov's were written over a period of more than two years, without any obligatory thematic links between them except his general "pilgrim's progress." Yet, arranged as they are in this book in relation to the other poet's poems, they develop a second set of meanings. This fact constitutes a striking instance of the cyclical principle as Bryusov practiced it. This work is a tour de force both of cyclization and of communication of the sort the Symbolists loved.

Balmont's first poem in the exchange shows the final ray of light at sunset as it touches the valley briefly before departure for "the eternal heights / Where there are no grasses, no dreams, no fragrance." The poem ends with an exclamation that establishes the metaphor: "Oh, yes, I recall! I was once alive!" Like the ray, the poet's spirit has left the grasslands for loftier spaces where the things of earth are not; life's random charms are no longer his concern. The poem was dedicated to Bryusov, whose opening poem, reciprocating the dedication, was written in the same verse form. Composed the December night Bryusov arrived in Petersburg, his poem begins: "I fear not Night or Winter." Full of

---

51.   In early January 1899, Bal'mont came to Moscow. There he read his lecture "Kal'deronovskaja drama ličnosti" (*Gornye veršini* [Moscow, 1904], pp. 26–42). In this essay Bal'mont seemed to reject the tenet that "life is a dream" and the parallel message of *The Voice of the Silence* insofar as they contradicted individualism. It may be possible to see the effect of Brjusov's arguments here.

optimism, it is addressed to one who shares the dark and cold. To him the poet offers fellowship of spirit and hope of coming bliss. But Balmont's second poem tells his brother poet that earthly joy and love are not for them: "Dear brother, you and I — / We are only Beauty's dreams," drops of dew in the eternal chalices of flowers that will not wilt in gardens that will not die. The sentiment, like the image, recalls Balmont's involvement with Shelley, who in "The Sensitive Plant" wrote of a life "Where nothing is, but all things seem, / And we the shadows of the dream." In Balmont's thought, poets are not creators but mere reflectors of unearthly beauty.

Bryusov's second poem responds in a more active tone. The poet's duty is to his own soul and to life: "The ways of perfection are endless, / O preserve every instant of being!" For Bryusov the flight into boundlessness is purposeful. Balmont's reply evokes another kind of boundlessness, the sea, where the poets are pictured as mere shadows on the waves, never reaching the shore. In his third poem Bryusov challenges the disdain for life that he finds in Balmont's poems. Here he addresses both the first and the third poems of Balmont's cycle. "We are brothers to all things," Bryusov's poet chants; we embrace all those grasses and sensations deserted by the "last ray." Rather than ripples on a boundless sea, "We are flowing waters / On the spaces of nature." In short, Bryusov is on the side of "life"; he urges fellowship of kindred spirits in the search for brighter, fuller being on this earth. But Balmont warns what may await the searchers. His fourth poem, in the spirit of "Dead Ships," shows them sailing "without end, without end," until they find a truth that blinds and reduces them to "sleeping phantoms," who never know they have reached their goal. This horrifying picture is one that Bryusov cannot counter directly. Instead, he responds with his "Still to hope is madness." Composed in the near-despair of May 1897, here it serves another purpose. For him, even despair does not cut one off from human company. "Make peace, submit and understand," he admonishes. Let your union with men be sealed. They too will in time grow to understand; be patient and wait. Balmont's answer is the famous "Scorpion," in which the poet flaunts his outcast state, refuses to submit, and insists that he will perish like the scorpion, proud, free and untamed. But Bryusov reiterates his previous admonition, reminding his interlocutor that "For the chosen there are years of silence."

In Bryusov's vision thus far, poets are an elite company who must endure their trials together. For Balmont the poet is essentially alone. His sixth poem, "The South Pole of the Moon," is a dazzling statement of his image of the poet's spiritual homeland: lifeless, barren, brilliant, beyond petty humanity. Here the poet can penetrate to "the unimaginable life of beauty" with the merciless clarity of vision his isolation gives him. Bryusov now counters with his own secret, which sustains him in times of darkness. The intensely lyrical "Not colors, not rays, nor fragrances" is written in the same meter and verse form as the opening poems of both cycles and uses a line from Balmont's first poem to emphasize the link. The first stanza has no verb, but consists of a series of negations: neither colors, nor rays, nor fragrances, nor many-colored fish nor wilted roses, nor even dreams of debauch, nor tears. None of these images which have appeared in his own past poems is essential to his song. The torrent of harmonies carries away all words and images, and the very darkness gives comfort: what is essential is the sheer joy of creating the poem.

Balmont's four remaining poems pursue his theme of withdrawal from life. The image of paschal boughs is interpreted as evoking not resurrection but "easeful death." A swan swims away in the moonlight and draws the poet's soul after him. Finally, brightly sad angels in disgrace stand at a tomb, presumably the poet's, his soul having gone on to other realms. Bryusov, on the other hand, uses his last four poems to bid farewell to the Muse they both once followed, and to chart his present course. "Once I struggled and grieved, / But now I wait" was a poem fresh from the author's pen, dated January 1899. It ends with a gust of Balmontian alliteration and an allusion to the waves of Balmont's third poem. The poet has won his battle with the waves: "Tak menja— / Bezvol'no volna / Voznosit v vys'.—Thus the wave carries me will-lessly upward." The next poem, "I could die with secret joy," confesses occasional nostalgia for the old ways. The final pair, while harkening back to the Muse glimpsed in *Me eum esse*, affirm his new intentions. This early Muse seems to be identified directly with Balmont in the tenth poem. That this is a translation of Maeterlinck's "Et s'il revenait un jour" is especially appropriate, given Balmont's devotion to Maeterlinck.[52] It is in effect a message to Balmont and to that earlier Muse that the partner is no longer waiting.

Bryusov's eight remaining poems are a showcase of his best recent poetry. At first it seems odd that he should have simply added them to a clearly self-contained cycle of ten. However, the logic becomes clear once one has grasped the argument he has urged on Balmont: the poet's place is everywhere, in life, in history, in the reaches of thought and fancy. Balmont opened his contribution with a cycle stating his position; Bryusov closes not with a cycle but a series, a deliberately open-ended form. Of course neither Bryusov's predilection for "life" nor Balmont's for "death" can be taken at face value. Among Decadents, Balmont's viewpoint was the more common, though his espousal of Eastern philosophy was relatively original.[53] However, Bryusov was not arguing for "realistic" poetry devoted to themes and scenes from ordinary life. It is one of the curious aspects of that loosely de-

52. Bal'mont had recommended Maeterlinck to Brjusov (*Dnevniki*, p. 24). Later, in *Vesy* no. 2 (1905): 1–12, Bal'mont published a study of Maeterlinck entitled, "Tajna odinočestva i smerti."

53. Brjusov had noted very early Bal'mont's preoccupation with death (*Percovu*, pp. 59–60). This topic was treated by Ellen Chances, "Bal'mont—Poet of the Existential Void," *Russian Language Journal* 31, no. 110 (1977): 65–75.

fined attitude called Decadence that it contained, as well as the more generally noted infatuation with the morbid and the life-negating, also the positive, future-oriented aspect represented by Bryusov.[54] This was the aspect Bryusov expressed with such excitement in the final paragraphs of *About Art*. And it was this that he urged upon Balmont.

Of Bryusov's series of eight poems, several later reappeared in the *Tertia Vigilia* cycle called "Favorites of the Ages," that gallery of great spiritual explorers. Among those poems which did not reappear, two are especially relevant to his formal concerns discussed earlier in this chapter. And both illustrate the way the poet's inspiration works with the humble images that life supplies. The first poem grew directly out of concern for the poetic line and its relation to folk poetry. "For the New Bell," later renamed "The Almsgatherers' Song," was written soon after Dobrolyubov's visit in August 1898, and its first recitations caused consternation. "Gentlemen! This is the question: is this a search for new ways or something else?" shouted one listener.[55] "But if that will do, we'll wind up putting the songs of beggars into our verses!" exclaimed another.[56] Bryusov did not bother to explain that this was exactly what he had done. In fact, his notebook for that period contained several pages of such transcriptions, along with notes on their prosodic features.[57] And very soon, in *Tertia Vigilia*, he would show much more fully his interest in contemporary urban folk verse.

The second poem, which listeners found markedly experimental in form, was "Demons of Dust" [I, 209]. (This poem reap-

54. See Chapter Three, footnote 36, and Introduction.
55. *Dnevniki*, p. 55. The speaker was S. A. Safonov, a minor poet and belletrist a few years older than Brjusov.
56. Ibid., p. 50. The speaker was Brjusov's "half-friend, half-poet" Kursinskij. Brjusov's reaction was "O Sancta simplicitas!"
57. Ašukin, *Brjusovskie čtenija 1963 goda*, p. 535.

peared in the section "Little Book for Children" in later editions
of *Tertia Vigilia*.)

> Est' démony pýli,
> Kak démony snéga i svéta.
> Est' démony pýli!
> Ix odéžda bagránogo cvéta,
>   Gorít ognëm.
>   No sérym plaščëm
> Oní's usméškoj eë zakrýli.

> There are demons of dust,
> Like demons of snow and of light.
> There are demons of dust!
> Their garments of crimson hue
>   Burn like flame.
>   But with a gray cloak
> They cover them, with ironical smiles.

The demons of dust hide in cupboards, lie in corners, "recalling
in their sleep that they have conquered." And eventually they
will be monarchs of all. It is an intricately structured poem of
four seven-line stanzas. The number of stresses per line varies
from two (in the four short lines of each stanza) to four, including
secondary ones, in the longest, but the distribution in lines is
constant from stanza to stanza. On the other hand, the number of
syllables per line varies from four to twelve, and the pattern is
different in each stanza. The rhyme-scheme is ABABccA, and
rhyme A is constant throughout all stanzas. Repetitions and
sound-orchestration reinforce the poem's structure. Technically a
poem of mixed binary and ternary meters, the interplay of fixed
and variable elements in "Demons of Dust" suggests a freer form.
At a reading in Petersburg the poem had great success, even with
Dmitri Merezhkovsky. Impressed by the poem (and perhaps by its
reception by his fellow poets), Konstantin Sluchevsky invited

Bryusov to contribute it to a volume being prepared for the Push-kin centenary. "That was unwise on his part," Bryusov observed, suspecting that on closer inspection Sluchevsky, or perhaps his fellow editors, would find the poem formally too bold.[58] He was right: the poem was rejected on these grounds.

This rejection gave Bryusov the opportunity to make a state-ment to members of the literary establishment in Petersburg set-ting forth his new convictions about the appropriate form for Russian poetry. He wrote to Sluchevsky that, first of all, he did not accept the notion that meters should be learned from a text-book, that he judged his own poems not by their literal confor-mity to one meter or another but by their sound. His main point went further:

> Studying our popular poetry I have come to the conclusion that the German syllabo-tonic line is not suitable to the Russian language, or at least no more suitable than the Polish-French syllabic line. Folk songs are composed without the wearying and monotonous alterna-tion of stress with equal intervals of unstressed syllables. Syllabo-tonic verse is dear to us because Pushkin, Baratynsky, and Tyutchev used it, but it is alien, borrowed. And this is felt. We handle it much more timidly and observe its rules much more exactly than do the Germans and the English, to whom it is native. As far as I am con-cerned, I would like to bring my verse close to the truly Russian, to that which the folk discovered, meditating for centuries on how to compose its songs most harmoniously.[59]

In his defense of this poem Bryusov stops short of his notion of the line being measured by "images." He may have felt that a less daring argument had a better chance of acceptance, as indeed time shows it had.

By the middle of 1899 Bryusov had come out on the other side

58.   *Dnevniki*, p. 65.
59.   Letter to Konstantin Slučevskij, 26 March 1899, *Literaturnyj kritik* no. 10–11 (1939): 235.

of the long period of travail and uncertainty that had afflicted him ever since the completion of *Me eum esse*. That spring he took his final examinations at the university and received his degree. His diary account of the weeks just preceding shows that, beside the struggling poet, the budding man of letters, and the bold new rebel in art, Bryusov's personality accommodated another facet: the student who worried over Old Church Slavic and Russian history and celebrated success together with his classmates. After all this he joined his wife and family in another vacation trip to the Crimea. Looking back, it seemed to him that not only his personal happiness but also his success had begun about the time of his marriage. His first publications, his acquaintance with the world of poets in Petersburg, his passing of the exams (for which he admitted he was woefully unprepared—not hard to believe in the light of his other activities): all of this added up to a new epoch in his life.[60] Again, frightened by his happiness, he invoked Polycrates.

He felt himself at last ready to begin his real work. He had finished more than one course. While he would have felt keenly the disgrace of failure at his university exams, his education there seemed to him of little value, especially when compared to that other education in the school of poetry he had also completed. This school had imposed greater trials, but the rewards were greater. He turned now to exploring the sum of what he had learned in that school. Released from the vow of abstention from poetry he had laid upon himself in November 1897 and to which —with the exception of *A Book of Meditations*—he had largely been faithful, he was now ready to reenter formally the ranks of publishing poets.

60. *Dnevniki*, pp. 73–74.

SEVEN

The Third Watch

ON 19 JUNE 1900 Bryusov wrote to Anna
Shesterkina in Moscow:

> I am on the shore of that sea which the Varangians sailed of yore, I
> am on the cliffs where ruins of the bandit nests of the Knights of the
> Order are still visible, I am in the cathedrals which have come down
> to us from the Middle Ages, in the venerable sharp-gabled buildings
> of the triumphant burghers of the sixteenth and seventeenth cen-
> turies. . . . The past has a strange hold on me.[1]

Bryusov and his wife spent June and July 1900 near the quiet
Baltic city of Reval (Tallin), where he was both fascinated and
amused by modern German *Akkuratesse* against the background of
a heroic past. To Manya Shiryaeva he wrote marvelling at the order, "which it is useless to dream of in even the best Moscow
hotels. There is no dust, everything is in its place: every drawer
locks, the loop for every hook is whole; there is a doily under
every glass, etc., etc."[2] At first the Bryusovs adopted a routine
almost Germanic.[3] In the mornings he translated the *Aeneid;*
in the afternoons they sat in the park and read, and in the evenings he worked on his autobiography. At the beginning of July,
Peter Bartenev and his daughter arrived, and life changed. The

1. Letter to Anna Šesterkina, *LN* 85, p. 624.
2. V. S. Dronov, "Pis'ma Valerija Brjusova k Marii Pavlovne Širjaevoj,"
Russkaja literatura i Kavkaz (Stavropol', 1974), p. 109.
3. *Dnevniki*, p. 88–89.

eighty-one-year-old editor and publisher of *Russian Archive*, besides being a living source of literary history, turned out to be an extremely lively and sociable man. Moreover, he knew how to exploit a work force when it was at hand. In no time both Bryusov and his wife were copying his journal material for the printers. Bryusov had already published seven short pieces on Russian poets in *Russian Archive*, and after this summer probation he was taken on as Bartenev's assistant, an arrangement which lasted until 1902. This internship established a modest beginning for Bryusov's published literary scholarship.

It was a summer of stock-taking. Bryusov's third volume of poems, *Tertia Vigilia*, had been sent off to the censor.[4] During these months he was preparing an autobiography for simultaneous publication with the poems.[5] As fully convinced as ever that a poet's life and work are inseparable, he desired to give an account of himself as he reached his maturity as a poet. Indeed there was reason to do this, given the close connection between his biography and his poetry, but the autobiographical genre may not have seemed adequate to the task. The plan was abandoned, and the burden fell on the poetry itself.

Passing university examinations in spring 1899 meant for Bryusov in some sense drawing a line beneath the events of his career so far. This is paradoxical in that he had apparently paid relatively little attention to his formal university courses over the

4. Jurij Bartenev, Petr's son, had just been named Moscow censor. Brjusov considered the cuts severe and called Bartenev's comments on the manuscript "curious" (*Dnevniki*, p. 89). However, the censor's copy preserved in IRLI shows to what extent Bartenev saved his book from still greater butchery. The first censor, appropriately named Ostroglazov ("of the sharp eyes"), wielded his pencil with abandon, but in many cases Bartenev overrode him. The poem "Christmas," inoffensive and orthodox as it seems, was cut out by one censor, restored by Bartenev, and sent on to the ecclesiastical censor. It finally appeared in the book (IRLI, fond 444, no. 11).

5. It appeared posthumously as "Moja junost'. Povest'," in the volume *Iz moej žizni*, pp. 9–85.

last several years. He had taken six years, 1893 to 1899, to complete his degree with first honors in the historical-philological faculty.[6] His early concentration had been on classical philology, with considerable time given to philosophy as well, but his formal specialization was history. Yet from his own record it seems that much of his energy went into education of a less formal sort, at best co-curricular. As we have seen, his single-minded goal was to be a poet in the fullest sense of the word. Seemingly, he could not give himself comfortably or steadily to writing poems while questions about the nature and form of poetry remained unsettled in his mind. The last three years of his university studies were years of vigorous working-out of satisfying answers in these matters. The two processes of maturation, literary-poetic and academic-intellectual, moved at their own paces but were completed simultaneously. It would be curious if his whole career had awaited a signal from the degree-granting authorities of Moscow University. Other explanations for the coincidence seem more reasonable. Bryusov had prolonged his stay at the university well beyond the normal four years, for reasons that may not have been completely clear to himself. It might be argued that some aspect of his studies was feeding the poet in him, or that he was unready to face the external question of a career until he had reached some internal conclusions on the same matter. At any rate, by mid-1899 he was ready to add up the items in the column of experience, failures, missteps, and achievements, and, finding a positive total, to invest that sum in his future.

The next few months were devoted first to rest, then to explorations of various sorts. The family vacationed in the Crimea again in the summer of 1899. A plan to spend winter 1899–

6.   In his "Avtobiografija" Brjusov stated that he spent five years in the university, but he also erred in saying that he finished Polivanov's gymnasium in 1892, not 1893, and he correctly gave 1899 as his year of completion of his university course. Other authors have accepted his statement regarding the five years.

1900 in Germany was displaced by a project fateful for both Bryusov's future and that of Russian Symbolism.[7] That summer Balmont introduced Bryusov to the young Lithuanian poet Jurgis Baltrušaitis and to Sergei Polyakov. Polyakov came from a wealthy merchant family engaged in manufacturing. Trained as a mathematician, he knew several languages, translated Hamsun, Nietzsche, Przybyszewski—in short, he was totally engrossed in esthetic matters while other relatives added to the family millions. With his new artistic friends Bryusov, Balmont, and Baltrušaitis, Polyakov established Scorpio, devoted to publishing the best of modernist literature, Russian and Western, in appropriately elegant form. In Bryusov he found an associate with the energy and special talents for realizing this idea. By the end of 1899 Scorpio was in business, and among its early publications was *Tertia Vigilia*.

By 1900 Bryusov was ready for new, expanded activity. An amazing flow of self-confidence, strength, and assurance—some would call it arrogance—had come out of the travail of the last several years. However, he had fought personal intellectual battles with his whole university education in history and philosophy and was now satisfied that his own position was tenable.[8] He was not especially grateful for what he had received. For him the uses of history were not those advanced by the academic world. Just before his examinations he complained in a letter to Samygin that the rush of preparation left no time to think deeply about the pa-

7.   Ioanna Brjusova, "Materialy k biografii Valerija Brjusova," in *Valerij Brjusov, Izbrannye stixi,* pp. 130–31.

8.   Professors of the history faculty of Moscow University in Brjusov's time were likely to have received their own formation during the historiographical debates of the 1860s, which centered on free will and determinism. Especially prominent was Vladimir Guerrier, whose "Očerk razvitija istoričeskoj nauki" appeared in the journal *Russkij vestnik* in 1865. An account of the state of ideas on history in that period is given by Boris Ejxenbaum, *Lev Tolstoj,* 2 vols. (Leningrad, 1928–1931), 2, pp. 318ff. (reprinted Munich: Wilhelm Fink Verlag, 1968).

rade of "emperors, ages, peoples" that marched before his eyes.
He resented rote memorization of facts and arguments to support
positions with which he could not agree. Moreover, he resisted a
conclusion that went against his own convictions. If history is a
science, he complained to Samygin, then there is no room for the
dominant personality; necessity rules. But, he concluded triumphantly, "I know another truth, to which I have come by another path. Both are true. There are many truths, and often they
contradict one another. One must accept this and understand."[9]
He and Samygin had often exchanged views of this sort. Now he
continued, "Yes, I have had this in mind for a long time. Our
striving for unity of forces or principles or truth has seemed comic
to me. My dream has always been the pantheon, the temple of all
gods. Let us pray there to both day and night, to both Mithra and
Adonis, to Christ and to the Devil. The 'I' is the central point
where all differences pale and all limits are reconciled. The first
commandment (although lower) is love of oneself and worship of
oneself. Credo."

This seems like pure Nietzscheanism, but it was reached
through a process of thought both independent and eclectic. On
one point he was now vehement: science and scholarship could
not give him the answers he wanted. Nor could Marxism. His old
school friend Stanyukovich, who had left Moscow, was in the
thick of Marxist discussions in Kharkov. Writing to him that
same spring, Bryusov rejected Marxism for its materialism and its
historical determinism.[10] He then went on to repeat in almost the
same words he had used to Samygin his belief in the plurality of
truths and his ideal of the pantheon. And to Ivan Bunin, who was
a sympathetic spirit, Bryusov inveighed against the "scientific
method" in contemporary scholarship, which threatened to "take
away independence of thought, to level all and replace the pen-

9.   *Dnevniki*, p. 61.   10.   *LN* 85, pp. 746–47.

etrating powers of genius by a calculating machine. No! I believe
that the conquest of knowledge is not accomplished in this way,
that the roads to truth are other!"[11] Clearly remembering his recent ordeal by examination, he fumed at "these little men, these
ants crawling along the marked road, taking two steps and brag-
ging that they have advanced knowledge." Life seemed too short
for all this.

Suddenly, at twenty-five, standing on the threshold of maturity, the urgency that had attacked him at earlier stages now
seized him with even greater force. He *must* go forward, and now
he was ready to do so. A remarkable letter written to Samygin
during July from Reval spells this out in full:

> "So. My noon has come." Pushkin's words. I feel and recognize my
> strengths. Now I am unable to write an insignificant piece. It is all
> the same, whether an article, a drama, or a long poem. In them I
> will be a creator at the height of his powers, and I will speak as a
> teacher. I could fill hundreds of volumes, if I wanted to say every-
> thing [that I might]. I am not concerned now with form—form in
> the widest sense. Now I have truly achieved that which I have talked
> about since childhood. I do not need—I speak sincerely from the
> depths of my soul—any recognition, any readers. That is a matter of
> indifference. Do you understand the total freedom which this knowl-
> edge gives? It is not hard to rise above mockery, but it is necessary to
> stand above all enthusiasms and above all convictions, one's own and
> those of others. Only then can one be a creator. I have found my
> highest point.[12]

A variant of this text, perhaps to another addressee, begins: "I
feel in myself powers and exuberance. I know that in me now are
concentrated all the secret threads of human thought from the
earliest days." And it concludes: "I understand everything with
stunning clarity, even that which I consider the most sublime.

11.   *LN* 84, 1: 445.   12.   IMLI, fond 13, op. 3, no. 12.

And therefore I go to people, mingle with them, fraternize with them."[13]

These statements will probably not surprise most of those who already know Bryusov's later reputation and certain often-quoted poems. Moreover, they seem all of a piece with the mood of the times. One is less apt to read them as stereotypical and more apt to attend to their content if one remembers the road by which he had come to this point. The question of Bryusov's Nietzscheanism arises pointedly here.[14] All things considered, he had not created his image cheaply. Nietzsche had indeed played a role, but Bryusov's Nietzscheanism was more than ordinarily selective. The notion of the superman, if it came from Nietzsche, was so internalized as to seem the outgrowth of his own inner beliefs and experience, dating even from early childhood. He had fought his way through self-doubt, uncertainty, and opposition with the help of the Leibniz-inspired conviction that every soul's truth is priceless because it is individual and unrepeatable. He now believed that new discoveries awaited the exceptionally gifted contemporary spirit in an ever-unfolding world. The pursuit of knowledge as a teleological process was discredited by Nietzsche. For Bryusov this meant that the imagination was freed for exploration in all directions. As he told Samygin, striving for unity of truth was an unnecessary, even wrong-headed, endeavor. Yet this did not lead in him to an enervating skepticism. Instead, variants of the doctrine of progress allowed the adventurous spirit to propose his own course, open to discoveries. And the doctrine of the

13.   Quoted in Ioanna Brjusova, p. 131.
14.   This matter is treated in part by Edith W. Clowes, "The Nietzschean Image of the Poet in the Early Works of Konstantin Bal'mont and Valerij Brjusov." Brjusov also affirmed his belief in Nietzscheanism in a 1906 letter to Nina Petrovskaja (*LN* 85, p. 191; see also Chapter Ten below). A curious undated fragment filed with the censor's copy of *Tertia Vigilia* in IRLI (fond 444, no. 11) and presumably a draft for a foreword complains that certain figures like Verlaine and Nietzsche changed their faiths so often as to be "shaky prophets."

plurality of truths relieved him of the worry of reconciling his findings.

Whatever may be said of Bryusov's powers as a thinker, so strong and independent a personality would have scorned accepting any world-view ready-made. His thinking, as has been shown, was eclectic in the extreme. Evaluating Nietzsche's influence on him without further evidence is difficult, but Bryusov's affinity for the spokesman of individualism, estheticism, and personal freedom, as Nietzsche was then perceived in Russia, cannot be doubted. He saw himself, like Zarathustra, descending from the mountain to mingle with men. This had been the burden of his last three years. But possibly to avoid a vulgar paraphrase of Nietzsche's prophet, in his letter to Samygin he instead had recourse to Pushkin: "My noon has come." The message, however, not only of these epiphanies to his friends but of the title of his newest book of poems, was the same as Zarathustra's: "Zarathustra has ripened, my hour has come: this is *my* morning, *my* day is breaking: *rise now, rise, thou great noon!*" [15] Again, perhaps to avoid the too obvious allusion, the title *Tertia Vigilia*, referring to the third watch of a Roman sentry's night, is not specifically mentioned in the poems of the first edition. But in a poem dated October 1900 and included in the 1901 volume of Scorpio's miscellany *Northern Flowers*, as well as in later editions of *Tertia Vigilia*, the meaning of this title is elucidated. The poem "I was a child not knowing terror" [I, 143] traces in particularly charming images the poet's path until "at last, in the third watch," the eastern sky crimsons: *his* day is breaking.

With *Tertia Vigilia* Bryusov's lyrical persona found his characteristic voice. Like the persona of *Me eum esse* this "I" is the Poet in full panoply. His vision and his intonations have changed, but the "history of a poet's soul" continues. In its first edition the

15.   Friedrich Nietzsche, *Thus Spoke Zarathustra*, tr. Walter Kaufmann (Harmondsworth: Penguin, 1980), p. 327.

book had five sections. Both then and later, most attention was paid to the first two, a fact that should have vexed Bryusov, given his esthetic convictions about the integrity of a book of poetry. The first was "Favorites of the Ages" and the second, "The City." "Favorites of the Ages" is devoted to the lyrical hero's pantheon. The protagonists of many of these poems are great or memorable figures of ages past—Assarhadon, Solomon, Rameses, Alexander, Cleopatra, Dante—whose lives and fates in some sense embodied the poet's dream, mood, or ideal. This was not, as one critic interpreted it, a flight to the past to avoid the trivialities of the present.[16] A letter to Pertsov dated November 1898 explained Bryusov's point of view. Pertsov had insisted that the poet's business was with current realities. But of course, replied Bryusov. However, "I hope that you don't insist on social questions. For certainly 'reality' is also the personal life of the poet. Every feeling, as long as it is sincere, is unique and worthy of expression. In what images? This seems to me a secondary matter. Simply in the most suitable ones."[17] And in some cases these will come from history or legend. "For example, it is natural to embody the consciousness of prophetic sight in the figure of [Cassandra]; or can one not convey one's mood by picturing Moses breaking the tablets?"[18]

Despite his complaint that study had allowed no leisure for meditation on events and personages of history, Bryusov had used his time to stock his imagination with figures to express his moods and feelings. In some poems the poet addresses the chosen fig-

---

16.　V. F. Savodnik, "Sovremmennaja russkaja lirika," part two, *Russkij vestnik*, no. 9 (1901), p. 129. The review was an enthusiastic one. Savodnik was a minor poet of Brjusov's circle.

17.　IMLI, fond 13, op. 3, no. 17.

18.　Both "Kassandra" and "Moisej" were written in spring 1898, though the latter did not appear in the first edition of *Tertia Vigilia*. Brjusov wrote here "Kleopatra," but the context indicates that he meant "Kassandra."

ures—Alexander, Cassandra. In others he uses the form that has been called the mask lyric: "I am chief of earthly kings and king— Assarhadon." [19] The effect of course is to identify the poet's "I" with the speaker, creating the image of the lone adventurer who shares the passions, longings, and possibly the destinies of these figures of literature, myth, and history. The first poem of the book makes explicit this desire of sharing. "To the Scythians" throws down an almost boyish challenge to "my distant ancestors" to accept into their warlike ranks him who would have excelled their own sons in sport, combat, and love. This opening to the cycle sets the paradigm of heroic yearning and promise of epic achievement. "The Chaldean Shepherd" emphasizes the theme of spiritual daring. Here the poet places himself on the bare hillside from which a remote predecessor puzzled out the secrets of the planets' movements, devised the signs of the zodiac, and knew the happiness of solitary exploit. One after another come figures who dared fate and, whatever their ultimate destinies, held mysterious power over others. A subcycle centers on the poem "Don Juan," where the Don too is portrayed as a seeker "thirsting for new lands, other flowers, / strange dialects," and, of course, other women. For him every woman conquered is also a new soul with a new secret to be possessed. The poet as such appears intermittently in the cycle. Tellingly he is allied to the seer and solitary outcast Dante.

The *poèma* "To the King of the North Pole" epitomizes the preceding cycle. The dreamer-adventurer is apotheosized in its hero, the Viking Sven. This *poèma*, reminiscent of Balmont's "Dead

19. See Ralph Rader's discussion of this form: "The Dramatic Monologue and Related Lyric Forms," *Critical Inquiry* (Autumn 1976): 140ff. A companion piece to "Assarhadon" is Brjusov's translation of Victor Hugo's "Solomon," placed next but one in the series and using the same basic meter—iambic hexameter— though with a final trimeter in each quatrain. In the first edition of this book Brjusov used translations freely where they fit the design of a section.

Ships," was dedicated to Ivan Konevskoy,[20] whose "Varangians" are kin to Bryusov's Sven. In form Bryusov's work resembles Balmont's, being composed of several sections in different stanzaic forms and meters. However, it is longer and in a sense more ambitious. It is also very different in its underlying idea. Contemporary readers must have seen the Norse heroes of both poems as inspired by Fridtjof Nansen and the twelve members of his expedition to the Pole. The Nansen expedition set off in the ship *Fram* ["Forward"] from Christiania on 24 June 1893 and was not heard from for three years. According to Nansen's plan, the specially constructed ship was to be frozen into the floating ice at sea and carried by currents which he expected to pass close to the Pole. The *Fram* returned to Norway in August 1896 with much valuable scientific information, but without Nansen. With one companion Nansen had left the ship to pursue his goal by a land route, when it became clear that the ship could not reach the Pole. They pushed further north than any known explorers hitherto had done. The expedition's outcome was not known when Balmont wrote his poem, leaving him free—as he would have been in any case—to mythologize. In Balmont's version, human daring meets its nemesis and is transformed into the eternal silence that swathes the globe. Bryusov's poem also mythologizes, but in a different vein. Sven the Viking sets off northward with his chosen band. Among these wanderers and fighters, Sven alone is a dreamer, held in thrall by the Polar Star. As her betrothed, he must overcome all passions except the one that draws him toward her, knowing all the while that death awaits him at the Pole. Sven perishes last of all his party, when he looks on "the dead charm of the Polar Star." After attaining his goal he is carried to Valhalla. At first glance the fate of Bryusov's heroes does not seem

20.   The "heroes of measureless personal pride" who appear in Konevskoj's "Varjagi" are kin to Sven. (Ivan Konevskoj, *Sobranie sočinenij* [Moscow, 1904; reprinted Munich: Wilhelm Fink Verlag, 1971], pp. 117–18.)

to differ much from that of Balmont's. Both perish in their striving toward the unknown. But Balmont's faceless voyagers blend with the Voice of the Silence (as the epigraph indicates), while Bryusov's individualized heroes meet death each in his characteristic fashion. And Sven is singled out as a victor: "You have died not in the day of battle, / But in the day of triumph!" sings his bard.

The date of composition of "To the King of the North Pole" is carefully specified: "Begun in September 1898. Completed in May 1900." That is, it was begun just after publication of "Dead Ships" as the lead piece in Balmont's *Stillness* and completed just in time for *Tertia Vigilia*. Bryusov had of course known Balmont's poem earlier, but its appearance in the book coincided with Bryusov's growing conviction that he and Balmont were pursuing different paths, and that Balmont's led nowhere. A poem "To Balmont," which he composed in late August 1898 but did not publish, expresses hopelessness over his "poor friend's" plight: "And the very abyss— / It is you!"[21] In "To the King of the North Pole" he approaches his point more obliquely and more effectively. The poem's frame distances action and characters and moves the theme to the foreground. The two brief introductory lyrics dwell on the lure of the unknown northern land that for ages has drawn the mad and the brave to their ruin and made them the subject of song. The poet here injects his own longing, which by implication makes him the fellow of Sven. The *poèma's* final song, after the narration of Sven's fate, offers a new message: a Voice announces that truth is in men's spirits, not in the vast expanses. Moreover, there are as many "truths" as there are human thoughts and utterances; the universe will not run out of secrets. But man must discover them. From the perspective advanced by Balmont, man is insignificant and powerless. Balmont had tried for a compromise: "He, the Unmoving, He, the Un-

21.   "Pogasni, izčezni" first published in III, 250.

thirsting, — and I." Bryusov now replied unequivocally: "Understand! — the whole world and all secrets are in us, / In us are Darkness and Dawn."

"To the King of the North Pole," then, exalted the adventurer of the spirit. Its inspiration in Nansen's voyage recalls that in childhood Bryusov had devoured tales of real-life heroes. Nansen's single-minded, fanatic daring epitomized the spiritual daring Bryusov demanded of the real poet. Moreover, Sven did not withdraw from the human world in order to lose himself in pure beauty. He sought life's secret, to be imparted at the Pole: "I am a messenger, standing on the threshold." He willed to extend the edges of the known at any risk.

Though taking its formal organization from "Dead Ships," Bryusov's *poèma* went even further in the variety of verse forms employed in its ten sections. Moreover, his experiments with rhyme and rhythm took him some distance beyond the regular meters and rhymes used by Balmont. This is seen at once in the introduction's two parts. The first lyric is written in conventional trochaic tetrameter with dactylic endings but unconventional rhyme. The second uses the classical elegiac distich. The first section following the introduction draws on his recent experience with and interest in folk poetry—appropriately, since the work is meant to suggest a saga. This section's twenty-three lines move easily through four verse forms. A catalogue of Sven's chosen followers is given in eight lines somewhat reminiscent of the *bylina*, with grammatical rhymes and such features as repetition and parallelism. This passage is followed by a three-line proverb about those left behind and their short-lived grief. The final lines voice the adventurers' exuberance in short rhymed couplets followed by a concluding quatrain, all in masculine rhyme. Other sections of the *poèma* exhibit other curious features, including echoes of Balmont such as the eight-foot trochaic meter of Part III and the voices of the elements in Part VII, which may go back through

Balmont to Shelley. The total effect is a fluid melding of verse and meaning.

Two other tales in verse complete the book's first section. "Aganatis [later 'Aganat']. A Phoenician Tale" is the story of a girl who becomes a hetaira in the service of the goddess of love when her lover fails to return from the sea. Their reunion years later threatens to become tragic until the goddess Asherah rolls back the years to the time of Aganatis's innocence. In "The Legend of a Bandit" Peter covets a monastery's riches for himself and his band. Entering it disguised as a monk, he is perceived by the nuns as a holy man. And indeed miracles begin to happen, the greatest but not the first of which is his conversion. In both poems truth is shown to be mutable, or possibly multiple.

"The Legend of a Bandit," based on a tale from the collection of pious tales called the *Prologue*, brings the section that depicts the poet's lyrical persona to a somewhat unexpected close. Contemporary criticism saw it as an expression of Bryusov's admiration for spiritual courage wherever found, or perhaps of his attraction to the marvellous.[22] Maxim Gorky singled it out for its fidelity to both the spirit and the form of folk poetry, declaring that "he did not ornament this legend with any patterns from contemporary thought."[23] The poem was written shortly after the memorable visit of Alexander Dobrolyubov. It sustains its *bylina* features throughout, showing again Bryusov's sympathy with forms of folk poetry as well as his discrimination in employing them.

The second section of *Tertia Vigilia*, entitled "The City," marks an important step in the author's career and a momentous beginning for twentieth-century Russian poetry. The urban theme,

22.   Savodnik, "Sovremennaja," p. 130.
23.   Quoted in Ašukin, p. 144. Brjusov described in his diary his first meeting with Gor'kij, during which Gor'kij read this poem aloud (*Dnevniki*, p. 94).

so important in the Futurist movement, is properly traced to Bryusov's poetry of the city. What has yet to be thoroughly explored, as Vladimir Markov noted, is the linkage this theme provides between Decadence and Futurism and possibly other later developments.[24]

One of Bryusov's earliest attractions in modern European poetry was to the work of Emile Verhaeren, the Belgian who made an antipoetical age itself a central theme for his poetry. Bryusov's enthusiasm for Verhaeren grew apace in the last months of 1899, as he explored new themes and forms to express contemporary moods. Later, especially in poems written during the Russo-Japanese War and the 1905 Revolution, Bryusov's imagery showed the influence of Verhaeren's tumultuous visions; now the influence seems to have been broadly thematic and possibly formal. Verhaeren's use of *vers libre* may have encouraged Bryusov's metrical experiments. Possibly, too, Verhaeren's impressionistic method suggested to Bryusov a mode for conveying his own feelings about and perceptions of the city. In 1900 *"les villes tentaculaires"* lay largely outside Bryusov's or any Russian's experience. However, the boom of industry and railroads in the 1890s was impressive enough to make residents of Moscow and Petersburg aware that a new era was well under way. It also generated feelings of excitement and apprehension on the part of the more imaginative. Fortunately, Bryusov did not try to adapt Verhaeren's vision of the seething metropolis to either of the Russian capitals: his inspiration was largely personal and spontaneous. In March 1899 Bryusov wrote to Ivan Bunin, exulting in the city spring: "Roofs sparkling with the morning sun, rushing streams of water, full puddles in which clouds pass by. . . . You don't like a city spring, but it is nearer to my meditations than country mud and bare branches stripped of snow. We pay little attention to the city,

24.   Vladimir Markov, "K voprosu o granicax dekadansa v russkoj poèzii (i o liričeskoj poème," pp. 486–87.

we merely live in it and call only paths in a garden 'nature,' as if sidewalk stones, the narrow perspectives of streets, and a bright sky with the outlines of roofs were not also nature." [25] Then in a prophetic mood he looked ahead to a transformed city "in far-off days, in the days of a life overflowing with ecstasy. Then people will find and recognize all the beauty of telegraph wires, graceful walls, and iron grills."

The prophetic note—destined for further development—was relatively new, but Bryusov's esthetic attraction to the city was not so new. His dedication of this section to Balmont surely referred to their earlier nighttime roamings through Moscow. But Petersburg had also contributed to his store of city images. In January 1897 he recorded the visual impressions of his winter visit. It was not the picturesque Neva and its embankments but the great avenues with their modern architecture that impressed him—and, even more, the details dictated by the needs of modern urban populations. "Artist, find beauty in shops, in staircases, in chimneys! You don't need columns." [26] Even business signs should contribute to the city's beauty: "And it can be done!" Bryusov's fascination with the city merged with the interest in Moscow's history he developed in connection with *A History of the Russian Lyric*. His latest plan for that project had included a study of Moscow life in the seventeenth century. Out of his research for that chapter, apparently, grew the plan for a guide to the city of Moscow, which, like the *History*, fell by the wayside but left its mark on other works.

The section of *Tertia Vigilia* entitled "The City" opens with a short *poèma*, "In an Unfinished Building," and continues through twenty-three lyrics, including two translations. Most of these are descriptive but employ the subjective manner, in which mood and object are barely separable. The prophetic note is intermittent and tentative, yet it receives some prominence from the ar-

25. *LN* 84, 1: 441.   26. *Dnevniki*, p. 27.

rangement of poems in the cycle. The opening *poèma* conveys claustrophobic fear before a future which may see the human race immured by its self-chosen limitations. Several lyrics circle about this theme. "Of conceptions strict and bold" reinforces the apprehensions, portraying the city first as ravening beast, then as tomb. "I foresee proud shadows" takes a more positive view but is still ambivalent. The poet there foresees a time when the city, massive, upward-reaching, essentially lifeless, nonetheless will contain a life in which every moment is portentous and men's desires are without measure. The closing lyric, "Corona," retreats into the vaguest possible intimations of a future unveiling of mysteries.

More interesting because more original are the poems that pursue the theme of limitation.[27] They use a more personal, less Orphic voice. The poet may be a prophet, but he is also contemporary man. As artist he shares, perhaps more than he wishes, the spiritual limitations of his breed and his time. For him walls are not always barriers. They can also be shelter from immensity, from the glare of infinity, and as such, they inspire affection. The phrase "I love" occurs in many of Bryusov's city poems. In the first of these he wrote, "I love the trueness of lines, / I love in dreams their limits. / . . . . / I love not cliffs but houses." Self-irony this may be. But there are compensations for finitude, and acute sensibilities are open to the most delicate intimations: "Crystals are dear to me, / And the sting of slender wasps." The second "I love" poem contains no hint of irony but, rather, a justification: "I love great houses and narrow city streets." City squares are celebrated, especially because they are surrounded by walls. Here another limit is invoked: twilight, the hour when the street lights are not yet lit and the stars glitter only faintly. In this

27.   A valuable treatment of this topic is that of Irene Masing-Delic, "Limitation and Pain in Brjusov's and Blok's Poetry."

hour, out of the rumble of traffic and the city's singing sounds, the poet's song is born: "In ecstasy already I hear rhyme."

The third lyric, "When the blinds are lowered," pursues the analysis of personal limitations and their positive benefits. "I need no brilliant splendor, / No beauty nor grandeur of skies." The lowered blinds shut out the world and leave the poet alone with his books and the singing meters. "Yes!" he exclaims. "I know how sweet are chains / In the depths of exitless caverns." Yet he is no desiccated hermit, and the present is no dungeon. His imagination can penetrate spiritual walls. "Evening Light," one of the most effective "I love" poems, shows how this happens. The pale dusk transforms the gaze of people passing in the still shadow, and the poet feels a sudden tenderness for these sad, thoughtful brothers who glide with him "on the rims of dreams." However, a paradox arises: is this dreamy poet the spiritual kin of Scythians and Vikings? "We have grown unused to bright colors." We live, we poets, in dusty rooms, treasuring our single lines and isolated instants of inspiration, while our dreams are wild and terrible: blood, screams, and war. The paradox is not immediately resolved. Yet, these instants of inspiration which come upon him in city streets at twilight, at the end of winter, resonate with common human experience. Moreover, many of them make highly satisfactory poems. These are primarily poems of the present, not the future, and the best of them are personal lyrics, in which the poet confesses that his inspiration comes from weakness as well as strength. As such they provide a complement to the portrait delineated in the book's first section.

The third part of *Tertia Vigilia*, "A Little Book for Children," was not quite what it pretended ("What kind of children are these?" blustered the censor Yuri Bartenev), but the title was not cynical. From the little green worms of "How desirable in a tedious hour" to the sand squeaking underfoot in "Drenched with nighttime rain," these lyrics are fresh in tone and diction. Some are indeed simple enough for children, though they have layered meanings. Fully five of the sixteen are devoted to religious or quasi-religious themes. "In an Old Temple" (St. Basil's in Red Square) evokes a service beneath the low painted arches, the air filled with incense and antiphonal chants. The monotonous anapestic quatrains with regular feminine rhymes suggest church singing, and dark faces of icons "gaze from the ages." The poem "Christmas" is a completely orthodox rendition in a few seemingly artless stanzas of the Christian mysteries from the annunciation to Mary to the calling of the first of Jesus' disciples. But "Easter, the Feast of Feasts" is an outright rejection of asceticism in favor of earthly joys, up to the final stanza where churchbells summon sinners.

After the book's first two cycles, the structure of this one seems loose. A clue to its plan may lie in the final two poems, though this cannot be certain without further evidence. The last poem is untitled but dedicated to "E. I. Pavlovskaya." So in later editions is the preceding poem, "The Vigil Lamp," and so was the poem "Christmas" in autograph.[28] The first two of these were dated 7 September and 28 August 1897 respectively, that is, shortly before Bryusov's marriage. Evgenia Pavlovskaya was governess in the Bryusov household for a short time during which she apparently made a deep impression on Bryusov. She was a lover of poetry, and their relationship seems to have been intellectual, artistic, and emotional, but probably not sexual. Not long before her death of tuberculosis, Bryusov went to Sorochintsy to see her for the last time. The occasion revived many memories—"of our past, our happy hours, our best moments." He later wrote to Balmont, "She was the best woman I ever met—unique." Though

28. I, 599, 600. The account given here [I, 599] is drawn from unpublished sections of the diary. In the letter to Samygin where he discusses his forthcoming marriage, Brjusov speaks of "Evgenija Il'inična, with her tortured thoughts of human happiness, of goodness, of God" (Ioanna Brjusova, p. 127).

formally dedicated to Bryusov's friend the German poet Georg Bachmann, the cycle may have been a private memorial to her.

"Pictures of the Crimea and the Sea," the fourth section, marks Bryusov's formal admission of error. A note calls it an addition to the "Travels" cycle of *Me eum esse*, but it is equally an apology to the beauties of nature, which he had scorned in his earlier book. These twenty-one poems are characterized by attentive, sympathetic observation, but they have little emotional content. The lyrical persona has become merely watcher and listener. Bryusov's real contribution as a poet of nature had to wait for the "Saima" cycle in *Stephanos*. In *Tertia Vigilia* the final lyric, "I lie on a rock, warmed by the sun," confesses that nature and he do not communicate. It concludes: "I shall not understand the secret meaning of the stirring, / And the sea will not understand my questions."[29]

The fifth and last section of the book is the longest, with an introduction and thirty poems. It is called "Repetitions," though in fact only one of the poems had already appeared, in *A Book of Meditations*. It might equally well have been called "Continuities." Thematically it seems to fall into three parts of equal length. The first ten poems form a subset serving a function now almost mandatory: they review the "pilgrim's progress" over the three years since *Me eum esse*, with special reference to the relationship with Balmont, which continued to serve Bryusov as a point of reference. The entire section is prefaced by an important programmatic poem, "The Return," in which the lyrical hero gives an allegorized account of past adventures, announces his present stance, and reaffirms his total dedication to poetry. Presumably the flight from the fleshpots of *Chefs d'œuvre* to the austerities of *Me eum esse* and the long sojourn in the desert are past.

29. The section was dedicated to Bunin, and several of these poems were first published with the help of Bunin in the newspaper *Južnoe obozrenie*. This was the first of Brjusov's works not printed at his own expense. See *Dnevniki*, pp. 62, 74.

At the summons he has taken up his rightful role as leader: "I have resumed the purple." The consort at his side is a new Muse, more voluptuous than the tantalizing spirit of *Me eum esse*. However, if the poet has learned one lesson, it is the obligation of moving on when called. Now, should the trumpet call interrupt even a passionate embrace, he will spring up, tearing free from all that holds him. The portrait is complete. The lyric hero whose outlines took shape in "Favorites of the Ages" now stands forth in his own lineaments.

The ten lyrics following elaborate this theme. The first, with very slight revision, is that which opened Bryusov's section in *A Book of Meditations*. Now dedicated not to Balmont but to Baltrušaitis, his colleague at Scorpio, "I know the fleetingness of Night and Winter" serves as a rallying call to kindred spirits. The next three lyrics call these fellow spirits to share in whatever is to come, victory or extinction, though the presumption favors the former. Emphasis soon shifts back to the exalted individual and his pilgrimage. Two lyrics dedicated to the early *Russian Symbolists* and *Me eum esse* stress how far the poet has travelled. He has reached his prime: "My spirit has not flagged in the murk of contradiction." He has won freedom: this is the crux. But freedom for what? This poem, later entitled simply "I," is the poetic expression of his personal manifesto to Samygin and others. "And to all gods I dedicate my lines." The key lies in the central stanza. Though the poet has sat at the feet of many teachers, his allegiance is to none of them: "But I myself have loved only the linking of words." The freedom he proclaims is the total freedom of the artist to serve no master except art itself. For Bryusov, as we have seen, the conviction that truth is multiple, that many truths may coexist, was a source of energy, and the spirit who possessed this "truth" possessed a rich source for his song. Only when avenues of spiritual exploration were closed off was the poet in danger of perishing as poet.

This was the core of his quarrel with Balmont, whom he considered to have become trapped in his own contradictions. "My spirit has not flagged in the murk of contradiction," viewed in the context of their dialogue, is a pointed reproach. Their ongoing correspondence, reinforced by Balmont's newest poems, convinced Bryusov that Balmont was as desperately confused as ever. The first cycle within "Repetitions" was capped by the sonnet "To the Portrait of K. D. Balmont."[30] The sonnet form was well chosen: the octet contains the indictments, while the sestet softens them with fellow feeling, though returning to the charge in the final lines. "Gloomy visage, convict's stare!" the poem opens. This is an outsider, "a hideous phantom" in our midst, who has fallen in love with his own temptations and has chosen a path leading to shame. But the poet recalls how they two together had taken the road to forbidden lands. He concludes: "I love you because you are all falsehood. / Because you yourself do not know where you are going, / Because you yourself consider the heights a deception." A letter from Bryusov to Andrei Bely written four years later provides the best gloss to this poem.[31] All of us, he told Bely, are unfaithful to our ideals. We make excuses for clinging to our pedestrian ways and not taking the great leap into heroism. To this he counted two possible exceptions: Alexander Dobrolyubov, by then confirmed as the ascetic wanderer, and Balmont. "And Balmont, with all the triviality of his 'derring-do' and all the ugliness of his 'freedom,' and his constant self-

30.   This placement suggests that these ten poems are part of the ongoing dialogue between Brjusov and Bal'mont. A detailed discussion is out of place here, but it can probably be demonstrated that the debate between the two on the nature and role of the poet continued through *Gorjaščie zdanija* and *Tertia Vigilia*. The portrait in question is presumed to be a studio portrait of Bal'mont taken in 1899 (*Stixotvorenija i poèmy*, p. 742). Ninov may have this in mind when he speaks of a photograph with a lilac branch in the background, presented by Bal'mont to Brjusov (*Neva*, 6/79, 114). The poem was probably written between 29 August and 5 September 1899. This suggests that the portrait by Durnov of Bal'mont overlooking the city by moonlight [I, 598] was inspired by this poem.

31.   *LN* 85, pp. 378–79.

deception which he has come to take for truth, nonetheless strives to reach some goal, if not by the direct route, at least by a round-about path." [32] At the end of 1899 Bryusov was pleading with Balmont to free himself from the traps into which he seemed to have blundered. What probably most irritated and distressed him at this point was Balmont's self-advertisement as a free soul, a "Scythian," and his failure, in Bryusov's opinion, to go anywhere at all. [33]

"Sonnet on Woman" announces the next set of poems. Woman is characterized in traditional ways as the enslaving divinity, the inscrutable mystery. The second poem, "Love," embodies Bryusov's philosophy of love, or passion. Love is not to be re-sisted; the cup is to be drunk, whoever offers it, for through love the spirit is "blended with the universal source." If the soul is a Leibnizian monad, it is encased within itself, for monads have no windows. But Bryusov posited communion with another in love as the escape from self and even more, the opening into other spheres. Passion, he later wrote, "is that point where the earthly sphere touches other realms of being; it is always closed, but there is a door." [34] Woman is the scroll on which secrets are written, and love, or passion, is the key to decoding them. The third poem of the series establishes a method for which Bryusov is famous or notorious: the architectural metaphor for sexual love. [35] The point of "By cold, familiar steps" seems to be that all is less grand than it had once seemed. The arches, the courts, the passages are di-

32.   Ibid., p. 379.

33.   See Bal'mont's poem "Skify" in the journal *Žizn'* at the end of 1899 (K. D. Bal'mont, *Stixotvorenija* ed. Vl. Orlov [second ed. Leningrad, 1969], pp. 150–51, 621). It boasts, in the first person, of the complete freedom of nomads, whose sole pride is in their tireless horses.

34.   *Vesy* no. 8 (1904): 25.

35.   Bal'mont became famous for a similar device. Vladimir Markov re-marked, "It is difficult now not to smile at the Victorian daring of Balmont's 'alcoves,' and on the whole his eroticism is inferior to the somber precision of Briusov's": "Balmont: A Reappraisal," *Slavic Review* 28, 2 (June 1969): 230.

minished, though the secret door still exists. Another poem utters the now familiar renunciation of earthly pleasures for the sake of a higher call.

Not all of Bryusov's poems about love are metaphorical and abstract. This cycle contains several that are personal, dedicated by initial: two to Eda, his wife, and one to "A." This is almost surely Anna Shesterkina. Wife of a Moscow artist of Bryusov's acquaintance, Mme Shesterkina may have been the first woman with whom Bryusov formed a serious extramarital relationship.[36] They began an extensive correspondence in 1899. The poem placed here shows a couple as they greet the morning in a cold, silent street, the sky just beginning to grow light. A moment of unearthly silence entrances them. It is an effective piece, lyrically stated and full of fresh, genuine emotion. The first "Eda" poem portrays a different and enigmatic relationship, where an inverted reminiscence of Dostoevsky's final scene from *The Idiot* may be intended: "And when you kill me, / You will don a white dress." The second "Eda" poem ostentatiously employs rhyme words from the lexicon in which Bryusov and Balmont were wont to communicate highly abstracted mental states: *more/bezbrežnost'/gore/nežnost'* (sea, boundlessness, grief, tenderness). They are revived here, where the similes are simple and close to life. Eda, serene and tender, is likened to the quiet shore on which the waves break gently. Ending the group dealing with women and

36. *Dnevniki*, p. 79, where Brjusov wrote of the encouragement of a Mme Š., and of his general weariness with that sort of thing. However, according to many sources he overcame his weariness (see *LN* 85, p. 622). Also, long after, Ioanna Brjusova's younger sister remembered as a schoolgirl having seen Brjusov in a sleigh attentive to "Mme Š." in a red cloak and then having disturbed the family at tea by reporting what she had seen (B. Pogorelova, "Valerij Brjusov i ego okruženie," *Novyj žurnal* no. 33 [1953]: 183). Many years later, Brjusov drew up a "Don Juan list," on which the functioning headings range from "I courted" to "It seemed to me I loved." Under the latter he listed, with relevant years, his wife, Anna Šesterkina, Nina Petrovskaja, and Nadežda L'vova. Šesterkina's years were 1899 to 1903. (This list is in a private collection.)

love is a translation of Verhaeren's "La Dame en noir" as "Woman at the Crossroads," where the eternal harlot is associated with forgetfulness and death.

The section's closing series contains several poems that convey a sense of mystery beneath the surface of life. Of these the most interesting is "The Fern," related—as some of Bryusov's most vivid poems of mystery are—to eerie personal experience.[37] "The Fern" portrays a twilight moment in a nut grove, when the poet is seized by a spell. The experience is almost inexpressible: "And for an instant in the spirit's depths / (Where many-visaged terror is) / There slips by listlessly, dully, / The tremor of life uncouth and pitiful." Suddenly a giant fern springs up, and in flight from it the poet meets monstrous people and beasts. "All the wraiths of all superstitions" laugh as he runs with terror in his heart, and the face of "life uncouth and pitiful" nods at him like an old hag. As dusk falls the heavens listen to ancient secrets, and a mockingbird sings. The unnamed, many-visaged terror sitting at the heart of the poem is presumably the inner, shadowy fear in all men, hidden until evoked by some seemingly innocent thing. The diction, in the choice of rhyme words especially, is vivid and precise, if such terms can be applied to such visions. The nut grove, the mockingbird, and the fern are not the phantom images of a Symbolist landscape but pregnant symbols of an inner experience.

Toward the end of the section the circle is closed by resumption of the dialogue with Balmont. Balmont's *Burning Buildings* was published in May 1900, just as *Tertia Vigilia* was going to the censor. Several years later Bryusov was to call *Burning Buildings*, somewhat ambiguously, the peak of Balmont's achievement.[38]

37.   Brjusov's sister Nadežda remembered how, when they gathered mushrooms, they regarded certain ones, presumably non-poisonous, as "enemies" and fled them, and that Brjusov also fled from ferns. Nadja reported, "Valerij genuinely feared them" [I, 601].

38.   Four articles by Brjusov on the books of poetry Bal'mont published between 1903 and 1909 appeared collected in his book of essays on literary fig-

However, at this moment he held a special viewpoint. Markov has called *Burning Buildings* "a book of storm and thunder, of 'dagger words,' a book that sings paeans to animalism and glorifies violence and is permeated by the color red—from red poppies and carnations to the blood-stained lips of the vampire."[39] Balmont subtitled it "poetry of the contemporary soul." Bryusov accepted this, but with reservations. He never questioned the "contemporary" nature of Balmont's strivings and soul-searchings, but he felt it to be wrong for Balmont to ensnare others in the traps in which he himself was caught. A poem called "The Tempted Brothers" took its epigraph from Zarathustra: "What is great in man is that he is a bridge and not an end."[40] The lyric exhorts brother poets to remember what unites them: they strive not for the "dead idol of Beauty" but toward an ever-moving goal. They are voyagers who do not rest.

A late addition to the closing section, written in August 1900, is "The eternal foundations of reason." Placed after "The Tempted Brothers," it builds on its theme. This final poem is a warning against the kind of madness invited by Balmont's latest poems. All these diabolic writings give only temporary flashes of vision bought at great price. Whoever is willing to forego the Pythian orgies and await the Bright Spirit will win the brighter, bolder

---

ures, *Dalekie i blizkie* (Moscow, 1912). *Gorjaščie zdanija* was praised retrospectively in the review of *Zlye čary* and *Žar-ptica* [VI, 265]. An attempt to survey all Brjusov's writings on Bal'mont from 1895 to 1913 is the article by T. V Ančugova, "Brjusov—kritik (Stat'i V. Ja. Brjusova o K. Bal'monte)," *Brjusovskie čtenija 1971 goda*, pp. 244–69. In later years Brjusov more than once tried to sum up his thoughts on Bal'mont in an article which in one version he called "Čto takoe Bal'mont?" [VI, 482–92]. This was written in 1921 and first published by D. E. Maksimov in 1956 with an introduction (*Učenye zapiski* 18, 5 [Leningrad, 1956]): 233–41. Another version, so far unpublished, was prepared in 1923 [VI, 638]. Both documents show the prejudices nursed by their author over long years.

39.   Markov, "K voprosu," p. 229.
40.   Nietzsche, *Thus Spoke Zarathustra*, p. 15.

vision. Later, Bryusov wrote of how difficult it was in those days for poets to remain independent of Balmont's overpowering influence.[41] Bryusov had himself experienced this influence. Now, however, he felt himself not only free of that hypnotic, confining spell, but ready to lead others into the freedom he enjoyed. He had no misgivings about what he could offer: "Gold I have created, gold."

41.   VI, 265.

EIGHT

Urbi et Orbi

IN LATE 1903 Bryusov published his fourth
volume of poetry, *Urbi et Orbi*, addressed, as he later explained,
not merely to the narrow "city" of his fellow Symbolists but to
the wider "world" of Russian readers.[1] The man who affirmed in
the summer of 1900 "My noon has come" anticipated by only a
little. *Urbi et Orbi* established Bryusov in the front rank of Russia's contemporary poets. Critical approval, lagging as always behind changes in artistic fashion, had begun to shine on Bryusov—
though far from unanimously.[2] More important, the field of his
influence was widening appreciably, both through broader publication of his work and through the chain of literary projects into
which he poured his seemingly endless energy.

The publishing house Scorpio was the launching pad for a
number of these. Along with sponsoring volumes of Russian and
foreign authors, Bryusov helped initiate Scorpio's series of miscellanies named for a famous predecessor, *Northern Flowers*.[3] The
first three volumes, published in 1901, 1902, and 1903, gathered
between their covers contributions from contemporary writers
representing both Symbolism and the larger literary world. Chekhov, Bunin, and Sluchevsky appeared beside Zinaida Gippius,

1. "Avtobiografija," p. 115.
2. Ašukin, pp. 170–77, quotes from contemporary reviews giving a
cross-section of opinion.
3. *Severnye cvety 1901 g.* (Moscow, 1901). The editors' foreword speaks of
"renewing after a seventy-year interruption the miscellany *Northern Flowers* (it
was last published in 1832 for the benefit of Delvig's family)."

Merezhkovsky, Sologub, Balmont, and Bryusov, as well as newer figures such as Blok and Bely. Scholarly items including unpublished materials of Pushkin, Fet, Tyutchev, as well as critical essays, found place, so that the new series defined itself advantageously in terms of literary culture as well as creative variety. Behind the scenes Scorpio's founding members, especially Bryusov and Polyakov, chased author after author to beg stories and poems, and they edited the volumes as well. Disappointments notwithstanding, they were sufficiently encouraged to formulate in 1903 another, much more ambitious project, a monthly journal of criticism with an international flavor. Its only Russian predecessor, Diaghilev's opulent *World of Art*, which was oriented especially toward the visual arts, offered a model of artistic format. The first literary review of its kind in Russia, *The Balance* compared well with its Western models.[4] The first issue appeared in January 1904. For the next six years, despite ups and downs and internal tensions, this handsome, cosmopolitan journal was the most prestigious forum for Symbolist criticism and debate as well as, after an enlargement of scope in 1906, the vehicle for some major Symbolist works. Its de facto editor was Bryusov.

Meanwhile, along with his work for *Russian Archive*, which continued through 1902, Bryusov was now invited to publish in a variety of periodicals. *World of Art* solicited his contributions. In 1902 the Merezhkovskys, Peter Pertsov, and Dmitri Filosofov were planning a monthly to be called *New Way*, and Bryusov was

4.　Special attention is given to the foreign connections of the journal *Vesy* by Georgette Donchin, *The Influence of French Symbolism on Russian Poetry* (The Hague: Mouton, 1958), ch. 2. A detailed account of the history of *Vesy* is given in K. M. Azadovskij and D. E. Maksimov, "Brjusov i 'Vesy' (k istorii izdanija)," *LN* 85, pp. 257–324. Like its publishing house, the journal was named for a zodiacal sign: Libra. However, in its multilingual advertising, it referred to itself as "La Balance," "Die Waage," and "The Balance." (See, for example, *Vesy* no. 2 [1904]: 92.)

elected secretary.[5] *New Way* was a hybrid. During its brief life in 1903 and 1904 it carried, besides the latest fiction and poetry, political articles—oddly, allotted to Bryusov—and the minutes of the meetings of the Religious-Philosophical Assembly, in which its editors were active. Bryusov resigned as secretary of *New Way* at the end of 1903, but some of his most important poems continued to be printed there.

Besides coinciding with Bryusov's natural taste, all this activity in the literary arena fit his conception of the poet's larger role and responsibility to be a leader and breaker of new paths. His early programmatic poems were largely addressed to other poets, encouraging them in the struggle toward new goals. In more recent ones such as "The Return" in *Tertia Vigilia*, the poet-figure emerged as an unmistakable torchbearer.

In the winter of 1902–1903 Bryusov found another medium besides the printed word for spreading the good news. Early in 1898 a group of prominent Moscow artists and art patrons established the Moscow Literary-Artistic Circle.[6] The performances, readings, and other activities that took place in the Circle's chambers in its first few years excluded the new art. Nonetheless, Bryusov began visiting there early in 1902 and soon was elected to the Circle's literary committee, an immediate charge of which

5.   *Dnevniki*, p. 123. Bryusov's relations with *Novyj put'*, including correspondence with one of its organizers, Percov, are described by D. Maksimov, "Valerij Brjusov i 'Novyj Put','" *LN* 27–28, pp. 276–98.

6.   Ašukin, p. 161. "Every day there gathered at the Circle writers, theatrical artists, painters. It was a club where, not only in public programs but also in private literary conversations, questions important for writers were discussed, and along the way practical publishing and journalistic matters were settled"; *Istorija Moskvy*, 6 vols. (Moscow, 1952–1959), 5, p. 523. Accounts of the Moskovskij Literaturno-Xudožestvennyj Kružok appear in many memoirs, including those of Zinaida Gippius, Andrej Belyj, Vladislav Xodasevič, V. V. Veresaev, N. Telešov, and Boris Zajcev. An account of its founding and development by Prince A. I. Sumbatov appeared in the *Izvestija Moskovskogo Literaturno-Xudožestvennogo Kružka*, beginning with no. 13 (March 1916): 6.

was to arrange the Tuesday night literary meetings.[7] Consequently, throughout the 1902–1903 season the "Tuesdays" provided a platform and debating ground for the ideas and productions of the new poets. The atmosphere of ferment and, often, scandal that accompanied these meetings created at least the illusion that tremendous strides were being taken in the name of Symbolism. Bryusov and Balmont were the leading figures. In his diary Bryusov described the series of readings and lectures by the two that February and March as "The Battle in Moscow."[8] Writing much later, Andrei Bely conveyed the color, heat, excitement, and enjoyment of the events.[9] However little conversion of public taste was accomplished on the spot, the fact that through these gatherings a number of younger talents were brought into direct personal contact with Balmont and Bryusov has importance. Moreover, by this time Bryusov had begun to hold his *jours fixes* in the apartment on Tsvetnoy Boulevard, and some of the activity carried on there was significant for Russian poetry in the immediate future, in ways to be discussed below.

When *Urbi et Orbi* was published, then, Bryusov had already become a central figure on the literary scene in Russia. Though some of the poems in *Urbi et Orbi* had appeared in *Northern Flowers* and *New Way*, many were new and, as always with Bryusov's books, the volume in its totality constituted a poetic statement. It was fortuitous but fateful that among the reading audience for Bryusov's new offering were some who would be major figures on the same stage within a short time. More than any of his previous books, *Urbi et Orbi* defined Bryusov for the second generation of Russian Symbolist poets and determined the nature of his influence upon them.

In *Urbi et Orbi* Bryusov employed a principle of organization apparently different from that of his previous books. Where *Tertia*

7.   *Dnevniki*, p. 122.
8.   Ibid., pp. 130–31.
9.   Andrej Belyj, *Načalo veka*, pp. 208–215.

Vigilia and *Me eum esse* had been organized into sections with thematic headings, the new volume was divided by genre. True, *Chefs d'œuvre* had accommodated both types of ordering, and formal designations had not been totally disregarded in *Tertia Vigilia*, yet the change was significant. *Me eum esse* was the book that most purely and obviously narrated a spiritual experience through its cyclical construction: "Counsels," "Visions," "Wanderings," "Love," "Intimations of Death," "In the Battle." Titles of sections in *Urbi et Orbi* are opaque by comparison: "Meditations [*Dumy*]: Premonitions," "Songs," "Meditations [*Dumy*]: Searchings," "Ballads," "Elegies," "Sonnets and Tercets," "Pictures: On the Street," "Anthology," "Odes and Epistles," "Poems [*Poèmy*]." But insisting that content always evoked form, Bryusov set out to realize a structure more complex than any he had used before. The foreword opened with his strongest statement on the nature of a book of poetry, one which echoed throughout the decade and beyond:

> A book of poems must be, not a random *collection* of poems of various types, but precisely a *book*, a closed whole, unified by a single thought. Like a novel, like a treatise, a book of poems reveals its content in successive steps from the first page to the last. A poem taken out of the common linkage loses as much as a single page taken out of a coherent discussion. The sections in a book of poems are no more nor less than chapters, one illuminating the other, which cannot be interchanged arbitrarily.
>
> [I, 604–605]

The conception that had been growing in him since the days of *Chefs d'œuvre* is here stated in full. Besides its general importance, it forms a challenge of sorts to the reader. In *Urbi et Orbi*, genre designations are to be understood as integral to meaning and total intended effect.

The *duma* is a lyric genre of no set form and of meditative content adopted by turn-of-the-century poets from the Romantics.

Bryusov's *dumy* continue one of the central themes of his poetry: a poet's reflections on what it means to be a poet. The attempt to define this role was almost an obsession with Bryusov. In *Tertia Vigilia* he had established the figure of poet-explorer, adventurer, even monarch. In "The Return" he had announced the most essential trait of such a leader: the readiness, even the thirst, to leave all when the hoped-for summons to further discoveries arrived. Should it not come, the poet would cease to be a poet. For in Bryusov's code, as we have seen it develop, the essence of poetry was discovery. "Overture," the first poem of the section "Meditations," subtitled "Premonitions," recapitulates the varied and novel visions of *Tertia Vigilia*. The lines are long—amphibrachic heptameter—and they move with vigor, especially in the last couplet. Here the poet reaffirms his essential nature:

> Ja sózdal, i ótdal, i pódnjal ja mólot, čtob snóva snačála kovát'.
> Ja sčástliv i sílen, svobóden i mólod, tvorjú čtoby kínut' opját'.

> I created and yielded up [my creation], and lifted the hammer to forge once again from the start.
> I am happy and strong, free and young, I create to cast away once more!

[I, 296]

"Premonitions" exhibits the lyrical hero, full of energy and daring, nonetheless stopping to ponder his course and weigh his resources of personality and strength. Capable though he feels himself, there is peril in this continual upward striving. "Stairs," the second poem, recalls the image, common currency in early Symbolism, of an aerial ladder over the abyss. But the earlier camaraderie with other travellers of Bryusov's own "Pale shadows entwine" (*Chefs d'œuvre*) is missing. The solitary traveller, having come a great distance in this perilous ascent, looks down and shudders: is he after all to end as a "falling star in the heaven of being"?

Bryusov had climbed far enough in his career to experience vertigo. To go dry or stagnant, to repeat himself—this would be to fall. Moreover, from his present position a fall would be conspicuous: a scandal and discouragement to the younger followers he had attracted, and a justification to opponents. But the greatest damage would be to the image of the poet he had so carefully nourished in himself and before the public. He now brought his doubts and questions forward. Given his premise that the poet must move ever beyond previous successes and discoveries, he might well ask where it would all end. In "The Last Desire" he asks this frightening and exhilarating question. Where will that last desire be satisfied, that last "unthought-of knowledge" come to him? Will it be in a monastery cell, or at the barricades of a city, or as a prisoner among his own books? These queries raised certain problems about his own nature. For the centrifugal and the centripetal warred in his personality. The drive to move outward in all directions in search of new truths was counterbalanced by the inward pull to the scholar-poet's cell. Bryusov was painfully aware of this ambivalence. In 1900, during his first meeting with Gorky, he recognized someone who did not seem to suffer from that problem. Wistfully he put the question to Gorky: "Could you live for twenty years among books and only books?" [10] To Gorky's amazed negative, Bryusov answered that that was just what he had done, though "I can't do it either." A strong note of self-irony sounds in the closing lines of "The Last Desire," where he pictures how "like a hungry prisoner, / I look on freedom from a window." But in "At Home" he affirms his intention of moving on. Looking for the last time at the familiar wallpaper, the rows of books, and at his old self, "as a snake [looks] at its discarded

10.   *Dnevniki*, p. 94.

skin," he resolves to set out toward the unknown mountaintops and the singing springtime. In "Flight" he casts one final look from that high window at the "many-headed crowd" that draws him forth. And in "Work" he is already learning in practice the "secrets of wise and simple life."

It is tempting to see in this series of poems a step in that progress away from Decadence to the poetry of real life which so many critics have looked for in Bryusov's career. There is no question that, beginning with *Tertia Vigilia*, Bryusov found a wide new sphere of poetic inspiration for himself and many Russian poets to come in his poetry of the city. He reminds us of this in the opening lines of this section: "Along narrow streets, in noise and at night, in theaters, in gardens I've roamed." However, much of Bryusov's urban poetry thus far dealt with what he called the mysteries of the city rather than with daily life as such. The poet preferred to stroll along those narrow streets at twilight, when only outlines were visible and inner secrets were more easily guessed as outer features were obscured. Most of all it should be remembered that the "secrets" in question were inevitably tied to the poetry that would be written out of them. In "Work" the poet asks, "What melodies will come to me" under the sooty stable roof? "What questions will arise, / What words will intoxicate" the poet while he mows? This is no Tolstoyan hero seeking moral betterment from menial tasks, yet there is a parallel. Bryusov's poet, like Tolstoy's Levin, hopes for revelation. But where Levin looks for *the* truth about life, the poet looks for an endless series of "truths" closely bound up with the words and melodies that will flow from them. Nor, despite Bryusov's by now frequent use of folk motifs, was he wed to the notion of finding his true sphere in the simple life or poems about it. "The Searcher" stresses his absolute lack of prejudice in regard to the locus of inspiration. What occupies the poet is the hope and the risk: what discoveries await him in the wilderness, and will he perish there? Or perhaps he will emerge on the shore, where multiple revelations wait when the sea will gaze at him with her "million eyes." This narrative line carries over easily to the following poem, "Ariadne's Thread," which underlines the perils of the quest. Then, as if pointing to the universality of his theme, Bryusov turns to a new set of images, this time biblical. The moving "Prodigal Son" with its epigraph from Pushkin departs from the traditional reading. It is not the biblical youth but the poet who contemplates a return to the pure springs of his youth. Having squandered his resources and drunk all the world's poisons, he recalls with regret the holy childhood shrine of feelings. The paternal home stands before him, but he cannot truly go home again.

The fear of spiritual desiccation and loss of spontaneity must haunt any poet. It attacked Bryusov with peculiar poignancy as he reached the peak of his powers. If they should fail, where was he to go for renewal? One of the poems most acclaimed by its first readers—and justly so—is "With the Earth." Despite the address to "Mother Earth," this is not a hymn of praise to nature and the simple life but, rather, a cry of spiritual weariness laden with Romantic overtones.[11] Lying on the earth, the poet begs her to betroth him to "the maiden stillness." He wishes to unite the two halves of his nature. "I am your son, I am also dust, / I like you am a link in creation." Whence, then, passion and terror and the endless fever of searching? Is betrothal to "the maiden stillness" the remedy for spiritual turmoil, or would such a betrothal mean death indeed?

The answer to the problem seems embedded in a paradox. The section "Premonitions" ends with the famous oxymoron "Onward, dream, my faithful ox! [vperéd, mečtá, moj vérnyj vól!]" Noted in its own right long before Marina Tsvetaeva's 1925 essay

11. The epigraph of "U zemli" is "Ja b xotel zabyt'sja i zasnut'!" from Lermontov's "Vyxožu odin ja na dorogu." Brjusov's poem, written in trochaic tetrameter (Lermontov used pentameter), conveys the same Romantic dividedness of soul as Lermontov's, but its imagery and meter suggest a closer link to folk poetry.

"Hero of Labor," the poem, entitled "In Answer," is a bold climax.[12] The imagery carries on the motif of physical labor and closeness to the earth appearing in other poems in this section. The premonitions occupying the poet were of two sorts. Some presaged new, unthought-of possibilities, while others hinted at a possible collapse of the poet's strength before that burden. For dream (*mečta*) in Bryusov's sense was no light play of fancy. The dreamers in his poems were Sven the Norseman and the like. Dream was strenuous spiritual exertion. Far as Bryusov was from mysticism in the usual sense, he could have understood the mystic's concept of spiritual exercise as a strenuous preparation for ecstasy. The moment of release from the rational self, so precious because so rare and fruitful, came only when the disposition had been prepared. The poet-plowman and his "*vernyj vol*" have their charge from a higher source, and they must not flag. But the reward also comes from that source. "And in that hour when darkness / Will hide the boundaries of this sphere, / Not I, but that Other, O my dream, / Will free you from the plough."

The section "Songs" following the first "*Dumy*" was an important departure for Bryusov in the direction of contemporary urban folksongs, *chastushki*. Several of the "Songs" are in this genre. Some contain small dramatic situations in which the singer is actor or observer: the factory worker watches his girl go home with another; another factory hand watches helplessly outside the

---

12.   Marina Cvetaeva, "Geroj truda (zapisi o Valerii Brjusove)." Selections appear in translation in *The Diary of Valery Bryusov (1893–1905)*, ed. and tr. with introduction by Joan Delaney Grossman (Berkeley and Los Angeles: University of California Press, 1980). Cvetaeva uses the famous phrase to illustrate her contention that Brjusov's genius was nine-tenths perspiration. Her essay is strongly colored by her personal contacts and personal disappointment with a would-be idol. She wrote: "And having strained my discernment to the utmost, I affirm: under the sincere guise of hatred I simply loved Bryusov, only more strongly in that aspect of love (repulsion) than I would have loved him in the simpler guise—attraction" (p. 172).

house where his love is dying of a fever, her dozing husband beside her; a girl decides to become a prostitute in order to secure gifts for her lover. There is the soldier's rehearsal of Russian victories in the manner of Lermontov's "Borodino"; the children's game; the prostitute's song of desperate gaiety. Bryusov's fascination with urban popular poetry led him to master its rhythms and lexicon. Some of the rhymes use city jargon tellingly and also provide the occasion for experiment with non-standard rhyme and rhythm. Four of the songs are in the standard *chastushka* quatrain, which Bryusov may have been the first to introduce into literary poetry.[13]

In "*Dumy*: Searchings" Bryusov experimented with freer forms for the poetic line. In some poems, as he noted in the foreword, he attempted to adapt features of *vers libre* to Russian. In others, while standard meters were used, line lengths, rhyme schemes, and stanza patterns varied with the meditative impulse. They are long poems, true meditations on the poet's inner life as well as on impressions drawn from without. A familiar pattern occurs in the structure of the section, with opening and closing poems offering question and response, problem and tentative solution. But the intensity of tone is new. The noonday devil attacked Bryusov with a vengeance in his maturity. The self-questioning that began in the first series of "Meditations" here develops into dismay, disgust, and worse. The opening poem, "L'Ennui de vivre," depicts a man horrified by the accumulated baggage weighing down his once free spirit. Weary of the persona made up of constantly shifting thoughts, longings, tastes, truths, rhymes, he cries: "I wish that I were not 'Valery Bryusov.'" Dragging behind him an ever-growing burden of time and memory, he is mocked all the while by his own poems and his unfulfilled desires. The bodies of women he has known, reveries and thoughts that pursue him,

13.   È. S. Litvin, "Valerij Brjusov i russkoe narodnoe tvorčestvo," p. 146.

books that have been teachers, friends, foes, and alter egos—all this unwieldy ballast makes him long to be without past or future, only to die and be reborn with each present moment.

The second poem provides relief and perspective. At first sight an account of the archangel's visit to the Virgin Mary, "Habet Illa in Alvo" offers a prolonged reflection on the mystery of motherhood and the succession of generations and meditates as well on the manner in which sin and goodness, passion and holy awe are intertwined in this mystery. A profoundly thoughtful poem, it is almost without link to any other poem of Bryusov's.[14]

The third poem, "Temptation," returns to the mood of "L'Ennui de vivre." It portrays a desert sojourn of doubt, disillusion, and above all disorientation, with imagery suggesting the desert trials of hermits and holy men. This hermit is also a pilgrim, now lured by mirages, now harassed by devils whispering their triumph over him. The classic trial of the desert father is his: the temptation to believe that his vision is false. The future promised by Nietzsche's prophet to one who believes in himself now threatens to fade. "Through the fingers the world's wisdom / Flows like water." And if beyond death is only the same aimless, sterile

14.   The manuscript bears the inscription: "Dedicated to Aubrey Beardsley" [I, 610]. This is thought to refer to a drawing of Beardsley's of a woman and an embryo that points at a page bearing the words "Incipit vita nova." The reference may also be in part autobiographical. His wife had several difficult pregnancies, and no child survived. Another possibility touches his intimate relationship with Anna Šesterkina, wife of the artist Mixail Šesterkin, in July 1902, the date of the poem. The account of Brjusov's relationship with Šesterkina and the selection of his letters to her over a period of fourteen years (LN 85, pp. 622–56) stop short of stating that Anna bore Brjusov a daughter in the summer of 1902. However, the editor, V. G. Dmitriev, notes that while Brjusov's letters to her usually avoid speaking directly of their relationship, hers to him are full of the strongest protestations of love. Dmitriev then quotes from a letter of Anna's to Brjusov dated 17 June 1914, in which she asked him to come to celebrate the twelfth birthday of her daughter: "You will have a look at our Nina" (p. 622). In June 1903 he sent birthday greetings and a present, speaking warmly and even longingly of the little girl (p. 653).

path? The voices of this mid-life desert all speak with equal persuasiveness—now urging him on, now mockingly suggesting
that neither exit from this tortured state nor extinction is possible. This is an absorbing, demanding poem which spoke eloquently to such readers as Bely.[15] Not consistently lyrical, with
few rhetorical flourishes, it shows the confident lyrical hero of earlier poems in a crisis not only of strength but of belief. This was
to be a recurring threat, as will be seen.

Two poems of this section are the fruit of Bryusov's travels to
Italy in 1902 and Paris in 1903. These were real, physical pil-
grimages. "Italy" and "Paris" combine descriptive passages with
reflections on the history and character of these places, as well as
on the pilgrimage's meaning for Bryusov. The penultimate poem
returns to Moscow. "A World" strikes a rare note in Bryusov's poetry, evoking the merchant milieu of his childhood. Dark ware-
houses with huge sacks, ladders, dusty windows, and over all,
that distinctive smell rising perhaps from hemp or from pitch:
"Forgotten world! I too breathed that poison / And shared that
fate." The outer world is contrasted with the still, dirty courtyard
disturbed now and again by a string of carts unloading goods into
trapdoors and by waiters collecting empty lunchpails. The memory's vividness is matched by the poignant realization that this,
his early world, is now lost forever. The same boy who crawled
over the sacks and played on the heavy scales also dreamed of
palm groves, unknown oceans, the polar regions, and interplane-
tary flight. Here perhaps is the key to Bryusov's duality: dreams
of conquering unknown spaces mingled with love of quiet familiar haunts. Now that old world is gone. Nostalgia overwhelms
the poet, and, in turn, the self-loathing of "L'Ennui de vivre"
threatens once more to engulf him.

However, for the time being a modus vivendi has been found,

---

15. Belyj quoted extensively from this poem and also from "V otvet" in
"Poezija Valerija Brjusova," *Noyj put'* no. 7 (July 1904), 134–36.

if we can judge by the final poem of the section. "In Hac Lac-rimarum Valle" is less lugubrious than the title suggests: from the vale of tears the poet sees the mountain peaks of gaiety and laughter. And he repairs there for a witches' sabbath of delights. From these he returns transformed and more sure of his gift and his call than ever: "I came into life a poet, I was chosen by fate, / And even against my will I shall remain myself" [I, 308].

These last lines should be read as a warning: this is my gift, take it as it is. The following two sections present what many have judged Bryusov's distinctive face, and they have been both lauded and reprobated. The six poems of the section "Ballads" are all erotic in theme and exotic in imagery. In form they are lyrical monologues. The Formalist critic Victor Zhirmunsky described Bryusov's method in these poems thus: "To put personal lyric excitement into the forms of his characters, who express both their own essence and the poet's imagining through lyrically ornamented narration in the form of a monologue addressed to an ideal hearer—such is Bryusov's favorite device."[16] Zhirmunsky, and after him many other critics, singled out this cycle as the heart of Bryusov's poetic creation. Observing that certain poems from the *Tertia Vigilia* section "Favorites of the Ages" and from the sections called "The Idols' Eternal Truth" in his next two books belong by theme and poetic method to his ballad genre, Zhirmunsky generalized from this category to the whole of Bryusov's work. From his analysis of the verbal categories, word combinations, rhythms, and rhymes of these poems he drew conclusions about the poetry as a whole. His discussion of Bryusov's craft is valuable in many respects. However, by his emphasis he created a one-sided image, and some of his statements are simply wrong when tested against poems outside the category he examined.[17] The excuse for Zhir-

16. Viktor Žirmunskij, *Valerij Brjusov i nasledie Puškina*, p. 10.
17. For example: "The fear of simple words forces Brjusov, like the French poets of the seventeenth and eighteenth centuries, to avoid the direct naming of objects, i.e., to replace the unpoetic concrete and individual word with descrip-

munsky's procedure lay in the originality and boldness with which Bryusov conceived this form as a vehicle for the theme of passion. Thus Bryusov was himself in part to blame, in this as in other ways, for the lopsided emphasis. As a result, in the eyes of generations of readers Bryusov has been for better or for worse what Zhirmunsky dubbed him, "poet of passion." [18]

As if to support this reading, a few months after *Urbi et Orbi* appeared Bryusov published in *The Balance* an essay entitled "Passion." [19] Perhaps precipitated by outcries against the "immorality" of his latest poetry, the piece provided a valuable gloss for the ballads. One of the great services of the new trends, Bryusov maintained, was to return to the human body its rightful place in the sphere of values. Nietzsche and the French Symbolists, he noted, came separately to see the need for this corrective. But where Nietzsche merely cried out, "Be true to the earth, my brothers," the Symbolists saw the body as yet another mystery to be plumbed. The new art recognized and fused two great human needs by rediscovering the power of the body through passion to open a door into the unknown. In his article Bryusov wrote that passion wore many masks in Greek mythology, but its true face could be seen only in the interval of changing from mask to mask. Presumably he attempted something like a series of glimpses into that mystery through this cycle he called ballads.

His "ballads" are related to the Romantic version of the genre by

tion by means of the more general, poetic word and the special generic sign" (p. 26). True as this is for the ballads, it is not at all true, for example, for the section "Na ulice: Kartiny" in such poems even as "Carica." There the ideal woman steps from a streetcar (*konka*), and after she disappears the poet finds himself looking at a string of streetlights (*fonari*). Examples like this can be multiplied almost indefinitely from all of Brjusov's books. They merely do not occur in the ballads.

18. Andrej Belyj had already used this title in a somewhat different form with decidedly different implications: "poèt—zdorovoj celomudrennoj strasti [poet of healthy, chaste passion]": "Brjusov," p. 200.

19. "Strast'," *Vesy* no. 8 (1904): 21–28.

the fact that they are lyrical-epic and favor the monologue form. The setting is usually vaguely ancient, and the speakers, both men and women, are anonymous or stylized types: a "queen," a "youth," a "slave," a Pompeian matron, Adam himself. The intent clearly is to distance the reader in order to focus on the essence of the narrated experience. "The Slave" is narrated by the servant of the "loveliest of queens." Her dark, burning glance glides over his prostrate form, but one day he lifts his scorching eyes to her face. In her wrath she condemns this defiler to a night chained to the bed where she disports with another. Forever after, toiling in the rock piles, he remembers that night, intended as torture, as one of unsurpassed bliss. "The Wayfarer" shows a king's daughter in a splendid garden bordering a dry and endless steppe, at the edge of which lies prostrate a handsome youth. Moved by pity and love, she invites him to share her bounty, but he refuses unless she will herself approach and offer him the cup. Angered, she turns away, and the mocking laughter of this unfortunate pursues her. In one case humiliation and pain only add to passion; in another both parties reject humiliation for love's sake and choose suffering. Possession, dominance, suffering and its delights, jealousy and its pains are all explored in these poems, whose force is in some cases considerable. The power of passion to reveal "the world's foundation," the basic movements of human nature, is the chief concern.

Bryusov certainly was not the first Russian poet to displace sentimental love poems by poems of passion. Mirra Lokhvitskaya's verse had ventured in this direction already in the 1890s.[20] But

20.   In one poem she wrote: "Ja ne znaju začem uprekajut menja, / Čto v sozdan'jax moix sliškom mnogo ognja (I do not know why they berate me / That in my creations there is too much fire)" (*Poèty 1880–1890-x godov*, ed. G. A. Bjalyj, series "Biblioteka poèta," [2nd ed. Leningrad, 1972], p. 592). Ivan Bunin wrote of her that the public thought her practically a bacchante because of her poems of love and passion, never suspecting that she was a married woman (I. A. Bunin, *Sobranie sočinenij*, 9 vols. [Moscow, 1967], 9, p. 289. She was closely connected with Konstantin Bal'mont in the later 1890s.

Bryusov made this type of lyric part of a larger conception of poetry and the poet's function. Not surprisingly, these poems added to his "decadent" image. But Bryusov's concept of Decadence, as we have seen, was not that of his early critics. For him its goal was penetration of the world's secret substructure through "other than rational means." That is, extremes of experience were necessary. And one of these extremes was passion. In this sense, then, as in others, *Urbi et Orbi* stands near the crest of Bryusov's Decadent poetry.

"Ballads" was followed by a section called "Elegies." Careful to note that he did not use this term in its conventional sense, Bryusov pointed to a derivation from ancient sources. Both the Alexandrian Greeks and Ovid used the elegy for erotic subjects. Bryusov's elegies indeed continued the erotic theme of the previous section, but where the ballads dramatized passion on a universal plane, the elegies are in a paradoxical way personal. The personal perspective is established by "To the Women," where the poet confesses with brutal frankness to the women in his life that individually their love was not enough. Private bliss is a paltry enticement compared to the real goal of entry into the extrarational sphere. Readers have often complained that his women have no names and no faces. Certainly in the elegies this is true and intentional, and here is the paradox. An essentially personal genre treats a personal experience with abstract imagery. The imagery in several of them is meant to shock—and many readers are repelled—by the juxtaposition of religious motifs with descriptions of physical love. The second elegy, "Rendezvous," which establishes this feature, is effective both as poem and as personal statement. The fatal encounter with passion is likened to Jacob's wrestling with the angel; the protagonist emerges lamed but marked for further revelations. In other poems crucifixion, miraculous conversion, and the performance of holy rites are invoked side by side with physical love. The jarring effect was intended to call attention to the profound mystery of a basic human experience. The climax of sexual embrace, the poet insists, *is* "our road to Damascus!"

The impersonality and coldness of which readers often complain in these poems of passion points to Bryusov's own ambivalence. The poet seems to be alone in his embraces, having rejected personal bliss to pursue the "mysteries." Yet in *About Art* he had written of the soul's need for communion and affirmed that "sexual love is the primary means of communion, . . . the sweetness of sensual pleasure lies in the momentary certainty that you are not alone" [VI, 52]. In a passage in "Truths" [VI, 59–60] which Alexander Blok found profoundly meaningful, Bryusov wrote of communion on the deepest level, which binds two beings together. *Shared* ecstasy was the ideal contemplated in several of the elegies. But "Farewell Gaze" already shows the inevitable rupture and failure. "Isolation" faces squarely the problem of the essential solitariness of human beings. Wings beat against an iron roof, the horizon is closed: "In passion itself we are alone!" The final note is nonetheless one of hope as the spiral of experience brings the poet out once more onto a higher plane. "To a Dear One" reaffirms the vision of solitary voyages of spiritual discovery yet manages to reconcile the two opposites of isolation and communion. Discoveries are made at the price of solitude and renunciation. But the end will bring resurrection of love and ultimate reunion with the loved one. This poem, which Bryusov thought one of his best, was truly a love poem, dedicated in manuscript to his wife.[21]

The section "Sonnets and Tercets" follows the pattern of genre designations for poems that develop common themes. However, these genres, unlike those of previous sections, have strict formal requirements. Bryusov did not try to alter them, but instead adapted them to his purposes. And one of his major purposes was

21.   Brjusov, *Stixotvorenija i poèmy*, p. 757. A letter of 26 January 1903 to Èda elaborated richly on the personal aspect of this poem.

to stress the continuous development of his poetic vision from *Chefs d'œuvre* down to the present moment. In *Chefs d'œuvre* the young poet created his first images of exotic passion in the sonnet "Premonition": "My love is as the burning noon of Java." In the long poem in tercets later called "Snows" he first merged earthly woman and Muse, passion and poetry. The ethereal love poems of *Me eum esse* chronicled the pursuit of the Muse. "Premonitions" of the understanding of passion and its relation to poetic illumination that informs *Urbi et Orbi* had already pervaded *Chefs d'œuvre*.

Of the three sonnets, one is a translation from D'Annunzio, one by its title refers to Maeterlinck's play *L'Intruse*, and the third many would say is pure Bryusov. In D'Annunzio's poem physical passion's aftermath is contrasted with the unattained ideal. In "The Intruder" this same ideal of passion—or is it poetry?—takes the poet for her own, turning him away from earthly women. One recalls the discarded heroines of the first elegy. Finally, "Rejection" tells how the poet's nature has alienated him from "Sparkling springtime, / Speeches of 'love,' the cherished trash of orators," and drawn him instead to the sordid, the criminal, the outcasts of society, in a word, to the "strange plants" of creation. The exploratory aspect of Bryusov's Decadence was here clearly in full flower.

The vampire-witch-Muse was no stranger to Bryusov's poetry.[22] Bely and Blok would speak of her as Astarte. The tercets begin with a variant on this motif in "The Forest Maiden." Dedicated to Lyudmila Vilkina, Minsky's wife and Bryusov's current extramarital interest, the poem uses folkloric motifs to convey the mingled delight and horror of being captured by this mysterious being. A firm link with his earlier poetry is established by the next poem, "Mon rêve familier," which specifically harks back to

---

22.   An outstanding early example that has its echoes here is from *Chefs d'œuvre* II: "I snova [And once again]," one of the poems Brjusov associated with the early days of his friendship with Bal'mont (*Dnevniki*, p. 50).

the early "Snows": "Once more alone as nine years earlier." [23] The
poet returns to solitary communion with the elusive love of that
earlier time. He now recognizes in her his one and only beloved,
the "creature of my dream"—in short, poetry: "In all I have ca-
ressed only you." It was an admission that Bryusov repeated in
one way or another throughout the most productive years of his
life. Whether or not his preoccupation with poetry was self-
defeating is a difficult matter to discuss and impossible to decide.
Without this passion much of his poetry presumably would not
have been written. Had his passion been a commoner one, he
might have written less but better, but there is no guarantee of
this. Meanwhile, in the concluding "Tercets to Booklists" he
showed a surprising capacity to be whimsical on the subject. The
personified booklist assures the poet that the only real immortality is in its power to give—the seven or eight lines that will
keep the poet's name alive forever. Not much, perhaps, but
Bryusov once said that he asked no more. [24]

"Pictures: On the Street" is a series of pictures of what might
be called everyday life. The urban theme, regarded as an innovation in *Tertia Vigilia*, now became a permanent part of Bryusov's
repertoire. The phrase *urban theme* has come to suggest factory
furnaces, mechanization, haunts of vice, and turbulent or down-
trodden crowds. While all these images appear occasionally in
Bryusov's poetry and more frequently in his translations from
Verhaeren, a careful reading of these thirteen "urban" poems in
Urbi et Orbi, as of those in *Tertia Vigilia*, gives a different impression. The urban sights and sounds are refracted through the sensibility of a brooding, whimsical stroller who prefers night to day.

23.   "Snega" (*Chefs d'œuvre*), subtitled "Terzini," also figured in these
recollections.
24.   Or less, as it was reported by Xodasevič: "I want to live so that there
will be in the history of world literature two lines about me. And there will be"
(Vladislav Xodasevič, *Nekropol'* [Paris: YMCA Press, 1976], p. 39).

"One thing I love: to roam aimlessly / Along noisy streets alone; / I love the hours of hallowed idleness, / Hours of revery and pictures" [I, 328]. Thus Bryusov sets the scene for the endlessly fascinating game of spying out the secrets of anonymous lives. For in this regard he was an incorrigible voyeur: "I gaze into the faces of passersby, / Drawn irresistibly into their secrets" [I, 328]. Ever alert for the sudden opening of a window into another soul, he finds his imagination works most fruitfully in the period from dusk to dawn. Tomblike houses in which people sleep like the dead, shadows which, like monsters lurking behind doors, make palpable the accumulated ills of life, and at last, in the final poem, hordes of workers stifling curses as they labor: these are some of the pictures he captures.

Night gives him two visions of his ambiguous ideal. In "Tsaritsa" she descends from an ordinary streetcar, a queenly beauty whom for a second he imagines celebrating a triumph in a conquered city. A moment later, alone on the empty sidewalk he sees only a diminishing row of streetlights. In "To a Passerby" he experiences another sort of encounter. "She" sweeps by, enveloping him in her perfume, her meaningful glance, and her bodily warmth. Then, suddenly, a burst of predatory laughter, and he is wrapped in the humid blackness of her loosened hair. An erotic fantasy no doubt, but is it not also night that bears down on the poet, wrapping its blackness around him and infusing him with its poetry? Daytime, too, has its images. The vivid, lively "At the Races" recalls Bryusov's childhood visits to the racetracks with his father, an enthusiastic player of the horses. The most often cited poem in this section is the famous "Stonemason." Working at building a prison, the laborer utters cryptic remarks that amount to social prophecy. "Stonemason" was a reworking of a poem by the noted Populist P. L. Lavrov, which Bryusov very likely knew from his schooldays and of which he may have been reminded by the reconstruction of a prison near his dacha in the summer of 1901.[25] The theme as well as the effective dialogue form of the poem (the latter borrowed from Lavrov) caused some critics to compare Bryusov to Nekrasov.

The combination of Verhaeren's influence and the mounting disturbances in Russian society in these years no doubt inspired the threatening notes in his city poems. The surprising thing is that they are so few. The impression is inescapable that these poems are what indeed they claim to be: not photographs, not agitation posters or banners, but *pictures*, impressionistic ones at that. It would take the building of barricades in the streets of Moscow in 1905 to evoke from Bryusov anything to compare with the revolutionary spirit of Verhaeren. The prophetic note is here heard only in the *poèma* section (discussed below).

The longest section in *Urbi et Orbi* is called "Anthology." While the title has classical associations, it seems here simply to designate a selection of poems touching various favorite themes but carrying no cumulative meaning. Several of these poems are dedicated to Bryusov's associates. A poem to Fedor Sologub is called "Voluptuousness." It features a woman who personifies that quality; she is crowned with purple poppies, and there is "something bestial" in her mien. Bryusov and Sologub had a long history of friendly relations based almost entirely on appreciation and understanding of each other's poetry. Several years earlier Sologub had dedicated to Bryusov a poem called "From the Evil Work of the Headsman," subtitled "Ballad," whose central figure yields nothing to any of Bryusov's sensuous heroines.[26] Daily at noon the queen leaves her luxurious surroundings to seek terrible amusements underground, where she takes the whip from the torturer and continues his work. Bryusov thanked Sologub for the

25. I, 612.
26. Fedor Sologub, *Stixotvorenija*, ed. M. I. Dikman, Biblioteka poèta (2nd ed. Leningrad, 1975), pp. 291–93.

dedication, saying, "And of course you are right. This ballad is congenial to me."[27]

"Stones" was dedicated to Alexander Dobrolyubov. During his visit to Bryusov in the summer of 1898, Dobrolyubov delivered himself of a curious theory about the wills of dead ancestors, the most ancient of which survive in stones.[28] Later he leaned to the idea that humankind had at one time passed through the stage of inanimate nature.[29] Bryusov's poem expresses brotherly feeling for these lower creatures and grants them resurrection on the last day. The poem probably echoes discussions with, or more likely monologues by, Dobrolyubov.

The poem dedicated to Zinaida Gippius, which closes the section, arose from conversations with her at the end of 1901. Dated December 1901, the poem takes its title from the first line: "In unshakable truth / I for a long while have not believed." Its most quoted lines are in the second stanza: "Both God and the Devil / I wish to praise" [I, 355]. In the compass of three quatrains Bryusov summed up the substance of his 1901 essay "Truths": no truth is absolute and all "truths" have something to offer the inquiring spirit. Gippius recalled the poem as having arisen from their talk about difficult rhymes. One word that challenged them was *istina*, "truth." But obviously more was at stake in their discussion. Writing years later as an émigrée, Gippius found it logical that a man who, to her mind, served only himself would

27.   Sologub, *Stixotvorenija*, p. 610. In 1910 Brjusov summed up Sologub's development as poet and seer, noting how Sologub had moved from tentative probing of life to ruthless exposure. "What was formerly quiet sadness became passion and turbulence of spirit: 'You, turbulent wind, my passion! [Ty, bujnyj veter, strast' moja!]'" (*Dalekoe i blizkoe*, VI, 286). Obviously they continued to share congenial themes. A parallel study of the poems of these two might uncover a dialogue that could fill out what is known of their relations. See also Fedor Sologub, "Speech in Memory of V. Ja. Brjusov."

28.   *Dnevniki*, p. 46.

29.   I, 615.

believe in nothing else.[30] Even during the years of their close association neither really liked or trusted the other. However, just at
the end of 1901 and in 1902 Gippius and Merezhkovsky tried to
convert Bryusov to their neo-Christianity and, apparently, for a
time Bryusov was disposed to listen. In a letter to Pertsov in
March 1902 he admitted that his Petersburg friends had shown
him new, unsuspected depths in Christianity.[31] But this was far
from a confession of faith, and this poem put the matter in
perspective.

One more poem with a personal dedication is of particular
interest. *"Terem"* drew partly on Bryusov's fascination with Moscow's historic places, which he visited extensively in 1899 and
1900. These included the Kremlin *terems*, or women's quarters.
On a more personal level it testifies to his awareness of the relatively confined and purposeless life Eda led, at home with his
mother and sisters, especially after the loss of their child in the
summer of 1901.[32] As an evocation of both the setting and the life
that must have gone on there the poem is particularly successful.

The poems in this section vary in tone as much as in content.
Some are light and charming, some are sensuous, some meditative. However, if the intent was indeed to provide a sampling of
Bryusov's poetry, one more type was needed, and it came in the
penultimate poem, "Disdain." Written originally in October
1900 during the depression that followed the publication of *Tertia Vigilia*, it is a particularly bitter personal confession. Con-
tempt for himself and for others, inability to love, recognition of
the illusoriness of all desires: it is *ennui de vivre* by another name.

30.   Zinaida Gippius, "Oderžimyj. O Brjusove," p. 89. That Brjusov was
"possessed" by ambition and self-love is the thesis of the essay.
31.   *LN* 27–28, p. 282.
32.   Testimony concerning Brjusov's devotion to his wife comes from an unlikely source. Zinaida Gippius recalled that when Èda was near death several
times in unsuccessful childbirth, Brjusov became so distraught as to be nearly
unrecognizable: *Živye lica*, p. 85.

That the mood was not a fleeting one is suggested by this poem's publication here three years later. That it was paired with "In unshakable truth" suggests its importance to him personally. Both poems seem to reflect consistent or recurrent states of mind.

The next section, "Odes and Epistles," is in part devoted to "favorites of the ages" such as Napoleon and Mary Stuart and to various faces of Venice, and it includes one poem on a Pan-Slavist theme anticipating the manner of poems Bryusov wrote during the Russo-Japanese War. The remainder, seven of the twelve, resume the attention to fellow poets begun in the previous section. The first two are addressed to Balmont. Over the past two or three years Bryusov's relations with Balmont had followed their previous tortuous pattern of close sympathy alternating with stormy episodes and periods of estrangement. The first part of 1901 belonged to the latter. However, Balmont's exile from the capitals at the end of June removed him temporarily from the scene, and a few months later he was allowed to go abroad. This separation renewed their friendship. No sooner was Balmont in Paris than Bryusov began receiving assurances of his affection.[33] In May of 1902 Balmont was in Oxford, and his letters grew in warmth and urgency. By winter he was back in Russia, in time to join Bryusov in the Moscow battle for the new art in the Literary-Artistic Circle and elsewhere. *Urbi et Orbi* was dedicated to "K. D. Balmont, poet and brother." These two epistolary poems elaborate this dedication. The mutual admiration of the two seems at this time to have been at its peak. Bryusov's earlier passionate exhortations to Balmont to free his spirit were answered in Balmont's "Freedom [Volja]," dated January 1902 and dedicated to Bryusov. Here he promised to be true to his own inspiration. Bryusov responded promptly with encouragement and congratulations in the first of these poems, written in Balmont's style

33. Letters of K. D. Bal'mont to V. Ja. Brjusov, CGALI, Moscow, fond. 56, op. 3, ed. xr. 6.

and quoting some of his expressions: "Ever free, ever young, / You are like the wind, like a wave" [I, 348]. The second poem must have pleased Balmont even more than the first.[34] It apotheosized Balmont as the supreme singer of the movement, the Arion, to be saved miraculously should all others perish. The stress here was on the word *singer*. Bryusov's review of Balmont's *Let Us Be Like the Sun* later that year showed the negative side of the image: Balmont was second to none as a singer, but he should be warned not to aspire to thought in his poetry.[35]

Other poems trace other aspects of Bryusov's relationships in those active days. Toward Jurgis Baltrušaitis, his colleague in the Scorpio enterprise and a fellow poet, he adopted the role of encourager. To V. I. Pribytkov, his fellow adept in spiritualism, he dedicated a poem written for a gathering of its Moscow followers. To the memory of Ivan Konevskoy, who had drowned in the summer of 1901, he dedicated a moving tribute setting out as effectively as any poem of that genre the unique gifts taken to the grave by a poet who died too young. Konevskoy's death left Bryusov with a sense of terrible loss for Russian poetry. A year later, as he became acquainted with Andrei Bely, he speculated that here might be the replacement for Konevskoy. "Probably the most interesting man in Russia," he wrote.[36] The last two poems of this section are directed to Bely and his young colleagues who were to form the new wing of Russian Symbolism, chief among whom was Alexander Blok.

Though Bryusov's interest in the *poèma* dated back to his early fascination with Poe's poetry, he had included no *poèma* so desig-

34.   I, 615–16. Bal'mont's letter of 31 August 1902 from Oxford protested his unworthiness of the accolade in the first of the epistles.
35.   *Mir iskusstva* no. 7–8 (1903): 29–36. The negative emphasis was much heavier when the piece was revised later to appear in *Dalekie i blizkie* (VI, 250–58).
36.   *Dnevniki*, p. 121n.

nated in any book since the second edition of *Chefs d'œuvre*. Two of the five *poèmy* there, "Snows" and "And once again," are recalled in other parts of *Urbi et Orbi*. Thus Bryusov used one more means of linking his latest with his early work. The three *poèmy* that close *Urbi et Orbi* form a prophetic triad. The first, "The Withdrawn Ones [Zamknutye]," grew out of his summer 1900 stay near the ancient Baltic city of Reval, which he found fascinating for its history but irritating for the seemingly limited imagination of its inhabitants. In this poem he pictures self-satisfied little people living complacent lives amidst relics of a heroic past. Yet even that impressive past speaks of isolation and secretiveness, and the poet is driven to flee both past and present, seeking the spot where another, freer wind blows: the harbor, with its feeling of liberty and its open horizon. Looking back to the city, he exhorts the populace: "Live, live! . . . Drink deep of truth and falsehood, / Love ecstasy and love pain." The first part is a very successful descriptive narrative, which renders with equal vividness the dusty museum exhibits—old boat prows and the beaks of ancient birds—and the rough songs of sailors and smell of tar. The second part elaborates an unflattering parallel between the deadly life of the secluded city and the life of which the poet himself is a part. In the latter all is pretense, masks are worn everywhere, "in art and in the drawing room," and people show their true faces only in gambling halls and brothels. It is a stifling picture. And from here he moves to the inevitable prophetic mood. Mechanization foretells the time when cities will be all-engulfing structures and their inhabitants like the withdrawn ones. The familiar picture of destruction that follows is given with eloquent brevity, as is the vision of a new world to come. Both visions are of course at least as old as the Bible and the classical poets, where Bryusov must first have seen them.

The second *poèma* is a diversion, taking off perhaps from the image of free-living sailors in the first. "City of Women" was

written in Venice in 1902, and the city of the poem is reminiscent
of Venice. Deserted but for the disturbing and finally maddening
olfactory hint of the presence of women, the city lures six seamen,
who remain forever. They never see their temptresses but are forever aware of their voluptuous presence. In manuscript this poem
was dedicated to Tennyson.[37] It may have been based on an episode in "The Voyage of Maeldune," already a source for Bryusov,
and possibly on "The Lotus Eaters." He of course goes beyond
what Tennyson allowed himself, even in the episode of the Isle of
Witches. And for Bryusov, besides the strongly sensual motif
there was an even more characteristic one. The poem deals with
the power of a mysterious enticement to make adventurous spirits
foresake certain contentment for an uncertain reward.

The closing poem, "The Last Day," blends Golden Age mythology with a kind of Decadent carnival of love. "It will come,
that world gone mad, / Which the poet praised." But Bryusov's is
a latter-day version undreamt-of by Vergil.[38] Strange, poisonous
perfumes fill the air, and not only men but flowers, birds, and
beasts display unwonted vitality. All tools of labor are laid down,
machines halt, prophets prophesy, and the language of nature is
understood by all. The great festival extends over all zones. Finally all parts of creation yearn for love and find it. The last
breath is one of ecstasy. The angel's trumpet is raised over a universe that ends with a universal sigh of love.

This vision stands in contrast to the more familiar one at the
end of "The Withdrawn Ones." The nineteenth and early twentieth centuries had grown inured to the picture of a world growing increasingly mechanized, bloodthirsty, effete, a world doomed

37. I, 619.
38. Brjusov's version of the return of the Golden Age is perhaps most
closely related to the dream of Versilov in Dostoevskij's *Podrostok*. There mankind, alone and without Christ, turns to universal love, which, paradoxically,
evokes the return of Christ. The specifically erotic note is Brjusov's addition.

to destroy itself. New life would replace the old, only to begin the cycle again. Early models for this are found in Plato and Ovid; modern developments provided new material to flesh out the plot. Bryusov himself later offered several versions.[39] Yet somewhere it should all come to an end, and Bryusov's vision of the last day offered an alternative to the varieties of catastrophe that human ingenuity had conjured up over the ages.

Eight years earlier Bryusov had begged Peter Pertsov to read *Chefs d'œuvre* straight through, "from the foreword to the table of contents inclusive, for everything has a fixed purpose."[40] The unity he had insisted on privately then was expressed in the new book's foreword. In another letter to Pertsov from the time of *Chefs d'œuvre* Bryusov wrote: "And they exist, these new, unknown forms [for poetry]! I foretold them in the foreword to *Chefs d'œuvre*, I feel them, but I don't know them."[41] The prediction consisted in his linking the development of form to a progressive emphasis on the artist's personality.

In the years since *Chefs d'œuvre* Bryusov had assisted this line of evolution with growing energy and conviction. Now in *Urbi et Orbi* he attempted to unite form and content in a single expression of the poet's persona. The book opens with "Meditations [*Dumy*]: Premonitions," where the genre's tradition underlines the subject of the poet's evolving role, always at the core of Bryusov's poetry. The series of eleven "Meditations" climaxes in the exaltation of his own conception, quite opposite to that of his chief rival Balmont, of the poet's imagination or dreams, *mečta*. Then he moves quickly into "Songs," which exhibit the play of his imagination. From these he returns to "Meditations," now subtitled "Search-

39. For example, the unfinished play *Zemlja*, first published in *Severnye cvety assirijskie* (1905) and several poems from *Stephanos*, to be discussed in Chapter Nine.

40. *Percovu*, p. 37.

41. Ibid., p. 32.

ings," for the poet cannot rest on his path. This serious genre
once more emphasizes the gravity of the problems explored, and
again the series climaxes in exaltation, this time of the new freedom the poet has attained. That new freedom is now expressed in
his treatment of conventional genres and in the boldest erotica yet
to appear in Bryusov's poetry. The lyrical monologues he calls
"Ballads" are celebrations of the poet's freedom to assume any
mask his imagination offers him. The ballad is traditionally a less
subjective form than the elegy, and, while he departed from the
common use of these genres, Bryusov kept this distinction. His
"Elegies" bring the erotic from the universal to the particular.
This cycle of erotica recalls his early work, and the return to "Sonnets and Tercets," forms favored in his first book of poetry, establishes the continuity of the poet's relationship with his earliest
Muse. At the same time, with their references to Western poets
like D'Annunzio and Maeterlinck, these genres reassert Bryusov's
links to Western Decadent poetry. The impressionistic "Pictures," with their fluid forms and varied subjects, demonstrate
the freedom of the poet's fancy to range, particularly in the relatively new direction of the urban theme. "Anthology" represents
the breadth and depth the poet has achieved in this, the high
noon of his work, and the poems that cap this section present the
"truths" from which his explorations have emanated and the new
positions to which they have led. He then turns to address his
fellow poets and spiritual comrades in forms traditional for that
purpose: odes and epistles. It is characteristic of Bryusov's poetic
persona that he should do this. Furthermore, the penultimate
section emphasizes the orientation of the book as a whole: toward
the city and the world. Finally, when he has gathered his listeners' attention for a final message, Bryusov frames that prophecy in a form of special importance for him and Balmont since
their early days—the *poèma*.

In this way Bryusov attempted to create in *Urbi et Orbi* not merely a thematic unity but a formal one, in the sense that the poetic forms he chose were intimately bound to the personality being expressed, in a way analogous to the tones of voice and phrasing of an orator. Except insofar as he gave certain genres an unaccustomed meaning, as with ballads, the forms themselves were not "new, unknown." Perhaps he had not yet been able to discover the forms he prophesied to Pertsov, or perhaps he found his need satisfied by the melding of form and purpose he achieved in *Urbi et Orbi*.

Despite the persistence of concerns from his early period, an important shift had taken place in Bryusov's views which made the relation of persona to poetry even more central. In effect they must expand together, as new reflections of the world are formed in the microcosm that is the artist's soul. We have seen the development of Bryusov's extreme individualist position. In *Tertia Vigilia* the poet defined himself in Nietzschean terms. In the final section of his 1901 essay "Truths," Bryusov had announced an important new stage in his thinking: "I have come to the view that the goal of artistic creation is not communication but simply self-satisfaction and self-knowledge. . . . The poet creates in order to clarify his reflections and emotional stirrings, to bring them to definition. . . . What happens after creation of a poem is another matter. It may serve also for communication. From this it follows once again that all true works of art are equally valuable" [VI, 60].

With this he had found a new set of reasons for the conclusion reached earlier about the all-inclusiveness of art. The idea that he spelled out with such conviction in "Truths" was contained in germ in the foreword to *Chefs d'œuvre*: "The essence of the work of art is the personality of the artist" [I, 572]. Now, in a logical conclusion to his thinking, the emphasis had been shifted. As Bryusov's awe before the complexity of the universe had grown, so too had his wonderment before the human personality. He now saw each soul as a unique refraction of the ever-changing cosmos.

Moreover, when the soul was highly refined—as was the artist's—it afforded glimpses of being that constituted an end in
themselves. Bringing these into clear resolution was a supremely
worthy goal.[42] *Urbi et Orbi* marked a new high in the development of Bryusov's individualism.

The publication of *Urbi et Orbi* occasioned a predictably mixed
response, which included parodies curiously recalling early days
when Vladimir Solovyov made merry over *Russian Symbolists*. If
Solovyov's remarks at that time had conferred recognition on a
poet hitherto unknown, present reactions confirmed the prominent position Bryusov now held. More than this, within the
growing circle of initiates his influence was all but hypnotic, and
Urbi et Orbi intensified that effect. Important in this regard are
Alexander Blok and Andrei Bely. Any assessment of Bryusov's
importance to twentieth-century Russian poetry must include an
examination of his relationship with these two poets, since so
much of later Russian poetry bore the imprint of one or the other.
Both Blok and Bely were seven years Bryusov's junior, and both
began writing poetry under other influences. But both fell under
his sway at an early stage and may be said to have reached their
maturity as poets only after passing through his school. Bely's
personal contacts with Bryusov began through the Solovyov family late in 1901 and soon blossomed into an association valued
perhaps as much by the older poet as by the younger.[43] Blok too
came to Bryusov's notice through the brother of the recently deceased Vladimir Solovyov, but since he lived in Petersburg, op-

42.   The example of Ivan Konevskoj had helped convince Bryusov that poetry was essentially "the clarification for the poet himself of his meditations and
state of feelings." Brjusov continued admiringly in his essay "Mudroe ditja":
"His poetry is a diary. He was unable to write of anything but himself—and as a
matter of fact, for no one but himself" [VI, 243].
43.   *Dnevniki*, p. 110.

portunities for contact between them were fewer, and in fact the two did not meet until 1904.[44] Blok's adulatory attitude by that time may have made personal relations difficult.

Bryusov's influence on Blok has long been considered to lie in his showing the younger poet the way to new content, notably the urban theme; and to new techniques, especially through his experiments with meter and rhythm and with free verse.[45] More recently one critic has noted the attraction that Bryusov's daring lyrical hero held for Blok.[46] Elsewhere I have discussed in some detail the nature of Bryusov's influence on Blok's *Poems about the Beautiful Lady [Stixi o Prekrasnoj Dame]*, which was published in October 1904 but had been begun late in 1900.[47] Blok became acquainted with Bryusov's work in the first issue of *Northern Flowers;* most of the items starred in Blok's copy were by Bryusov.[48] Other evidence from that time shows Blok trying to reconcile his attraction to what he perceived as Bryusov's Decadence with the mystical strivings fired in him by Solovyov.[49] He came to the tentative conclusion that the new art's great feat was boldly to uncover and gaze into the two abysses of light and darkness within man, long sensed but never so openly explored. It was a terrifying

44.   Aleksandr Blok, *Sobranie sočinenij*, 8 vols. (Moscow and Leningrad, 1960–1963), 8, pp. 82–84.

45.   Viktor Gol'cev, "Brjusov i Blok," *Pečat' i revoljucija* no. 4 (1928), pp. 33–46; no. 5, pp. 67–80.

46.   Pavel Gromov, *Aleksandr Blok: Ego predšestvenniki i sovremenniki* (Moscow and Leningrad, 1966), pp. 88ff.

47.   In my article "Blok, Brjusov, and the Prekrasnaja Dama."

48.   Aleksandr Blok, *Zapisnye knižki 1901–1920* (Moscow, 1965), p. 22.

49.   *Zapisnye knižki*, pp. 22–24; Blok, VII, 21–38. The latter is a sketch for an article on Russian poetry. It is interesting to compare Blok's thoughts with an 1839 poem of Baratynskij's, "Blagosloven svjatoe vosvestivšij!" The fifth and sixth lines are notable: "Dve oblasti—sijanija i t'my—/ Issledovat' ravno stremimsja my (Two spheres—radiance and darkness—/ We strive equally to probe)" (E. A. Baratynskij, *Polnoe sobranie stixotvorenij*, Biblioteka poèta [2nd ed. Leningrad, 1957], p. 193).

but fascinating revelation for Blok. What he now sought was an adventurous guide acquainted with the new terrain. He already suspected that Bryusov was that guide, and *Urbi et Orbi* confirmed his suspicions.

In the first months after its appearance Blok wrote two reviews of *Urbi et Orbi*. The first of these, not then published, focused on the image of the adventurer-poet. It also commented on Bryusov's use of *vers libre* and his employment of commonplaces of urban life as poetic images.[50] The second review, published in *New Way*, is much more revealing of the book's significance for Blok at that time.[51] The lessons Blok learned were clearly of two very different sorts. The first of these was the principle of structure Bryusov put forth in this book. The prevalence of that structural principle in later Russian poetry speaks strongly for the importance of Blok's perception of it. Blok's review opens with a paragraph quoted from Bryusov's foreword, in which he set forth his theory of the book of poetry as an integrated whole. Blok made much of the triumph of achieving this in a varied collection of poems written over a period of three years. It is significant that Blok was just then facing the same problem in *Poems about the Beautiful Lady*. He admired not only Bryusov's theory but its realization in *Urbi et Orbi:* "A book like a song, from which 'not a word can be discarded,' locked in all its nine parts, leaving only a narrow passage from section to section, as from chapter to chapter."[52] That Blok absorbed this lesson is evident not only in his first book but also in the foreword to the 1911 edition of his poems, where he paraphrased Bryusov's introduction to *Urbi et Orbi*.[53]

The second major point in Blok's review is a more difficult one, which students of Blok have avoided confronting. This is his en-

---

50. Blok, V, 534.
51. *Novyj put'* no. 7 (1904): 202–208; V, 540–45.
52. Blok, V, 541.
53. Blok, I, 559.

thusiastic claim for a spiritual kinship between Bryusov and Vladimir Solovyov.[54] That this was a central thesis is clear from the epigraphs Blok chose for his own book: one each from Solovyov and Bryusov for the first section, where the poet awaits the Beautiful Lady's apparition, and one from each for the two remaining sections, where hope, fear, and sense of loss mingle. The visionary Solovyov commemorated in his poem "Three Rendezvous" his three encounters with Sophia—the Divine Wisdom, World Soul, Eternal Feminine. Blok's "Beautiful Lady" was an elusive ideal of the Solovyovian type, who tantalized him with the hope of more and more explicit visitations. His correspondence with Bely in the summer of 1903 was full of mutual questioning and very tentative answers.[55] In Blok's view the World Soul would be approached chiefly through vision or dream. Poets thus clearly had a role in revealing her to the world. Hitherto they had addressed an esthetic ideal; now, under a new dispensation, more might be expected. In this quest Blok still regarded Solovyov as his chief mentor, but he was ready for other guidance as well. Blok's excitement over Bryusov's book indicated that he felt he had found this added guidance.

The question naturally occurs: what in *Urbi et Orbi* and in Bryusov's poetry generally could warrant such an interpretation? Nothing in Bryusov's conception of poetry coincided with Blok's notions, or so it would seem. Yet Blok was convinced that Bryusov not only pursued an ideal like his own but possessed knowledge of her not yet accessible to his younger colleagues.[56] Blok saw the ambiguous feminine figure who glimmers through Bryusov's poems from the earliest days as a Solovyovian visitant, rendered

54. Pavel Gromov has called Blok's suggestion *"Počti dikoe*—almost wild" (*Aleksandr Blok*, p. 102).
55. *Aleksandr Blok i Andrej Belyj: Perepiska*, ed. V. N. Orlov (Moscow, 1940), pp. 32–46.
56. Blok, VIII, 72; Letter to Brjusov, 26 November 1903.

complex and changeable by Bryusov's bold gaze into the two abysses. That she sometimes wore the mask of Astarte, the goddess of sexual love, was inconsistent with Blok's image of her, but he was willing to trust Bryusov's superior knowledge and experience. Moreover, this was not the only mask she wore in Bryusov's poetry. The poem from which Blok drew the epigraph for the first section of his book was Bryusov's closing elegy, "To a Dear One." Using imagery usually reserved for his programmatic poems, Bryusov there evoked cosmic spaces. Foreseeing his soul's future odyssey through "the timeless immeasurable," out of which new visions would arise as the dust of each successive past was shaken off, he envisioned a final revelation. The discarded past will rise again before his transfigured soul: "And as if once more beneath the starry vault, / From my fathomless height, / I will cast your name into the abysses, / And to my call will answer—you" [I, 315].[57] Whatever the autobiographical subtext to this poem, which was dedicated to his wife, it certainly enfolded other meanings: thus far Blok's sense was correct. For Blok, however, this poem was a clear acknowledgment that Bryusov served an ideal that was close to Blok's own, received from Solovyov, and it confirmed Blok's belief that Bryusov was the bearer of new spiritual secrets.

Bryusov soon understood what Blok's ecstatic reaction to his poems meant, and he firmly rejected the suggestion that he sought the Solovyovian vision. There were moments, indeed, when he seemed to envy the confidence of the younger poets. This feeling appears in "To the Younger Ones," the penultimate poem in "Odes and Epistles." The bride has entered with the groom and his company, made up of the younger men, while the older poet stands without on the cold stones with the door locked against him. Written in a moment when the spell of Blok's "Beautiful Lady" poems was strong upon him, the poem did not

57.   See also footnote 21 above.

truly represent Bryusov's attitude toward the younger poets' views.[58] Whatever their mystical experiences, Bryusov often expressed strongly his belief that it was not the business of poetry to serve theurgic or any other extrinsic goals. For some time, however, Blok suspected Bryusov of lack of candor. "Bryusov conceals his knowledge of Her. In just this he is sincere to the extreme. Moreover he deceives *everyone*, insisting that *Urbi et Orbi* is a rational book."[59] It took Blok years to realize that Bryusov's ideal was no transcendental being but poetry itself, which provided a vision of the world but was never for him the instrument of some higher revelation.

Andrei Bely's response to *Urbi et Orbi* was at least as enthusiastic as Blok's. In November 1903 he wrote to Blok: "Have you read *Urbi et Orbi*? After that volume there can be no argument about Bryusov: there is every reason to join his name to the names of Pushkin, Lermontov, Maikov, Polonsky, Tyutchev, Fet, Aleksei Tolstoy, Nekrasov, and Vladimir Solovyov."[60] He later repeated these praises, even shortening the list.[61] And he shared Blok's belief in Bryusov's vatic powers. However, unlike that of Blok, Bely's relationship with Bryusov was a personal one, and at the time of *Urbi et Orbi* it consisted of unclouded admiration. But in the second half of 1904 a bizarre series of episodes began that nearly issued in a duel between Bely and Bryusov. A reconciliation allowed them to work closely—though not always harmoniously—on *The Balance* throughout much of its existence. Their professional concerns during those years kept them in harness, though their differing approaches to Symbolism led to conflicts in

58. Cf. Petr Percov, "Brjusovskoe stixotvorenie 'Mladšim' (Iz literaturnyx vospominanij)," *30 dnej* no. 10–11 (1939): 127.

59. *Zapisnye knižki*, p. 65, entry of May 1904.

60. *Perepiska*, p. 58.

61. "Apokalipsis v russkoj poèzii," *Vesy* no. 4, (1905): 17. Also in Andrej Belyj, *Lug zelenyj* (Moscow, 1910; reprinted New York and London: Johnson Reprint, 1967). The revised list of significant poets reads: Puškin, Lermontov, Nekrasov, Tjutčev, Fet, Solov'ev, Brjusov, and Blok.

that area as well.[62] Nonetheless, they continued to respect each other as artists, and some of Bely's statements in the three or four years after *Urbi et Orbi* are particularly useful in assessing Bryusov's contribution to forming the poets of Bely's generation.

During the earlier years Bely and Bryusov saw each other often. Bely wrote much later of evenings in Bryusov's apartment when he and other young poets brought their work and received "unforgettable lessons . . . in stylistics, versification, and so on."[63] He also marvelled in retrospect at Bryusov's eagerness to listen to his ideas, no matter how they differed from his own. Possibly in those early days the two refused to admit that their points of view on poetry and its goals were irreconcilable. The poem "To Andrei Bely" ("Odes and Epistles"), if read in the light of 1903 and not of later events, suggests this. Open as he was to any probing of the limits of knowledge, Bryusov may have listened at first with real hope to Bely's visionary talk. Yet he was cautious. The poem warns that the speaker has believed and loved many times, only to be disillusioned. Thus it implies: let that one beware who proves unfaithful and misleads him again.[64]

Bely's first poem dedicated to Bryusov, called "Mage," dramatized his and Blok's awe of the older poet: "And there—a cliff, and you stand, / the unyielding mage crowned with stars, / and

---

62. Brjusov rejected Belyj's praise in "Apokalipsis," since it was based on premises he could not accept. He expressed his position in "V zaščitu ot odnoj poxvaly: (Otkrytoe pis'mo Andreju Belomu)," *Vesy* no. 5 (1905): 37–39. Belyj responded with "V zaščitu ot odnogo narekanija," *Vesy* no. 6 (1905): 40–42. The most famous and far-reaching debate of these questions, involving not only Brjusov and Belyj but also Aleksandr Blok and Vjačeslav Ivanov, appeared in the journal *Apollon*, no. 8 (Blok and Ivanov), no. 9 (Brjusov), and no. 11 (Belyj). Other poets commented elsewhere on the polemic, which is often considered to mark the demise of the Symbolist movement.

63. "Valerij Brjusov," p. 278.

64. At the time this was written no basis for real personal enmity yet existed. However, Brjusov's psychological ascendancy over Belyj already seems evident.

you gaze with prophetic smile."[65] Like Blok, Bely for a time refused to accept Bryusov's protest against such reverent treatment.
Eventually he came to see it as a refusal of grace. In 1907, Bely
challenged Bryusov to make his choice: Life or Death, black
magic or white, poetry in the service of religion or in the service
of a deified self.[66] Bryusov steadfastly refused to discuss the matter in these terms. He said what amounted to his final word in "In
Defense against Certain Praise," his reply to Bely's "Apocalypse in
Russian Poetry," where he was apotheosized."[67]

Meanwhile, along with other young Moscow poets, Bely bene-
fited by Bryusov's personal instruction in the technical aspects of
writing poetry. This he acknowledged repeatedly. Fortunately for
the record, not only did Bely learn from Bryusov but he thought
it worthwhile to articulate what he had learned. In his 1907 essay
Bely wrote, "Bryusov is the one great Russian poet of our time."[68]
He proceeded to examine the aspects of Bryusov's poetry that
"resurrect the eternal devices of poetic creation, which we so often
forget." After crediting Bryusov with having revived interest in
rhyme, he moved on to Bryusov's main concern: the importance
of the poetic line. "Bryusov was the first to revive for us an understanding of the intimate life of the line. The distinctive rhythm
of his meters is deepened by the brilliant choice not only of the
words as such, but also of the sounds in the words. To the music
of rhythm there corresponds the rhythm of thoughts and images."[69]

Bely here formulated concisely the lessons Bryusov had expressed in the 1900 essay "On Russian Versification." It will be

65.   Andrej Belyj, *Stixotvorenija i poèmy*, ed. T. Ju. Xmel'nickaja, N. B.
Bank, and N. G. Zaxarenko, Biblioteka poèta (2nd ed. Moscow and Leningrad,
1966), p. 117. A later poem under the same title is perhaps better known. It
begins: "Upornyj mag."
66.   *Lug zelenyj*, pp. 193–94.
67.   See footnote 62 above.
68.   *Lug zelenyj*, p. 181.
69.   Ibid., pp. 189–90.

recalled that Bryusov considered the line, not the metrical foot, to be the basic unit of the poem. In that essay he chose the term *image* [*obraz*] to describe the nodes of meaning and sound features with which the poet composes. He then discussed the advantageous arrangement of these images to make the effective line.[70] Though the word *image* apparently later resumed its usual meaning in Bryusov's vocabulary, the underlying conception was embodied in his own poetry and, surely, in the teaching sessions to which Bely referred. Thus we can deduce with near-certainty that Bryusov taught *how* to write memorable lines of poetry, lines where the delicate melding and balance of thought, emotion, and sound elements would impress the senses and minds of readers and hearers with their beautiful inevitability. This kind of art is usually attributed simply to inspiration and genius. It hardly needs saying that these qualities help greatly. Nonetheless, Bely remembered leaving Bryusov's study on those evenings exhilarated by his new knowledge: "I understood for the first time just what a specific, grammatically constructed line of poetry was. Bryusov's lesson was not in vain. I began for the first time to work hard at my own poetic form. Later I went on to study the rhythm of poets. And this work I published in [my book] *Symbolism*."[71]

Bely's evidence makes specific the commonplace about the effect of Bryusov's standards of craftsmanship, but probably the real "secret" can be seen only in application. Perhaps this is where the *jours fixes* in the fall of 1902 and after came in. It is not fanciful to suppose that one reason for the general rise in the quality of poetic production and poetic taste in the early years of the Symbolist movement was the opportunity for young poets to

70.   "O russkom stixosloženii," in Aleksandr Dobroljubov, *Sobranie stixov* (Moscow, 1900); reprinted in Aleksandr Dobroljubov, *Sočinenija*, introduction by Joan Delaney Grossman (Berkeley: Berkeley Slavic Specialties, 1981), pp. 129–30.
71.   "Valerij Brjusov," pp. 278–79.

profit from the instruction as well as the example of a few first-class poetic craftsmen.

One more contribution by Bryusov to the growth of Symbolism at this period should be considered. His essay "The Keys to the Mysteries" is regarded as possibly his most important statement about the movement of which he was now clearly the leader. Delivered as a lecture in Moscow and in Paris in March and April 1903, "The Keys to the Mysteries" appeared as the lead essay in the first issue of *The Balance* in January 1904 [VI, 78–93]. Obviously Bryusov's intent was to establish that Symbolism was a unified and distinct artistic movement, accorded its rightful place in the succession of esthetics he had described in previous writings. Three of the essay's four sections disposed of earlier theories of art: the utilitarian; "l'art pour l'art"; and the psychological, touching what we might now call reception theory and studies of creativity. Most of the arguments are familiar from his earlier essays. In the final section he triumphantly reiterated his own theory, for which he found support in Schopenhauer: "Art is the comprehension of the world [*postiženie mira*] by other than rational means" [VI, 91]. Yet the essay's concluding passages have suggested to some that Bryusov moved for a time in the direction of the followers of Vladimir Solovyov: "Works of art are the half-open doors to Eternity" [VI, 91]. We are not trapped in the visible world, the "blue prison," as Fet called it [VI, 92]; there are apertures through which we may catch glimpses of the world's essence. "And the basic task of art consists in seizing these instants of vision, of inspiration" [VI, 92].

Yet despite its hieratic vocabulary, "The Keys to the Mysteries" did not signal Bryusov's adherence, even briefly, to a theurgic concept of art. It in fact shows him hewing closely to the line of his earlier expositions of art's purpose and capacities. One notes, for example, that he did not equate art and revelation, but merely compared them: "Art is that which in other areas we call revelation" [VI, 91]. Nor is there any real ambiguity in his use of the word "Eternity." That "Eternity" which can be glimpsed through art was something different for Bryusov than it was for Blok and Bely, as indeed he had been at pains to explain to them. Balmont's "boundlessness," which Bryusov readily accepted, and Bryusov's own many invocations of limitlessness—temporal, spatial, moral —easily suggest the sense in which he used the term. It meant, in fact, "freedom," the freedom he had often claimed for the artist to explore in all directions. Like the word "mysteries," which Bryusov used so frequently, in another context it would not have been misunderstood.

Nonetheless, his essay's title was suggestive and surely deliberately so. It was calculated to appeal to those whose views on poetry he knew differed from his own. At this juncture Bryusov saw his task as unifying the forces of the new art. *The Balance* was to be their rallying point, and obviously he wished to reassure Bely, Blok, Vyacheslav Ivanov, and their like that it would offer a congenial forum for their talents. It should be remembered that, at the start of 1904, it was not obvious that the theurgic trend would soon dominate Russian Symbolism. Bryusov's chief message was, as it had always been, the necessity of freedom for art. Even to those "younger ones" whose mystical tendencies he did not share he offered the freedom to pursue by their own means what he perceived as their common goal. He concluded the essay: "Let contemporary artists consciously forge their works in the form of keys to the mysteries, in the form of mystical keys opening to mankind the doors out of his 'blue prison' into eternal freedom" [VI, 93]. This essay, then, directed specifically to the "city" of Symbolist poets, was a companion piece to the book that conveyed his poetic message "to the city and the world."

With the appearance of *Urbi et Orbi*, then, began the real noonday of Bryusov's poetic achievement and of his influence on the Symbolist movement. The first can be defined by the undeniable power and beauty of many of the individual poems in his book. But for Bryusov this achievement lay also in his sense of approaching the goal he had set years ago in *Chefs d'œuvre:* poetry as the perfect reflection of the artist's soul. This artist's soul was more occupied than were most with the idea of *being* an artist. The secret he offered was not hieratic, as some wished it to be. However, in terms of his own goals he had reached a high eminence. As usual, he had little idea of what new vistas might beckon. It was no wonder that he feared just now to become "a falling star in the heaven of being." But that time, if it was to come, lay in the future.

NINE

The Year 1905 and
Stephanos

THE RUSSO-JAPANESE WAR and the 1905
Revolution found Russian Symbolism nearing its prime. The
chief figures of the "older generation"—Merezhkovsky, Gippius,
Balmont, Bryusov, Sologub—were now established in reputation
and influence. The younger figures, notably Bely and Blok, were
reaching artistic maturity. Vyacheslav Ivanov had just published
his second book of poems. Moreover, the movement itself had
reached full stature. Since 1900 the publishing house of Scorpio
had provided a widening public with the best in Western and
Russian modernist writing and, since January 1904, with the
handsome monthly *The Balance*. One would have said that all was
well with Russian Symbolism at the start of 1905. Nonetheless,
changes were in the making. Some of these surely were related to
the external events of those times, though how they were so
linked is a complex question inviting further investigation. Of
the dramas—and traumas—of that year, Bryusov's is one of the
most interesting and instructive.

In 1904, when the war broke out, Bryusov had just turned
thirty. The success of *Urbi et Orbi* had brought his reputation to
its peak. His finger was in every literary pie involving Symbolists, and in some others besides. He had become a spokesman
to the public. His reaction to first the war and then the revolution
was at once symptomatic of his position and highly individual.

The leader of a movement that rejected pedestrian reality and glorified the moment of intense experience could be expected to romanticize the revolution, for a time at least. Moreover, Bryusov's personal attitudes guaranteed that he would find in these events stimuli to his emotional life and to his poetry. Yet his behavior fell far short of what some expected of him.

> I won't say I wasn't affected by our revolution. Of course I was. But I couldn't stand the compulsory requirement to fall into ecstasies over it and to be indignant with the government, which my associates, except for a very few, demanded of me. In general I can't bear pre-determined judgments. I had very serious clashes with many of them. I ended up with the reputation of being "rightist" and, with some people, of being one of the Black Hundreds.[1]

Thus some years later he summed up his experience of 1905. However, this was far from the whole story.

Given Bryusov's early acceptance of the Bolshevik Revolution and his active involvement in its treatment of literature, Soviet scholars understandably have interested themselves in defining his position in 1905. The prevailing view has been that stated in 1956 by E. S. Litvin: "The social enthusiasm of the early 1900s helped the poet to overcome the narrow, enclosed circle of purely Decadent moods, beyond the limits of which his first collections of poetry did not go."[2] This author and others have noted flaws in Bryusov's revolutionary thinking—his undervaluing of popular power, his disbelief in any constructive effects of the revolution—and his general political naïveté. Nonetheless, at the very least they have seen Bryusov in 1905 as turning away from Decadence and toward a more "healthy" art. The most cautious assessment was published in 1934 by I. Yampolsky, who noted that Bryusov's

---

1. *Dnevniki*, pp. 136–37.
2. È. S. Litvin, "Revoljucija 1905 g. i tvorčestvo Brjusova," p. 198.

revolutionary fervor lasted all of three or four months and that his attitude toward the revolution was chiefly esthetic.[3] D. E. Maksimov in 1969 summed up: "Bryusov's attraction to the revolution of 1905 was serious, but brief, elemental, and inwardly contradictory."[4] Yet the impression remains strong that 1905 marked a crisis in Bryusov's Decadent individualism, inducing in him a more receptive attitude toward contemporary reality that prepared him to accept the Bolshevik Revolution.[5] The picture is coherent and largely persuasive, but it is incomplete. And its incompleteness falsifies our image of Bryusov, not only for 1905 but for years to come.

In his diary under the heading "From 1904–1905" Bryusov wrote:

> For me that was a year of storms, a year of maelstrom. Never have I experienced such passions, such torments, such joys. The greater part of these experiences is embodied in my book of poems *Stephanos*. Some of them went also into the making of the novel *The Fiery Angel*. At times I was quite sincerely ready to throw over all my past life and take up a new one, to begin my whole life again.[6]

This passage is sometimes used to show how deeply, if briefly, Bryusov was stirred by the public events of 1904 and 1905.[7] However, it is difficult in the light of other evidence to make this confession apply primarily to his reaction to public happenings. He himself put matters in perspective in a well-known letter to

3. I. Jampol'skij, "Valerij Brjusov i pervaja russkaja revoljucija," p. 202.
4. D. E. Maksimov, *Brjusov: Poèzija i pozicija*, p. 176.
5. Ibid., pp. 178–79.
6. *Dnevniki*, p. 136.
7. A notable exception is the article by V. Dronov, "Kniga Brjusova 'Stephanos,'" *Brjusovskij sbornik* (Stavropol', 1977), pp. 63–111. Dronov, remarking that "bylo by ne sovsem verno" to draw this conclusion, gives full credit to the role of Brjusov's relations with Petrovskaja in evoking this turmoil (p. 69). However, his main thesis is directly opposite to that of this chapter. See footnote 59 below.

Peter Pertsov dated 24 September 1905: "For about a year you and I haven't met or talked or written. In regard to the last I am the more guilty. But for me this past year was a most exceptional one. I have 'lived' (I hate that expression of Nadson's) much. And all that against the background of the tragic sufferings of all Russia."[8] If Russia's tragic sufferings were the background, what was in the foreground? None of his intimates could have had any doubt, and with the assistance of *Stephanos* and *The Fiery Angel* all might surmise. In the fall of 1904 Bryusov began a seven-year love affair with Nina Petrovskaya. A young writer who frequented Decadent circles, sometime wife of the head of Scorpio's rival publishing house Gryphon, Nina Petrovskaya had shifted her affections from one Symbolist poet to another until her involvement with Bryusov. The relationship was in many ways fatal for both. Nina's memoirs show that she regarded it in retrospect as the central event of her life.[9] Its importance for Bryusov was much greater than those who have written about it tend to credit.[10] To consider any aspect of Bryusov's activity in 1905 without taking this relationship, which was then at its crest, into account is to misjudge the case gravely.

This is not to say that Bryusov's responses to the Russo-Japanese War and to the revolutionary wave were merely external and trivial or that the "passions" he referred to could not conceivably have been in part patriotic and revolutionary. However, there is no reason to believe that Bryusov's attitude toward poetry and toward himself as poet, built up over years and continually reaffirmed, was washed away in an access of civic enthusiasm. There is much reason to believe the contrary, that the experiences of these important years fuelled these attitudes as well as his po-

8.   "Materialy po istorii literatury. Desjat' pisem Valerija Brjusova k P. P. Percovu," *Pečat' i revoljucija* no. 7 (October–November 1926): 43.

9.   Excerpted in *LN* 85, pp. 773–89.

10.   The chief source for Western scholars has been V. F. Xodasevič, "Konec Renaty." See footnote 49 below.

etry. Here certain questions must be kept in mind and certain propositions tested. How emotionally and intellectually involved was Bryusov in the public events of that time? How did he perceive them? How did these perceptions and experiences interact with his personal drama? Did either his poetry or his conception of poetry change, and if so, in what direction? The judgment of many scholars that "this experience [of the revolutionary years] facilitated the process of Bryusov's continuing approach to reality and the outgrowing of his enthusiasm for Decadence"[11] cannot simply be swept aside.

When war with Japan broke out in January 1904, Bryusov showed himself in patriotic feeling as well as poetic style, to be the devoted pupil of Fyodor Tyutchev's political verse of the 1850s. For Tyutchev, Russia's "manifest destiny" was the absorption of all Slavs and the extension of her empire across Eurasia. His verse issued a summons to a holy war. And when Russia was defeated in the Crimea, Tyutchev's wrath turned first on the emperor.[12] Bryusov had had ample time to absorb Tyutchev's philosophy of history. His publications on Tyutchev had been appearing for several years.[13] The historical thinking of the two differed in that Tyutchev's view was Pan-Slavist with a strongly Orthodox religious cast, while Bryusov's Russian nationalism was tinged by his fascination with the Roman Empire. For Tyutchev, Russia's foe was Europe, while for Bryusov, in different historical circumstances, it was the East. But the sentiment was the same, as far as Russia's destiny was concerned. Bryusov's two previous volumes had contained poems in this vein that were explicitly

11.   Maksimov, *Brjusov*, pp. 178–79.

12.   For a discussion of Tjutčev's political poetry see Richard Gregg, *Fedor Tiutchev: The Evolution of a Poet* (New York and London: Columbia University Press, 1965), chs. 5, 6.

13.   Besides his early publications in *Russkij Arxiv* in 1898, since 1900 Brjusov had published there letters of Tjutčev to Čaadaev (no. 11 [1900]) and other items concerning Tjutčev's literary relations (see *Bibliografija*).

linked to Tyutchev.[14] Now his "To the Pacific Ocean," dated the day of Japan's attack at Port Arthur, put forth the doctrine of Russia's "manifest destiny" with a vengeance. Russia and the Pacific were portrayed as two giants destined to embrace, and woe to him who would try to separate them!

Meanwhile, Bryusov shared for some time the general expectation of a quick and easy Russian victory over the Japanese. When the first major Japanese victories came in April, he reacted strongly, though not in poetry. To Pertsov he wrote that Russia should have bombarded Tokyo long ago, for the Pacific belonged to Russia. "I love Japanese art—but let it fall in ruins. I'm for the barbarians, I'm for the Huns, I'm for the Russians!"[15] By autumn some in Russia were already beginning to agitate against the government, but Bryusov was not among them. When George Chulkov printed Bryusov's protest poem "The Dagger" in the October *New Way* without his permission, Bryusov was chagrined. It had been written several years earlier in, as he said, "other circumstances."[16] The reminiscence of Lermontov in its

14.   "Problesk" in *Tertia Vigilia* took its epigraph from Tjutčev's "Russkaja geografija" and ends with a stunningly Pan-Slavist vision: "Slavjanskij stjag zareet nad Car'gradom" [I, 227]. "Ijul' 1903," written after the assassination of a Russian consul in Turkey, was composed "in the spirit of Tjutčev," as Brjusov told Percov [I, 356, 618].

15.   "Materialy," p. 42. Publicly, as editor of the avowedly nonpolitical *Vesy*, Brjusov maintained a more reserved position. But political elements nonetheless were allowed to creep onto *Vesy*'s pages in various ways. Twice during 1904, in May and November, articles by Rémy de Gourmont containing crude anti-Japanese propaganda were reprinted from *Mercure de France* under the guise of surveying foreign journals. However, to demonstrate its lofty stance *Vesy* published in its October and November issues a lavish display of Japanese sketches and watercolors to remind its readers "of the Japan we love and value, the land of artists, not of soldiers" (no. 10, p. 39).

16.   In the note to "Kinžal" in the first edition of *Stephanos*, Brjusov referred to these circumstances and gave the date of composition as 1903. However, Čulkov remembered it differently. "Kinžal" had been composed, he said, as a result of his conversations with Brjusov at the end of 1901 when, in trying to win Brjusov over to the idea of revolution, he greatly exaggerated the strength of

title was appropriate, for it is an essentially Romantic statement of the poet's place in the heart of the storm. Bryusov was embarrassed to have it appear in fall 1904, when, as he wrote to Chulkov, "students in Moscow can think of nothing better to do than try to dissuade soldiers from going to war or boo the national anthem." [17]

In December Bryusov published two poems that voiced quite other sentiments. In "To My Fellow Citizens" he called out "Close the Forum!" It was no time for talk when Russians were dying at Mukden and Port Arthur. Moreover, weakening Russia at this crucial time was tantamount to selling her birthright to future greatness. The second poem, "For the New Year 1905" was clearly suggested by Tyutchev's "1856." Both of these poems called patriotically for a united Russia. However, Bryusov's national pride, like that of so many others, was badly shaken by the mounting defeats and the humiliating Dogger Bank incident, when Russian ships in the North Sea fired on two of their own, taking them for Japanese, and struck English fishing smacks instead. By December public disturbances had taken a more serious turn, and in Moscow there was enough activity to command Bryusov's interest, if not his active support. On 10 December he wrote to Pertsov, "And so, it's revolution!" [18] He followed with a vivid description of a Moscow demonstration viewed from inside a coffeehouse, where patrons were temporarily penned. Clearly stirred by Cossack and other brutalities, he told Pertsov that the December issue of *The Balance* would carry a drawing by a German artist T. T. Heine called "Spring Flowers." It showed policemen with swords bounding about a meadow to assault moth-

the revolutionary movement: Georgij Čulkov, *Gody stranstvij* (Moscow, 1930), pp. 102–3.

17.   Čulkov, *Gody stranstvij*, p. 321.

18.   Valerij Brjusov, "Pis'ma k P. P. Percovu," *Russkij sovremennik* no. 4 (1924): 233–34.

ers and small children picking flowers.[19] At Balmont's he had "docilely" signed some kind of protest document. He summed up his mood: "Everywhere nightmare, miasma. Port Arthur's ships sink, the Baltic fleet grows barnacles on its hulls. . . . The Japanese shout, 'Banzai! Down with Russia!'"

At the end of 1904 his country's situation inspired confusion, anger, and depression in Bryusov. Yet he was not ready to sympathize actively with revolution. In fact, after the New Year he fell silent on all such subjects. Bloody Sunday, the fall of Port Arthur, the general strike went unrecorded. It was to be midsummer 1905 before Bryusov took up his civic lyre again. In the meantime he was writing a good deal of poetry on another theme, love. Later Bryusov wrote to Nina Petrovskaya of how, after the publication of *Urbi et Orbi* in late 1903, he experienced an acute depression. He recalled how he had wanted to withdraw from all human contact, especially from those that forced him to think, act, and *feel*. He soon found himself fighting for his very life as a poet, and, given his convictions about poetry, his very identity. It was not simply that he needed a new theme for his poems. He needed a profound emotional experience to reveal new depths in his own soul. Only thus, he believed, could his poetry explore new reaches of the spirit. And without this for him there was no poetry.

At this crucial moment Nina had come into his life, bringing something utterly new: "Love, of which I had only written in poems, but which I had never known: a woman of the kind I had only read about in books (in your Przybyszewski) but had never seen. . . . My eyes suddenly opened, became a hundred times sharper; in my hands I felt new strength. I suddenly saw around me anew treasures which my previous vision had not discerned."[20]

19.   See *Vesy* no 12 (1904): 48.

20.   *LN* 85, p. 791. The Polish Decadent Stanislaw Przybyszewski apparently was one of her favorite novelists.

It was a resurrection of his poetic powers. He had known Nina for some time, and the acquaintance grew gradually into something more in the course of 1904, until by autumn he felt himself to be deeply in love. Two years earlier he had written to Lyudmila Vilkina of what he felt to be his greatest weakness: "No, I really do not know passion, i.e., blinding, frenzied. I cannot enter its domain. I only stand at its heavy gates. . . . Fate has refused me her best gift—the bliss of suffering!"[21] Here (allowing for typical Decadent language) Bryusov seems as close to the truth about himself as he could get. But now something had changed. With Nina he believed he could overcome the barrier.

Some of his best and certainly some of his most famous poems date from this period of his life. One can even suppose a connection between his passionate concern over his country's destiny and this new expansion of his emotional horizons. At any rate, toward the end of 1904 he was living the kind of heightened existence he had sung in his poetry and yearned for in private for many years. "A year of storms, a year of maelstrom," he called the period from late 1904 to late 1905. As his patriotic fervor lapsed into frustrated anger, his personal life reached a pitch of excitement beyond anything he had known. This condition arose not only from his passion for Petrovskaya but also from the triangular relationship among himself, Nina, and Andrei Bely, which had been taking shape for some time. Bryusov's relations with Bely were cordial in 1903 and well into 1904, made up as they were of mutual interest and admiration, along with common professional concerns. However, a potentially troublesome element began to surface very early. In 1903 Bely had published his poem "Mage," in which he portrayed the older poet as a seer to whom were known secrets only dreamed of by Bely.[22] Gradually he became

21.   IRLI, fond 39, ed. xr. 833. Letter dated December 1902.
22.   Andrej Belyj, *Stixotvorenija i poèmy*, Biblioteka poèta (Moscow and Leningrad, 1966), p. 117.

obsessed with the notion that Bryusov exercised domination over him psychologically by means of black magic and hypnotism.[23] Earlier in the year he had been greatly disturbed to find his rarefied relationship with Nina, in which he saw himself as her spiritual guide, turning into a common romance on her side. Henceforward he tried to extract himself from this position but succeeded in breaking off with her only in August. As he told it, he felt responsible for saving her soul. For a time both he and Bryusov were her confidants, a situation that produced highly dramatic developments.

There is no totally reliable witness to what happened in late 1904 and early 1905 between Bryusov and Bely. How Bryusov may have played on Bely's extreme sensitivities and why—to avenge Nina or for other reasons—cannot be known with any certainty, though Bely himself hinted at an explanation after the crisis had passed. The best-known evidence is in the poems exchanged by the two in December 1904. Bryusov's "Loki to Balder" draws on Scandinavian mythology to portray the victory of the dark forces over light. The dark and evil Loki treacherously pierces the god Balder with an arrow during play. Punished for his deed, Loki yet prophesies the final triumph of darkness over light in the universe: "Darkness, darkness is on my side!" Loki is of course Bryusov. Bely recalled later that Bryusov sent the poem to him folded in the form of an arrow. His reply, "To an Old Enemy," threatened that enemy with incineration by the sun.[24] One more poem by Bryusov was written 1 January 1905. In "To Balder II" Bryusov conceded moral defeat and, more than that, admitting his baleful influence on Nina, offered to surrender her to the light.[25] But the poem was never sent to Bely.

There was still another stage in the combat between the two

23.   *Aleksandr Blok i Andrej Belyj: Perepiska* (Moscow, 1950), pp. 113–17.

24.   Belyj, *Stixotvorenija*, p. 465.

25.   Brjusov, *Stixotvorenija i poèmy*, p. 502.

poets. This was almost a duel in the literal sense. It was provoked by Bryusov. Bely refused to accept the challenge, and the incident was over by the end of February.[26] However tempting it may be to see this as mere melodrama (Bely drew some very amateurish but violent caricatures of Bryusov during the incidents), there was in fact a powerful explosion of anxieties and hostilities on both sides.[27] Adequate evidence exists to show that both Bely and Bryusov suffered intensely through it all. In a letter to Blok less than a month later Bely recognized this: "Now I have learned certain purely biographical details explaining why Bryusov was so fierce toward me. I forgive him willingly. I unconsciously did him much harm. He revenged himself on me. Now I understand everything."[28]

26. *LN* 85, pp. 381–83. Brjusov apparently had used intemperate words about Merežkovskij in Belyj's presence. Belyj protested by letter and pointed to what he called Brjusov's quarrelsome character. Brjusov answered with the challenge, to which Belyj reacted with surprise and disclaimers of offensive intent. Earlier accounts of this episode, where the relevant letters have been inaccessible to the authors, tend to be inaccurate. (Cf. Oleg Maslenikov, *The Frenzied Poets*, p. 117.) Vjačeslav Ivanov, greatly exercised over the affair, wrote to Brjusov afterward that he knew Belyj would not fight but that he feared Brjusov might kill Belyj, in order afterward to punish himself: *LN* 85, p. 473.

27. Some of these caricatures can be seen in *LN* 85, pp. 385, 387, and in *Perepiska* after p. 176.

28. *Perepiska*, p. 126. Some further light is thrown on these "purely biographical details" by a letter of February 1905 from Brjusov to Petr Percov, reading in part: "In our house there is also war. The Christian [former Decadent, now sectarian preacher] Aleksandr Dobroljubov has moved in. He lives in my study, dines at my table, writes on my paper (letters to the Merežkovskijs, Minskij, Maeterlinck, Lev Tolstoj, Fr. Gapon, Svjatopolk Mirskij, [the deceased] O. Wilde (yes!), Verhaeren, [Count] Witte (all instructions about the necessity of believing in God), reads my books and manuscripts (including those in my desk), repeats like a parrot the three words 'brother-God-peace' and has perverted my sister and Ioanna Matveevna. At home now they read Ecclesiastes and say 'Przybyszewski and that sort of rubbish.' And finally Ioanna Matveevna is going off to live in New York. This is not exaggeration but the simple truth." Cited by E. V. Ivanova, "Valerij Brjusov i Aleksandr Dobroljubov," p. 264. Part of this passage also appears in P. Percov, *Literaturnye vospominanija (1890–1902 gg.)* pp. 239–40.

Much has been deduced about Bryusov's relationship with Nina Petrovskaya from the novel *The Fiery Angel*. But reading backward from a novel is not likely to give a complete and undistorted picture of actual events.[29] The sixteenth-century witch Renata, in love with the fiery angel and drawing the German soldier Ruprecht into her paradoxes and paroxysms, was certainly modeled on Nina. But this source must be supplemented by others wherever possible. Nina's memoirs describe the fall of 1904 in Symbolist language drawn from Bryusov's poem "The Goblet." "That autumn Bryusov offered me a goblet of dark, astringent wine in which, like Cleopatra's pearl, his soul was dissolved, and said 'Drink!' I drank it down and was poisoned for seven years."[30]

Bryusov rendered his experience similarly in other poems of November and December 1904. One of these, "Again my soul is riven," he sent to Lyudmila Vilkina with the note, "A photograph of my soul today" [I, 627].[31] As in all such movements, the Symbolists had their own vocabulary and intonations for conveying experience, and they regarded personal experience as a mystery to be probed through poetic language. However, along with this very personal poetic idiom, they often portrayed what they lived through in imagery drawn from myth, history, or romance. When Chulkov asked Bryusov early in 1905 for poems for his journal *Problems of Life*, he was looking for civic poems. Bryusov sent him instead "Achilles at the Altar," explaining that the burdens of *The Balance* and "purely personal matters" kept him from producing any others.[32] In May, still with the same tale to tell, he offered the cycle "Winter Crop" as the fruit, as it were, of his fall sowing. Three of its five poems drew on myth or ancient settings.

29.   The most complete account of the biographical connections of Brjusov's novel is that of S. S. Grečiskin and A. V. Lavrov, "Biografičeskie istočniki romana Brjusova *Ognennyj Angel.*"

30.   CGALI, fond 376, op. 1, ed. xr. 3.

31.   Brjusov also sent the poem to Ivanov "vmesto pis'ma." *LN* 85, 469 n. 1.

32.   Čulkov, *Gody stranstvij*, pp. 322–23.

He described these as "antique images, but animated by the contemporary soul." Then somewhat defensively he continued, "All speak of love. In these days when Rozhdestvensky's fleet has gone to the bottom and with it all of old Russia . . . love remains a matter of contemporary concern, even burningly so."[33]

That winter seems to have been an especially dramatic one for Bryusov. Much later, Nina asked, "What did Valery Bryusov see in me then? . . . He sensed in me the organic kinship of soul with one half of his own, with that—*mystery*, which those about him knew nothing of, with that in himself which he both loved and more often fiercely hated."[34] In January of that year Nina wanted to die. This was one of several occasions when, as she recalled, Bryusov proposed joint suicide.[35] This motif recurred in several poems of that time. The most striking is "Cleopatra," a dramatic monologue that rewrote history in Decadent fashion. Antony exhorts Cleopatra to release the asp so that they may escape the humiliation of slavery and meet their fate together in ecstasy. Later Nina marvelled: would anyone believe that at the height of his fame Bryusov would so "thirst for the instant of ecstatic death?"[36] Symbolism, Khodasevich wrote, was "a series of attempts, sometimes genuinely heroic, to find the fusion of life and artistic creation, a sort of philosopher's stone of art."[37] Bryusov and Nina at this stage of their romance perhaps felt that they were close to this goal. In a letter to Bely in August 1904, Bryusov had lamented their generation's tendency to talk about "ecstasy and frenzy" but to be unwilling to pay the price of such experiences.[38] He was now paying generously and reaping some of

33. Ibid., p. 324.
34. *LN* 85, p. 782.
35. CGALI, fond 376. Nina dated these events January 1904, clearly by mistake.
36. Ibid., with reference to the poem "Axilles u altarja."
37. Xodasevič, p. 8.
38. *LN* 85, p. 378.

the harvest. The ultimate test may have been the ability to die by one's own hand in order to experience the final ecstasy. Nina was no stranger to the thought of suicide. In 1928 at forty-four, in a poor hotel in Paris, she finally ended her life. Bryusov possibly had too robust a nature to take the final step.[39] But during these months he was living only with that half of his soul which Nina claimed as kin to her own.

In May they left Moscow for a month in Finland on Lake Saima, already hymned by Vladimir Solovyov.[40] A new mood now appeared in Bryusov's poetry. The "Saima" cycle is a miracle of harmony. The turbulent being who had "sought madness, begged for alarms" is cast by fate on a quiet shore where peace and tenderness flow over him and into him. The tranquillity of this place not only soothed his soul but made it more sensitive to Saima's delicate, changing beauty. Nina herself, enveloped by the blue peace, was transformed for the time into Renata in her most angelic mood.

Bryusov subsequently described the month on Saima as a summit never to be regained.[41] However, the decline, if decline there was, was not immediately apparent. What was obvious was a change in Bryusov himself. Parting from Nina at the end of June, he went directly to Tarusa, where his family was spending the summer. There he plunged immediately into work of all sorts. (He was sometimes in Moscow, but Nina wrote bitterly of her failure to find him on these occasions.)[42] Clearly there was a great deal to catch up on. The events from Bloody Sunday through Tsushima and into the final days of the war were like piled-up

39.   See also Chapter Four.
40.   Vladimir Solov'ev, *Stixotvorenija i šutočnye p'esy*, Biblioteka poèta, second edition ed. Z. G. Minc (Leningrad, 1974), pp. 105–107.
41.   CGALI, fond 376, op. 1, ed. xr. 4, letter with the date deleted, following that of 29 August 1905.
42.   CGALI, fond 56, op. 1, ed. xr. 95, letter dated "July 17 [1905], evening."

newspapers, awaiting belated attention. His first worries had to do with *The Balance*, the editorship of which he was considering leaving.[43] Nonetheless, the poetic surge that had lasted through winter and spring and into the summer did not recede now but only widened its scope. He began to attend once again to what was happening in Russia. With the Portsmouth Peace conference putting the period to Russia's immediate plans for expansion, the question of "What now?" confronted even diehard imperialists like Bryusov. Along with it, the question of the poet's public role again became vital. In July, Bryusov's younger brother, Alexander, wrote a Latin epistle reproaching him with political indifference.[44] In response Bryusov wrote "To One of the Brethren," in which he took up the message of "The Dagger": the poet will be where he is needed to proclaim the cause of freedom. However, where others break down walls, the poet prepares the souls of men and releases them from their imprisonment.

Before Bryusov could turn fully to this task, he owed one poem to the war just concluded. Somewhat tardily, he wrote "Tsushima" (later dated "June 1905"). In majestic cadence the poet there mourned not only the loss of life and ships at Tsushima, but the end, for the foreseeable future, of Russia's great hope for "Both the scepter of the Far East / And the crown of the third Rome!" The other side of the coin showed his wrath at those responsible for Russia's disgrace. He wrote "To Them: Occasioned by the Conclusion of Peace with Japan and Other Causes," ending with the line: "The poet crowns you with shame." The poem "Julius Caesar" announced a change of position: borne on the winds of the latest events, Bryusov crossed his Rubicon. The poem, dated August 1905, chiefly expresses his disgust with the government and the behavior of public officials. Nor was he

43. *LN* 85, p. 477, letter from Vjačeslav Ivanov protests Brjusov's intention.
44. This incident is recounted by Aleksandr Brjusov, "Vospominanija o brate," *Brjusovskie čtenija 1962 g.*, pp. 293–301.

pleased with all that he found among the opposition. In "To
Those Close to Me" he wrote, "No, I am not yours! Your goals are
alien to me," and ended with words that reveal much: "To tear
down—I will be with you! To build—no!"

In the famous "The Coming Huns," also written in late summer 1905, the poet sees very well that he has no place among the
new cohorts. The solution, at whatever cost to civilization, was
self-sacrifice for the probable good of the future. The idea, even
then not new to Bryusov,[45] was expressed again in "To the Happy
Ones." Strongly influenced by Verhaeren, this was one of Bryusov's fullest utopian statements. It is hard to credit Bryusov with
a genuine desire for a state of affairs where all is settled and no
challenges remain. The most significant lines are probably·those
that echo "The Coming Huns." The present generation is only a
fleeting dream or nightmare. "So be it!" says the poet. "I was! I
am! I do not need eternity!"

This period of exuberant creativity formed both a break and a
continuity with the profound emotions of the previous months.
To Vyacheslav Ivanov Bryusov wrote on 1 September:

> I feel myself dying in one part of my soul and reviving again in an-
> other. Reviving in that part which you best know. I am working very
> hard, as I haven't worked for a long time. Already I am sending *Prob-
> lems of Life* a whole heap of poems, and to *Journal for Everyone* and
> *Conversation* as well. I'm writing articles, stories, a novel. Am trans-
> lating Byron. And I have enough ideas for a whole life, if not for
> two. I am printing my *Stephanos*, in which you will find many new
> things. In general in my work I feel a fresh vigor, strength, the pos-
> sibility of anything at all—the wingedness of a clear morning when
> it is possible to reach what I strove for in vain both in the flaming
> evening and the will-less night. I have written, have achieved much
> that I dreamed of hopelessly during *whole* years. And if in *vigor* of

45.   It had already appeared in the play "Zemlja," published in the spring
of 1905 in *Severnye cvety assirijskie* (Moscow, 1905). The subtitle was "Tragedija
iz buduščix vremen."

powers I compared this time to morning, I would have been equally correct comparing it to noon in *fullness* of strength, feeling, the consciousness that I have reached full power over all that is in me, that the years of gathering are finished, that it is time to spend.[46]

The centerpiece of it all was *Stephanos*. It represented a summit in his artistic life like that of Saima in his personal life. But the person with whom he had shared that exhilaration was not interested in sharing this one. During the weeks after their return a classic situation took shape. Nina ardently tried to recapture the mood of Saima.[47] To Bryusov it seemed irretrievable. At the end of August he tried earnestly to explain the situation. Assuring her of his continued love, he begged her to believe "that love is not always madness and that madness is not always love!"[48] If only she could see the clarity of his horizons, feel his "thirst to breathe, work, be, live!" And if only she could be satisfied with what he now had to offer: "All of myself as I now am: without madness, with a stubborn, unquenchable thirst for work, but with undying love for you." That this was no idle offer is abundantly borne out in Bryusov's letters to Nina over the next several years, most of which are yet unpublished.

Vladislav Khodasevich has been until recently, along with Bely, the chief source of information on Bryusov's relations with Nina. He pictured Bryusov as dropping Nina callously after he no longer needed her as a model for Renata.[49] Nina remembered it differently. Her memoirs reveal that in retrospect she under-

46.   *LN* 85, p. 481.
47.   CGALI, letters of Nina Petrovskaja to Brjusov, dated 3 and 4 July 1905.
48.   CGALI, Brjusov to Petrovskaja, 29 August 1905.
49.   Xodasevič wrote: "That which was still life for Nina had become for Brjusov a used-up plot. It was tedious for him endlessly to relive the same chapters" (*Nekropol'*, p. 20). In his essay "Brjusov" he added that "with deliberate callousness [Brjusov] made clear his wish to break it off once and for all" (ibid., p. 40). Nina's memoirs and Brjusov's unpublished letters to her, especially those of 1908 and 1909, cast doubt on this version.

stood Bryusov's strengths and weaknesses far better than she had in 1905. Then she felt she was fighting for her life and begging for a miracle. Bryusov, on the other hand, had passed the moment when he was ready to throw over his past life and begin again. The part of his soul that was "dying," as he told Ivanov, was clearly the part capable of that "madness" which he as well as Nina had prized not long before.

Meanwhile Bryusov's progress in his new poetic vein met with a check. On 20 August he offered Chulkov a cycle of seven poems entitled "From the Present." Owing to censorship, only three of these poems appeared in the September *Problems of Life*.[50] He poured out the sum of his frustrations to Pertsov. The war still oppressed his imagination, and the fateful sense of a new era bore down upon him. He was especially vexed by the seeming obliviousness of his fellow Decadents:

> With us everything is as it was. Balmont has written a book of "elfin" poems and keeps on telling the world: "People! I am tender!" . . . All the rest along with Bely are locked up in the society "Argo," where with "pure" spirit they talk once a week on Fridays about virtue. . . . Seryozha Solovyov, nephew of a famous uncle, is getting fat. The young hangers-on of Balmont, Bryusov and *The Balance*, the Khodaseviches, etc. [*pod-bal'montiki, pod-brjusniki, i podvesniki, Xodaseviči, etc.*] overflow with assurances that the time of realism has passed, that the world is a mystery, that only great writers are incomprehensible, that sin is sweet and that the university was established for learning, not for revolution.—Almost before your eyes you see how everything around is growing rigid, dying.[51]

Nor was he satisfied with the other side: "Revolution. . . . A fine way they make a revolution. Their active people are completely without talent!" Not to make use of the Potemkin incident! Not

---

50. Čulkov, *Gody stranstvij*, p. 352. Brjusov withdrew one of the poems himself, though it is not clear which.

51. "Materialy," pp. 43–44.

to exploit fully the disturbances in the Caucasus! Not to produce in sixteen months one orator, one tribune. The most remarkable figure was Father Gapon. Bryusov damned the government equally: "The cowardly, hypocritical government, yielding all and everywhere! The emperor concluding a shameful peace. . . . One sees whipped dogs: an unpleasant sight. But a whipped emperor of all Russia!"[52]

Bryusov's frustration exemplified a widespread mood. No doubt so also did his reaction when the general strike broke out on 7 October. To Chulkov he then wrote, "I greet you in the days of revolution."[53] This letter is often quoted to show Bryusov's support for the October Revolution, particularly the remark "revolutionary action suits me." He wrote: "As much as I have always despised (and still do despise) liberal *chatter*, so much does revolutionary *action* suit me. But for the time being I am only an observer."[54] This is hardly a decisive statement of position. He then asked Chulkov not to use the new freedom of the press to print the poems turned down a few months earlier by the censor. "I will write new ones worthier of the time." Chulkov did print the rejected poems in his October–November issue, possibly because Bryusov's renewed output was not plentiful after all.[55]

What Bryusov did write at this time, however, was significant. And probably the most significant is "To the Satisfied," dated the day after the October Manifesto established a constitutional government of sorts. Addressed to those who were satisfied with the gains, it is in the tradition of Lermontov's expression of bitter civic scorn which he called his "iron verse." It begins: "I am

52. Ibid., p. 44.
53. Čulkov, *Gody stranstvij*, p. 335.
54. Ibid., pp. 335–36. The quoted remark was: "mne po duše revoljucionnoe dejstvie."
55. The poems published in *Voprosy žizni*, nos. 10–11, were "Lik Meduzy," "Mjatež" (an adaptation of Verhaeren's "La Révolte"), and "Znakomaja pesn'." Several Brjusov translations of Verhaeren appeared in the same number, along with poems by Ivanov, Sologub, and Čulkov on related themes.

ashamed of your congratulations, / I am terrified by your proud words!" Their satisfaction is that of a herd with a cud to chew. Then come the lines most revealing of Bryusov's attitude toward revolution and power, both in 1905 and in the future: "Splendid in the might of terrible power / Is the Eastern king Assarhadon, / And also the ocean of popular passion, / Shattering the fragile throne to splinters!" For Bryusov *either* extreme was splendid in its threatening power; the key word here is "splendid." Even at the height of his civic fervor Bryusov himself recognized that much of his excitement was esthetic. The poem contains another telling statement: "Half-measures are hateful." Those who adopt them are the biblical "lukewarm," to be spat out of the mouth. "To the Satisfied" closes with an impassioned invitation to the mob, the "children of flaming day," to rise like a whirlwind and "shatter life—and with it me!" "To the Satisfied" tells much about Bryusov's position in October 1905.

Essentially Bryusov dreamed of a freedom that was more inner than outer. He apparently felt no gratitude for practical gains such as the abatement of censorship. He wanted men transformed into free beings; he wanted poets to soar on wings of power. For a very brief time, the fury he saw unleashed in the streets of Moscow seemed an exhilarating elemental force. In "Face of the Medusa" Bryusov identified these "days of fire and blood" with primeval chaos. Not that he ever carried the red flag, as did Alexander Blok on the day of the Manifesto. In Bryusov there was no confusion of roles. The poet's place was in the storm, but with only a lyre in hand.

During the Moscow riots he was never anything but an observer, though an active one. What risks he took were in the interests of his art.[56] Writing to Chulkov on 28 October, he related: "Amid the whoops of Cossacks, between strolls along the

56.   Cf. letter from Ivanov of 24 October 1905 (*LN* 85, p. 487), in which he chides Brjusov for going too far in this direction.

lighted and barricaded streets, I have continued to work on my novel. And somehow the work goes very well. All the more so because in the opening chapters I have to describe the religious-revolutionary movement in Germany in 1533."[57] At about the same time, he wrote to Anna Shesterkina: "The revolution interests me only as an observer (though I came under Cossack fire in Gnezdikovsky Lane). . . . I will be a poet even during the terror, even in the days when they will break up museums and burn books—and that is inevitable. Revolution is beautiful and, as an historical phenomenon, magnificent, but it is hard for poor poets to live in it. They are unnecessary."[58]

In November *Stephanos* was still in press and Bryusov was still inserting his latest poems. Even with these, he was aware that his book was not quite timely. "My poor book!" began his short introduction [I, 620]. A piece earlier destined for this function was published separately as "Contemporary Thoughts" [VI, 110–11]. It countered criticism directed at poets who do not rally their talents to the cause. To the question of whether a poet must fulfill his civic duty *as* poet, he replied, "Perhaps in some periods the poet as citizen is obliged to go to the barricades, but he is not obliged to describe this in a special poem." Nor, he noted, are poets relieved of military duty for writing a book of soldiers' songs. In fact, he continued, there is no evidence that poetry has any appreciable effect on social movements. And surely the public can tolerate only so many "Marseillaises." Bryusov's quarrel was not with poetry treating social themes but, rather, with poetry *serving* any cause but its own. Art, he repeated, has its own sphere —the human soul. Concerning itself with those mysteries, art cannot be estranged from life, for "all our life is nothing other than the series of our spiritual experiences. . . . Of course the day's events are contemporary, but the questions of Love, Death, the Aim of Life, Good and Evil are also contemporary, to our days

57. Čulkov, *Gody stranstvij*, p. 337.
58. *LN* 85, p. 654.

as to the times of Orpheus" [VI, 111]. Bryusov obviously saw no contradiction between his own civic poetry and this principle.[59] The free poet draws his inspiration solely from those things that touch his inner life, whether they be public events or no.

Striking evidence of Bryusov's consistency in these views came in the article "Freedom of the Word," in *The Balance* for November 1905.[60] It was an answer to Lenin's "Party Organization and Party Literature" (*New Life*, no. 12 [1905]). Never reprinted though occasionally refuted, Bryusov's article is a fascinating document. Lenin's article had been directed primarily at shaping a genuine Bolshevik literature in the new condition of a legal Social Democrat press and the Bolshevik-Menshevik split. Bryusov technically misrepresented some of Lenin's words by assuming, despite Lenin's protestations, that he had in mind the control, not only of party literature, but of literature in general. He quoted from Lenin's article with certain unmarked elisions (indicated here) to emphasize what he took to be Lenin's basic point: "The literary enterprise may not be [an instrument of profit for persons or groups, it may not be in general] an individual enterprise, independent of the proletarian enterprise. Down with non-Party literary people! Down with the supermen of letters! The literary enterprise must become [in part a general-proletarian enterprise,] the 'wheel' and 'screw' of one single great Social Democratic mechanism."[61]

59. Most commentators have done so, however. See VI, 591, and Dronov's article (footnote 7 above). Dronov sees *Stephanos* as epitomizing the conflict that he finds in Brjusov at that time. The Decadent author of the section "Iz ada izvedennye," which treats the love affair in Decadent fashion, is seen as struggling against the author of the civic poems, who is reaching out toward reality. This approach completely fails to take into account Brjusov's conception of the poet and of the scope of poetry.

60. *Vesy* no. 11 (1905): 61–66; signed "Avrelij," Brjusov's most frequently used pseudonym. The reference was to Aurelius d'Aquapendente, a follower of Agrippa von Nettesheim, the sixteenth-century scholar, alchemist, and occultist, whose career fascinated Brjusov.

61. Ibid., p. 61. V. I. Lenin, "Partijnaja organizacija i partijnaja literatura," *Polnoe sobranie sočinenij*, fifth edition, 55 vols. (Moscow, 1960), 12, pp. 100–101.

Lenin exhorted his colleagues to shun the kind of writing that appeared in the bourgeois press and to create a new literature free from the taint of "bourgeois-anarchist individualism." Bryusov took this as a direct attack on his own camp and sensed behind Lenin's somewhat ambiguous statements a more general threat. It was evident, Bryusov wrote, that the Social Democrats were interested in freedom only for themselves. Moreover, under Lenin's regime there would be no room for variant views even within the party, making the new censorship worse than the old. Agreeing with Lenin and his party about the ugliness of certain features of the existing system, Bryusov gave no quarter on the question of freedom. "Insofar as you demand *faith* in prepared formulae, insofar as you consider that there is no more truth to seek because you have found it—you are the enemies of progress, you are our enemies." As for poets of his own kind, he prophesied: "If there came into being a social 'classless,' as it were, 'truly free' society, we would turn out to be the same outcasts, the same *poètes maudits* as we are in a bourgeois society."[62] Whatever misinterpretation was involved, his intuition was correct. Only much later, in the 1930s when the doctrine of Socialist Realism was promulgated, was his prophecy fulfilled.

Whatever Bryusov's sympathy with the "children of flaming day," it seems unwarranted to assume, as some have done, that these words convey the same spirit of romantic submission to the new race as was expressed in "The Coming Huns" or "To the Happy Ones."[63] It was one thing to envision in verse the poet and his lyre swept into the bloody chaos out of which would emerge humanity's new day. It was quite another to contemplate in a realistic way political organizers decreeing that poets should have their artistic freedom curtailed in the interests of the proletariat.

Given Bryusov's reaction to Lenin's pronouncements and his

62.   "Avrelij," ibid., p. 66.
63.   B. A. Bjalik, "Rossija v 1901–1907 gg.," in *Russkaja literatura konca XIX-načala XX v. 1901–1907* (Moscow, 1971), pp. 40–41.

reservations about the revolutionary movement in 1905, it seems appropriate to ask what it was about revolution per se that attracted Bryusov. Bryusov lagged behind many of his fellows in support of the 1905 Revolution. But he was the only major Symbolist writer who actively cooperated with the new regime after 1917, even to the point of accepting an official post. On the other hand, there is no record of the sick and prematurely aging Bryusov roaming the streets of Moscow in October 1917 as he had in October 1905 to feel himself in the heart of the action. It is, of course, important to note the difference in circumstances, but there seem to have been some common features which make this question meaningful.[64]

As has already been noted, Bryusov was disgusted with the Tsarist government's conduct of the war and humiliated by its outcome. He responded to the early stages of the 1905 revolution with scorn and distrust. It seemed petty and impotent. Only in the late summer and early autumn of 1905, when street riots and violent clashes between demonstrators and Cossacks heightened the excitement of daily life, did Bryusov find his creative energies roused. At the time he admitted that esthetic values figured largely in his response. Closely allied to his attraction to revolution as spectacle was his conviction that a poet must immerse himself in contemporary reality. Witnessing the 1905 street clashes gave him a sense of being so immersed. In 1917 the case seems to have been different. By then he had been a war correspondent and had seen much more "contemporary reality" in the form of war and its effects on the population. And he was older. Nonetheless, there is no reason to discount the strength of revolution's appeal in a new historical setting. Again, as in 1904 and 1905, he felt disgust and utter dismay by 1917 at the direction

---

64. It is beyond the scope of this argument to account definitively for later development of Brjusov's political attitudes. What continuities there may have been between his behavior in the two revolutionary situations are to be discussed largely on the psychological level.

the war was taking. Much more strongly than in 1905 Russia sensed a coming change. The yearning expectation of apocalypse that had marked Bely, Blok, and other followers of Vladimir Solovyov in 1905 and formed their first perceptions of 1917 did not touch Bryusov in any direct way. His vision of the future had always been different from theirs. The expectation of world catastrophe followed by a great revelation, with Russia playing a central role, was alien to him. Yet his early and continuing infatuation with change and with the poet's function in unrolling the future was probably one of the strongest links between his attitudes in the two revolutionary periods.

When the second revolution showed that it was here to stay, that indeed it intended to tear down the old and build the new, Bryusov seized the opportunity to have a say in that building, out of which might come, among other things, a new art. His yearning to discover or at least to be among the first to reach a new artistic frontier still burned within him. Bryusov's attitude toward these matters somewhat resembled that of the Futurist poet Vladimir Mayakovsky. One great difference, of course, lay in age and all that comes with it: nearly twenty years had passed since Bryusov was perceived as a young rebel. By now, through his association with Lunacharsky and the Commissariat of Education, he was a member of the establishment. But traces of the young Bryusov who, envisioning a new kind of art in Russia, had sworn that its leader "will be I! Yes, I!" still lived in the older man. Years earlier he had written to Ivan Konevskoy of his sympathy with the nihilists of the 1860s: "I love their violent exuberance and overturning of all idols, the permitting of all freedoms."[65] He added a revealing sentence, however: "Rules are even pleasing to me, but on the condition that I feel my power over them." Beneath Bryusov's exaltation of individual freedom, and never

65. "Iz neizdannyx pisem Valerija Brjusova k poètam: Ivanu Ivanoviču Oreusu (Konevskomu)," published by Valentin Dmitriev in *V. Brjusov i literatura konca XIX–XX veka* (Stavropol', 1979), p. 141.

completely concealed, lay his authoritarianism. Along with his worship of dynamic change was the worship of and identification with strength. The Assarhadons and Alexanders of his poems were ideals, even masks, of his lyric persona. The poet desired to be, if not Assarhadon, one of those close to that source of power. The deep-lying contradiction in Bryusov's character became most apparent when at last he accepted authority from an authoritarian regime.

Stephanos finally appeared in the last days of 1905. Bryusov wrote in his diary of how he walked with the Moscow psychiatrist and dilettante Nikolai Bazhenov through the riot-torn streets and later, in Scorpio's offices, presented him with a copy of *Stephanos* just off the press.[66] Its appearance was followed closely by the revolution's collapse. Moscow's street fighting was in its last stages. And Bryusov's year of tremendous creative energy was also over: there remained only the book that was the fruit of it all. In its first edition *Stephanos* had five sections, followed by three *poèmy*, besides the poems of dedication and conclusion. One is struck, in view of Bryusov's sensitivity at that time to the charge of irrelevance, with the choice of opening section. "Evening Songs," with an epigraph from Verlaine ("De la musique avant toute chose") is a remarkably sustained set of poems, musical indeed, that climaxes in the "Saima" cycle. The setting for the most part is in nature, so that these poems form both a continuation of and a contrast to the city poems of *Tertia Vigilia*, where evening reveals mysteries in the city and in the poet's soul. The dominant notes here are peace and calm, repose, receptivity to quiet revelations. The poet's "Greeting" reaches out to all his fellows in the half-world that is in shadow, who gaze with him into the night sky's abyss. These poems are not unpeopled, but there is a consistent etherealizing of living beings, so that they interchange easily

66. *Dnevniki*, p. 137.

with phantoms. Two poems employ similarly effective metaphors for nighttime phenomena. "The air becomes blue" portrays the rapid onset of night, so that blue becomes black as "Black riders drive / Millions of black bulls— / A herd of midnight shadows!" "Fog" is built entirely on a metaphor: a file of maidens drift by trailing white veils, and white horsemen in white cloaks rise from a canal to carry them away. In "I remember the evening, remember the summer" two lovers roam old Cologne and feel themselves figures in a poem by Heine.[67]

Vyacheslav Ivanov's favorite poem of this series was "Healing," where the poet's frenzied will is made quiescent by the evening silence.[68] Ivanov congratulated Bryusov generally on the tone of *Stephanos*, the "Crown," which he felt manifested the "calm of noonday" achieved by his talent. In this cycle, the adventurous persona of *Tertia Vigilia* and *Urbi et Orbi* has retired. Repeatedly the poet's "I" is absorbed into a shadowy realm where the will does not need to operate. Even the love poems focus on the less tempestuous first and last stages of love. "First Meetings" looks back with nostalgia on timid beginnings, while "Love's Dying" rejoices in an afterglow where passion is gone but closeness remains. The seven "Saima" poems bring these moods together on "this quiet shore where Fate has thrown" the poet. Here his love, his sense of history, and the healing power of nature work together to bring him peace. When Bryusov revisited the southern shores and mountains of the Crimea in 1898 with his new bride, not only had his earlier disdain of nature been recognized for the pose it was, but he was then, as he wrote, in a state of bliss which he fondly thought would be permanent.[69] Now, seven years later, this northern lake surrounded by moss, pines, and rocks, reflecting the pale sky of the midnight sun, touched him similarly, but

67.   Brjusov wrote to Anna Šesterkina that this poem was addressed to his wife. They visited Cologne en route to Paris in May 1903 [I, 622].

68.   *LN* 85, p. 490.

69.   *Dnevniki*, pp. 29, 37.

this time he knew the happiness would pass. One senses in these harmonious poems not only the achieved calm of which Ivanov spoke but an underlying exhaustion.

Alexander Blok wrote that "Evening Songs" was the section of *Stephanos* that was "closest and most precious" to him, but that the finest sections were the next two, "The Idols' Eternal Truth" and "From Hell Delivered." [70] The epigraph to the first of these takes its title from a line by Konevskoy. (See Appendix A for the Russian text of this cycle.) These are the "antique images" expressing contemporary emotions, some of which poems Bryusov had offered to Chulkov. Though the autobiographical references are clear, as they were intended to be, the poems have the self-sufficient strength and grace of Greek sculpture. To a degree they recall the "Favorites of the Ages" in *Tertia Vigilia*, but they are more dramatic. "To Demeter" calls the seeds of passion and suffering that have been sown to come alive in song. The poems that follow are related in form: two dramatic dialogues, "Adam and Eve" and "Orpheus and Eurydice"; a dramatic monologue with prologue and epilogue, "Medea"; another with epilogue, "Theseus to Ariadne"; "Achilles at the Altar," where the hero meditates on the death he is about to meet, and "Loki to Balder," a prophetic cry of triumph and revenge. "To the Olympians" marks a shift away from the dramatic method toward the poet's own persona. The mood of mingled rebellion and weariness, which makes all victory paltry and turns ecstasy to shame and pain, causes the poet to address Prometheus, the only Olympian with whom he feels in sympathy. The final poem, "Orpheus and the Argonauts," written in November 1904, may have been a friendly message to Bely and his "Argonauts," the group of young idealists whose aims in art Bryusov came to oppose so strongly.

Of the nine poems, five relate to love and its transformations.

70. Aleksandr Blok, *Sobranie sočinenij*, 8 vols. (Moscow and Leningrad, 1960–1963), 8, p. 148; 5, p. 617.

Possibly the most effective is "Orpheus and Eurydice," one of the more memorable renditions of this legend in European poetry. Bryusov's talent for dramatization and compression shows itself in this spare dialogue, where the coming separation of the two lovers becomes more certain at each step. Eurydice follows dutifully though uncertainly as Orpheus calls back: "Upward! Upward! Every step we climb / Leads toward sounds, to light, to the sun! / There the shadows will melt from your sight, / There, where my love waits!" Eurydice warns that he is leading a mere shade, but Orpheus encourages her: "Trust me! Trust me! At the threshold / Like me you will greet the spring!" Yet Eurydice protests: "What is spring to one who has seen the sowing / In the land of asphodels!" Nor can she remember their nights of love; she has forgotten his face—a challenge Orpheus cannot resist. He turns, and "—Eurydice! Eurydice!— / Groan the echoes of the shades." This poem was first published in August 1904 in *New Way*. Bely, recalling his struggles of that year to save Nina from herself and remembering how they had compared themselves to Orpheus and Eurydice, was sure that Bryusov's poem was written about them.[71] Bryusov's own letters to Nina of 1908 and 1909 echo the same kind of plea, but simply and without the poetic apparatus. Yet whatever the underlying biographical text, the poem stands as one of Bryusov's finest achievements.

The section "From Hell Delivered" suggests that the story of Orpheus and Eurydice is capable of another ending. Here, according to the epigraph, the goddess Astarte takes a hand. This cycle of seventeen poems acts as a centerpiece to the book. In the sequence linking "The Idols' Eternal Truth" with this section Bryusov followed the procedure he had used in *Urbi et Orbi* with his "Ballads" and "Elegies": the emotions universalized in the first set are made explicitly personal in the second. The opening "At Noon," sent to Ivanov in September 1905, no doubt prompted

71.   Andrej Belyj, *Načalo veka*, p. 282.

his comment about the confident stance of this book. "At Noon" stands in the line of self-assessments with which Bryusov marked his poet's progress. "It is accomplished! Youth is finished!" But this poem had undergone transformations to match its author's state of soul. In September 1903, in the depression that followed completion of *Urbi et Orbi*, Bryusov had written a poem "To Youth," which began with the same words. There he pictured himself once winged, now wingless, faced with making a life in the abyss [I, 626–27]. In Finland he rewrote the poem: the "rainbow of love" and the "wings of passion" had changed his lot. Yet the closing stanza is ambiguous: "I fall," but at the same time "with my whole being I drink in the heights." Three poems which follow this give an eerie and probably insightful picture of Nina. "Portrait" shows her as a spiritual waif, wounded by reality, withdrawn, the shade of death upon her: Eurydice, in fact. The two poems dedicated "To the Moon Priestess" contain in germ the plot of *The Fiery Angel*. This dreamy creature is alien and even hostile to this world. Discovering her bewitchment the poet cries out: "You are in Astarte's power, / You are hers, you are not mine!" These poems are followed by "The Goblet," the poem Nina selected years later to describe her enthrallment to Bryusov.

Among the remaining dozen poems of this section are most of those that cause readers to associate Bryusov with Decadent themes such as necrophilia, the bliss of pain, double suicide. The Decadent principle of extreme individualism dictated that *any* emotion or experience was worthy of art. In practice this often meant: the more perverse, the better. Bryusov had given only sporadic attention to most of these motifs in his earlier books. But with the entry of Nina into his life came a love of which he had only written in verse, of which he had only read in authors like Przybyszewski. In "The End of Renata," Khodasevich painted a picture of Nina Petrovskaya as a "natural" Decadent. To Bryusov she now seemed a being from a world illumined by an unholy light. At last he was plunged into the "other" stream of Decadence, where the poet-hero-individualist was submerged in sulphurous flames. The proud individualist's fate is portrayed in "Antony," the central poem of this central cycle. The poem is written in Bryusov's earlier manner, where he addresses a hero of the past and interprets sympathetically a key event of his life. Antony stands for him like a giant on the horizon, a conqueror and ruler of men, who threw all his spoils on the scale and found that love outweighed them all. Conveniently, the words for "power" and "passion" rhyme in Russian: *vlast'*/*strast'*, but *strast'* is the slightly weightier word. Nor was the parallel with Bryusov's personal situation left to suggestion. The poem ends with a prayer to the god of love that the poet may draw the same lot and send his ship "Vsled za egipetskoj kormoj!" [less effectively in English: "After the Egyptian (barge's) stern!"]. This abandonment to an overwhelming passion seemed to Bryusov to open new spheres of experience and at the same time to offer the dreamed-of escape from the closed monad of self.

Bryusov's experience in this affair suggests a curious parallel with that of Tyutchev in his "last love" with Elena Denisieva. The fact that Bryusov himself may have seen such a parallel is significant. The pattern of Tyutchev's love affair and his emotional reaction to it are vividly embodied in the poems which several generations of scholars have identified with Denisieva. Bryusov was of course familiar both with the poems and with Tyutchev's biography. It is an intriguing thought that the stimulus he derived from Tyutchev's political poems of this period may have extended to the love poems. As Richard Gregg has noted, at least one poem revealing Tyutchev's conception of love closely anticipates the Decadent attitude.[72] The final stanza of his "There are twins—for

---

72.   Richard A. Gregg, *Fedor Tiutchev: The Evolution of a Poet*, pp. 180, 231 n. 49, where he notes the similarity of this poem, "Est' bliznecy-dlja zemnorodnyx," to Baudelaire's later published "Les deux bonnes sœurs" and raises the question of Tjutčev's relation to the Decadent movement. Gregg's seventh chapter, "The 'Last Love' in a New Key," provides material helpful in exploring the point I have addressed. I have used Gregg's translations of Tjutčev's poems.

the earthborn" reads like a Decadent grammar of love: "And who in an overflow of feelings, when the blood seethes and freezes, has not known your temptations—Suicide and Love."

Whatever guidance in his poetry and his life Bryusov may have derived from Tyutchev, suicide from love was not in store for either. The question of where his passion would lead, other than to the writing of poems, was a problem Bryusov may have pondered even when the affair was at its height. The death in ecstasy which he created for Antony and Cleopatra and which by Nina's evidence he considered with her as an ideal solution was not to be his. Once before, in the Caucasus, he had considered death as the logical step for the poet who has reached his earthly goal. In *Tertia Vigilia* Sven the Norseman died contemplating the Polar Star. But the poet must go on writing poetry. The "other half" of Bryusov's nature, of which he wrote to Ivanov, demanded to be heard.

After the interlude on Saima, Bryusov returned to the noisy life of Moscow, where newspapers shouted the humiliating terms of the Portsmouth Treaty and where protest demonstrations were leading to the erection of barricades. The last half of his book is made up of two sections, "The Everyday" and "The Present," and four *poèmy*. "The Everyday" finds the poet in his usual city haunts, once more pursuing the unique instant in random encounters. Some of his civic poems found place in this section, but most are in the following one. Finally come three *poèmy* in which the prophetic mood reaches its crest. "Praise to the Crowd" shows the influence of Verhaeren's "La Révolte," which Bryusov was then translating. "Spirits of Fire" is in the same mood and style, in free verse and irregular stanza form. "Pale Horse," the most famous of these, was written in a different manner. With four sections of three quatrains each in trochaic heptameter, the poem's conventional formal regularity is challenged by vocabulary and cadence. The scene narrated contains a corresponding contradiction. The poem describes a momentary apparition of unearthly horse and rider in a somewhat futuristic city setting. The rider carries a banner bearing the word "Death." The onlookers are stunned, but as soon as the apparition is gone, all return to their ordinary business, except for two. The harlot and the madman remember, but they are lost in the crowd. Obviously apocalyptic (its epigraph is from St. John), this poem has nothing to do with revolution as such. As the climax of a series it puts a definite interpretation on all of Bryusov's "revolutionary" poems. The poem especially impressed Bely, Blok, and Sergei Solovyov, and Blok acknowledged its influence on his poem "The Last Day" [I, 637].

Considering the "storms and maelstrom" of the year past so richly reflected in this book, the poem that Bryusov selected for his conclusion seems at first a strange choice. "From the Songs of Maeldune" returns to Tennyson. "The Voyage of Maeldune" is its ostensible source, but the sentiment is closer to his "Ulysses."[73] Tennyson's Maeldune wandered with his men among many exotic isles, only to learn from an old hermit the folly of taking vengeance. Bryusov's Maeldune draws a different lesson from his wanderings: the pleasures he and his men have experienced along the way are not enough reward for those who are born and sworn adventurers. The New World beckons; tomorrow when the sun rises they will sit down again at the oars. Maeldune's exhortation to his men echoes that of Ulysses, who held out hope of reaching the Happy Isles. Tennyson's Ulysses held up the ideal: "One equal temper of heroic hearts, / Made weak by time and fate, but strong in will / To strive, to seek, to find, and not to yield." Thus Bryusov concluded *Stephanos*, the "Crown" of his work thus far. This final poem announces that the poet-adventurer has returned to the helm of his boat and means to move on. The frame he provided for his book makes clear its total meaning and places it firmly in the context of his other work. "From the Songs of Maeldune" is set apart in tone and subject from the poems pre-

73. Alfred Lord Tennyson, *Ballads and Other Poems*, ed. Hallam, Lord Tennyson (London: Macmillan, 1908), pp. 166–76; "Ulysses," *Poems II* (London: Macmillan, 1908), pp. 26–29.

ceding it, but it reaches back to the dedicatory poem addressed to Vyacheslav Ivanov. Whatever Ivanov's political views at that time, it is notable that the book is dedicated to him as "poet, thinker, friend." In his foreword Bryusov firmly distances his poetry from current matters. "My book, you will resemble a mad singer who has wandered onto the field of battle, in the smoke, under fire,—with only a harp" [I, 620]. And in the dedication he offers Ivanov his grateful thanks for returning him to the dear and familiar horizons of classicism and offering the model of the poet who rises above the immediate concerns of life.

Deeply as the events of the past year had stirred him as a man, they only reinforced his conception of poetry and of his role as poet. Ulysses/Maeldune had visited the isles of love and the city of strife. Now he must strike out for a new world. The challenge of the next journey made the following years of Bryusov's life very difficult ones.

TEN

The Death of a Poet?

THE JANUARY 1905 ISSUE of *The Balance* carried Bryusov's article "A Holy Sacrifice," one of his most important statements on art made during the Symbolist years.[1] Although critics have seen in this piece the influence of Bely and Ivanov, the statement clearly developed out of Bryusov's early thinking on Symbolism and Decadence. In various efforts in the mid-1890s to define the two terms, he had concluded that Symbolism was the artistic method that had emerged to express the new world-view that was Decadence. For some time, he believed the chief virtue of Decadence was its contemporaneity: "It is moving ahead, developing, and the future belongs to it, especially when it finds a worthy leader."[2] From that early stage when he saw Decadence as a possible road to fame, Bryusov deepened his thinking and carved out a literary position that became identical with his self-concept. Extreme individualism, the kernel of Decadence, was for him no mere pose, but the essential and unchanging feature of his philosophy. We have seen how, after his almost instinctive adoption of this stance, he found its philosophical justification in Leibniz and others; how he cast aside the basically romantic search for pure beauty as offering too narrow a scope for the modern poet; and how he argued passionately with Balmont on the poet's need to immerse himself in contemporary reality. Some critics have dismissed Decadence as the earliest stage of

1. "Svjaščennaja žertva," *Vesy* no. 1 (1905): 23–29; VI, 94–99.
2. *Dnevniki*, p. 12.

Bryusov's career, largely outgrown by the early 1900s. "A Holy Sacrifice" sets the record straight.

Nineteenth-century Romanticism, Bryusov wrote—clearly envisioning French literature only—spawned two movements, Parnassian and Realist. The former, aside from lessons of form, had little to teach its successors. Not so the latter:

> Leaving the Parnassians to gather their *Trophées*, the Decadents departed from them into all the turbulence, all the grandeur and lowness of life, from dreams of the rajahs' splendid India and the ever beautiful Greece of Pericles to the fires and hammers of factories, to the rumble of trains (Verhaeren, Arno Holz), to the common surroundings of contemporary rooms (Rodenbach, Rimbaud), to all the painful contradictions of the contemporary soul (Hoffmannsthal, Maeterlinck), to that contemporary condition which the Realists also hoped to embody.
>
> [VI, 96–97]

It was no accident, he concluded, that the city, a theme first explored in the Realist novel, had found its best singers among the Decadents. However, if the Realists brought the contemporary world in its entirety into literature, the Decadents added their distinctive point of view. The common subject was life, but the Realists looked outward for their subject matter and their artistic stimulation, whereas the modern writer, the Decadent, looked within: *"The whole world is in me"* [VI, 97]. The realization Bryusov had come to after his Caucasian summer is reiterated in "A Holy Sacrifice": the poet must fill not his notebooks but his soul. This meant throwing himself into life, erasing any line between the poet and the man. The epigraph to this piece and its title were taken from Pushkin's "The Poet,"[3] by way of a polemic. In Pushkin's view as expressed in this poem, until the poet is called to

3. A. S. Puškin, *Polnoe sobranie sočinenij*, 10 vols. (Moscow, 1956–1958), 3, p. 22.

"holy sacrifice" by Apollo he is free to bury himself in the trivia of life. When the call comes he must flee the distractions of life and men, to be alone with his inspiration. In Bryusov's view, today's poet must remain in the midst of life and himself become the "holy sacrifice." "We demand of the poet that he constantly bring his 'holy sacrifices' not only in his verses but in every hour of his life, every feeling—his love, his hate, his achievements and falls. Let the poet create not his book but his life" [VI, 99].

This characteristically Symbolist attitude was rooted firmly in Bryusov's understanding of Decadence. Whatever the Decadent poet's theme—cities, factories, wars, loves—he looked inward to see how that theme was experienced in his soul. As long as his soul was thriving, his source of poetry was endless.

Writing at the end of 1904, Bryusov could speak confidently of these matters. Both he and the movement were at their height. By the middle of 1906 he saw the situation differently. *Stephanos* was published toward the end of 1905. That a period of dryness and depression should set in afterward was entirely predictable. Additional reasons for Bryusov's depression at this period were numerous and weighty: the aftermath of the unsuccessful war and the revolution; serious ideological problems within the Symbolist movement, especially the opposition to his views offered by his friend Vyacheslav Ivanov and worries connected with *The Balance;* and a new, troubled phase of his love affair with Nina Petrovskaya. It all added up to a state of crisis that was, in certain important respects, unlike anything he had experienced in the past.

A series of letters to Nina Petrovskaya in May and June 1906 described the situation.[4] The month-long stay at Lake Saima the year before had been, as Bryusov had predicted, the high point of their relationship. By May 1906, misunderstandings and difficulties had mounted, though the attachment continued strong on

---

4.   These letters appear in part in *LN* 85, pp. 789–98. Some passages are supplied from archival sources.

both sides. Now she left Moscow with the hope, which Bryusov shared, that separation would mend matters. Her absence was the occasion for Bryusov to pour out long, emotional letters that showed much not only about the relationship but about his state of mind. On 27 May he wrote of his need for "some sort of resurrection, some rebirth, some fiery baptism, in order to become myself again, in the best sense of the word. What am I good for in *this* state! A machine for composing fine verses! An apparatus for brilliant translations of the poems of Verhaeren!"[5] The chilling thought had occurred that at thirty-two he might have run through the whole range of his possibilities. A few days later, on 2 June, he complained that his spiritual temperature, measured by his poetic production, had fallen very low—no more than ten poems in the last five months, and those very mediocre. "To stop writing poems is for me completely equivalent to spiritual death. And I have stopped writing poems."[6] He knew what Nina's advice would be: "'Change your whole life! Throw over everything! Become mad!'"[7] "Madness" was the term they used for the ecstatic frenzy with which they lived their love affair in its best moments. Bryusov had already warned her that this was not a state he could long sustain, that his love and his life normally flowed in more regulated fashion. Now he assured her that he had no spiritual strength for such changes. "In the life of my spirit these ten months have been only a descent, a slow rolling downhill into an abyss. I must fall to the bottom. Only then can a rebirth take place."[8] It could not be long now, it seemed. With this dim hope he began to examine his past life. He saw that he had lived with an inner intensity that had brought him to early exhaustion.

5.   *LN* 85, p. 789.
6.   Ibid.
7.   CGALI, fond 376, op. 1, ed. xr. 4. Petrovskaja's letters to Brjusov are also in CGALI (fond 56, op. 1, ed. xr. 95) but are largely unavailable because of archival restrictions.
8.   Ibid.

"*Urbi et Orbi* took everything that was in me. *Stephanos* climaxed my poetry, truly crowned it."[9] He saw it as impossible to go on in the same way, repeating himself as he considered Balmont to be doing. And at this crucial moment, when all his strength was needed to break through to new paths, Nina spoke to him of love! He had no strength for either. Whatever his love for her—and he assured her that it still existed—he made abundantly clear in this letter that the frenzied love and revolutionary excitement that had fed his poetry over the last year would serve no longer. Frantically he reached for something else: "There are some kinds of truths—beyond Nietzsche, beyond Przybyszewski, beyond Verhaeren, ahead for contemporary man. Whoever will show me the way to them, that one I will follow."[10]

Four days later, on 10 June, another letter went out in response to one of hers. Here Nina seems to have challenged some of his most treasured convictions. Recriminations began: he reminded her that he knew that she had never read *Stephanos*, the book devoted in large part to their love! In short, she valued him as lover more than as poet. Moreover, she seems to have reproached him, and perhaps his poetry, for lack of political relevance. "It is possible," he wrote, "that in art the thought expressed is more important than the artistic significance of the work. But I cannot believe this! For me the sole measure in poetry (everywhere, in all) remains artistic quality. To me, an artist, a political party's urgency seems nonsense, but to abuse poetry is to abuse my divinity."[11] He was driven to one of the strongest and most personal assertions of his creed: "Poetry for me is *everything!* All my life is given only to serving it. I live insofar as it lives in me, and when it dies in me I will die. In its name, without a second thought I will sacrifice everything: my happiness, my love, myself."[12]

On the night of 13–14 June Bryusov wrote a letter in which

9.   *LN* 85, pp. 789–90.   10.   Ibid., p. 790.   11.   Ibid.
12.   Ibid., p. 791.

he detailed what he thought had happened to him. *Urbi et Orbi* had exhausted him, but his meeting with Nina had brought to light new resources in himself and the world around him. *Stephanos* was a final burst, after which there was nothing else. Here he came to the crux of his problem:

> I can no longer live by worn-out beliefs, by those ideals which I have gone beyond. I can no longer live by "Decadence" and "Nietzscheanism," in which I believe, believe. . . . You once said that in my soul I was a hermit, a monk, that in the Middle Ages I'd have gone into a monastery. Yes! Yes! I have to believe in that which I serve, completely, to the end, and I have to serve something. I pretend to be a skeptic.[13]

The mask he had donned for his public career was paining him. He had chosen to play the role of Decadent poet, and now he felt trapped by the consequences. These words, written off in the middle of the night to a person to whom he was accustomed to reveal his most private thoughts, cannot be said to belong to the category of public pose. The contradiction in them seemed to arise out of a deep and painful contradiction in his spirit. "Decadence" and "Nietzscheanism" (note his use of quotation marks) were outworn beliefs—probably in the sense that they were no longer productive for him. His extreme individualism had defined his world as a series of unrolling prospects accessible to the poet-adventurer. Now the poet-adventurer faced a blank wall. And yet he still believed. Where was he to go?

Physically and emotionally drained, Bryusov left a few days later with his wife for a stay on the island of Gotland. Ten days after arrival he wrote to Nina: "I am still the same, exhausted, without will or strength. More and more I submit to a will not my own but another, which wants to take command of me."[14] It

13. Ibid., pp. 791–92.
14. CGALI, fond 376, letter of 27 June 1906.

is impossible to interpret this cryptic allusion with any assurance. However, it was apparently around this time that Bryusov became addicted to morphine.[15] Nina, herself a drug-taker from early years,[16] wrote to him in 1911 that she had watched him pass through a total change of personality, and "I know the role, terrible for me, that morphine has played in it."[17] It is probable that then if not before, in these terrible months when he felt the core of his existence going dead, he resorted to this artificial stimulation. Drug-taking was of course part of the Decadent way of life, but it is likely that in this as in much else Bryusov had remained largely an observer until his liaison with Nina.[18]

In spite of these inward afflictions, Bryusov continued to be active in the literary arena. We cannot here trace the conflicts and rivalries among factions within Symbolism or Bryusov's part in them as chief pilot for *The Balance*.[19] However, the contents of that journal to a certain extent reveal Bryusov's efforts to find a way out of his labyrinth. In particular, the debate concerning Decadence and the writings about and by René Ghil and his "poésie scientifique" deserve attention.

The dating of the disintegration of Symbolism, or Decadence, is subject to various interpretations. The movement, made up almost from its beginnings of truly disparate attitudes toward art, was for a few years held together by outside forces. As long as it seemed a beleaguered garrison attacked from all sides, differences

15. His later addiction is mentioned in various sources, including V. F. Xodasevič, *Nekropol'*, p. 60.

16. CGALI, fond 376, op. 1, ed. xr. 3, p. 65, "Vospominanija N. I. Petrovskoj o V. Ja. Brjusove."

17. CGALI, fond 56, op. 1, ed. xr. 95, letter of 12 February 1911.

18. In a review signed "Avrelij" of Rafail Solov'ev, *Filosofija smerti*, Brjusov cites the aphorism: "Poetry is morphine, awakening our consciousness": *Vesy* no. 5 (1906): 82–83.

19. This is done in great detail by K. M. Azadovskij and D. E. Maksimov in "Brjusov i 'Vesy' (k istorii izdanija)," *LN* 85, pp. 257–324.

were more or less buried. But by 1906 the small fort had been transformed into a large field, open to everyone. Contests of greater or lesser ferocity were taking place on various parts of the extended territory. When Bryusov wrote "Decadence" and "Nietzscheanism" in quotation marks, he may have been referring in part to the fashionable trends going by those names. For him, Decadence was a profoundly serious matter. He disagreed strongly with his friend Vyacheslav Ivanov, who wrote during the exchange in *The Balance* over the mystical-anarchist miscellany *Torches* begun by Ivanov and Chulkov, "In my view, 'Decadence' is only a conventional and popular tag."[20] Bryusov's own conception, based on years of honing, had been lost in the turmoil of the development of the movement or had simply not been accepted by some of his closest associates. Decadence now meant to many nothing more than the writers grouped around *The Balance*, and even on its pages the term was used variously. In a 1906 article, "Decadence and the Public Concern," signed by Dmitri Merezhkovsky but written by Zinaida Gippius, Decadence was distinguished from individualism.[21] Decadents were those who were so far removed from consciousness of the rest of life as to be oblivious of it, whereas individualists were potential unifiers because of their religious view of life. Ivanov's argument for mystical anarchism was less clear-cut. Accepting the appellation Decadent for himself, Ivanov wrote that mystical anarchism expressed a striving away from isolation to spiritual oneness, and that it was opposed to Decadence only if the latter was a synonym for isolation. The tendency in both of these pieces was of course unacceptable to Bryusov. A year later *Russian Thought* carried an essay by the philosopher Nikolai Berdyaev entitled "Decadence and Mystical

20. "O 'fakel'ščikax' i drugix imenax sobiratel'nyx," *Vesy* no. 6 (1906): 55.

21. "Dekadenstvo i obščestvennost'," *Vesy* no. 5 (1906): 30–37; Z. N. Gippius, *Literaturnyj dnevnik* (St. Petersburg, 1908; reprint Munich: Wilhelm Fink Verlag, 1970), pp. 327–46.

Realism" which, while it chiefly attacked mystical anarchism, also attacked some of Bryusov's own convictions.[22] At base it was a call for art once more to serve worthy ends, which in this case meant religion.

In *The Balance* for September 1907 Bryusov published under the pseudonym V. Bakulin the conclusions he had reached about the Decadent movement.[23] "The Conquerors' Triumph" borrowed its title from a recent article published elsewhere that described how Decadence had won the field by a cheap victory, which consisted in becoming a popular fad. Bryusov agreed completely, noting that even within its own confines Decadence harbored vulgarians. "It is time now for those [Decadents] who have preserved boldness of gaze and readiness for new struggle to laugh bitterly."[24] He insisted, as he always had, that Decadence is not merely a style of writing but a world-view. Then he put the crucial question: have the original Decadents remained true to extreme individualism? They had not: the schism within the school, he now admitted openly, marked the beginning of the end. But if Decadence was dying, none of the pretenders now on view deserved to be its replacement. " 'Decadence' is waiting to hand its scepter in the world of art to a new group of artists connected to it by right of succession, and, if it is fated to close its eyes before that group arises, to answer as did Alexander the Great the question of to whom he was leaving his kingdom: 'To the most worthy.' "[25]

Although he did not put his own name to this declaration, the signature "V. Bakulin" (from his mother's maiden name) was to most readers no disguise. A year earlier he had revealed to Nina Petrovskaya the depth of his attachment to what he considered to

22.   "Dekadentstvo i mističeskij realizm," *Russkaja mysl'* no. 6 (1907): 114–23.

23.   "Toržestvo pobeditelej," *Vesy* no. 9 (1907): 53–57.

24.   Ibid., p. 54.

25.   Ibid, p. 57.

be Decadence. The school that now claimed that name hardly fitted his notion of it, but he would have preferred not to write its
obituary just yet. To George Chulkov early in 1907 he had expressed the same view as in this article, but with an addition
valuable for defining his present position: periods of consolida-
tion, he wrote, were necessary in the evolution of art. "'Decadence' and 'Symbolism' and 'the new poetry,' all these schools
have died (for a normal truth lives, say seventeen, eighteen, or at
the most twenty years), but that element in these schools which
was alive must now be allowed to put up its shoots." [26] This is the
period when academies are founded. (Various critics claimed that
Bryusov was heading toward the academy.) "I confess that the role
of eternal conqueror, of eternal 'nomad of beauty' is much more
attractive . . . , but submitting to this historical moment, I say,
like the legendary Roman legionnaire: *sta, miles, hic optime man-
ebimus.*" [27] However, events seemed to be crowding the once "new
art," and in his public statement Bryusov apparently thought it
as well to anticipate its demise.

This was the moment Bryusov chose to prepare a full collected
edition of his published poetry. [28] The title, *Roads and Crossroads*,
was full of meaning, for he indeed felt himself at an important
crossroad in his career. Two volumes came out in 1908; the third,
All Melodies, in 1909, contained poems written in 1906–1909.
Drawing a line beneath the sum of his past achievements implied
a new departure. Though he urged on the wayward Chulkov the
virtue of due consideration before action, he nonetheless was anxiously looking about for the new path to follow. His recent successes in prose fiction, the novel *The Fiery Angel* (1908) and his
collection of stories and dramatic scenes called *The Earth's Axis*

26. Georgij Čulkov, *Gody stranstvij. Iz knigi vospominanij*, p. 347.
27. Ibid., p. 348. The Latin means: "Halt, soldier, here we will best
remain."
28. *Puti i pereput'ja. Sobranie stixov*, 3 vols. (Moscow, 1908, 1909).

(1907), were in his old vein. Moreover, he still and always saw himself as a poet, though at present a poet uncertain of his next steps.

For a number of years Bryusov had been attracted by the work of the Belgian Emile Verhaeren. In 1906 he published a volume of Verhaeren's poems in Russian, including not only those he had translated during Russia's turbulent period of the last two years but many more. Although he had known Verhaeren's work earlier, Bryusov's real appreciation of him apparently dated from 1899 and played a decisive part in turning his imagination away from the unpeopled realms he had earlier explored with Balmont to wider spheres. "Verhaeren spread the limits of poetry so wide that he included in it the whole world," Bryusov wrote in 1904.[29] Verhaeren confirmed Bryusov's feeling that the poet's soul offered a much more powerful lens than his predecessors had thought: anything in the world might be visible through it. Few of Bryusov's poems are reminiscent of Verhaeren's, but the latter opened vistas in all directions and thereby merited Bryusov's warmest praise: "His work is in the best sense contemporary."[30]

Associated with Verhaeren in other minds besides Bryusov's was a much less significant poet but a figure striking in a different way, René Ghil. It is not quite certain when Bryusov first heard of Ghil (he told Ghil that it was as early as 1891, but he may well have exaggerated).[31] However, in 1904 he received a letter from Ghil offering to become the French correspondent for *The Balance*, the first issue of which Ghil had discussed with Maximilian Voloshin.[32] Always a missionary of sorts, Ghil no doubt saw promise

29. Review of E. Verhaeren, *Les villes tentaculaires* (Paris, 1904), in *Vesy* no. 3 (1904): 54.
30. Ibid., p. 55.
31. Letter of Brjusov to Verhaeren, 14 February 1904, cited by A. E. Margarjan, "Valerij Brjusov i Rene Gil'," *Brjusovskie čtenija 1966 goda*, p. 524. In this letter Brjusov effusively accepted Ghil's offer to write for *Vesy*.
32. Ibid., pp. 523–24.

here of spreading to a new audience his ideas about scientific poetry, including his theory of "l'instrumentation verbale." The latter was an extreme development of the notion of the musicality of poetry in which Ghil hypothesized a precise relation between phonetic features of language and auditory and visual sensations, which he tried to elevate into a system. For this he found followers, though not in large numbers, and created a certain polemical stir.[33] Of more far-reaching appeal were his pronouncements about poetry's place at the forefront of modern life. It was chiefly here that Ghil was allied with Verhaeren. His name was sufficiently well known for Bryusov to seize gladly on Ghil's interest in writing for *The Balance*. Bryusov assured him of the delight of the staff and allotted him from sixty to seventy pages a year for his reviews and articles.[34]

In the final issue in 1904, Bryusov supplemented Ghil's five lengthy "letters on French poetry" and sundry reviews with a study of Ghil's theories and career.[35] The occasion was the publication of Ghil's poetic work *Œuvre*, along with the fourth edition of his treatise on poetry. It is clear from Bryusov's essay that he was bent on pleasing Ghil and at the same time impressing readers with the importance of this contributor. But it is also obvious that some—though not all—of Ghil's ideas did attract him greatly. Ghil's efforts to eliminate chance from art by subjecting inspiration to laws amounted, as Bryusov put it, to bridling Pegasus.[36] But Ghil's insistence "that poetry must stand at the summit of the contemporary scientific world understanding" was

33. An interesting account of the debate concerning this theory in one country is found in Herman Braet, *L'accueil fait au Symbolisme en Belgique 1885–1900* (Brussels: Palais des Académies, 1967), ch. I, "L'affaire Ghil: l'instrumentation verbale."

34. Margarjan, "Brjusov i Gil'," pp. 524–25. Brjusov's letters initially suggest that Ghil may have wanted even more space; Brjusov had to remind him that this was after all a Russian journal.

35. "Renè Gil'," *Vesy* no. 12 (1904): 12–31.

36. Ibid., pp. 25–26.

at least a cousin to his own ideas on art's necessary contemporaneity.[37] Moreover, he found in Ghil an even more ambitious notion of the integrity of a poet's work than his own recently expounded theory. Not only must a book of poems be treated as a whole, but a poet's entire *œuvre* should be conceived in the same way. Ghil provided the example by the ongoing publication of the work called simply *Œuvre*, a series of poems the goal of which was, as Bryusov put it, "to survey the entire universe from the viewpoint of contemporary man in all the manifestations of being, in nature and in man."[38]

Bryusov's interest in Ghil did not abate (he offered to write another article on him for Chulkov's journal the following year),[39] but his next published study did not appear until 1909. Meanwhile, on the pages of *The Balance* Ghil continued to expound his ideas in reviews of French poetry. Some of his views must have struck Bryusov forcefully in the days of his own uncertainty. For example, a review by Ghil in 1906 stressed the word "new." He spoke of "new dogmatics, new ethics, and a new consciousness that will reign over mankind as a new holy step on the eternal stairway of the world's development."[40] And he repeated that "a new conception of the world cannot avoid creating a new poetic language adequate to it."[41] These words echoed principles Bryusov had worked out in his youth. True, the insistence on science was new, but Ghil often noted that science and poetry reach the same goal, only by different means. Later that same year in a review of *Plus loin* by Vielé-Griffin, a poet whom Bryusov valued highly, Ghil attacked Symbolism. He observed how Vielé-Griffin was breaking the bonds of Symbolism and going even beyond Ver-

37. Ibid., p. 18.
38. Ibid., p. 30.
39. Čulkov, *Gody stranstvij*, p. 327.
40. *Vesy* no. 1 (1906): 78.
41. Ibid.

haeren.[42] The following year Ghil continued the attack. He wrote in an article on new French poetry: "We are not the center of the world, as we imagine our ignorance and our naïveté, poet-egotists, trying to embrace infinity in our finite beings and to make our 'I' the measure of the unmeasurable world evolution!"[43] He went on to invite these benighted souls to join the movement toward the future.

Ghil's words attacked a position Bryusov had long held but about which he was already troubled, as his letter to Nina Petrovskaya of June 1906 shows. In January 1907 Bryusov wrote to Ghil: "The more deeply I study your work, the more I am enraptured by its grandeur and worldwide significance. I have already published five books of poetry and several volumes of prose . . . — I see that I have come to the bounds of your 'scientific poetry.' Its principles seem to me more and more unshakeable and doubtless one fine day I shall surprise my friends by my unexpected conversion."[44] A few months later he reported to Ghil that he had presented Ghil's theory in a public lecture. But he was still cautious: "Of course I will have to study it more deeply and think more seriously before I begin with my accustomed zeal to spread this theory. But perhaps that time is not so distant."[45] The following summer, 1908, Bryusov was in France and made the personal acquaintance of Ghil and his followers of the group "L'Abbaye." Here he no doubt clarified his impressions further.

In 1909 René Ghil published in Paris a more popular exposition of the ideas he had first proposed in 1886 and had elaborated in notoriously difficult language over the intervening years. *De la poésie scientifique* offered Bryusov the opportunity for a more considered treatment of Ghil's work. He chose to place his review

42.   *Vesy* no. 8 (1906): 59–62.
43.   *Vesy* no. 6 (1907): 85.
44.   Margarjan, "Brjusov i Gil'," p. 529.
45.   Ibid., p. 530.

article of Ghil's book in *Russian Thought* rather than *The Balance*.[46]
In it Bryusov presented for consideration a conception of poetry
and the poet that contradicts many, though not all, of the positions he had held heretofore. According to Bryusov, Ghil rejected
the view of contemporary poets that their own emotions are supremely worth recording. Only a few people, he said, possess any
really interesting emotions. Moreover, most poets continue to operate with the literary conventions of bygone times, incongruous
in an era of telegraphs, ocean liners, and stock exchanges. To the
notion of poetry as the random expression of impressions and
emotions Ghil opposed the ideal of a conscious, thinking art that
knows its goals and is tightly linked to the contemporary period.
His basic idea was that "poetry is the supreme act of thought"
[VI, 167]. The poetic image is the result of the synthesizing powers of our mind. And while the proper work of poetry is not to
express in verse the findings of astronomy or sociology, it should
address by its own methods the same contemporary problems.
"Acquaintance with scientific facts should open to the poet new
horizons," wrote Bryusov, summarizing Ghil's views, "should
procure for him an inexhaustible, constantly increasing supply of
new themes for his creative work, not personal, not local, but
general, worldwide" [VI, 167]. Poetry was not to be the hand-
maiden of science; the two approaches to the world were to be
complementary.

    The appeal for Bryusov of this invitation to explore new hori-
zons is surely understandable. It is even credible that he could
accept Ghil's violent criticisms of "poet-egotists" in view of his
strong approval of "poet-philosophers." Emotion was not rejected
but was seen to rise from thought. Above all, there was the challenge to the poet to become fully contemporary. It was still true
that the poet was born not made, but he "must stand at the level

    46.   "Naučnaja poèzija," *Russkaja mysl'* no. 5 (1909): part II, pp. 147–58;
VI, 160–75.

of contemporary knowledge and possess a conscious world-view" [VI, 169]. For all his stress on intellect, Ghil did not reject intuition. Bryusov noted carefully that Ghil had worked out the roles of the conscious and the subconscious in inspiration. And for his own part he recalled that Pushkin had said: "Inspiration is needed in geometry the same as in poetry" [VI, 171].

After an exposition which, while objective, is clearly sympathetic, Bryusov set about evaluating Ghil's theories. He made acceptance of them dependent on two factors: (1) how realizable they were; and (2) how the interrelation of art and science was viewed. Ghil regarded his theory as a logical step in the evolution of poetry, finding his closest predecessors in Lucretius, Goethe, and Shelley. As for the present, it was too early to evaluate the success of its application, said Bryusov, though the theory need not stand or fall on this criterion. Making clear that "l'instrumentation verbale" strictly interpreted was not to be regarded as an essential part of Ghil's doctrine, Bryusov nonetheless praised Ghil's own "Œuvre" for its cosmic scope. And Verhaeren, while not explicitly a propagator of Ghil's ideas, was close enough to his group to cast luster on its members.

It was when Bryusov faced the second of his two criteria that his own position became apparent. His experience over the last ten years or more had brought him to a crossroads.

> Obviously, the newest criticism definitely destroys all of the teachings on the final *goal* of art which have been set forth up to this time, including the theory of "imitation" (mimesis) stemming from Aristotle, Hegel's theory of "Beauty," Schiller's and Spencer's theory of "play without purpose," the sensualist theory of special "esthetic satisfaction," and the theory of "communication" defended by Tolstoy. Thus the field is cleared for the theory set forth by A. Potebnya of art as a special method of cognition. [VI, 174]

As long ago as *About Art*, where he had implicitly challenged Tolstoy, Bryusov had demonstrated an acquaintance with the

theories of Potebnya, though he had then leaned much more on
Schopenhauer to bolster his ideas. In his memoirs Bely associates,
with an irritating indefiniteness as to time, Bryusov's enthusiasms
for Ghil and Potebnya.[47] (There is evidence here and in other
writings to make Bryusov one of the earliest twentieth-century
literary theorists in Russia, if not the first, to be attracted to the
work of this linguist, who was in some ways an important forerunner of the Formalist critics.)[48]

Bryusov's earlier conceptions were being transformed under a
variety of pressures into very different ones, but threads of consistency run throughout. His passionate belief that the poet belongs
on the forefront of human development made him vulnerable to
Ghil's arguments attacking so many of his other convictions.
Only after many years, in his last two published books of poetry,
Mea and *Distances*, did Bryusov formally declare himself for scientific poetry and endeavor to practice its precepts so far as language
and theme were concerned.

One other, largely unpublished work should be considered under the heading of Ghil's influence. First conceived in 1909 and
begun in 1911, this project was described by Bryusov in his
1913 autobiography as "a large book of poems (four volumes are
planned) 'Dreams of Mankind,' which is intended to present 'lyrical reflections of the life of all peoples and all times.'"[49] It was to
be dedicated to René Ghil. Of a different genre and greater mag-
nitude, "Dreams of Mankind" recalls the "History of the Russian
Lyric" in the kind of thought and preparation Bryusov devoted to
it. His archive contains elaborate plans and drafts of introductions.[50] Only twenty-five of the poems were published in his life-

47.   Andrej Belyj, *Načalo veka*, p. 165.
48.   See Victor Erlich, *Russian Formalism: History—Doctrine* (third ed. New
Haven and London: Yale University Press, 1981), pp. 23–26.
49.   "Avtobiografija," p. 118.
50.   II, 459–64.

time, though a volume was planned in 1916–1917.[51] It is difficult to judge this work on its fragments or imagine the impact even the one planned volume might have had if it had been published at that time. It belongs by rights to a later period of Bryusov's career; its relevance here is to the influence of Ghil and to Bryusov's efforts to find a new voice. The project recalls in scope not only Ghil's *Œuvre* but Victor Hugo's *La légende des siècles*.

Thus at the end of the decade that had seen his rise to the heights of literary fame, Bryusov found himself in a hiatus, the difficulty of which was aggravated by the breakup of the Symbolist movement. In 1919, in an outline for an autobiography, he headed the period beginning after *Stephanos* with the word "*Uklon*."[52] Usually understood as "change of direction," or "deviation," it can also mean "downward slope." In the context the last meaning seems to be the one intended. The subheadings Bryusov gave referred to personal involvements and journeys. Then comes the provocative word *gibel'*, "ruin." The final section, which begins before the 1917 Revolution, is headed "The End." The first subtopic is "Slow Decline," and the last is "Waiting It Out," *Doživanie*. That he perceived his later course as essentially downward motion seems inescapable. There is no question that Bryusov sought a change of direction after *Stephanos*.

Bryusov's near-conversion to "poésie scientifique" in 1907, whatever fruit it bore at a later date, seems a part of his desperate struggle in those years to find new stimuli and a new direction for his art. To Nina he had written that it was impossible to go on in the same way, repeating himself, however effectively. Yet the poetry he wrote between 1906 and 1909, fine as much of it is, showed little by way of new departures. The foreword to *All*

51. II, 465. A reconstruction of this volume from archival materials is presented in II, 313–93.
52. E. N. Konšina, "Tvorčeskoe nasledie V. Ja. Brjusova v ego arxive," *Zapiski Otdela rukopisej*, Lenin State Library no. 25 (Moscow, 1962), p. 86.

Melodies was a dignified admission of this fact. There he wrote: "In the poems of this volume are found the same devices, perhaps somewhat more perfected, the same circle of attention, perhaps somewhat broadened, as in the two previous volumes [of *Roads and Crossroads*, i.e., all his earlier published poems]" [I, 637]. He considered this particular road travelled to its end and hoped not to return to it. "I am certain that in poetry, and not only Russian poetry, there still exist an infinite number of tasks which no one has completed, of themes hardly touched, and of means completely unused" [I, 637]. He hinted, clearly, at hoped-for new departures in his own work.

Some critics have found the poems of *All Melodies* and his 1912 *Mirror of Shadows* among the best that Bryusov wrote. In both the habit of recording and reacting to the events of his life—notably, his love affairs—continues. His poems follow the tortuous course of his relationship with Nina Petrovskaya until her final departure from Russia in November 1911. A prominent place is given also to his briefer connection with the famous actress Vera Kommissarzhevskaya and later to his ultimately tragic tie with Nadezhda Lvova. The links to his earlier books take many forms. For example, the use of distinctive genres for erotic themes in *All Melodies* goes back to *Urbi et Orbi*. Many section titles likewise proclaim their earlier connections: "Evening Songs," "In the City," "The Idols' Eternal Truth," "Women."

However, *Mirror of Shadows* departs markedly from all his earlier books in one way: it has no foreword and no formal conclusion beyond one simple lyric. The poet-persona is still at the core of the book, but there is relatively little stress on the act of searching. New explorations of life simply begin: the self-as-adventurer is not at center-stage. One of the new themes is the drug experience. Titles such as "To the Tempter" (with an epigraph from De Quincy) and "Le paradis artificiel" show the experience for what it was, without exalting it. Perhaps one of the most moving poems in the book is "Little withered flower, my soul!" (1911). Its second image, a fish thrown up on the sand and writhing in agony, may have come from Hölderlin's *Hyperion*, but if so it is one of Bryusov's most successful borrowings. The poem is in eight rhymed couplets, with the last repeating the first: "Little withered flower, my soul! / We two are once more alone—you and I."

The poems of these collections often show a theme or method fully matured. Wherein, then, lay the *"uklon"*? In "Decadence and the Public Concern" Zinaida Gippius opined that there are those who are Decadents from their mother's womb, so to speak, and nothing can be done to change their ways.[53] In a rather different tone something similar might be said of Bryusov. From early on he was convinced that he was to be a poet. His conception of what it meant to be a poet in his time and place united with a personality that fell apparently naturally into the stance of extreme individualism, or Decadence. What initially was partly a pose and continued in part to be such was in its deeper meaning profoundly tied to his identity. "Other times, other manners" only superficially applied to a man of Bryusov's character. Decadence might go out of style, but his words written to Nina Petrovskaya on that night in June 1906 express the dilemma that trapped him for years to come: "I can no longer live by 'Decadence' and 'Nietzscheanism,' in which I believe, believe."[54] To be a poet meant for Bryusov, leaving aside all matters of craft, a supreme faith in one's own soul that amounted to extreme individualism. Certainly life in all its variety was his subject, but that reality could not be approached directly. Throwing oneself into life did not imply for Bryusov anything like complete abandon, as every critic of Bryusov has pointed out.

A poem written in December 1907 and one of those most often anthologized (and often taken as typifying Bryusov's point of view) is best interpreted in the light of the struggle he was under-

53. *Literaturnyj dnevnik*, 337–38.
54. *LN* 85, p. 791.

going in those years after *Stephanos*. It is addressed, similarly to one written years earlier for *Me eum esse*, "To the Poet."[55] In literal translation it runs:

> You must be proud, like a banner;
> You must be keen, like a sword;
> Like Dante, the underground flame
> Must scorch your cheeks.
>
> Be a dispassionate observer of all things,
> Bend your gaze on all.
> Let your virtue be—
> Readiness to climb onto the bonfire.
>
> Perhaps all in life is but a means
> For vividly singing verses,
> And from joyful childhood onward you
> Must seek the linking of words.
>
> In moments of love's embraces
> Compel yourself to dispassion,
> And in the hour of merciless crucifixions
> Praise the maddening pain.
>
> In morning's dreams and evening abyss
> Catch what Fate whispers to you,
> And remember: in all ages
> The poet's fated crown is one of thorns.

Likening him to a monk or hermit, Nina Petrovskaya had caught more than a glimpse of the essential feature of Bryusov's character expressed in this poem, one that he confirmed to her over and over. The asceticism demanded of the poet according to this formulation amounts to heroism. The image of Dante is invoked purposefully, not merely to justify the "underground flame"—for the poet must be ready to explore both heaven and hell. Dante is also the image of the dedicated poet, the "captive soul and gentle

55. The reference is to "Junomu poètu (To a Young Poet)," 1896 [I, 99–100].

lover," who had a vision of his heart being fed to his ideal.[56] The
chosen poet must restrain his impulses so that his eye may be
clear. The courage required by this restraint may amount to burning at the stake. Perhaps all in life must be subordinated to his
calling, and, like the pious medieval child-saint, even his earliest
years must be given to learning his craft.

The opening lines of the fourth stanza epitomize the attitude
toward love that so many readers have found objectionable in
Bryusov. Writers have often complained that their work inter-
feres with the directness of their experiences. Chekhov's Trigorin,
mediocre writer though he must have been, tells Nina Zarech-
naya in *The Seagull:* "I catch myself and you in every phrase, in
every word, and hurry as quickly as possible to lock up all these
phrases and words in my literary cupboard: maybe they'll be
useful!"[57] Bryusov turned this necessary evil into a virtue. He believed that it must be so and even flaunted it as a badge of his
special calling. Without attempting to account for this fact psychologically, in Bryusov's case or any other, we may at least credit
his belief. "To the Poet" is the opening poem of *All Melodies*,
published in 1909. Thus we may observe the consistency of his
notion of the poet, as supreme individualist and proud ascetic,
which was formed in its essential outlines fifteen years earlier and
not greatly changed, though elaborated, over the intervening
years. Whether we admire it is of course another matter.

Was this, then, the end of Bryusov as a poet? Obviously it
would be rash to say so, and many poems of subsequent years
challenge any such assertion. What was surely in mortal agony in
the years between 1906 and 1909 was Bryusov's confidence in the
public identity he had built up over the years. That identity was

56.   Dante Alighieri, *La Vita Nuova*, tr. Barbara Reynolds (Harmondsworth: Penguin, 1978), p. 32.
57.   A. P. Čexov, *Polnoe sobranie sočinenij i pisem*, Sočinenija vol. 12–13
(Moscow, 1978), p. 29.

challenged both inwardly and outwardly. As Tynyanov put it, for a certain part of his career the tide of literary development ran with him, but after a certain point it ran against.[58] Or as Boris Eikhenbaum's 1915 review of the republished poems of Bryusov's prime conveyed, no one needed prophets any more, at least not prophets of Bryusov's generation, who, whatever they might say or do, bore the imprint of their time.

Besides continuing to write poetry, Bryusov remained for several years an arbiter of the newest poetry. His apparent liking for the Futurist school no matter how much it reviled all its predecessors was in character. The very name "Futurist" appealed to that deep yearning within him to ride the crest of the future. That some of the Futurists themselves felt ties with Decadence is evinced by the rehabilitation of Decadence undertaken by the Ego-Futurist organ *The Enchanted Wanderer* in the fall of 1913.[59] That Bryusov's interpretation of Decadence occasionally struck sympathetic chords in the avant-garde movements of that period may be explained in part by the "cult of the future" which permeated his writings well beyond his period of leadership.

The other major poetic movement that sprang up with the demise of Symbolism was Acmeism, or as it sometimes called itself, for its emphasis on elemental things, Adamism. Its rejection of its predecessor's other-worldly orientation hardly touched Bryusov, whose insistence on exploration of *this* world had already set him apart from the other Symbolists. Moreover, in his esthetic views he was close to such Acmeists as Kuzmin and Gumilev. Bryusov stood outside this new creative current, in spite of their common concerns and despite the fact that the final lines of his 1908 poem "The Sower" proclaimed the program it would take up soon after: "Once more like Adam in paradise I shall see the

58.   Jurij Tynjanov, "Valerij Brjusov," p. 523.

59.   See Vladimir Markov, *Russian Futurism: A History* (Berkeley and Los Angeles: University of California Press, 1968), p. 97.

whole world unfamiliar and new, and I shall conjure up with simple and prophetic word all the mysteries of being!" The phase of Bryusov's career that had the greatest meaning for subsequent Russian poetry was over by 1910 or before. Inwardly he knew this.

It will be argued that a new and important phase of his career began in 1910 or even later. The achievements of his later phase lie beyond the scope of this study, the main concern of which has been the conception of poetry and the poet that Valery Bryusov held before the eyes of the coming generation of Russian poets, along with its most immediate results. There is more to be said even on this subject. Another study might investigate how members of the generation that ushered Symbolism and Decadence into Russia and embodied it in their lives and writings coped in the post-Symbolist period. The change of sensibility that occurred after 1910 and was so greatly accelerated by the war experience put tremendous pressure on them to remake their poetic personalities. Bryusov was probably the most visible figure among these writers.

His reception by such new critics as Eikhenbaum and Jakobson suggests that his success in this endeavor—if this was in fact his goal—was only partial. In this light a review of his 1916 *Seven Colors of the Rainbow* by Vladislav Khodasevich is revealing in several ways.[60] Himself a relatively late product of the Symbolist period, Khodasevich understood at first hand that for Bryusov "to live means to be a poet." He cited a 1912 poem in which Bryusov anticipated in a positive way his later negative judgment on this period of his life: "What should I regret on this poor earth? / . . . / I have thought enough! I have accomplished enough!"[61] Noting how this poem answered sentiments of the period of *Me eum esse*

60. Vladislav Xodasevič, "O novyx stixax. Valerij Brjusov, *Sem' cvetov raduji. Stixi 1912–1915 g*," *Utro Rossii* (no. 141), 21 May 1916, p. 5. II, 417–18. I am indebted to my colleague Robert P. Hughes for calling my attention to the authorship of this review.

61. "Letom 1912 goda," II, 95.

when the young poet rebelled at the thought of dying before enough was accomplished, he saw a cycle of Bryusov's life and career as completed. Now the new book seemed to him to offer hope of a new beginning. Seemingly for the sake of emphasis, Khodasevich treated Bryusov's career up to that time as set in the spirit of *Me eum esse*, ignoring that Bryusov's view of poetry's goals shifted sharply after that book. And he welcomed what he now perceived as a dramatic change: Bryusov the "not quite real, 'ideal' Bryusov" of Bely's "Mage" and the Vrubel portrait seemed on the verge of becoming a real man. In that possibility he rejoiced. However, he set before a future biographer of Bryusov the task of reckoning with the "difference between the ideal, premeditated Bryusov and the Bryusov who lived in our reality. Perhaps," he suggested, "precisely in connection with this difference will be revealed the tragedy of his creative work."

This study is not strictly speaking a biography. Yet it cannot ignore such questions, especially when put by such a shrewd contemporary as Khodasevich. Obviously there is much value in his observations and those of younger contemporaries such as Marina Tsvetaeva about the iron will that Bryusov put at the service of poetry. Yet Khodasevich showed the bias of the moment at which he wrote, perhaps most of all in the notion that there were two Bryusovs, the man and the mask. Bryusov's early remarks to Bunin (quoted at the start of this book) showed his awareness that he was assuming an exacting role and assuming it permanently. To Khodasevich and his peers, engaged at this juncture in overcoming all traces of the Symbolist mystique in themselves, Bryusov's concept of poetry as an all-embracing vocation seemed unconvincing. Khodasevich seemed to be saying, "If only Bryusov could have lived in a different, more 'natural' and spontaneous mode, he might have been a greater poet." Yet had he lived in other historical circumstances, he might not have been a poet at all.

Such questions are of course futile. Bryusov's career was a

unique product of time, place, and personality. In the sudden change of atmosphere in the years under consideration Khodasevich might read the opening poems of *Seven Colors of the Rainbow* as signifying a shift in Bryusov away from the artificial to the real. Yet for at least fifteen years, since *Tertia Vigilia*, Bryusov had reiterated that his subject was life in all its guises—of course, as reflected in his soul. The poet who now cried "Sed non satiatus" expressed the same thirst for new experience that he had expressed in those early days. Khodasevich thought he now heard the man, not the poet, speaking. In his own Symbolist days he may not have sufficiently understood the man Bryusov, so closely fitting the mask but not identical with it. Knowing that for Bryusov "to live means to be a poet," he did not reflect what might be the consequences of Bryusov's abandoning *his* notion of poet. The poet for Bryusov was a "holy sacrifice," a burnt offering. Perhaps this meant destruction of something human in him, but it is not quite the "tragedy" of which Khodasevich wrote. His 1916 assessment of Bryusov is interesting most of all as the comment of one esthetic upon another.

Possibly only now can readers of Russian poetry put both esthetic modes in their proper perspective. Possibly, too, Bryusov's poetry can now be read without the hitherto obligatory comparison with Blok's or with that of the great poets of the generation that followed: Pasternak, Marina Tsvetaeva, Mayakovsky, and the others—some of whom may yet be found to owe unrecognized debts to Bryusov. Best of all, from the point of view of scholars and readers alike, perhaps the complex and many-sided phenomenon that was Russian Symbolism and Decadence is on its way to being better understood and appreciated. This will occur when some of its major figures such as Bryusov, Zinaida Gippius, Fyodor Sologub, and Konstantin Balmont are retrieved from the handbooks of literature and given the careful attention that both their works and their places in the history of modern Russian literature deserve.

APPENDIXES

APPENDIX A

"Pravda večnaja kumirov," from *Stephanos*

"PRAVDA VEČNAJA KUMIROV" [The Idols' Eternal Truth]" is the second cycle of Bryusov's *Stephanos* (1906). It is reproduced here from *Puti i pereput'ja* [*Roads and Crossroads*] (volume 2, 1908), the first collected edition of Bryusov's poems. Some of the poems of this cycle have long been regarded as among his best and most characteristic and consequently have often been anthologized. The present book has argued that Bryusov's poems yield up their full measure of meaning and artistry only when read in relation to one another in the cycle of which they form a part. With this in mind, one complete cycle is offered here in the original and in translation to illustrate the discussion found in Chapter Nine. The 1908 version, it will be noted, differs slightly from that of the first edition.

Like *Stephanos*, *Puti i pereput'ja* was produced by Scorpio, the publishing house of which Bryusov was co-founder and in the physical design of whose publications he took an active interest.

These translations make no pretense at replicating the verbal texture of the poems. Bryusov normally wrote in stanzaic rather than free verse form. Furthermore, he is noted for innovative practice with rhythm and rhyme, as well as for rich sound instrumentation. I have been able to retain only the external organization of the poems, while striving to preserve as much of the meaning and mood as essentially prose renditions can capture.

ПРАВДА ВѢЧНАЯ КУМИРОВЪ.

Позналъ ты правду вѣчную кумировъ.

Ив. Коневской,

I. КЪ ДЕМЕТРѢ.

Небо четко, небо сине,
Жгучій лучъ палитъ поля;
Смутно жаждущей пустыней
Простирается земля;

Губы вѣющаго вѣтра
Ищутъ, что поцѣловать...
Низойди въ свой міръ, Деметра,
Воззови уснувшихъ, мать!

Глыбы взрыхленныя черны,
Ихъ вспоилъ весенній снѣгъ.
Гдѣ вы, дремлющія зерна,
Замышляйте свой побѣгъ!

Званы вы на пиръ вселенной!
Стебли къ солнцу устремя,
Къ жизни новой, совершенной,
Воскресайте, озимь!

THE IDOLS' ETERNAL TRUTH

You have come to know the idols' eternal truth.

Iv. KONEVSKOJ

1. TO DEMETER

The sky is clear, the sky is blue,
A burning ray scorches the fields;
Like a hazily thirsting desert,
The earth stretches without end;

The lips of the wafting wind
Seek something to kiss . . .
Descend into your world, Demeter,
Mother, summon those who have fallen asleep!

The loosened clods are black,
The spring snow has fed them.
Where are you, slumbering seeds?
Lay plans for your escape!

You are called to the feast of the universe!
With your stalks straining toward the sun,
Toward a new and perfect life,
You who have slept through the winter, arise!

И въ душѣ за ночью зимней
Тоже—свѣтъ, и тоже—тишь.
Что жъ, душа, въ весеннемъ гимнѣ
Ты проснуться не спѣшишь?

Какъ засѣянное поле
Простираются мечты,
И въ огнистомъ ореолѣ
Солнце смотритъ съ высоты.

Брошенъ былъ порой осенней
И въ тебя богатый сѣвъ,—
Зерна страсти и мученій,
Всколоситесь какъ напѣвъ!

Время вамъ въ движеньяхъ метра
Прозвучать и проблистать.
Низойди въ свой міръ, Деметра,
Воззови къ уснувшимъ, мать!

2. АДАМЪ И ЕВА.

ЕВА.

Адамъ! Адамъ! приникни ближе,
Прильни ко мнѣ, Адамъ! Адамъ!
Свисаютъ вѣтви ниже, ниже,
Плоды склоняются къ устамъ.

In the soul, too, after winter's night
There is light, and there is hush.
Why do you not hasten, O soul,
To awake in a hymn of spring?

Like the sown field
Dreams stretch endlessly.
And in a fiery halo
The sun gazes from above.

Into you, also, in autumn time
Rich seed was cast—
Seeds of passion and anguish,
Sprout forth as melody!

It is time for you in meter's movements
To sound forth and shine.
Descend into your world, Demeter,
Summon those who have fallen asleep, O Mother!

2. ADAM AND EVE

Eve

Adam! Adam! press nearer,
Cling to me, Adam! Adam!
The boughs droop lower, lower,
The fruit bends to our mouths.

АДАМЪ.

Приникни ближе, Ева! Ева!
Темно. Откуда темнота?
Свисаютъ вѣтви справа, слѣва,
Плоды вонзаются въ уста.

ЕВА.

Адамъ! Адамъ! кто вѣтви клонитъ?
Кто клонитъ, слабую, меня?
Въ пѣвучихъ волнахъ тѣло тонетъ,
Твои касанья—изъ огня!

АДАМЪ.

Что жжетъ дыханье, Ева! Ева!
Едва могу взглянуть, вздохнуть...
Что это: плодъ, упавшій съ древа,
Иль то твоя живая грудь?

ЕВА.

Адамъ! Адамъ! я—вся безвольна...
Гдѣ ты, гдѣ я?.. все - сонъ иль явь?
Адамъ! Адамъ! мнѣ больно, больно!
Пусти меня—оставь! оставь!

АДАМЪ.

Такъ надо, надо, Ева! Ева!
Я—твой! Я—твой! Молчи! Молчи!
О, какъ сквозь вѣтви, справа, слѣва,
Потокомъ ринулись лучи!

Adam

Press nearer, Eva! Eva!
It is dark. Whence this darkness?
Boughs droop from right, from left,
The fruit plunges into our mouths.

Eve

Adam! Adam! Who bends these boughs?
Who bends me, so feeble?
My body sinks in singing waves,
Your touch is of fire!

Adam

What burns my breath, Eva! Eva!
Barely can I glance, or gasp. . .
What is this: fruit fallen from the tree,
Or your living breast?

Eve

Adam! Adam! All of me is without will. . .
Where are you, where am I? Is this dream or waking?
Adam! Adam! This hurts me, hurts me!
Let me go—oh, cease! cease!

Adam

So it must be, Eva! Eva!
I am yours! Yours! Be silent! Silent!
Oh, how through the branches from right, from left,
The sun's rays pour in torrents!

ЕВА.

Адамъ! Адамъ! мнѣ стыдно свѣта!
О, что ты сдѣлалъ? Что со мной?
Ты позабылъ слова запрета!
Уйди! уйди! дай быть одной!

АДАМЪ.

Какъ плодъ сорвалъ я, Ева, Ева?
Какъ раздавить его я могъ?
О вотъ онъ, знакъ Святого Гнѣва,—
Текущій красный, красный сокъ!

3. ОРФЕЙ И ЭВРЕДИКА.

ОРФЕЙ.

Слышу, слышу шагъ твой нѣжный,
Шагъ твой слышу за собой.
Мы идемъ тропой мятежной,
Къ жизни мертвенной тропой.

ЭВРЕДИКА.

Ты—ведешь, мнѣ -- быть покорной,
Я должна итти, должна...
Но на взорахъ—облакъ черный,
Черной смерти пелена.

Eve

Adam! Adam! The light shames me!
What have you done? What has happened to me?
You forgot the words of the commandment!
Leave me! Leave me! Let me be!

Adam

How did I tear off the fruit, Eva, Eva?
How could I crush it so?
Oh, there is the sign of Holy Wrath—
The flowing red, red juice.

3. ORPHEUS AND EURYDICE

Orpheus

I hear, I hear your gentle steps,
I hear your steps behind me.
We follow a troublous path,
A barren path to life.

Eurydice

You lead, I shall submit,
I must go, I must. . .
But before my gaze is a black cloud,
The shroud of black death.

ОРФЕЙ.

Выше! выше! всѣ ступени,
Къ звукамъ, къ свѣту, къ солнцу вновь!
Тамъ со взоровъ стаютъ тѣни,
Тамъ, гдѣ ждетъ моя любовь!

ЭВРЕДИКА.

Я не смѣю, я не смѣю,
Мой супругъ, мой другъ, мой братъ!
Я лишь легкой тѣнью вѣю,
Ты лишь тѣнь ведешь назадъ.

ОРФЕЙ.

Вѣрь мнѣ! вѣрь мнѣ! у порога
Встрѣтишь ты, какъ я, весну!
Я, заклявшій лирой — бога,
Пѣсней жизнь въ тебя вдохну!

ЭВРЕДИКА.

Ахъ, что значатъ всѣ напѣвы
Знавшимъ тайну тишины!
Что весна, — кто видѣлъ сѣвы
Асфоделевой страны!

ОРФЕЙ.

Вспомни, вспомни! лугъ зеленый,
Радость пѣсенъ, радость пляскъ!
Вспомни, въ ночи — потаенный
Сладко жгучій ужасъ ласкъ!

Orpheus

Upward! Upward! Every step we climb
Leads toward sounds, to light, to the sun!
There the shadows will melt from your sight,
There, where my love waits!

Eurydice

I dare not, I dare not,
My spouse, my friend, my brother!
I but drift like a light shadow,
You lead back but a shade.

Orpheus

Trust me! Trust me! At the threshold,
Like me you will greet the spring!
I, having invoked God with my lyre,
Will breathe life into you with song!

Eurydice

Ah, what do melodies mean
To those who have known the mystery of quiet!
What is spring, to one who has seen the sowing
In the land of asphodels!

Orpheus

Remember, remember! the green meadow,
The joy of songs, the joy of dancing!
Remember, at night the hidden
Sweet-burning terror of caress!

ЭВРЕДИКА.

Сердце — мертво, грудь—недвижна.
Что́ вручу объятью я?
Помню сны,—но непостижна,
Другъ мой бѣдный, рѣчь твоя.

ОРФЕЙ.

Ты не помнишь! ты забыла!
Ахъ! я помню каждый мигъ!
Нѣтъ, не сможетъ и могила
Затемнить во мнѣ твой ликъ!

ЭВРЕДИКА.

Помню счастье, другъ мой бѣдный,
И любовь, какъ тихій сонъ...
Но во тьмѣ, во тьмѣ безслѣдной
Блѣдный ликъ твой затемненъ...

ОРФЕЙ.

— Такъ смотри! — И смотритъ дико,
Вспять, во мракъ пустой, Орфей.
— Эвредика! Эвредика!—
Стонутъ отзвуки тѣней.

4. МЕДЕЯ.

На позлащенной колесницѣ
Она свергаетъ столу съ плечъ
И надъ дѣтьми безумной жрицей
Возноситъ изощренный мечъ.

Eurydice

My heart is dead, my breast unmoved.
What can I give to an embrace?
I remember dreams, but I cannot grasp,
My poor friend, your words.

Orpheus

You do not remember! You have forgotten!
Ah, I remember every instant!
No, not even the tomb
Can blot out your face for me!

Eurydice

I remember happiness, my poor friend,
And love, like a quiet dream. . .
But in darkness, in darkness without trace
Your pale countenance is lost to me. . .

Orpheus

—Then look!—And Orpheus peers wildly
Back into empty darkness.
—Eurydice! Eurydice!—
Groan the echoes of the shades.

4. MEDEA

In the gilded chariot
She casts her stole from her shoulders
And over her children, like a mad priestess,
Raises the honed sword.

Узду грызущіе драконы,
Взметая крылья, рвутся въ высь;
Сверкнулъ надъ ними бичъ червленый,—
Съ земли рванулись, понеслись.

Она летитъ, бросая въ долы
Куски окровавленныхъ тѣлъ,
И мчится съ нею гимнъ веселый,
Какъ туча зазвенѣвшихъ стрѣлъ.

„Вотъ онъ, вотъ онъ, вѣтеръ воли!
Здравствуй! въ уши мнѣ свисти!
Вижу бездну: море, поле—
Съ окрыленнаго пути.

„Мнѣ лишь снилось, что съ людьми я,
Сонъ любви и счастья сонъ!
Духъ мой, пятая стихія,
Снова сестрамъ возвращенъ.

„Я ль, угодная Гекатѣ,
Ей союзная, могла
Возлюбить тщету объятій,
Сопрягающихъ тѣла?

„Мнѣ ли, мощью чародѣйства
Ночью зыблившей гроба,
Засыпать въ тиши семейства.
Какъ простой женѣ раба?

The dragons, champing at their bridles,
Strain upward, flapping their wings.
Over them the crimson whip flashes—
They break free from the earth and rush away.

She flies, casting into valleys
Fragments of bloodied bodies,
And a cheerful hymn speeds with her,
Like a cloud of ringing arrows.

"There it is, there, freedom's wind!
Hail! Whistle in my ears!
I see the abyss: sea, field—
From my winged path.

"I merely dreamed that I was among people,
A dream of love, a dream of bliss!
My spirit, the fifth element,
Is once more returned to its sisters.

"Could I, a favorite of Hecate,
Her ally, could I
Come to love the futility of embraces,
Coupling bodies?

"Could I, who through magic's power
Troubled graves by night,
Doze in the quiet of a family circle,
Like the simple wife of a slave?

„Выше, звѣри! хмелемъ мести
Я дала себѣ вздохнуть.
Мой подарокъ—на невѣстѣ,
Жжетъ ей дѣвственную грудь.

„Но, дробя тѣла на части
И бросая на земь ихъ,
Я позоръ послѣдней страсти
Отрясаю съ чреслъ моихъ.

„Выше, звѣри! взвейтесь выше!
Не склоню я внизъ лица,
Но за моремъ вижу крыши,
Верхъ Ээтова дворца“.

Вожжи брошены драконамъ,
Круче въ воздухѣ стезя.
Поспѣшаютъ за Язономъ,
Обезумѣвшимъ, друзья.

Каждый шагъ—предъ нимъ гробница,
Онъ лобзаетъ красный прахъ...
Но, какъ огненная птица,
Золотая колесница
Въ дымно-рдяныхъ облакахъ.

"Higher, beasts! I have allowed myself to breathe
The drunkenness of vengeance.
My gift is upon the bride,
Burning her virginal breast.

"But by cutting the bodies to pieces
And casting them on the earth,
I have shaken from my loins
That final passion's shame.

"Higher, beasts! Soar higher!
I shall not bow my head,
But beyond the sea I see the roofs,
The peak of Aeetes's castle."

With reins abandoned to the dragons,
The airy path grows steeper.
His friends rush in pursuit
Of Jason gone mad.

With every step before him is a grave.
He kisses the red dust.
But like a fiery bird
Is the golden chariot
In the smoky-roseate clouds.

5. БАЛЬДЕРУ ЛОКИ.

Свѣтлый Бальдеръ! мнѣ навстрѣчу
Ты, какъ солнце, взносишь ликъ.
Чѣмъ лучамъ твоимъ отвѣчу?
Опаленный, я поникъ.
Я взбѣгу къ снѣгамъ, на кручи:
Ты смѣешься съ высоты!
Я взнесусь багряной тучей:
Какъ звѣзда сіяешь ты!
Припаду на тайномъ ложѣ
Къ алой ласковости губъ:
Ты метнешь стрѣлу,——и что же!
Я, дрожа, сжимаю трупъ.

Но мнѣ явленъ Нертой мудрой
Призракъ будущихъ временъ.
На тебя, о златокудрый.
Лукъ волшебный наведенъ.
Въ часъ веселья, въ ясномъ полѣ,
Я слѣпцу вручу стрѣлу,—
Вскрикнешь ты отъ жгучей боли,
Вдругъ повергнутый во мглу!
И когда за темной Гелой
Ты сойдешь къ зловѣщимъ снамъ,—
Я предамъ, со смѣхомъ, тѣло
Всѣмъ распятьямъ! всѣмъ цѣпямъ!
Пусть въ пещерѣ ядъ змѣиный
Жжетъ лицо мнѣ,—я въ бреду
Буду пѣть съ моей Сигиной:
Бальдеръ! Бальдеръ! ты въ аду!

5. LOKI TO BALDER

Radiant Balder! Like the sun you raise
Your visage toward me.
How shall I answer your rays?
Scorched, I droop.
When I race upward to the snows, to the mountain peaks,
You laugh from the heights!
When I soar like a crimson cloud,
You shine like a star!
When I sink on the secret couch
To the scarlet caress of lips,
You shoot an arrow—and lo!
I, trembling, embrace a corpse.

But the wise goddess Nerta has shown me
The phantom of times to come.
Toward you, o golden-haired,
A magic bow is aimed.
In the hour of mirth, in the open field,
I will deliver an arrow to the unseeing one—
And you will scream from burning pain,
You, suddenly cast into darkness!
And when you follow the dark goddess Hel
Down into ominous dreams—
With laughter I will yield my body
To all tortures! all chains!
Let the poison of serpents
Burn my face in the cave—in delirium
I will sing with my Sigina:
Balder! Balder! You are in hell!

Не вотще вѣщали норны
Мнѣ таинственный обѣтъ.
Въ пыткахъ вспомнитъ духъ упорный:
Нѣтъ! не вѣченъ въ мірѣ свѣтъ!
День настанетъ: огнебоги
Сломятъ мощь небесныхъ силъ.
Рухнутъ Одина чертоги,
Рухнетъ древній Игдразилъ.
Выше радуги священной
Встанетъ зарево огня,—
Но послѣдній царь вселенной,
Сумракъ! сумракъ!—за меня.

6. ТЕЗЕЙ АРІАДНѢ.

„Ты спишь, отъ долгихъ ласкъ усталая,
Предавшись дрожи корабля,
А все растетъ полоска малая,—
Тебѣ сужденная земля!

„Когда сошелъ я въ сѣнь холодную,
Во тьму излучистыхъ дорогъ,
Твоею нитью путеводною
Я кознь Дедала превозмогъ.

„Въ борьбѣ, меня твой ликъ божественный
Властнѣй манилъ, чѣмъ дальній лавръ...
Разилъ я съ силой сверхъестественной, —
И палъ упрямый Минотавръ!

Not in vain did the norns
Make me a secret vow.
In torment the stubborn spirit will remember:
No! Light is not eternal in the world!
That day will come: the firegods
Will break the might of the heavenly powers.
Odin's towers will fall,
The ancient tree Yggdrasil will fall.
Higher than the sacred rainbow
The glow of fire will rise—
But the last king of the universe,
Darkness, darkness! is on my side.

6. THESEUS TO ARIADNE

"You sleep, weary from long caresses,
Yielding yourself to the ship's vibration,
And the tiny strip grows ever larger—
The land which is your fate!

"When I descended under the cold canopy
Into the darkness of radiating paths,
By your guiding thread
I overcame the snares of Daedalus.

"In the battle your divine countenance
Beckoned more powerfully than the distant laurel. . .
I struck with supernatural force—
And the stubborn Minotaur fell!

„И сердце въ первый разъ извѣдало,
Что есть блаженство на землѣ,
Когда свое біенье предало
Тебѣ—на темномъ кораблѣ!

„Но всѣмъ судило Неизбѣжное,
Какъ высшій долгъ,—быть палачо мъ.
Друзья! сложите тѣло нѣжное
На этомъ мху береговомъ.

„Довольно страсть путями правила,
Я въ даръ богамъ несу ее.
Намъ, какъ маякъ, давно поставила
Аѳина строгая—копье!"

И надъ водною могилой
Въ отчій край, гдѣ ждетъ Эгей,
Вѣютъ черныя вѣтрила—
Крылья вѣстника скорбей.

А надъ спящей Аріадной,
Словно сонная мечта,
Богъ въ коронѣ виноградной
Клонитъ страстныя уста.

"And my heart for the first time knew
That there is bliss on earth
When it yielded its beat
To you—on the dark ship!

"But the Inexorable meted out to everyone
As his highest duty—to be an executioner.
Friends! Lay the tender body
On this shore's moss.

"Passion has ruled my ways enough,
I bear her to the gods as a gift.
As a beacon for us, stern Athena
Long since has set her spear!"

And over the watery grave
To his native land, where Aegeus waits,
Stream the black sails—
Wings of grief's messenger.

And over the sleeping Ariadne,
Like a drowsy dream,
A god in a crown of grapes
Bends his passionate lips.

7. АХИЛЛЕСЪ У АЛТАРЯ.

Знаю я, во вражьемъ станѣ
Изогнулся мѣткій лукъ,
Слышу въ утреннемъ туманѣ
Тетивы пѣвучій звукъ.

Всталъ надъ жертвой облакъ дыма,
Пѣсня хора весела,
Но разитъ неотвратимо
Аполлонова стрѣла.

Я спѣшу склонить колѣна,
Но не съ трепетной мольбой.
Обрученъ я, Поликсена,
На единый мигъ съ тобой!

Всѣмъ равно въ глухомъ Эребѣ
Годы долгіе скорбѣть.
Но прекрасенъ ясный жребій—
Просіять и умереть!

Мать звала къ спокойной долѣ...
Нѣтъ! не выбралъ счастья я!
Прошумѣла въ ратномъ полѣ
Жизнь мятежная моя.

7. ACHILLES AT THE ALTAR

I know that in the enemy's camp
A well-aimed bow is bent,
I hear in the morning fog
The bowstring's singing sound.

A cloud of smoke has risen above the sacrifice,
The song of the chorus is joyful,
But Apollo's arrow
Never misses its mark.

I hasten to bend my knee,
But not in trembling prayer.
I am betrothed to you, Polyxena,
For but a single instant!

In dim Erebus all are equally fated
To grieve long years.
But splendid is the bright fate—
To shine forth and die!

My mother urged me to a quiet lot. . .
No! It was not happiness I chose!
On the field of battle
My turbulent life resounded.

И, вступивъ сегодня въ Трою
Въ блескѣ царскаго вѣнца,—
Предъ стрѣлою не укрою
Я спокойнаго лица!

Дай, къ устамъ твоимъ приникнувъ,
Посмотрѣть въ лицо твое,
Чтобъ не дрогнувъ, чтобъ не крикнувъ,
Встрѣтить смерти острiе.

И, не кончивъ поцѣлуя,
Клятвы тихiя творя,
Улыбаясь, упаду я
На помостѣ алтаря.

8. ОРФЕЙ И АРГОНАВТЫ.

Боги позволили, Арго достроенъ,
Отданъ канатъ произволу зыбей.
Станешь ли ты между смѣлыхъ, какъ воинъ,
    Скалъ чарователь, Орфей?

Тифисъ, держи неуклонно кормило!
Мели выглядывай, зоркiй Линкей!
Тиграмъ и камнямъ довольно служила
    Лира твоя, о Орфей!

And entering Troy today
In the gleam of a king's crown,
I will not shield my calm face
From that arrow!

Let me cling to your lips,
Let me look on your face,
So as, neither trembling nor crying out,
To meet the sharp point of death.

And not ending the kiss,
Making quiet vows,
On the altar's dais,
Smiling, I shall fall.

8. ORPHEUS AND THE ARGONAUTS

The gods permitted it, the Argo was completed,
Her cable given over to the ripples' whim.
Will you stand among the bold like a warrior,
      Orpheus, charmer of cliffs?

Typhœus, hold fast the helm!
Look out for shallows, keen-eyed Lynceus!
Tigers and rocks your lyre has served,
      O Orpheus, sufficiently!

Мощенъ Гераклъ, благороденъ Менотій,
Мудръ многоопытный старецъ Нелей, —
Ты же провидѣлъ въ священной дремотѣ
    Путь предстоящій, Орфей!

Слава Язону! руно золотое
Жаждетъ вернуть онъ отчизнѣ своей.
Въ день, когда вышли на подвигъ герои,
    Будь имъ сподвижникъ, Орфей!

Славь имъ восторгъ достижимой награды,
Думами темныхъ гребцовъ овладѣй,
И навсегда закляни Симплегады
    Гимномъ волшебнымъ, Орфей!

9. КЛЕОПАТРА.

Нѣтъ, какъ рабъ не буду распятъ,
Иль какъ плѣнный врагъ казненъ!
Клеопатра!—Вѣрный аспидъ
Намъ обоимъ принесенъ.

Вынь на волю изъ корзины,
Какъ союзницу, змѣю,
Полюбуйся мигъ единый
На живую чешую.

Heracles is powerful, Menoteus is noble,
Wise is the elder, much-experienced Neleus—
You have previsioned in holy trance,
      Orpheus, the way that lies before.

Glory to Jason! The golden fleece
He thirsts to bring back to his fatherland.
On the day when the heroes set out on their exploit,
      Orpheus, be their fellow adventurer.

Praise the ecstasy of a reward within their reach,
Rule the thoughts of the dark oarsmen
And cast a spell forever on the Simplegades,
      Orpheus, with your magic hymn!

9. CLEOPATRA

No, I will not be crucified as a slave,
Nor put to death as a captured foe!
Cleopatra!—The faithful asp
To us both is brought.

Draw forth the serpent,
Like an ally, from the basket,
Admire for a single moment
The living scales.

И потомъ на темномъ ложѣ
Дай припасть ей намъ на грудь,
Сладкимъ холодомъ по кожѣ
Въ быстрыхъ кольцахъ проскользнуть.

Не любовь, но смерть намъ свяжетъ
Узы тягостныя рукъ,
И. скрутясь, межъ нами ляжетъ
Нашъ послѣдній тайный другъ.

Губы въ губы, — взглядъ со взглядомъ, —
Встрѣтимъ мы послѣдній судъ.
Два укуса съ жгучимъ ядомъ
Сжатыхъ рукъ не разомкнутъ.

И истома муки страстной
Станетъ слабостью конца,
И замрутъ, дрожа согласно,
Утомленныя сердца.

Я какъ рабъ не буду распятъ,
Не покорствуй какъ раба!
Клеопатра!—Вѣрный аспидъ—
Наша общая судьба.

And then, on the dark couch,
Let it press to our breasts,
With a sweet chill on our skin
Let it slide in swift rings.

Not love but death will bind
Our hands with heavy fetters,
And coiled between us will lie
Our last and secret friend.

Lips to lips—gaze into gaze—
We will meet the final judgment.
Two bites with burning poison
Will not unlock our clenched hands.

And the languor of passion's torture
Will become the weakness of our end,
And our weary hearts,
Trembling together, will grow numb.

I will not be crucified as a slave,
Do not you, like a slave, submit!
Cleopatra!—The faithful asp
Is our common fate.

10. АНТОНІЙ.

Ты на закатномъ небосклонѣ
Былыхъ, торжественныхъ временъ,
Какъ исполинъ стоишь, Антоній,
Какъ яркій, незабвенный сонъ.

Боролись за народъ трибуны
И императоры—за власть,
Но ты, прекрасный, вѣчно юный,
Одинъ алтарь поставилъ—страсть!

Побѣдный лавръ, и скиптръ вселенной,
И ратей пролитую кровь
Ты бросилъ на вѣсы, надменный,
И перевѣсила любовь!

Когда вершились судьбы міра
Среди вспѣненныхъ боемъ струй,—
Вѣнецъ и пурпуръ тріумвира
Ты промѣнялъ на поцѣлуй.

Когда одна черта дѣлила
Въ вѣкахъ величье и позоръ,
Ты повернулъ свое кормило,
Чтобъ разъ взглянуть въ желанный взоръ.

10. ANTONY

Against the evening sky
Of former triumphant times,
Like a giant, Antony, you stand,
Like a vivid, unforgettable dream.

Tribunes fought for the people,
Emperors fought for power,
But you, O splendid, ever young,
Set up one altar—to passion!

The victor's laurels, the universe's sceptre,
The outpoured blood of legions
You, haughty one, threw on the scales,
And love outweighed them all.

When the world's fates were being decided
Among the battle's foaming streams—
The wreath and purple of a triumvir
You traded for a kiss.

When a single line separated
Eternal grandeur and shame,
You turned your helm
To look once more at the desired gaze.

Какъ нимбъ, Любовь, твое сіянье
Надъ всѣми, кто погибъ, любя!
Блаженъ, кто вѣдалъ посмѣянье,
И стыдъ, и гибель—за тебя!

О дай мнѣ жребій тотъ же вынуть,
И въ часъ, когда не конченъ бой,
Какъ бѣглецу, корабль свой кинуть
Вслѣдъ за египетской кормой!

Like a nimbus, Love, is your radiance
Over all who have perished, loving!
Blessed is he who has known mockery,
And shame, and ruin—for your sake!

O let me draw that same lot,
And in the hour when the battle still goes on
Like a fugitive let me speed my vessel
After the Egyptian ship.

Tables of Contents, First Editions of Bryusov's Books of Poems

For the convenience of the Russian reader, the tables of contents of Brjusov's poetry collections treated in this book are offered below. Since first editions of Brjusov's works are rare, the poems' locations in Volume I of the seven-volume *Sobranie sočinenij* (1973–1975) are given in the second column. Certain poems appear in revised form in later editions or with different titles (indicated here in brackets). A few poems were omitted from the 1973–1975 edition.

CHEFS D'ŒUVRE

ОСЕННИЙ ДЕНЬ

MÉDITATIONS

CHEFS D'ŒUVRE, 2nd ed.

КРИПТОМЕРИИ

ПОСЛЕДНИЕ ПОЦЕЛУИ

ПОЭМЫ

ME EUM ESSE

ЗАВЕТЫ

ВИДЕНИЯ

TERTIA VIGILIA

ЛЮБИМЦЫ ВЕКОВ

I. ЛЮБИМЦЫ ВЕКОВ

КНИЖКА ДЛЯ ДЕТЕЙ

КАРТИНКИ КРЫМА И МОРЯ
[У МОРЯ]

ПОВТОРЕНИЯ [МЫ]

URBI ET ORBI

ДУМЫ

ЭЛЕГИИ

СОНЕТЫ И ТЕРЦИНЫ

КАРТИНЫ

АНТОЛОГИЯ

ОДЫ И ПОСЛАНИЯ

ПОЭМЫ

STEPHANOS

ПОСВЯЩЕНИЕ

ВЕЧЕРОВЫЕ ПЕСНИ

ПРАВДА ВЕЧНАЯ КУМИРОВ

ИЗ АДА ИЗВЕДЕННЫЕ

ПОВСЕДНЕВНОСТЬ

СОВРЕМЕННОСТЬ

СЛАВА ТОЛПЕ

ДУХИ ОГНЯ

КОНЬ БЛЕД

ЗАКЛЮЧЕНИЕ

APPENDIX C

Contributions of Konstantin Bal'mont and Valerij Brjusov to *Kniga razdumij* (1899)

К.Д. БАЛЬМОНТ

Where pages are given, these poems are to be found in K. D. Bal'mont, *Stixotvorenija*, second ed., ed. VI. Orlov (Leningrad, 1969).

ЛИРИКА МЫСЛЕЙ

СИМВОЛИКА НАСТРОЕНИЙ

ВАЛЕРИЙ БРЮСОВ

Unless otherwise marked, all page numbers refer
to Volume I, *Sobranie sočinenij.*

РАЗДУМЬЯ

Selected Bibliography

THE BIBLIOGRAPHY of primary and secondary sources below takes into account the fact that a comprehensive bibliography of works by and about Valery Bryusov in Russian up to 1974 is available to researchers. It has been thought impractical to analyze the contents of serial volumes devoted to Bryusov, which sometimes include hitherto unpublished biographical material, including letters.

PRIMARY SOURCES

BASIC COLLECTED EDITIONS OF BRYUSOV'S POETRY AND CRITICAL ESSAYS

Brjusov, Valerij. *Puti i pereput'ja. Sobranie stixov*, 3 vols. Moscow, 1908–1909.

———. *Dalekie i blizkie. Stat'i i zametki o russkix poetax ot Tjutčeva do našix dnej*. Moscow, 1912.

———. *Polnoe sobranie sočinenij i perevodov*, vols. 1–4, 12–13, 21 [of 25 projected]. Moscow, 1913–1914.

———. *Izbrannye sočinenija*, ed. I. M. Brjusova, A. A. Il'inskij, N. S. Ašukin, intro. by A. S. Mjasnikov, 2 vols. Moscow, 1955.

———. *Stixotvorenija i poèmy*, second ed., comp. D. E. Maksimov, ed. M. I. Dikman. Leningrad, 1961.

———. *Sobranie sočinenij*, ed. P. G. Antokol'skij et al., 7 vols. Moscow, 1973–1975.

AUTOBIOGRAPHICAL SOURCES AND LETTERS

Brjusov, Valerij. "Avtobiografija," in *Russkaja literatura XX veka*, ed. S. A. Vengerov, 3 vols. Moscow, 1914–1918. I, pp. 101–119.

―――. *Dnevniki 1891–1910*, ed. I. M. Brjusova, N. S. Ašukin. Moscow, 1927.

―――. *Iz moej žizni*, ed. S. V. Baxrušin, M. A. Cjavlovskij. Moscow, 1927.

―――. *Pis'ma V. Ja. Brjusova k P. P. Percovu*, ed. P. Percov. Moscow, 1927.

―――. "Pis'ma k F. Sologubu," ed. V. N. Orlov, I. G. Jampol'skij. *Ežegodnik Rukopisnogo otdela puškinskogo doma 1973* (Leningrad, 1976): 104–125.

―――. "Pis'ma k L. N. Vil'kinoj," ed. S. S. Grečiškin, A. V. Lavrov. *Ežegodnik Rukopisnogo otdela puškinskogo doma 1973* (Leningrad, 1976): 126–135.

Bunin, Ivan. "Perepiska s V. Ja. Brjusovym (1895–1915)," *Literaturnoe nasledstvo. Ivan Bunin*. Vol. 84 (2 parts), ed. V. R. Ščerbina et al. (Moscow, 1973), 1: 421–470.

SECONDARY SOURCES

BIBLIOGRAPHICAL AND ARCHIVAL GUIDES

Binyon, T. J. "Bibliography of the Works of Valery Bryusov." *Oxford Slavonic Papers* 12 (1965): 117–140.

Danieljan, È. S. *Bibliografija Valerija Jakovleviča Brjusova 1884–1973*, ed. K. D. Muratova. Erevan, 1976.

Konšina, E. N. "Tvorčeskoe nasledie V. Ja. Brjusova v ego arxive." *Zapiski Otdela rukopisej*, Lenin State Library no. 25 (Moscow, 1962): 80–142.

―――. "Perepiska i dokumenty V. Ja. Brjusova v ego arxive." *Zapiski Otdela rukopisej* no. 27 (Moscow, 1965): 5–42.

―――. [Correction and addition to article in no. 27]. *Zapiski Otdela rukopisej* no. 29 (Moscow, 1967): 264.

WORKS ABOUT BRYUSOV

Ajvazjan, K. V., et al., eds. *Brjusovskie čtenija 1962*. Erevan, 1963.

―――. *Brjusovskie čtenija 1963*. Erevan, 1964.

―――. *Brjusovskie čtenija 1966*. Erevan, 1968.

―――. *Brjusovskie čtenija 1971*. Erevan, 1973.

―――. *Brjusovskie čtenija 1973*. Erevan, 1976.

Ašukin, N., ed. *Valerij Brjusov v avtobiografičeskix zapisjax, pis'max, vospominanijax sovremennikov i otzyvax kritiki.* Moscow, 1929.

Belyj, Andrej. "Brjusov." Pp. 178–205 in *Lug zelenyj. Kniga statej.* Moscow, 1910. Reprint, New York and London: Johnson Reprint, 1967.

———. *Načalo veka.* Moscow and Leningrad, 1933. Reprint, Chicago: Russian Language Specialties, 1966.

———. "Valerij Brjusov." *Rossija* 4 (1925): 263–280.

Binyon, T. J. "Valery Bryusov and the Nature of Art." *Oxford Slavonic Papers* 7 (1974): 96–111.

———. "Valery Yakovlevich Bryusov: Life, Literary Theory, Poetry." Dissertation, Oxford, 1969.

Brjusova, I. M. "Materialy k biografii Valerija Brjusova." Pp. 119–149 in V. Brjusov, *Izbrannye stixi.* Moscow and Leningrad, 1933.

Clowes, Edith W. "The Nietzschean Image of the Poet in Some Early Works of Konstantin Bal'mont and Valerij Brjusov." *Slavic and East European Journal* 27 (Spring 1983): 68–80.

Cvetaeva, Marina. "Geroj truda (zapisi o Valerii Brjusove)." Pp. 203–270 in *Proza*, New York: Chekhov Publishing House, 1953.

Čulkov, Georgij. *Gody stranstvij. Iz knigi vospominanij.* Moscow, 1930.

Donchin, Georgette. *The Influence of French Symbolism on Russian Poetry.* The Hague: Mouton, 1958.

Dronov, V. S. "Pjatigorskoe leto Valerija Brjusova." Pp. 158–177 in *Literatura i Kavkaz.* Stavropol', 1972.

Dronov, V. S., et al., eds. *Brjusovskij sbornik.* Stavropol, 1974.

———. *Brjusovskij sbornik.* Stavropol. 1975.

———. *Brjusovskij sbornik.* Stavropol, 1977.

———. *V. Brjusov i literatura konca XIX–XX veka.* Stavropol, 1979.

Erlich, Victor. "The Maker and the Seer: Two Russian Symbolists." Pp. 68–119 in *The Double Image: Concepts of the Poet in Slavic Literatures.* Baltimore: Johns Hopkins, 1964.

Gindin, S. I. "Brjusov o Nekrasove." *N. A. Nekrasov i russkaja literatura.* Kostroma, 1974.

———. "Brjusov o Nekrasove." *N. A. Nekrasov i russkaja literatura.* Jaroslavl', 1975.

———. "Neosuščestvlennyj zamysel Brjusova." *Voprosy literatury* no. 9 (1970): 189–203.

———. "Iz istorii stixovedenija. Vzgljady V. Ja. Brjusova na jazykovuju priemlemost' stixovyx sistem i sud'by russkoj sillabiki (po rukopisjam 90-x godov)." *Voprosy jazykoznanija* no. 2 (1970): 99–109.

Gippius, Zinaida. "Oderžimyj (o Brjusove)." Pp. 73–117 in *Živye lica*. Prague: Plamja, 1925. Reprint, Munich: Wilhelm Fink Verlag, 1971.

Gofman, M., ed. *Poèty simvolizma*. St. Petersburg and Moscow, 1908. Reprint, Munich: Wilhelm Fink Verlag, 1970 (Slavische Propyläen Bd. 106).

Grečiskin, S. S., and A. V. Lavrov. "Biografičeskie istočniki romana Brjusova *Ognennyj angel.*" *Wiener Slawisticher Almanach* 1 (1978): 79–107; 2 (1978): 73–96.

Grossman, Joan Delaney. Pp. 159–177 in "Blok, Brjusov and the Prekrasnaja Dama." *Aleksandr Blok Centennial Conference*, ed. Walter N. Vickery and Bogdan Sagatov. Columbus, Ohio: Slavica Publishing House, 1984.

Gudzij, N. "Iz istorii rannego russkogo simvolizma. Moskovskie sborniki 'Russkie simvolisty.'" *Iskusstvo* 3, no. 4 (1927): 180–218.

———. "Tjutčev v poètičeskoj kul'ture russkogo simvolizma." *Izvestija Otdelenija russkogo jazyka i slovesnosti*, Akademija Nauk SSSR 3, no. 2 (1930): 465–549.

Holthusen, Johannes. *Studien zur Ästhetik und Poetik des russischen Symbolismus*. Göttingen: Vandenhoeck und Ruprecht, 1957.

Ivanova, E. V. "Valerij Brjusov i Aleksandr Dobroljubov." *Izvestija Akademii nauk. Serija literatury i jazyka* 40, 3 (1981): 255–265.

Jakobson, Roman. "Brjusovskaja stixologija i nauka o stixe." *Naučnye izvestija Akademičeskogo Centra Narkomprosa* 2 (1922): 222–240.

Jampol'skij, I. "Valerij Brjusov i pervaja russkaja revoljucija." Pp. 201–220 in *Literaturnoe nasledstvo* 15. Moscow, 1934.

Kuljus, Svetlana Konstantinovna. "Formirovanie filosofsko-èstetičeskix vzgljadov V. Brjusova i ego tvorčestvo 1890-x godov." Dissertation, Tartu State University, 1982.

Literaturnoe nasledstvo. Vols. 27–28 [Simvolizm]. Moscow, 1937.

Literaturnoe nasledstvo. Valerij Brjusov. Vol. 85. Moscow, 1976.

Litvin, È. S. "Revoljucija 1905 g. i tvorčestvo Brjusova." Pp. 198–245 in *Revoljucija 1905 g. i russkaja literatura*. Moscow and Leningrad, 1956.

———. "Valerij Brjusov i russkoe narodnoe tvorčestvo." Pp. 136–152 in *Russkij fol'klor* 7. Moscow and Leningrad, 1962.

Maksimov, D. E. *Brjusov. Poèzija i pozicija*. Leningrad, 1969.

———. *Poèzija Valerija Brjusova*. Leningrad, 1940.

Mantorov, G. V. "Èvoljucija èstetičeskix vzgljadov rannego Brjusova

(1890-e gody)." *Učenye zapiski Moskovskogo gosudarstvennogo pedago-gičeskogo instituta im. Lenina* 328 (1969): 27–56.

Markov, Vladimir. "K voprosu o granicax dekadansa v russkoj poèzii (i o liričeskoj poème)." Pp. 485–498 in *American Contributions to the Eighth International Congress of Slavists*, vol. 2, ed. Victor Terras. Columbus, Ohio: Slavica Publishers, 1978.

Masing-Delič, Irene. "Limitation and Pain in Bryusov's and Blok's Poetry." *Slavic and East European Journal* 19, 4 (Winter 1975): 388–402.

Maslenikov, Oleg A. *The Frenzied Poets: Andrei Biely and the Russian Symbolists*. Berkeley and Los Angeles: University of California Press, 1952.

Močul'skij, Konstantin. *Valerij Brjusov*. Introductory essay, "Brjusov čerez mnogo let," by Wladimir Weidlé. Paris: YMCA Press, 1962.

Percov, P. *Literaturnye vospominanija (1890–1902 gg.)*. Moscow and Leningrad, 1933.

Poggioli, Renato. *Poets of Russia, 1890–1930*. Cambridge, Mass.: Harvard University Press, 1960.

Rice, Martin P. *Valery Briusov and the Rise of Russian Symbolism*. Ann Arbor: Ardis, 1975.

Schmidt, Alexander. *Valerij Brjusovs Beitrag zur Literaturtheorie. Aus der Geschichte des Russischen Symbolismus*. Slavistische Beiträge Bd. 7. Munich: Otto Sagner, 1963.

Setschkareff [Setchkarev], V. "The Narrative Prose of Brjusov." *International Journal of Slavic Linguistics and Poetics* 1/2 (1959): 237–265.

Sologub, Fedor. "Speech in Memory of V. Ja. Brjusov," ed. Joan Delaney Grossman. Pp. 421–424 in *Slavica Hierosolymitana* vol. 5–6. Jerusalem: Magnes Press, Hebrew University, 1981.

Solov'ev, V. S. "Russkie simvolisty. 1895." [Three review articles on Brjusov's *Russkie simvolisty*.] Pp. 159–170 in *Sobranie sočinenij*, ed. S. M. Solov'ev and È. L. Radlov, second edition, vol. 7. St. Petersburg, n.d. Reprint, Brussels: Foyer Oriental Chrétien, 1966.

Struk, Danylo. "The Great Escape: Principal Themes in Valerij Brjusov's Poetry." *Slavic and East European Journal* 12, 4 (1968): 407–423.

Tardov, V. G. "Eres' simvolizma i Valerij Brjusov." Pp. [3]–85 in his *Otraženija ličnosti. Kritičeskie opyty*. Moscow, 1909.

Tixančeva, E. P. *Brjusov o russkix poètax XIX veka*. Erevan, 1973.

Tynjanov, Jurij. "Valerij Brjusov." Pp. 521–540 in his *Arxaisty i novatory*. Leningrad, 1929. Reprint, Munich: Wilhelm Fink Verlag, 1967 (Slavische Propyläen Bd. 31).

Vengerov, S. A., ed. *Russkaja literatura XX veka 1890–1910.* Three vols. in one. Moscow, 1914–1916. Reprint, Munich: Wilhelm Fink, 1972 (Slavische Propyläen Bd. 115).

West, James. *Russian Symbolism: A Study of Vyacheslav Ivanov and the Russian Symbolist Aesthetic.* London: Methuen, 1970.

Xačikjan, Ja. I., et al., eds. *Brjosovskie čtenija 1980.* Erevan, 1983.

Xodasevič, V. F. "Brjusov." Pp. 26–60 in his *Nekropol'.* Brussels: Editions Petropolis, 1939. Reprint, Paris: YMCA Press, 1976.

———. "Konec Renaty." Pp. 7–25 in his *Nekropol'.* Brussels: Editions Petropolis, 1939. Reprint, Paris: YMCA Press, 1976.

Žirmunskij, Viktor. *Valerij Brjusov i nasledie Puškina. Opyt sravnitel'no-stilističeskogo issledovanija.* St. Petersburg, 1922. Reprint, The Hague and Paris: Mouton, 1970.

Index

Designer:	Mark Ong
Compositor:	G&S Typesetters, Inc.
Text:	11/13 Garamond
Display:	Trump Mediaeval & Garamond
Printer:	Braun-Brumfield, Inc.
Binder:	Braun-Brumfield, Inc.